Benefit-Cost Analysis
Financial and Economic Appraisal using Spreadsheets

This text offers the perfect introduction to social benefit-cost analysis. The book closely integrates the theory and practice of benefit-cost analysis using a spreadsheet framework. The spreadsheet model is constructed in a truly original way which contributes to transparency, provides a check on the accuracy of the analysis, and facilitates sensitivity, risk and alternative scenario assessment.

A case study incorporating the various issues is progressively developed on a spreadsheet with the links between each stage thoroughly explained. The complete case study spreadsheet can serve as a template for the reader's own appraisal of projects in the field. In addition to the worked examples in the text some exercises are appended at the end of each chapter.

The book has several unique features:
- the close integration of spreadsheet analysis with analytical principles;
- the spreadsheet approach provides an invaluable cross-check on the accuracy of the appraisal;
- the book is structured in a way that allows readers to choose the level of analysis which is relevant to their own purposes.

The text is suitable for people with a basic understanding of elementary economics who wish to learn how to conduct a social benefit-cost analysis.

Harry Campbell and **Richard Brown** are both in the School of Economics at The University of Queensland. They have extensive experience in teaching and applied benefit-cost analysis and have between them held academic positions at universities in North America, Europe, Africa and Australia.

For: Jenny, Jamie and Astrid
Kathy, Ben, James, Oliver and Alex

Benefit-Cost Analysis

Financial and Economic Appraisal using Spreadsheets

Harry F. Campbell and Richard P. C. Brown
The University of Queensland

CAMBRIDGE
UNIVERSITY PRESS

CAMBRIDGE UNIVERSITY PRESS
Cambridge, New York, Melbourne, Madrid, Cape Town, Singapore, São Paulo

Cambridge University Press
477 Williamstown Road, Port Melbourne, VIC 3207, Australia

Published in the United States of America by Cambridge University Press, New York

www.cambridge.org
Information on this title: www.cambridge.org/9780521528986

First published 2003
Reprinted 2005

Printed in Singapore by Craftprint

Typeface Goudy (Adobe) 10.5/13 pt. *System* QuarkXPress® [MK]

A catalogue record for this publication is available from the British Library

National Library of Australia Cataloguing in Publication data
        Campbell, Harry F. (Harry Fleming), 1945– .
        Benefit-cost analysis: financial and economic appraisal
        using spreadsheets.
        For university students
        ISBN-13 978-0-521-52898-6 paperback
        ISBN-10 0-521-52898-4 paperback
        1. Cost effectiveness – Textbooks. I. Brown, Richard P.C.
        II. Title.
658.1554

ISBN-13 978-0-521-82146-9 hardback
ISBN-10 0-521--82146-0 hardback
ISBN-13 978-0-521-52898-6 paperback
ISBN-10 0-521-52898-4 paperback

Contents

Figures

Tables

Preface

This book is intended for people with a basic understanding of elementary economics who wish to learn how to conduct a social cost-benefit analysis. We use the term *social benefit-cost analysis* to refer to the appraisal of a private or public project from a public interest viewpoint. We follow professional practice in using the terms *benefit-cost analysis* and *cost-benefit analysis* (with or without the *social* prefix) interchangeably.

A social cost-benefit analysis of a publicly funded project may be commissioned by a municipal, state or federal government, or by an international agency such as the World Bank, IMF, UN or OECD. Proponents of private projects which have significant social impacts may also commission an economic analysis of this type in order to support an application for approval to proceed with the project. Sometimes the scope of the required analysis is broader than the evaluation of economic benefits and costs: an impact analysis may also be required to determine the effects of the project on employment and economic growth; an environmental impact statement may be required; and a social impact analysis dealing with factors such as crime and impacts on families may be sought. This book concerns itself mainly with the economic benefits and costs of projects, although it does touch on the question of economic impact. The main questions addressed are: Do the benefits of the project exceed the costs, no matter how widely they are spread? And which group benefits and which bears the costs?

Social cost-benefit analysis relies mainly on microeconomic theory, although some understanding of macroeconomics is also useful. The person whose background should be sufficient to allow them to benefit from this book is someone who did a principles of economics subject as part of a commerce, arts, science or engineering degree; a person with an undergraduate economics training will find the organizational principles set out in the book to be innovative and of considerable practical use.

The book has several unique features: the close integration of spreadsheet analysis with analytical principles is a feature of some financial appraisal texts, but is unusual in social benefit-cost analysis; the particular layout of the spreadsheet is unique in offering an invaluable cross-check on the accuracy of the appraisal; and the book is structured in a way that allows readers to choose the level of analysis which is relevant to their own purposes.

The book emphasizes practical application. It develops a template based on spreadsheet analysis which is recommended for use in conducting a social cost-benefit analysis and which provides a check on the accuracy of the analysis. The template is presented in the form of a case study of a social cost-benefit analysis of a proposed private investment project in a developing economy. The case study, together with reference to the necessary economic principles, is developed stage by stage in Part 1 of the book, consisting of the first six Chapters. At the completion of Part 1 the reader should be capable of undertaking a cost-benefit analysis of an actual project.

Part 2 of the book introduces some complications which were ignored in Part 1: input or output price changes caused by the project under analysis; imperfections in foreign exchange markets; risk; and the cost of public funds. The analysis of many projects does not require consideration of these matters, and because they tend to be a little more complicated they are deferred to this second Part of the book. The treatment of these issues in practical benefit-cost analysis is illustrated by amendments to the case study developed in Part 1.

Part 3 of the book looks at broader issues, including income distribution issues from an atemporal and inter-temporal perspective, valuation of non-marketed goods, and economic impact analysis.

Note to the Instructor

The book is intended as the required text for a sequence of two courses in benefit-cost analysis. It provides a framework for courses involving practical application and leading to the acquisition of a valuable set of skills. It can be supplemented by a range of other readings chosen to reflect the emphasis preferred by the Instructor. It includes exercises and a major benefit-cost analysis problem which can be assigned for credit.

A one-semester undergraduate or postgraduate course can be based on Chapters 1–6 of the book, or Chapters 1–7 if issues of consumer and producer surplus are to be included. We suggest a weighting of 50% credit for examination of the principles put forward in the Chapters, 10% for a selection from the small Exercises that follow each Chapter, and 40% for completing the benefit-cost analysis assignment presented in the Appendix. Chapter 14, dealing with the way in which a benefit-cost analysis should be reported, can also be assigned as reading. The text can be supplemented with other reading, including reference to chapters in other benefit-cost texts which cover some issues in more detail. Some classes might benefit from a set of lectures on the basic microeconomic principles upon which benefit-cost analysis draws, together with reference to a text in microeconomics or public finance.

A more advanced course can be built around Chapters 7–13 and selected parts of Chapters 1–6, together with references to further reading. We teach the higher level course in 6–8 weeks in the second half of the semester, with completion of the basic course as a prerequisite. We use a weighting of 65% credit for examination of principles and 35% for completion of the Exercises. However, a term paper on a particular issue in benefit-cost analysis could be assigned for part of the credit.

For the purposes of the more advanced course the text needs to be supplemented by a significant amount of further reading. In our course we recommend to our students some chapters in some of the benefit-cost analyses texts referred to in our brief suggestions for further reading, but the choice is very much a matter of individual taste.

Our teaching of the basic course is based on two hours of lectures and class discussion per week plus a one-hour computer lab session. To start with we use the lab session to make sure everyone is comfortable with using spreadsheets and is able to access the various financial subroutines. We then spend some time developing the benefit-cost analysis of the case study project as an example of the practical application of the approach. After 6–7 weeks of lectures and lab work students are ready to undertake the benefit-cost analysis assignment in the Appendix. In the second part of the semester we use the class and lab times for consultations with students who require help with the major assignment. As indicated by the sample case study report, which was prepared by one of our students and is included in Chapter 14, a high standard of work can be expected.

We use a similar teaching pattern for the more advanced course. The lab sessions are used to provide help with the assignments, and consultation sessions can also be provided for this purpose and for assistance with preparing a term paper. The benefit-cost analysis assignment in the Appendix could be expanded, as illustrated in the Appendices to Chapters 7–10, and further development of the report prepared in the basic course could be the subject of a significant assignment.

The text will be supported by a link on Cambridge University Press' website (http://academic.cambridge.edu.au) which will provide the Instructor with access to spreadsheets, problem solutions and powerpoint presentations.

Acknowledgements

We have benefited greatly from teaching benefit-cost analysis over many years in several universities and we would like to thank our students, both past and present, for their contribution to our understanding and presentation of the concepts which are the topic of this book. In particular we would like to thank Angela McIntosh for permission to include her case study in Chapter 14. We would like to thank the School of Economics at The University of Queensland for the opportunity to teach benefit-cost analysis in a diverse and stimulating environment. We have enjoyed excellent support from all members of the School's administrative staff in the preparation of the manuscript and, in particular from Gloria Barr who has incorporated our frequent revisions with patience and efficiency. We received helpful comments on earlier drafts from several anonymous reviewers, and from Dale Squires. We would like to thank these people for their suggestions and to absolve them from any responsibility for any remaining errors.

Benefit-Cost Analysis: Introduction and Overview

Introduction

Social benefit-cost analysis is a process of identifying, measuring and comparing the social benefits and costs of an investment project or program. A program is a series of projects undertaken over a period of time with a particular objective in view. The project or projects in question may be public projects – undertaken by the public sector – or private projects. Both types of projects need to be appraised to determine whether they represent an efficient use of resources. Projects that represent an efficient use of resources from a private viewpoint may involve costs and benefits to a wider range of individuals than their private owners. For example, a private project may pay taxes, provide employment for the otherwise unemployed, and generate pollution. These effects are termed social benefits and costs to distinguish them from the purely private costs and returns of the project. Social benefit-cost analysis is used to appraise private projects from a social viewpoint as well as to appraise public projects.

It should be noted that the technique of social benefit-cost analysis can also be used to analyse the effects of changes in public policies such as the tax/subsidy or regulatory regimes. However a very broad range of issues can arise in this kind of analysis and, for ease of exposition, we adopt the narrower perspective of project analysis in this study.

Public projects are often thought of in terms of the provision of physical capital in the form of infrastructure such as bridges, highways and dams. However there are other less obvious types of physical projects that augment environmental capital stocks and involve activities such as land reclamation, pollution control, fishery management and provision of parks. Other types of projects are those that involve investment in forms of human capital, such as health, education, and skills, and social capital through drug-use and crime prevention, and the reduction of unemployment. There are few, if any, activities of government that are not amenable to appraisal and evaluation by means of social benefit-cost analysis.

Investment involves diverting scarce resources – land, labour and capital – from the production of goods for current consumption to the production of capital goods which will contribute to increasing the flow of consumption goods available in the future. An investment project is a particular allocation of scarce resources in the present which will result in a flow of output in the future: for example, land, labour and capital could be allocated to the construction of a dam which will result in increased electricity output in the future (in reality there are likely to be additional outputs such as irrigation water, recreational opportunities and flood control but we will assume these away for the purposes of the example). The cost of the project is measured as an opportunity cost – the value of the goods and services which would have been produced by the land, labour and capital inputs had they not been used to construct the dam. The benefit of the project is measured as the value of the extra electricity produced by the dam. Chapter 2 discusses the concept of investment and investment appraisal in more detail.

The role of the benefit-cost analyst is to provide information to the decision-maker – the official who will appraise or evaluate the project. We use the word "appraise" in a prospective sense, referring to the process of actually deciding whether resources are to be allocated to the project or not. We use the word "evaluate" in a retrospective sense, referring to the process of reviewing the performance of a project or program. Since social benefit-cost analysis is mainly concerned with projects undertaken by the public sector the decision-maker will usually be a senior public servant acting under the direction of a minister. It is important to understand that benefit-cost analysis is intended to inform the existing decision-making process, not to supplant it. The role of the analyst is to supply relevant information about the level and distribution of benefits and costs to the decision-maker, and potentially to contribute to informed public opinion and debate. The decision-maker will take the results of the analysis, together with other information, into account in coming to a decision. The analyst's role is to provide an objective appraisal or evaluation, and not to adopt an advocacy position either for or against the project.

An investment project makes a difference and the role of benefit-cost analysis is to measure that difference. Two as yet hypothetical states of the world are to be compared – the world **with** the project and the world **without** the project. The decision-maker can be thought of as standing at a node in a decision tree as illustrated in Figure 1.1. There are two alternatives: undertake the project or don't undertake the project (in reality there are many options, including a number of variants of the project in question, but for the purposes of the example we will assume that there are only two).

The world without the project is not the same as the world before the project; for example, in the absence of a road-building project traffic flows may continue to grow and delays to lengthen, so that the total cost of travel time without the project exceeds the cost before the project. The time saving attributable to the project is the difference between travel time with and without the project, which is larger than the difference between travel time before and after the project.

Which is the better path to choose? The **with-and-without** approach is at the heart of the benefit-cost process and also underlies the important concept of **opportunity cost**. **Without** the project – for example, the dam referred to above – the scarce land, labour and capital would have had alternative uses. For example, they could have been combined to increase the output of food for current consumption. The value of that food, assuming that food production is the best (highest valued) alternative use of the scarce resources, is the opportunity cost of the dam. This concept of opportunity cost is what we mean by "cost" in social benefit-cost analysis. **With** the dam project we give up the opportunity to produce additional food in the present, but when the dam is complete it will result in an increase in the amount of electricity which can be produced in the future. The benefit of the project is the value of this increase in the future supply of electricity over and above what it would have been in the absence of the project. The role of the benefit-cost analyst is to inform the decision-maker: if the **with** path is chosen additional electricity valued by consumers at $X will be available; if the **without** path is chosen extra food valued at $Y will be available. If X>Y the benefits exceed the costs, or, equivalently, the benefit/cost ratio exceeds unity. This creates a presumption in favour of the project although the decision-maker also has to take distributional effects into account – who would receive the benefits and who would bear the costs?

How do we measure the benefit of the additional electricity produced by the project? The gross value of the project output is measured by the amount consumers are willing to pay for it. In the case of a small increase in output **willingness-to-pay** (WTP) is measured by market price. However where the project output is substantial, relative to the original quantity of the good produced and consumed, willingness-to-pay for additional units of the good will be lower than market price because of the downward slope of the demand curve. In these circumstances marginal willingness-to-pay (WTP for an additional unit of output) declines as a result of the project and consumer benefits are measured as an area under the demand curve known as **consumer surplus**.

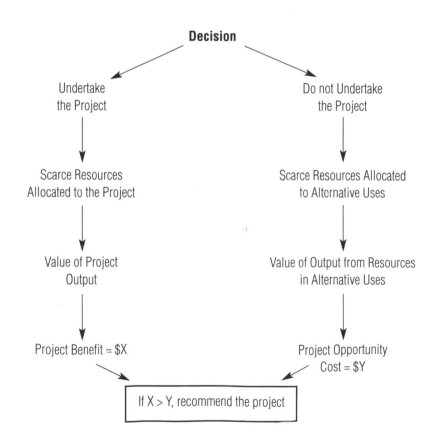

Figure 1.1 The "With and Without" Approach to Benefit-Cost Analysis

The concepts of consumer surplus, and the corresponding measure of **producer surplus**, which measures benefits or costs to suppliers, are discussed in detail in Chapter 7, in particular the concept of consumer surplus is illustrated by Figure 7.1. We now explain why we defer discussion of these important economic concepts until later in the book.

Traditional expositions of benefit-cost analysis usually start with the notion of consumer and producer surplus. However these concepts are relevant to the analysis only if output or input prices (or, in the case of non-marketed output, imputed prices) change as a result of undertaking the project. In many cases, including the case study which is developed in the Appendices to Chapters 4–6, no price changes can be identified. However all social benefit-cost analyses face the difficult task of social accounting – working out how the overall net benefits (or net costs) of the proposed project will be shared among the interested parties, including foreign and domestic, public and private, and consumers and producers. Entitlement to shares in net benefits is governed by a complex array of fiscal, regulatory and financial arrangements. Failure to understand these relationships can lead to fundamental errors of omission and double-counting in social benefit-cost analysis, and we have given these matters priority in the order of presentation.

The example of the electricity project was presented as if the benefit-cost analysis directly compares the value of extra electricity with the value of the forgone food. In fact the comparison is made indirectly. Suppose that the cost of the land, labour and capital to be used to build the dam is $Y. We assume that these factors of production could have produced output (not necessarily food) valued at $Y in some alternative and unspecified uses. We will consider the basis of this assumption in detail in Chapter 5, but for the moment it is sufficient to say that in a competitive and undistorted market the value of additional inputs will be bid up to the level of the value of the additional output they can produce. The net benefit of the dam is given by $(X–Y) and this represents the extent to which building a dam is a better (X–Y>0) or worse (X–Y<0) use of the land, labour and capital than the alternative use.

When we say that $(X–Y)>0 indicates a better use of the inputs than the best alternative use we are applying a measure of economic welfare change known as the **Kaldor–Hicks criterion**. The K–H criterion says that, even if some members of society are made worse off as a result of undertaking a project, the project confers a net benefit if the gainers from the project could compensate the losers. In other words, a project does not have to constitute what is termed a **Pareto improvement** (a situation in which at least some people are better off and no one is worse off as a result of undertaking the project) to add to economic welfare, but merely a **potential Pareto improvement**. The logic behind this view is that if society believed that the distributional consequences of undertaking the project were undesirable, the costs and benefits could be redistributed by means of transfer payments of some kind. The problem with this view is that transfers are normally accomplished by means of taxes or charges which distort economic behaviour and impose costs on the economy. The decision-maker may conclude that these costs are too high to warrant an attempt to redistribute benefits and costs. We return to the issue of the distributional effects of projects in Chapter 11.

Since building a dam involves costs in the present and benefits in the future the net benefit stream will be negative for a period of time and then positive, as illustrated in Figure 1.2. To produce a summary measure of the net benefits of the project all values have to be converted to values at a common point in time, usually the present. The net present value is the measure of the extent to which the dam is a better (NPV>0) or worse (NPV<0) use of scarce resources than the best alternative. Converting net benefit streams, measured as net cash flows, to present values is the subject of Chapters 2 and 3.

When we compute present values for use in a social benefit-cost analysis we need to make a decision about the appropriate rate of discount. The discount rate tells us the rate at which we are willing to give up consumption in the present in exchange for additional consumption in the future. A riskless market rate of interest, such as the government bond rate, provides a measure of the marginal rate of time preference of those individuals participating in the market. However it can be argued that future generations, who will potentially be affected by the project, are not represented in today's markets.

In other words, in using a market rate of interest as the discount rate, the current generation is making decisions about the distribution of consumption flows over time without necessarily consulting the interests of future generations. This raises the question of whether a social discount rate, as opposed to a market rate, should be used to calculate the net present values used in public decision-making. This issue is considered further in Chapters 10 and 11.

Much of what has been said to this point also applies to projects being considered by a private firm: funds that are allocated for one purpose cannot also be used for another purpose, and hence have an opportunity cost. Firms routinely undertake investment analyses using techniques similar to those of social benefit-cost analysis. Indeed the appraisal of a proposed

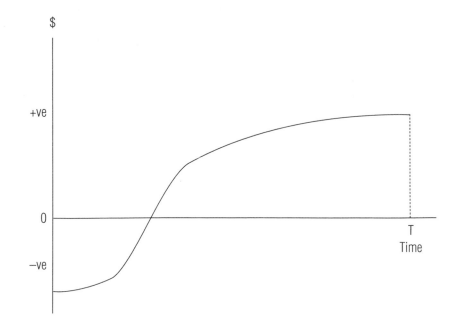

Figure 1.2 Typical Time-Stream of Project Net Benefits

project from a private viewpoint is often an integral part of a social benefit-cost analysis, and for this reason the whole of Chapter 4 is devoted to this topic. A private investment appraisal takes account only of the benefits and costs of the project to the private firm – its effect on revenues and costs and hence on profit. The project may have wider implications – environmental and employment effects, for example – but if these do not affect the firm's profits – its "bottom line" – they are omitted from the analysis. In contrast a social benefit-cost analysis takes a wider or "social" perspective – it measures and compares the costs and benefits experienced by all members of "society". In the context of social benefit-cost analysis "society" is to be interpreted in a relatively narrow way: it is simply that group of individuals deemed by the decision-maker to be relevant, and it is usually termed the **referent group**. Before undertaking a social benefit-cost analysis the analyst needs to ascertain from the decision-maker the composition of the referent group. Often the referent group consists of all the residents of a country, but it may be more narrowly defined in terms of sub-groups such as residents of a State or region, or social groupings such as the poor, unemployed, elderly, or people of Aboriginal descent.

It is clear that benefit-cost analysis can be conducted from different viewpoints: for example, it can take account of only the benefits and costs to the owners of the equity (the shareholders) in a private firm; an analysis from this perspective shall be referred to in this book as a **private benefit-cost analysis**. Alternatively, it can be broadened to include all benefits and costs to members of the referent group.

In what we term a **project benefit-cost analysis** estimates of all project benefits and costs are calculated at market prices; the project analysis tells us whether, in the absence of loans and taxes, the project has a positive NPV at market prices. The project NPV calculated in this way is neither the private NPV (the value of the project to private equity holders) nor the social NPV (the value of the project to the referent group). The equity holders do not stand to receive all the benefits of the project or incur all of the costs: for example, taxes may be due on project income, and loans may be obtained to finance part of the project, with consequent outflows in the form of interest payments. Whether the return to equity and debt holders is relevant in a social benefit-cost analysis depends on whether these groups are part of the referent group, but tax revenues paid by the project to the domestic government are certainly social benefits. Furthermore, by pricing inputs and outputs at market prices the project benefit-cost analysis ignores various types of referent group effects such as employment benefits, measured as the project wage bill less the opportunity cost of supplying the labour. It also excludes the benefits or costs of non-marketed commodities such as pollution. We discuss the former type of benefits and costs in detail in Chapter 5, and the latter in Chapter 12.

The important concept of the referent group is illustrated in Figure 1.3, which deals with an example which will be developed in Chapters 4–6 of this book. Suppose that a wholly foreign-owned company proposes to set up a factory in a developing country. The government wishes to appraise the proposal from the point of view of residents of the host country – the referent group. The firm has two questions to consider. First, is the overall project efficient from a market viewpoint? This is determined by the project benefit-cost analysis which compares the benefits and costs associated with undertaking the project, where benefits and costs are calculated at market prices; the present value of the net benefits is represented by

Area A+B in Figure 1.3 (the interpretation of the breakdown of the project net present value into the components A and B will be explained shortly). Second, is the project profitable from the perspective of the firm's owners, or, equity holders? This is determined by the private benefit-cost analysis. If the project is to be wholly internally financed the answer to this second question is obtained by deducting tax payments from the project NPV. However we will assume that there is to be some debt participation in the project in the form of a loan from a financial institution in the host country. The amount of the loan must be deducted from the project cost and the loan repayments and interest charges deducted from the project's after-tax benefits to give the benefits and costs of the project to the equity holders; the private benefit-cost analysis.

In this example we shall assume that the firm's equity holders are not considered part of the referent group. This being so, in Figure 1.3 Area A represents the net present value of the project net benefits to the members of the referent group: the lenders of the firm's loan (the bank) and the recipients of the firm's tax payments (the government). The net benefit of the project to the non-referent group members, the firm's equity holders, expressed as a net present value, is represented by Area B. Only if the net benefit to equity holders is positive is the project worthwhile from the firm's viewpoint. Areas A and B together amount to the project NPV.

As noted above the project may have a wider impact than that summarized by the project benefit-cost analysis. The project may generate benefits or costs to various groups within the host country. For example, some people who would otherwise have been unemployed may obtain jobs: the pay that they receive from the firm may be higher than the value

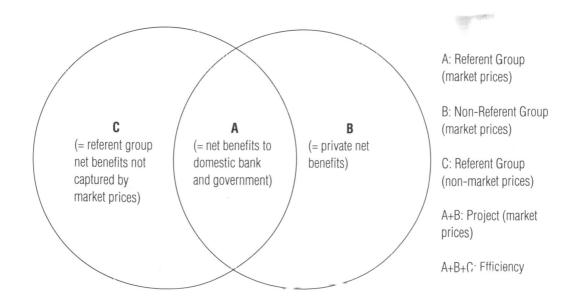

Figure 1.3 Relationship between the Project, Private, Efficiency and Referent Group Net Benefits

of their time in some non-market activity, thereby resulting in a net benefit to them. The firm may purchase various goods and services, such as water and electricity, from government agencies, paying prices in excess of the production costs of these inputs, again generating net benefits for this section of the referent group. The project may generate pollution which imposes health and other costs on residents of the host country. In Figure 1.3 Area C represents the set of net benefits (present value of benefits net of costs) accruing to the referent group as a result of divergences of market prices from referent group valuations of benefits or costs, or as a result of non-marketed benefits and costs. We shall refer to these as **non-marketed net benefits/costs** accruing to members of the referent group. The total referent group net benefit is given by Area A+C.

What then does the whole area, A+B+C, represent? This can be thought of as representing the **efficiency net benefits** of the project – the present value of benefits net of their opportunity cost, and irrespective of whether they accrue to members of the referent group or not. Area B represents the net benefits to the non-referent group equity holders, which will determine the firm's decision whether to undertake the project or not. Area A+C represents the net benefits to the referent group, which will determine the government's decision as to whether or not to allow the project to proceed. Referent group net benefits are a subset of the efficiency net benefits. The composition of the referent group follows from the definition of the scope of the benefits and costs to be counted. As noted earlier, it is essentially a policy decision as to who the relevant stakeholders or referent group members are. The composition of the referent group net benefit is the main issue which the benefit-cost analyst is called upon to address, although in negotiating with the firm the decision-maker may also be interested to know how attractive the project is from a private viewpoint. It should also be noted that the definition of the referent group can be controversial especially in situations where there are transboundary externalities such as pollution affecting citizens of other states or countries.

Apart from measuring the aggregate referent group net benefit, the analyst will also need to know how this is distributed among the different sub-groups as the decision-makers will, most probably, want to take into consideration the distribution of net gains and losses among the referent group members: this is referred to as the **referent group analysis**.

In summary, the hypothetical project discussed above (or any other project) can be appraised from four different points of view:

(i) the **project** benefit-cost analysis: this is represented by Area A+B and is obtained by valuing all project inputs and outputs at private market prices;

(ii) the **private** benefit-cost analysis: this is obtained by netting out tax and interest and debt flows from the project appraisal, and, if the firm's equity holders are not part of the referent group as in our example illustrated in Figure 1.3, it will be given by area B: which, in this example, is the non-referent group project net benefit;

(iii) the **efficiency** benefit-cost analysis: this is represented by Area A+B+C and is obtained in a similar way to the project appraisal, except that the prices used to value inputs or outputs are shadow- or accounting-prices, which are discussed in Chapter 5, or are derived from the application of non-market valuation techniques as discussed in Chapter 12;

(iv) the **referent group** (or social) benefit-cost analysis: this is represented by Area A+C and can be obtained in two ways as noted below – directly, by enumerating the costs and benefits experienced by all members of the referent group; or indirectly, by subtracting non-referent group net benefits from the net benefits calculated by the efficiency analysis. In our example, the non-referent group net benefits are summarized by the private appraisal (Area B), although in other cases the private project owners may be part of the referent group.

In the course of undertaking a complete social benefit-cost analysis the project analyst will therefore need to follow a sequence of steps:
- First, calculate the **project** cash flow at market prices (Area A+B in Fig. 1.3)
- Second, calculate the **private** cash flow at market prices (Area B in Fig. 1.3)
- Third, recalculate the **project** cash flow at **efficiency** prices (Area A+B+C)
- Fourth, disaggregate the efficiency cash flow among the **referent group** (and non-referent group) members.

It is clear that there are two ways of going about the task of estimating Area A+C – the net benefits to the referent group: directly, by listing all the benefits and costs to all members of the referent group – in this example, labour, government organizations, and the general public – and measuring and aggregating them; or indirectly by measuring the efficiency net benefits of the project and subtracting from them the net benefits which do not accrue to the referent group. Under the first approach Area A+C is measured directly; under the second approach Area A+B+C is measured and the net benefits to those not in the referent group (represented in the example by Area B) are subtracted to give Area A+C.

At first sight it might seem strange to consider using the indirect approach. However as we will see in Chapters 4 and 5 it is relatively easy to measure the net benefits represented by areas A+B+C and B respectively. The net efficiency benefits of the project are obtained by valuing all project inputs and outputs at marginal values to the world economy: these marginal values may be represented by accounting- or shadow-prices which are artificial rather than observed market prices, and which are relatively easy to calculate, as discussed in Chapter 5, or by prices obtained from the application of non-market valuation techniques as discussed in Chapter 12. The net private benefits are obtained by using market prices which are directly observable, and deducting tax and debt flows: this calculation simply mimics the process which the firm undertakes internally to decide whether or not to proceed with the project. Measuring Area A+C directly is more difficult because each subset of the referent group which is affected by the project has to be identified and their costs and benefits measured. In summary, the indirect approach produces an aggregate measure, whereas under the direct approach the social net benefits are measured in disaggregated form and assigned to various groups. While the disaggregation provides important information which relates to the income distributional concerns of the decision-maker it is more difficult to obtain than the summary figure.

In this book we advocate the use of both approaches: measure Area A+C as A+B+C less B, and then measure its component parts directly and sum them to get Area A+C. If the same answer is not obtained in both cases an error has been made – some benefits or costs to members of the referent group have been omitted or incorrectly measured. A check of this nature on the internal consistency of the analysis is invaluable.

An analogy which may assist in determining what is to be measured and where it belongs in the analysis is to think of the project as a bucket. Costs go into the bucket and benefits come out: however the range of benefits or costs which go in or come out depends on the perspective that is taken. In the **efficiency analysis** we count all the costs and benefits measured at the appropriate shadow-prices, and the latter minus the former – the net benefits of the project – is equivalent to Area A+B+C in Figure 1.3. The **project analysis** is similar to the efficiency analysis except that all the costs and benefits are measured at market prices, where these exist, to obtain an estimate of Area A+B, and non-marketed benefits and costs are ignored. In the **private analysis**, which, in the example, measures non-referent group net benefits accruing to the foreign firm, we count all sums contributed or received by the firm's equity holders to calculate the non-referent group net benefits (Area B). In the example this consists of the project cost less the loan obtained from the domestic bank, and the project revenues less the interest and principal repayments, and the tax payments to the host country. In the **referent group** analysis we count all contributions and receipts by referent group members to estimate Area A+C: in our example this consists of Area A – the capital contribution of the domestic financial institution, together with the loan repayments and interest payments, and the taxes received by government, and Area C – the employment benefits received by domestic labour. (If there are other, non-marketed net benefits or costs accruing to *non-referent group* members, we would need to add this as an additional category, say D, which would be included in the efficiency benefit-cost analysis, but, like area B, deducted from the aggregate efficiency net benefit to arrive at the total referent group net benefit. This is considered in more detail in Chapter 6.)

At this point it should be stressed that many projects will not correspond exactly to the above example, and what is to be included in Areas A, B and C will vary from case to case. Furthermore, additional categories of project effects may be required. For example, suppose, as in the case study developed in the appendices to Chapters 4–6, that part of the cost of the project was met by a loan from a foreign bank which is not part of the referent group. To incorporate this possibility we would add the foreign bank's net benefits to Area B in Figure 1.3. Area B still forms part of the efficiency benefit-cost analysis but this area has to be subtracted from the total efficiency NPV to calculate the referent group NPV. Another possibility is that instead of paying taxes the foreign firm receives a subsidy. Areas A and B would then need to take account of the subsidy: as a credit item in Area B and a debit item in Area A. A comprehensive framework which takes account of all possible categories of benefits and costs is presented in Chapter 6.

We have discussed four ways of looking at a benefit-cost analysis, and the interrelationships among these four points of view. The client for whom we are conducting the analysis will rarely attach equal importance to each. For example, an international organization such as the IMF or World Bank may be primarily interested in the best use of scarce resources, as summarized by the efficiency analysis. A regional organization, such as a regional development bank, will also be interested in efficiency but will want to know how the host country – the referent group – is affected. The host country will be primarily concerned with referent group effects but, where a private firm is involved, may also be concerned with the viability of the project from a private viewpoint for negotiation purposes. The private firm will similarly be interested in the referent group analysis as it tries to obtain favourable terms from the host country.

The Use of Spreadsheets in Social Benefit-Cost Analysis

An important theme of this book is the use of spreadsheets in benefit-cost analysis. This theme is developed in detail in Chapters 3–6. However, since the structure of the spreadsheet directly reflects the various points of view accommodated in the social benefit-cost analysis, it is instructive to consider the layout of the spreadsheet at this point.

The spreadsheet is developed in five parts in the following order:

(i)   a data section containing all relevant information about the project – costs, outputs, prices, tax rates etc. This is the only part of the spreadsheet which contains the raw data pertaining to the project. All the entries in the remaining four parts of the spreadsheet consist of references to the data in this first section;

(ii)   a section containing the **project** benefit-cost analysis;

(iii) a section containing the **private** benefit-cost analysis;

(iv)   a section containing the **efficiency** benefit-cost analysis;

(v)   a section containing the **referent group** benefit-cost analysis.

The relationships among these sections can be illustrated by means of the following simple example. Suppose that a foreign company proposed to invest $100 in a project which will produce 10 gadgets per year for a period of 5 years. The gadgets will sell for $10 each. To produce the gadgets the firm will have to hire 20 units of labour per year at a wage of $3 per unit. The project is located in an area of high unemployment and the opportunity cost of labour is estimated to be $2 per unit. The firm will pay tax at a rate of 25% on its operating profit (defined here as its total revenue less its labour costs). There are no other costs or allowances, such as depreciation allowances, and the project has no effect on the market price of any input or output.

Figure 1.4 illustrates the structure of the spreadsheet. The project data, consisting of the capital cost, the output and input flows, the prices and shadow-prices, and the tax rate are entered in Section 1. In Section 2 the project benefit-cost analysis is conducted: the flows of costs and benefits, valued at market prices, are calculated for each of the five years of the project's life, using Section 1 as the source of the data. A net benefit stream, represented by a net cash flow, summarizes the effects of the project, and net present values at a range of discount rates, and an internal rate of return are calculated. In Section 3, the private benefit-cost analysis is conducted, again with reference to the data in Section 1. In this simple example, the benefits of the project to the private firm consist of the after-tax returns. Again the performance of the project is summarized in the form of a net cash flow, and net present values and the internal rate of return are calculated. In Section 4 the efficiency benefit-cost analysis is conducted which involves using shadow-prices where appropriate. In the simple example, the only shadow-price required is that of labour, which is $2 per unit. As in Sections 2 and 3 of the spreadsheet the net benefit stream is calculated from the data in Section 1 and expressed in the form of a net cash flow. Net present value is calculated for the chosen range of discount rates and an internal rate of return is calculated.

Section 5 contains the referent group benefit-cost analysis. In this case it is assumed that the referent group consists of the government and workers of the host country, and does not include the foreign equity holders of the private firm. The first line of the referent group

Section 1: Project Data						
Capital Cost	$100	Product Price	$10	Tax Rate	25%	
Output Flow	10	Wage	$3	Dis. Rate	5%	
Labour Input	20	Shadow Wage	$2	Dis. rate	10%	

Enter values for all project variables in "Project Data" table

		Year				
	0	1	2	3	4	5
Section 2: Project Cost-Benefit Analysis						
Benefits		100	100	100	100	100
Operating Costs		-60	-60	-60	-60	-60
Capital Costs	-100					
Net Benefit	-100	40	40	40	40	40
NPV@5% = $73.18		**NPV@10%** = $51.63		**IRR** = 29%		

Set up *Project Cash Flow* drawing on data in Section 1 (A+B in Fig. 1.3)

Section 3: Private Cost-Benefit Analysis						
Benefits		100	100	100	100	100
Operating Costs		-60	-60	-60	-60	-60
Capital Costs	-100					
Taxes		-10	-10	-10	-10	-10
Net Benefit	-100	30	30	30	30	30
NPV@5% = $29.88		**NPV@10%** = $13.72		**IRR** = 15%		

Derive *Private Cash Flow* by adding taxes to project costs (B in Fig. 1.3)

Section 4: Efficiency Cost-Benefit Analysis						
Benefits		100	100	100	100	100
Operating Costs		-40	-40	-40	-40	-40
Capital Costs	-100					
Net Benefit	-100	60	60	60	60	60
NPV@5% = $159.77		**NPV@10%** = $127.45		**IRR** = 53%		

Derive *Efficiency Cash Flow* using shadow wage (A+B+C in Fig. 1.3)

Section 5: Referent Group Cost-Benefit Analysis						
Referent Group Aggregate Net Benefits						
	0	30	30	30	30	30
Referent Group Net Benefit Allocation						
Govt. (taxes)		10	10	10	10	10
Labour (rent)		20	20	20	20	20
Total		30	30	30	30	30

Net Present Values	5%	10%
Govt.	$43.29	$37.91
Labour	$86.59	$75.82
Total	$129.88	$113.72

Allocate *Referent Group Net Benefits* to referent groups, "*Government*" and "*Labour*"

Figure 1.4 The Benefit-Cost Analysis Spreadsheet

analysis is simply the difference between the efficiency net benefit stream and the private net benefit stream. While this calculation gives us the aggregate net benefits to the referent group, we want some information about the distribution of these benefits. The two groups of beneficiaries are the government and labour and we enter the net benefit streams accruing to each: tax revenues to government, and rent to labour – wages in excess of those which could be earned in the alternative activity. When these two benefit streams are added we get an alternative measure of the referent group net benefit stream.

If the referent group net benefit measures obtained by the two methods of calculation are inconsistent in any year, an error has occurred, perhaps in shadow-pricing or in identifying or measuring benefits or costs to referent group members. Once any discrepancy has been accounted for and corrected, summary measures of the performance of the project from the viewpoint of the referent group can be prepared. In this case net present values only are presented because the referent group net benefit stream does not have an internal rate of return, for reasons discussed in Chapter 2.

In summary, we have developed a template for conducting a social benefit-cost analysis, using a spreadsheet, which contains an internal check for accuracy. Because project data are entered in Section 1 only, we can use our model to perform sensitivity analyses simply by changing one cell entry in the data Section. For example, suppose the tax rate were increased to 40%, would there still be sufficient inducement to the foreign firm to proceed with the investment, while providing a reasonable net benefit stream to the referent group? To answer this question, all we need do is change the tax rate cell in Section 1 to 40% and review the new set of results.

The Rationale for Public Projects

It was suggested above that a set of accounting-prices (usually termed shadow-prices), or a set of prices obtained by use of non-market valuation techniques was required to calculate the efficiency net benefit stream of the proposed project. This raises the question of what is wrong with market prices, or why markets do not exist for some commodities which affect economic welfare, and indirectly raises the issue of the rationale for public projects – and social benefit-cost analysis.

It would be appropriate to use market prices to calculate the efficiency net benefit stream of a project if these prices measured the benefits (opportunity costs) of all project outputs (inputs). This condition would be satisfied if markets were competitive (in the sense that no market participant can have any individual influence on price), undistorted (by taxes and public regulation, for example) and complete (in the sense that everything that contributes to economic welfare is traded in a market). If we lived in such a world, market prices would accurately measure social benefits and costs, and since participants in markets are assumed to be utility or profit maximizers, every scarce input would be allocated to its highest value use. The economy would be working efficiently in the sense that no reallocation of scarce resources could make anyone better off without making someone else worse off to a greater degree.

What then would be the role of the public sector? While governments might be concerned with the fairness of the income distribution generated by the market economy the argument that public intervention, either in the form of undertaking projects or requiring modifications to proposed private projects, could lead to a more efficient allocation of resources would be unsustainable. In other words, if markets are perfect and the existing distribution of income is deemed optimal, there is no need for public projects, social benefit-cost analysis, and social benefit-cost analysts!

In fact, as discussed in detail in Chapter 5, in most economies markets are non-competitive, distorted and incomplete to a greater or lesser degree. Even the so-called "free market economies" are rife with market imperfections – budding social benefit-cost analysts can breathe a sigh of relief! Proposed private sector projects are not necessarily in the public interest, and projects which are in the public interest will not necessarily be undertaken by the private sector and will require government involvement. However market imperfections constitute a double-edged sword: because some markets are imperfect to a significant degree we cannot trust the prices they generate to accurately measure the efficiency benefits and costs of a proposed project. This means that for the purpose of undertaking a project appraisal, the analyst needs to modify observed market prices in various ways to ensure that they reflect efficiency values, or, in cases in which the market does not exist, to generate them in other ways. It should be stressed that these modifications are for the purpose of the social benefit-cost analysis only: the accounting- or shadow-prices are not actually used to pay for project costs or charge for project benefits.

It was suggested above that even if the market economy succeeded in achieving a completely efficient allocation of resources there might still be a case for government intervention on income distributional grounds. Recalling that the decision-maker is a public servant acting under the instructions of a minister – an elected politician – it should come as no surprise that the income distributional effects of a public project – who benefits and who loses – will be an important consideration in determining whether or not the project should proceed. In Chapter 11 we outline some approaches to evaluating the income distributional effects of public projects. However we consider the social benefit-cost analyst's primary role to be identifying, measuring and evaluating the efficiency effects of the project – in particular, do the gains to the referent group outweigh the losses irrespective of who the gainers and losers are? – and to identifying and measuring, but not evaluating, the income distributional effects of the project. The former role is fulfilled by means of the aggregated approach to measuring the social net benefits of a project, whereas the latter role requires the disaggregated approach to referent group net benefit measurement described earlier.

The social benefit-cost analysis should identify sub-groups among the referent group who are significantly affected by the project – for example, a proposed new airport will benefit air travellers but will inflict costs on residents in the vicinity of the proposed site. The analyst needs to identify the nature of these effects – reduced travel time for passengers, and increased noise for residents – to measure them in physical units – hours saved, additional decibels endured – and to quantify them in dollar terms as far as possible. The role of the decision-maker is then to determine whether X dollars worth of gain for one group justifies Y dollars worth of pain for another.

The Role of the Analyst

To this point we have described the analyst's role as if she was a passive actor in the benefit-cost process – called in to provide information about a particular proposal and then dismissed once the report has been submitted. This view neglects a very important function of the analyst – that of project design – a function which emerges during the process of scoping the analysis. Suppose that the analyst is contacted by the Department of Agriculture: "We are considering building a 30 metre dam at the end of Headless Valley to provide irrigation water to farmers. We would like you to do a benefit-cost analysis." At the first meeting with Department officials the analyst needs to ask: why a 30 metre dam? Why Headless Valley and not somewhere else? Why is the dam not also producing electricity? What provisions have been made for recreational access? And so on. In the process of this meeting it may emerge that all these questions have been carefully considered and that in fact the proposed project design is the best option. However often it turns out that in the process of determining exactly what is to be appraised the analyst is able to assist the Department officials in clarifying their objectives and refining their proposal. In other words, benefit-cost analysis is not limited to a linear process of project design, from appraisal to implementation, but can be a feedback process as illustrated in Figure 1.5.

Project evaluation – the retrospective assessment of project benefits and costs – may also play a part in this process by providing valuable information about the appropriate design of

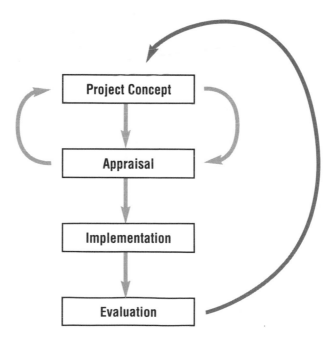

Figure 1.5 Project Appraisal and Evaluation as a Continuous Process

future projects. However, it is worth noting that government agencies seldom commission retrospective project evaluations, suggesting that governments are more inclined to use benefit-cost analysis as a tool to support current decisions than for assessing their performance in implementing past decisions.

It has been suggested that the analyst may be able to help the client formulate a better proposal – one which has a higher net present value to the referent group than the original proposal – although this does not guarantee that the revised project can be recommended on efficiency grounds. However the analyst may also be able to assist with the income distributional aspects of the project: these are sometimes difficult to identify and may emerge only during the drafting of the report. At this stage the analyst may be in a position to suggest measures which may offset the losses which some sub-groups would experience if the proposal went ahead. For example, Headless Valley may be a prime area for wild-life viewing and birdwatching. Is there an alternative area which could be developed as a substitute? This would reduce the net loss suffered by the nature viewing group and make the project more "fair" in terms of its distributional effects. It might incidentally, and of interest to the politician, reduce the level of political opposition to the proposed project.

Further Reading

Most introductory- or intermediate-level microeconomics texts contain sections devoted to the three main economic issues arising in this Chapter: the notion of scarcity and opportunity cost; how to identify a change in the level of economic welfare; and the failure of markets to allocate resources efficiently. The latter two issues are the main topic of welfare economics, about which many books have been written, some of which are quite technical. An advanced text with a focus on practical issues is R. E. Just, D. L. Hueth and A. Schmitz, *Applied Welfare Economics and Public Policy* (Prentice Hall, 1982). See also A. E. Boardman, D. H. Greenberg, A. R. Vining, and D. L. Weimer, *Cost-Benefit Analysis: Concepts and Practice* (Prentice Hall, 2001) Chs. 1 and 2.

Exercises

1. The Casino has given you $100 worth of complimentary chips which must be wagered this evening. There are two tables – roulette and blackjack. The expected value of $100 bet on roulette is $83, and the expected value of $100 bet on blackjack is $86. What is:
    (i) the opportunity cost of betting the chips on roulette?
    (ii) the opportunity cost of betting the chips on blackjack?

2. Suppose you have been offered a choice of two part-time jobs: 10 hours a week stacking shelves at the supermarket for $10 an hour; or 12 hours a week working in the bar of the local hotel for $8 per hour plus a free case of beer once a week. Assuming that you will take one and only one of the jobs, what is:
    (i) the opportunity cost of taking the supermarket job?
    (ii) the opportunity cost of taking the hotel job?

3. A foreign firm is considering a project which has present values of benefits and costs, at market prices, of $100 and $60 respectively. If the project goes ahead, tax of $20 will be paid to the host country, and pollution costing the host country $10 will occur. Assuming that the owners of the foreign firm are not part of the referent group, what are the net present values generated by:
    (i)   the project benefit-cost analysis;
    (ii) the private benefit-cost analysis;
    (iii) the efficiency benefit-cost analysis;
    (iv) the referent group benefit-cost analysis?

4. Suppose that the economy consists of three individuals, A, B, and C, and that there are three projects being considered. The net benefits, measured in dollars, received by the three individuals from each of the three projects are reported in the following Table:

Individual	Project		
	1	2	3
A	−10	+20	+5
B	+5	+1	−5
C	+10	+1	−1

Which of the projects, if any, can be described as follows:
(i)   a Pareto improvement
(ii) a potential (though not an actual) Pareto improvement
(iii) neither a potential nor an actual Pareto improvement.

2
Investment Appraisal: Principles

Introduction

This Chapter provides a simple introduction to the principles of investment appraisal. It starts with an outline of the logic of the investment appraisal process from the viewpoint of an individual considering a very simple type of project. During the course of the discussion of this process such concepts as the discount rate, discount factor, present value, benefit/cost ratio, marginal productivity of capital and internal rate of return are developed. The discussion then shifts to the economy as a whole and the role of investment appraisal in allocating resources between investment and the production of goods for consumption. The simple algebra of various investment decision-rules applied in the latter part of the Chapter is then presented, followed by a numerical example. Following this, some special concepts, such as annuities, economic depreciation, inflation and risk, are discussed in the context of investment appraisal.

In the following chapter (Chapter 3), the discussion shifts to applications of the various investment decision-rules. Some of the applications rely on the simple algebraic concepts already discussed in Chapter 2, while some are developed using the basic tool of the benefit-cost analyst – the spreadsheet. Some issues already raised in this Chapter, such as the time value of money and the calculation of present value and internal rate of return, are explored further, while new concepts, such as comparison of projects and capital rationing are introduced and discussed.

Investment Appraisal from a Personal Viewpoint

Economists start from the proposition that an individual's economic welfare in a given time period is determined by the quantity of goods and services she consumes in that time period; consumption of goods and services is taken to be the ultimate goal of economic activity. However sometimes it pays to use scarce resources – land, labour and capital – to produce capital goods in the present so that the flow of consumption goods and services (hereafter referred to as "consumption goods") can be augmented in the future. Two important processes are at work here: saving – which is refraining from consumption so that scarce resources are freed up for a use other than producing goods for current consumption; and investing – which is the process of using scarce resources to produce goods for future consumption. Sometimes an individual undertakes both activities – for example, instead of spending all of her income on current consumption goods an individual spends part of it in refurbishing the basement of her house so that it can be let. However often the connection between saving and investment is made through a financial intermediary such as a bank: the individual saves, lends to the bank, the bank lends to the investor who uses the money to construct the capital good.

How is an individual to decide whether a particular investment is worthwhile? Take the example of the person considering investing in refurbishing part of their house for letting. There are two options under consideration: do not undertake the investment and the required saving, in which case all income received in each period can be used to purchase consumption goods; or undertake the investment, in which case the value of consumption will be lower in the current period by the amount of the saving required to finance the investment, but higher in future periods by the amount of the rent net of any letting costs. To make it simple, suppose that there are only two periods of time – this year and next year – and assume that all payments and receipts occur at the end of the year in question (this is an assumption about the "accrual date" to which we will return later), and that the reference point (the "present" in a present value calculation) is the end of this year (now). This means that benefits or costs assumed to occur at the end of this year are not discounted, and those occurring at the end of next year are discounted by one period back to the present.

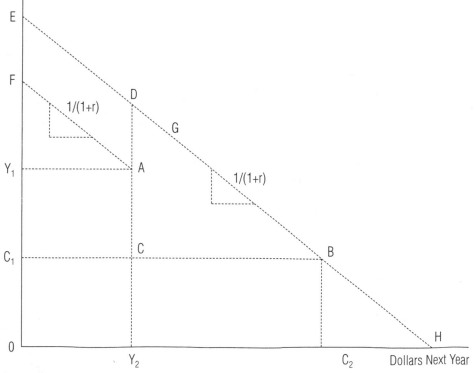

Figure 2.1 Investment Appraisal – a Private Perspective

The two options available are illustrated in Figure 2.1. The individual's income levels in the two years, from sources other than the investment, are given by Y_1 and Y_2, represented by point A. The consumption level in the first year is Y_1 if the investment is not undertaken. The cost of the investment is Y_1-C_1, where C_1 represents the consumption level in year 1 if the investment is undertaken (income of Y_1 less savings of Y_1-C_1); this is represented by the length AC in Figure 2.1. Undertaking the investment provides a return which allows the individual to spend more on consumption goods in year 2 than her income from other sources. Consumption in year 2 is C_2 and this means that the return on the investment is C_2-Y_2, represented by length BC in Figure 2.1.

How is the investor to decide whether it is worthwhile undertaking the project? To be worthwhile, clearly the project must be at least as good an investment as putting the money to be expended on the project in the bank instead. How does the return on the investment compare with the alternative of placing the savings in the bank? There are two main ways of answering this question: the rate of return on the proposed investment can be compared with the rate of return on money deposited in the bank; or the cost of the project, Y_1-C_1 in Figure 2.1, can be compared with the present value of the project return – the sum of money which would have to be deposited in the bank now to yield a future return equal to the project return, C_2-Y_2 in Figure 2.1. Both these approaches recognize the "time value of money", which means that dollars at different points of time cannot be directly compared.

If the individual puts \$AC in the bank this year she will have the principal plus interest available to spend on consumption goods next year: this amounts to \$AC(1+r) where r is the annual **rate of interest** the money earns in the bank. If \$AC(1+r)<BC then the return from the bank is less than that from the investment. Put another way, if BC/AC>(1+r) the investment is worth undertaking. BC/AC is the **marginal productivity of capital** – the ratio of the return on the investment to its cost – and the **internal rate of return**, (BC−AC)/AC, is given by the marginal productivity less 1 which we will denote by r_p. It can readily be ascertained from the above relationships that the investment is worth undertaking if r_p>r – if the internal rate of return (IRR) on the investment is greater than the rate of interest, r.

While the internal rate of return is often calculated as part of a social benefit-cost analysis, it is not as frequently relied upon as the **net present value** of the project, for reasons discussed later in the Chapter. The condition for the project yielding a higher rate of return than that offered by the bank can be rewritten as BC/(1+r)>AC, where BC/(1+r) is the **present value** of the project, AC is its opportunity cost, and r is the rate of interest paid by the bank. The present value is obtained by multiplying the project return, BC, by the **discount factor** 1/(1+r), where r is the **discount rate**. In terms of Figure 2.1 this is accomplished by projecting the length BC on to the vertical line through AC to get a point such as D, where DC is the present value; since DC=BC/(1+r) it is apparent that the slope DC/BC equals the discount factor 1/(1+r). The net present value (NPV) is the present value of the return less the cost of the investment: BC/(1+r) – AC, and is measured by the distance DA in Figure 2.1.

If the NPV is positive the present value of the project's return is greater than the present value of its opportunity cost and the project will make the individual better off. Another way of expressing the NPV>0 condition is in the form of a **benefit/cost ratio**: [BC/(1+r)]/AC>1.

Finally, note that the IRR can be defined as the discount rate which makes the NPV=0:

since r_p = BC/AC – 1, BC/(1+r_p) – AC = 0. Yet another way of assessing the project is to compare the project cost, AC, **compounded forward** at the rate of interest, with the project return, BC: if the future net value of the project, BC – AC(1+r)>0 the project is worthwhile undertaking. The project net benefit compounded forward (known as the terminal value) is seldom used although it does have a role in project selection under a budget constraint.

Instead of making a direct comparison of the cost, AC, and the present value of the return, DC, of the investment project, the project could have been evaluated indirectly by comparing the consumption streams with and without the project, represented by points A and B respectively in Figure 2.1. The present value of stream A is given by point F and the present value of B by point E. Since 0E>0F the individual is better off with the project than without it. This gives rise to a general rule (which applies when the lending and borrowing rates of interest are the same[1]): the individual can maximize economic welfare by maximizing the present value of consumption; whatever the individual's preference for present relative to future consumption is she should choose to produce at point B rather than at A because she can trade along the line BE (by lending or borrowing in the initial period) to reach a point superior to A, such as G for example, where she can consume more in both periods than the income levels Y_1 and Y_2 permit. This rule is very important in investment analysis: it means that the analyst does not need to know anything about the individual's preferences for present versus future consumption in order to recommend that a particular investment project be undertaken or not; if the net present value is positive the individual can be made better off by undertaking the project.

Investment Opportunities in the Economy as a Whole

Some important concepts in investment appraisal have been illustrated by means of a small project being considered by an individual – the discount rate, discount factor, net present value, internal rate of return, benefit/cost ratio and so on – but how well does the analysis translate to the economy as a whole? From the individual's point of view the rate of interest offered by the bank is the opportunity cost of the funds to be invested – if she decided not to refurbish the house she could earn interest on her money in the bank. In the wider economy the market rate of interest also measures the opportunity cost of funds since some investor is willing to borrow at that rate (otherwise it wouldn't be the market rate of interest); this means that if the NPV of the proposed project being appraised by the investor is positive using the market rate of interest as the discount rate, the present value of the benefits of the investor's project is greater than its opportunity cost.

It can be assumed that among all the investors' projects which are competing for funds there is one project which is marginal in the sense that its NPV is zero. The present value of

---

1 Individuals often face lower rates if they lend than the rates they pay if they borrow. In this case the NPV rule still holds if a lender remains a lender (use the lending rate as the discount rate), or a borrower remains a borrower (use the borrowing rate), but it no longer applies if a lender becomes a borrower, or a borrower becomes a lender, as a result of undertaking the project.

the net benefits of this project is the present value of using the required set of scarce resources in the particular way proposed by this investor. If the scarce resources are used in an alternative way – such as investing in refurbishing the basement of an individual's house – the opportunity cost of that alternative project is given by the present value of the benefits of the marginal project. In other words, discounting the alternative project by the market rate of interest and following the NPV>0 rule ensures that the benefits of the alternative project are at least as high as those of the marginal project it displaces.

It was suggested that, whatever the levels of income the individual earned in the two years, she could lend or borrow at the market rate of interest to obtain the desired consumption profile: this was described as trading along the net present value line passing through the point representing the income profile. At one extreme she could consume the entire NPV of her income stream this year (given by OE in Figure 2.1 if she undertakes the refurbishing investment), and at the other she could consume the first year's income plus interest plus the second year's income next year (given by OH).

Suppose the economy as a whole was considering the latter option: this would involve undertaking all the investment projects that could be funded by the scarce resources available this year. As many of us know to our cost, there are good investments and bad investments – projects with high IRRs and projects with low IRRs. In choosing projects to be undertaken this year it would pay to undertake the better projects first, but as more and more projects were undertaken, lower and lower quality projects would have to be accepted. This means that the

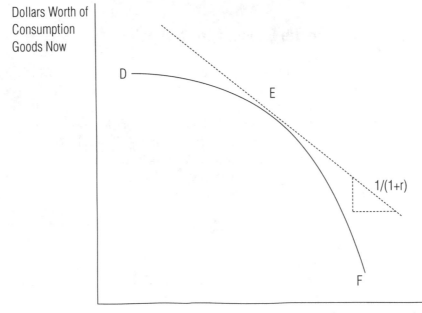

Figure 2.2 A Country's Inter-temporal Production Possibilities Curve

economy as a whole is unable to trade along an NPV line, rather it can undertake inter-temporal trades of the consumption goods it produces along a curve such as that illustrated in Figure 2.2 which shows an inter-temporal production possibilities curve (IPPC) – a curve showing all possible combinations of values of consumption goods which can be produced in the present and the future.

The IPPC starts at the consumption combination which would occur if no investment were undertaken in the current year, as represented by point D. The slope of the curve is the ratio of the cost to the benefit of the marginal project, which in the light of our earlier discussion (consider the ratio AC/BC in Figure 2.1) can be identified as a discount factor based on the project's IRR. As we move along the curve in the direction of increased output of goods in the future the internal rate of return on the next project in line falls (the slope of the curve, which is $1/(1+r_p)$, rises and hence r_p must fall) – this is termed **diminishing marginal productivity of capital**. As more and more investment projects are undertaken, production of consumption goods falls in the present and rises in the future until a point such as F is reached where present consumption is at subsistence level.

In reality the economy will not choose to be at either of the two extremes discussed above but somewhere in the middle, such as point E in Figure 2.2, where the slope of the curve measures a discount factor based on the IRR of the marginal project – the project for which NPV=0. However we know that when NPV=0 the IRR equals the discount rate. Hence the slope of the IPPC at the chosen point is the discount factor based on the market rate of

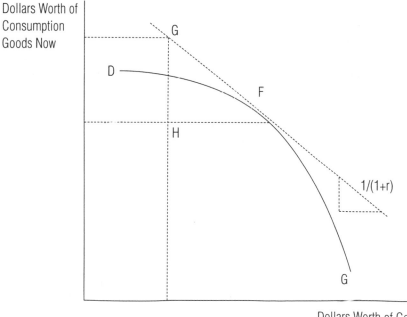

Figure 2.3 The Inter-temporal Effects of International Trade

interest. This is the interest rate which should be used in evaluating all projects – those with a positive NPV lie to the left of E and those with a negative NPV lie to the right. In summary, the role of the interest rate in investment appraisal is to ensure that no project is undertaken if its benefits are less than its opportunity cost, where opportunity cost is the value of an alternative use of the resources involved.

The above discussion neglects the possibility of international trade: countries can consume combinations of present and future goods which lie outside of the IPPC. In Figure 2.3 a country produces at point F but consumes at point G; it achieves this by borrowing GH in the present (a capital account surplus) and spending the funds on GH worth of imported goods and services (a current account deficit). In this two-period analysis the funds have to be repaid with interest the following year, consisting of an amount FH (a capital account deficit) which foreigners spend on exports from the debt repaying country valued at FH (a current account surplus). The ratio GH/FH represents a discount factor based on the interest rate which is established in international financial markets. Of course, in a multi-period world, it is possible to maintain a current account deficit for a long period of time.

The Algebra of Simple Net Present Value and Internal Rate of Return Calculations

So far the analysis has been in terms of two time periods; we now extend it to three. It will be assumed that there is a project capital cost in the current year (year 0) and a net benefit in each of years 1 and 2; a net benefit means a benefit less any project operating costs incurred in the year in question. As noted earlier, the assumption about the accrual date of benefits and costs is important.

Project benefits and costs generally accrue more or less continuously throughout the year. It would be possible to discount benefits and costs on a monthly, weekly or even daily basis using the appropriate rate of interest. However in practice such level of detail is unnecessary. Instead it is generally assumed that all costs or benefits experienced during the year occur on some arbitrarily chosen date: it could be the first day of the year, the middle day or the last day. This assumption converts the more or less continuous stream of benefits and costs to a set of discrete observations at one-year intervals. The annual rate of interest is then used to discount this discrete stream back to a present value.

There is no general rule as to which day of the year should be chosen, or whether the calendar or financial year is the relevant period. However we suggest that costs or benefits should be attributed to the last day of the calendar year in which they occur. For example, following this convention, the net cash flow of a project with a capital cost of $100 during the current calendar year, and net benefits of $60 in each of two subsequent calendar years would be treated as a cost of $100 on December 31 this year, and net benefits of $60 on December 31 in each of the two subsequent years. It should be noted that while this procedure tends to introduce a slight downward bias to a positive NPV calculation (assuming the firm has access to short-term capital markets), any other assumption about accrual dates also introduces bias.

In denoting the project years we generally call the current year "year 0" and subsequent years "year 1", "year 2" etc. Since we do not discount benefits or costs occurring in the current year, we are effectively choosing December 31 of the current year as the referent date – "the present" in the net present value calculation. Benefits or costs occurring in year 1 (by assumption on December 31) are discounted back one period, those occurring in year 2 are discounted back two periods, and so on. Thus the number used to denote the year tells us how the appropriate discount factor is to be calculated. This discussion might seem a bit laboured and trivial but consistency in the choice of accrual date is an important practical issue.

Using our assumption about the accrual date, our illustrative project has a capital cost now (K at time zero), and a net benefit one year from now (at the end of the first year), and two years from now (at the end of the second year). The resulting sequence, $-K$, B_1, B_2, can be termed a net benefit stream as illustrated in Figure 2.4. To calculate the project NPV we need to bring B_1 and B_2 to present values, sum them and then subtract the project cost, K, which is already a present value (since it is incurred in year 0).

The net benefit B_2 can be brought to a present value by using the interest rate in year 2 to bring it to a discounted value at the end of year 1, and then using the interest rate in year 1 to bring that discounted value to a present value. B_1 can be discounted to a present value using the interest rate in year 1:

$$NPV = -K + B_1/(1+r_1) + B_2/[(1+r_1)(1+r_2)]$$

In practice it is almost invariably assumed that the rate of interest is constant over time, so that $r_1 = r_2 = r$, in which case the NPV formula reduces to: $NPV = -K + B_1/(1+r) + B_2/(1+r)^2$.

To take a simple example, suppose the project costs \$1.6 and yields net benefits of \$10 after 1 and 2 years respectively, and that the rate of interest is 10%:

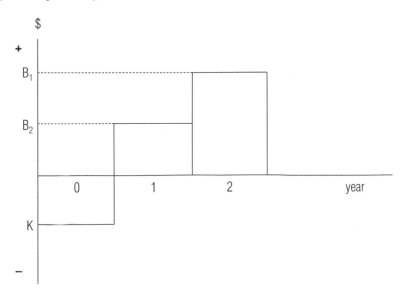

Figure 2.4 Net Benefit Stream of a Two-period Investment Project

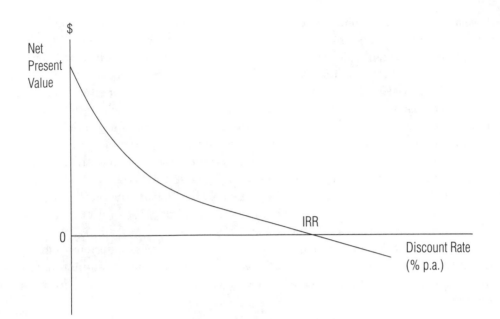

Figure 2.5 Net Present Value in Relation to the Discount Rate

$$NPV = -1.6 + 10*0.909 + 10*0.826 = 15.75$$

The values of $1/1.1$ and $1/(1.1)^2$ are obtained from a Table of Discount Factors, or by using a pocket calculator. The benefit/cost ratio is given by $17.35/1.6 = 10.84$ and the net benefit/cost ratio by $15.75/1.6 = 9.84$. (The mechanics of deriving discount factors and using discount tables are discussed in more detail in Chapter 3.) It can be seen from the NPV formula that the NPV falls as the discount factors fall, and hence as the discount rate rises; this relationship is illustrated in Figure 2.5.

It was explained earlier that the internal rate of return is the discount rate which reduces the project's NPV to zero, as denoted by IRR in Figure 2.5. It can be calculated by solving the following equation for r_p:

$$-K + B_1/(1+r_p) + B_2/(1+r_p)^2 = 0.$$

Multiplying both sides of this equation by $(1+r_p)^2$ gives an equation of the following form:

$$-Kx^2 + B_1x + B_2 = 0,$$

where $x = (1+r_p)$. This is the familiar quadratic form, as illustrated in Figure 2.6, which can be solved for x and then for r_p.

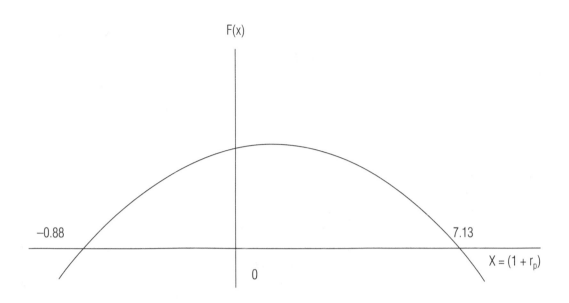

Figure 2.6 Calculating Internal Rates of Return – One Positive Value

More generally it can be noted that if we extended the analysis to include a benefit at time 3 we would need to solve a cubic, and if we further extended it to time 4 it would be a quartic equation, and so on; fortunately we will be solving only a couple of IRR problems by hand – the rest will be done by computer using a spreadsheet program.

To return to our example, we need to solve:

$$-1.6x^2 + 10x + 10 = 0.$$

Recalling our high school algebra, this is a quadratic equation of the general form:

$$ax^2 + bx + c = 0,$$

where a= –1.6, b=10, and c=10, and which has two solutions given by the formula:

$$x = [-b +/- SQRT(b^2 - 4ac)]/2a.$$

A bit of arithmetic gives us the solution values 7.13 and –0.88, which is where the function crosses the x-axis as illustrated in Figure 2.6 This means that r_p is either 6.13 (613%) or –1.88 (–188%). The negative solution has no meaning in the context of project appraisal and is discarded. Hence the IRR is 613%, which is very healthy compared with an interest rate of 10%.

Let us now change the example by making B_2 = –10. For example, the project could be a mine which involves an initial establishment cost and a land rehabilitation cost at the end of the project's life. When we calculate the IRR using the above method we find that there are two solutions as before, but that they are both positive: r_p = 0.25 (25%) or 4 (400%). Which is the correct value for use in the project appraisal process? The answer is possibly neither. As discussed above, when we use the IRR in project appraisal we accept projects whose IRR exceeds the rate of interest. In the current example the IRR clearly exceeds an interest rate in the 0–24% range, and it is clearly less than an interest rate in excess of 400%. But what about interest rates in the 25–400% range? We cannot apply the rule in this case, and it is for this reason that it is not recommended that the IRR be used in project appraisal when there is more than one positive IRR.

What would have happened if we had asked the computer to calculate the IRR in this case? The computer's approach is illustrated in Figure 2.7.

$F(x)$ is the value of the quadratic function, and setting $F(x)=0$ gives the solution values – these occur where the function crosses the x-axis. In the previous example this occurred once in the negative range of x and once in the positive range, and the negative value was discarded. However in the present case there are two positive values of x for which $F(x)=0$, 1.25 and 5. The computer solves the quadratic equation by asking for an initial guess, say $x = x_1$ in Figure 2.7. It then calculates the first derivative of the function at that value of x (the equation of the slope of the function at that point) and works out the value of x, x_2, that would set the first derivative equal to zero. It then uses x_2 as its guess and repeats the process until it converges on the solution value $x = 5$ ($r_p = 4$) in Figure 2.7.

If you had given the computer x_a, for example, as the initial guess it would have converged on the solution value $x = 1.25$ ($r_p = 0.25$). How would you know if there were two positive solutions? Some programs will report no solution or an error if there is more than one positive IRR. However a simple way of checking for the problem in advance is to count the

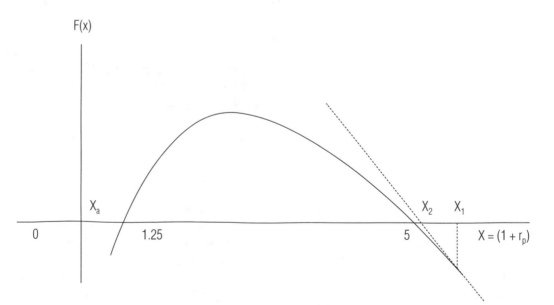

Figure 2.7 Calculating Internal Rates of Return –Two Positive Values

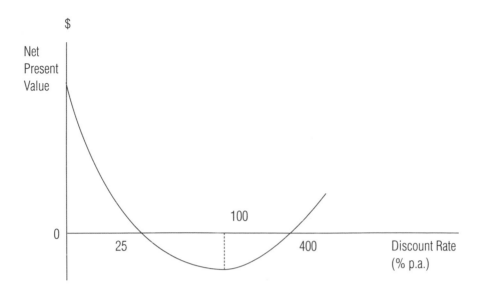

Figure 2.8 Net Present Value in Relation to the Discount Rate – the Two Positive Internal Rates of Return Case

number of sign changes in the net benefit stream. In the initial example we had a well-behaved cash flow with signs "– + +", i.e. one change of sign, hence one positive IRR. In the second example we had "– + –", i.e. two changes of sign and two positive IRRs. This is a general rule which applies to higher order equations – the number of positive solutions can be the same as the number of sign changes[2]. If you are analyzing a proposed project which has a net benefit stream (including costs as negative net benefits) with more than one change of sign, it is better not to attempt to calculate the IRR. The NPV rule will always give the correct result irrespective of the sequence of signs.

As illustrated in Figure 2.5, the IRR is the discount rate which reduces the project NPV to zero. The case in which there are two positive IRRs is illustrated in Figure 2.8, where the project NPV is positive at first, and falling as the discount rate rises, and then, after reaching some negative minimum value, it starts to rise and eventually becomes positive again. There are two points at which NPV = 0 and these correspond to the two positive IRRs. The discount rate at which NPV is a minimum, 100% in the example, can be solved for from the NPV equation.

Finally we consider a case in which no IRR can be calculated. Suppose that in the original example we change the initial cost of $1.6 to a benefit of $1.6. The net benefit stream now consists of three positive values and there is no value of the discount rate which can reduce the NPV to zero and hence no IRR. This case is illustrated in Figure 2.9 where the NPV continually falls as the discount rate increases, but never actually becomes zero.

---

2   In fact more than one change in sign is a necessary, but not a sufficient condition for the existence of more than one positive IRR. A sufficient condition is that the unrecovered investment balance becomes negative prior to the end of the project's life. The reader is referred to advanced texts for a discussion of this concept.

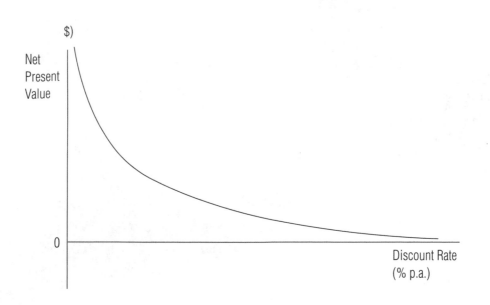

Figure 2.9 Net Present Value in Relation to the Discount Rate – the No Internal Rate of Return Case

Annuities and Perpetuities

To this point we have been considering net benefit streams consisting of three values – an initial cost (a negative net benefit) and then net benefits after one and two years respectively. Clearly it would be very tedious to do higher order examples by hand – we leave these until the following Chapter where we introduce the use of spreadsheets. However there are some additional steps we can readily take without needing the help of a computer. Suppose a project has a cost in year zero and then the same level of net benefit at the end of each and every subsequent year for a given time interval: the net benefit stream B_1, B_2, B_3 ... B_n, where $B_i = B$ for all i, is termed an **annuity**. The present value of the annuity (on December 31 of year 0) is given by:

$$PV(A) = B/(1+r) + B/(1+r)^2 + B/(1+r)^3 + ...+ B/(1+r)^n,$$

where B is the equal annual net benefit which occurs at the end of each year (the accrual date in this case). This expression is a geometrical progression – each term is formed by multiplying the previous term by a constant value – $1/(1+r)$ in this case. It is relatively easy to work out a formula for the value of the sum, S (try it as an exercise! hint: multiply S by $1/(1+r)$, subtract S from the result and rearrange). Having done this we can write the present value expression as:

$$PV(A) = B[(1+r)^n - 1]/[(1+r)^n.r],$$

which can readily be computed using a calculator. The expression $[(1+r)^n - 1]/[(1+r)^n.r]$ is known as an **annuity factor** and it can be obtained from a set of Annuity Tables. We sometimes refer to this expression as $AF_{r,n}$, where r denotes the interest rate and n denotes the length of the annuity. (The use of Annuity Tables is discussed in more detail in Chapter 3.)

In the previous example the accrual date was set at the end of each year in accordance with the normal practice. An **annuity due** is a similar stream of payments, but with the accrual date set at the beginning of each year. Its present value is given by:

$$PV(D) = B + B/(1+r) + B/(1+r)^2 + B/(1+r)^3 + \ldots\ldots + B/(1+r)^{n-1}.$$

It can be seen from the above expression that $PV(D) = PV(A) + B - B/(1+r)^n$. We can use this relation to modify the formula for the present value of an annuity to make it apply to an annuity due, or we can take the annuity factor from the Annuity Tables and add B and subtract $B/(1+r)^n$, obtained from the Discount Tables. Finally we can use the formula for the present value of an annuity to work out the present value of a **perpetuity** – an annuity that goes on forever. If we take the limit of PV(A) as n goes to infinity we get the following simple expression for the present value of a perpetuity:

$$PV(P) = B/r.$$

Where a project benefit stream takes the form of an annuity the Annuity Tables can be used to calculate the project IRR. We know that $NPV = -K + B.AF_{r,n}$, where K is project cost, B is the annual benefit and $AF_{r,n}$ is the annuity factor. To calculate the IRR we set NPV=0, giving $AF_{r,n} = K/B$. In other words, we divide the cost of the project by the annual benefit to obtain a value for the annuity factor, and then look up the column or row in the Annuity Tables which corresponds to the life, n, of the project under consideration to see which discount rate, r, corresponds to the annuity factor we obtained. That discount rate is the project IRR.

At this point it might be questioned why the various formulae discussed above are worth knowing about in the computer age. There are two main advantages: first, it is helpful to know what the computer is doing so that you can recognize an absurd result if it appears because of some programming error you may have made – such as asking for an IRR when there will be at least two positive values which may be difficult to interpret in the project appraisal. Secondly, you may be parted from your computer – it may have gone to New Caledonia while you went to Papua New Guinea (take it as hand luggage next time), or you may both be in New Caledonia but you forgot to take the adaptor plug and the batteries are low, or you were called unexpectedly into a meeting where you are supposed to provide a "back of the envelope assessment" of the project, but you left your computer at the hotel! In all these cases you will find that you can make quite a lot of progress using a pocket calculator and some elementary understanding of discounting annuities (if you forgot your pocket calculator, stick to perpetuities!).

Economic Depreciation and the Annual Cost of Capital

A useful illustration of the use of the concept of an annuity in investment analysis is the calculation of annual "economic depreciation" – not to be confused with accounting depreciation used in financial statements, as discussed in Chapter 4. Sometimes we want to express the capital cost of a project as an annual cost over the life, n years, of the project, rather than as an initial lump-sum cost, K. The annual capital cost consists of interest and depreciation, and as always in benefit-cost analysis, the cost is an opportunity cost. For simplicity we can think of the bank as the investment which is the alternative to the project being appraised. If K dollars are deposited in the bank the depositor will receive annual interest of rK at the end of each of n years, and at the end of the nth year will be repaid the principal, K. The amount rK is the annual interest cost of the capital investment. While there are various ways of computing annual economic depreciation, we need to distinguish between those methods which are mandated by the Taxation Office, and which may bear no close relation to opportunity cost, and economic depreciation. Expressed as a constant amount per year, economic depreciation is the sum of money, D, which needs to be deposited in the bank each year over the life of the project in order to recoup the initial capital investment at the end of n years.

The annual opportunity cost of the capital sum, K, is the sum of interest plus economic depreciation, and the present value of the interest plus depreciation equals the capital sum invested in the project:

$$AF_{r,n}\{rK + D\} = K,$$

where $AF_{r,n}$ is the annuity factor which brings an equal annual flow of payments over n years to a present value using the interest rate r. By rearranging this equation we can solve for the annual depreciation, D:

$$D = K\{1/AF_{r,n} - r\}.$$

Using the formula developed above for the annuity factor, D can be expressed as:

$$D = rK/\{(1+r)^n - 1\}.$$

If we want to express the capital cost of a project as an annual cost over the project life, rather than as a capital sum at the start of the project, we can do this by summing the annual interest cost, rK, and the annual depreciation cost, D, calculated according to the above formula.

It should be emphasized that the cost of capital should not be accounted for twice in a net present value calculation. When we include the initial capital cost of the project in the net benefit stream and use a discount rate reflecting the opportunity cost of capital we are taking full account of the cost of capital. If, in addition to this, we were to deduct interest and depreciation cost from the net benefit stream we would be double-counting the cost of capital. This can readily be seen by recognizing that if interest and depreciation costs have been correctly measured, their present value equals the initial capital cost. Thus to include them in the net present value calculation, as well as the initial capital cost, is to deduct the capital cost twice from the present value of net benefits of the project.

Treatment of Inflation in Investment Appraisal

We now turn to the problem of calculating present values when the values of future benefits and costs are subject to **inflation**. Inflation is a process which results in the nominal prices of goods and services rising over time. The existence of inflation raises the question of whether project inputs and outputs should be measured at the prices in force at the time of the appraisal – **constant prices** – or at the prices in force when the project input or output occurs – **current prices**.

It was argued earlier that the purpose of an NPV calculation is to compare the performance of a proposed project with the alternative use of the scarce resources involved. The alternative use is taken to be a project yielding an IRR equal to the market rate of interest – in other words, a project with an NPV=0 at the market rate of interest. The market rate of interest is generally taken to be the rate of return on a riskless asset such as government bonds. If you look up the government bond rate in the financial press it will be quoted at some rate, m, which includes two components – the **real rate of interest**, r, and the **anticipated rate of inflation**, i: m = r + i. In other words, the anticipated rate of inflation is built into the money rate of interest. For example, if the rate of interest on government bonds is reported as 5% (the financial press always quotes the rate of interest on money) this will consist of perhaps 3% real rate of interest and 2% anticipated inflation. The anticipated inflation rate cannot be observed, although it can be inferred from an analysis of a time series of money interest rates and rates of inflation. Often it is assumed that the anticipated inflation rate is the current rate, and that the real rate of interest is the money rate less the current rate of inflation.

When you calculate the present value of a commodity, such as a tonne of coal at time t, you calculate the value of the tonne of coal at time t, B_t, and then calculate the present value of that value, $B_t/(1+ x)^t$, where x represents the appropriate rate of discount. A simple rule, which it is vitally important to remember, is that **if you include inflation in the numerator of the present value calculation you must also include it in the denominator**. What does this mean? There are two ways of calculating the value of a tonne of coal at time t: we could use constant prices, which do not include the inflation which will occur between now and time t, or we could use the anticipated price at time t, incorporating inflation. Similarly, there are two ways of discounting the value of the coal back to a present value: we could use the real rate of interest – the money rate less the rate of inflation – or we could use the money rate. If inflation is included in the value of coal at time t the money rate of interest (which incorporates inflation) must be used as the discount rate; if inflation is not included, the real rate of interest must be used.

Which is the better approach? It can be shown that when the prices of all commodities inflate at the same rate the two procedures give the same result. At today's price, P_0, the value of a quantity of coal at time t, Q_t, is given by $P_0 Q_t$. The present value of the coal, using the real rate of interest, r, is given by $P_0 Q_t/(1+r)^t$. At the inflated price of coal its value at time t is given by $P_0(1+i)^t Q_t$ where i is the annual inflation rate. The present value, at the money rate of interest, m, is given by $P_0 Q_t (1+i)^t/(1+m)^t$, or $P_0 Q_t [(1+i)/(1+m)]^t$. Since $(1+i)/(1+m)$ is approximately equal to $1/(1+m-i)$, where $m-i = r$ is the real rate of interest, the two procedures give essentially the same result.

Are there any circumstances in which one approach is preferred to the other? Suppose that all commodities are not expected to rise in price at the same rate over time. For example, the income elasticity of demand for outdoor recreation services is thought to exceed unity; this means that as a consumer's income rises she spends an increasing proportion of it on outdoor recreation. In consequence, rising per capita incomes will result in a significant increase in demand for these services, relative to that for commodities with low income elasticity of demand, and hence, given supply limitations, in a rise in the price of outdoor recreation services relative to the prices of other commodities. Suppose you are appraising an outdoor recreation project and want to take account of the effect of the rising relative unit value of outdoor recreation services. If the unit value is expected to rise at a rate i_c, the present value of a unit of recreation service at time t is given by: $P_0 [(1+i_c)/(1+m)]^t$, where P_0 is the unit value at time zero; this value exceeds $P_0/(1+r)^t$ as long as $i_c > i$. (Note that P_0 is a shadow-price, as discussed in Chapter 5.) In this example, in which the rate of price increase of the output (or of a significant input) is expected to be different from the general rate of price inflation, omitting inflation from the evaluation will give an incorrect estimate of present value. Such cases are not unusual: as noted above, any good which has a high income elasticity of demand and faces significant supply limitations is likely to experience a relative price increase as per capita income rises.

Incorporating a Risk Factor in the Discount Rate

It is quite common for private investment projects to be appraised using a discount rate which includes a risk factor: if the money rate of interest is 5% the discount rate may be set at 8%, allowing 3% for project risk. We favour a more formal approach to risk analysis, which is described in Chapter 9, but here we examine the basis of this kind of adjustment for risk as the analysis is similar to the discussion of inflation which we have just completed.

Suppose that a project will yield a net benefit of B_t in year t, provided that some catastrophe has not occurred in the intervening years – for example, a dam will produce electricity if it hasn't burst in the meantime, or a forest will produce timber if it hasn't been consumed by fire, or an oil well will generate revenues for its private sector owners if it hasn't been nationalized in the meantime. Suppose that the probability of catastrophe is p per year – for example, a 2% chance (p=0.02) each year that the catastrophe will occur during that year. The expected value of the project net benefit in year t is given by: $E(B_t) = B_t (1-p)^t$, where $(1-p)^t$ is the probability of the catastrophe not occurring during the time interval to t. The present value of the expected net benefit is given by: $PV = B_t(1-p)^t/(1+r)^t$ or $B_t[(1-p)/(1+r)]^t$. Since $(1-p)/(1+r)$ is approximately equal to $1/(1+r+p)$ the expected present value of the net benefit in year t can be obtained by discounting by the interest rate plus the risk factor. There are two reasons why we don't advocate this approach to costing risk: firstly, the "risk" involved has a very special time profile which projects in general may not exhibit; and, secondly, if the normal economic view of risk as variance around an expected outcome is taken, the procedure doesn't deal with risk at all, but rather only with calculating the expected value of the outcome.

Further Reading

A classic work on the economic theory underlying investment analysis is J. Hirschliefer, *Investment, Interest and Capital* (Prentice Hall, 1970). A useful book which deals with practical problems involving NPV and IRR calculations, and issues such as depreciation is L. E. Bussey, *The Economic Analysis of Industrial Projects* (Prentice Hall, 1978).

Exercises

1. A firm is considering a project which involves investing $100 now for a return of $112 a year from now. What are the values of the following variables?
    (i)   the marginal productivity of the capital investment;
    (ii) the internal rate of return on the project;
    (iii) the net present value of the project, using a 5% discount rate;
    (iv) the project benefit-cost ratio;
    (v)   the project net benefit-cost ratio.

2. A project requires an initial investment of $100,000 and an annual operating cost of $10,000. It will generate an annual revenue of $30,000. If the life of the project is 10 years and the discount rate is 6%, decide whether to accept or reject this project using (i) NPV criterion, and (ii) IRR criterion.

3. Given the following information, use two different methods to calculate the present value of a tonne of coal to be received one year from now:

money rate of interest:	8% per annum
expected rate of general price inflation:	6% per annum
expected rate of increase in the price of coal:	2% per annum
current price of coal:	$25 per tonne

3
Investment Appraisal: Decision-Rules

Introduction

In this Chapter the discussion shifts to applications of the various investment decision-rules discussed in the previous Chapter. Some of the applications rely on the simple algebraic concepts already discussed in Chapter 2, while some are developed using the basic tool of the benefit-cost analyst – the spreadsheet. Some issues already raised in Chapter 2, such as the time value of money and the calculation of present value and internal rate of return, are explored further, while new concepts, such as comparison of projects under capital rationing, are introduced and discussed. Finally, the use of spreadsheets in project appraisal is discussed in detail.

Discounted Cash Flow Analysis in Practice

We now turn to evaluating multi-period investment projects – projects that have a net benefit stream occurring over many years. The remainder of this Chapter aims at familiarizing the reader with the practical application of discounted cash flow (DCF) decision-making techniques. At the end of the section the reader should know how decisions are made: to accept or reject a particular project; to select a project from a number of alternatives; and, to rank a number of projects in order of priority. Slightly different DCF decision-rules apply in each case. Although some examples are given to illustrate the use of these techniques, the exercises at the end of this section are also useful.

The widespread availability and relatively low cost of personal computers have transformed the task of the project analyst. Electronic spreadsheets such as *Excel, Lotus 1-2-3*, and *Quattro* have greatly facilitated the previously laborious, computational side to benefit-cost analysis. Repetitive, mechanical calculations can now be performed at will, which has the enormous advantage of allowing more project options and alternative scenarios to be considered than ever before. However, it should not be assumed that the PC spreadsheet program can assist in the design or setting-up of the framework for the project analysis. This requires both skill and art on the part of the analyst. This section aims at familiarizing readers with the necessary techniques, framework, and computer skills.

As noted earlier, benefit-cost analysis (BCA) is a particular method of appraising and evaluating investment projects from a public interest perspective. In later parts of this book, in particular in Chapter 5, we will examine the main differences between private and social benefit-cost analysis. At this stage these differences are not important because essentially the same principles and techniques of discounted cash flow analysis apply to both private and public sector investment analysis.

Common to all DCF analysis is the conceptualisation of an investment project as a net benefit stream as measured by a "cash flow". Economists define an investment in terms of the decision to commit resources now in the expectation of realising a flow of net benefits over a reasonably long period in the future. This flow of net benefits, measured in terms of a net cash flow, can be represented graphically as in Figure 2.4 in the previous chapter.

When resources (funds) are given up now, as investment outlays, the "cash flow" is negative, indicating that there is a net outflow of funds. Once the project begins operations, and benefits (revenues) are forthcoming, the cash flow becomes positive (hopefully), indicating that there is a net inflow of funds. What is represented here is a **net** cash flow, measuring the annual benefits less costs, so we should not forget that throughout the project's life there are also outflows in the form of operating costs.

It should also be noted that although we use the term *cash flow*, the monetary values assigned to the costs and benefits in BCA might be different from the actual pecuniary costs and benefits of the project. This point is taken up later in Chapter 5 when we discuss *Efficiency Benefit-Cost Analysis* and the principles and methods of *shadow-pricing*.

The process of project appraisal and evaluation can be considered in terms of three aspects of cash flow analysis:

(i) **identification** of costs and benefits
(ii) **valuation** of costs and benefits
(iii) **comparison** of costs and benefits.

In this Chapter we consider item (iii), assuming that the relevant costs and benefits of the project we are appraising have been identified and valued. Chapter 4 deals with items (i) and (ii) from a private perspective, Chapter 5 considers them from an efficiency perspective, and Chapter 6 considers them from the perspective of the referent group.

Discounting and the Time Value of Money

By this stage you should be familiar with the concept of the net cash flow of a project (NCF) and are aware that to compare benefits and costs accruing at different points in time, we cannot simply add up all project benefits and take away all project costs, unless of course we are assuming that the discount rate is zero. There is a need for **discounting** when comparing any flow of funds (costs and revenues or benefits) over time. To consider the process of discounting in practice, consider two investment projects, A and B. The net cash flows of these projects are given as:

Year	0	1	2	3
Project A	−100	+50	+40	+30
Project B	−100	+30	+45	+50

Remember the convention we use to denote the initial year of the project, "year 0". If project years are also calendar years, then all costs and benefits accruing during that year are assumed to accrue on 31 December of that year. Therefore, any costs or benefits accruing in the course of the next year, "year 1", are also assumed to accrue on 31 December of that year; i.e. one year from year 0. Similarly, "year 2" refers to two years from year 0, and so on. Of course, there is no reason why the chosen time period need be a year. It could be a quarter, month, week or day – the same principles hold whatever the time period used, but then of course the (annual) discount rate would have to be adjusted accordingly.

Our task is to compare projects A and B. Which would you prefer? A and B both have total costs of $100, but A's benefits total $120 while B's benefits total $125. Can we say that B is preferred to A because $125–$100 is greater than $120–$100? Obviously not as this calculation ignores the *timing* of cash inflows and outflows: they are not the same. We need to discount all future values to derive their equivalent **present values**.

How do we accomplish this? From the previous Chapter we saw that we need to derive the appropriate **discount factor**. What is the present value (PV) of $100 a year from now assuming a discount rate of 10% per annum?

$$PV = \$100 \times 1/1.1 = \$100(0.909)$$
$$= \$90.9$$

The value "0.909" in this example is the discount factor. It tells us the amount by which any value *one year from now* must be multiplied by to convert it to its present value, *assuming a discount rate of 10% per annum*.

What about the present values of benefit accruing in years beyond year 1? These values need to be discounted a number of times, and we will perform these calculations making the usual assumption that the discount rate is constant from year to year:

Example 3.1: Discounting a Net Present Value Stream

Year	0	1	2	3
Project A	−100	+50	+40	+30

PV of $50 = $50(0.909)
PV of $40 = $40(0.909)(0.909)
PV of $30 = $30(0.909)(0.909)(0.909)

By converting all future values to their equivalent present values (discounting) we make them directly comparable. For example, what is the PV of $40, 2 years from now?

$$PV \text{ in year } 1 = \$40 \times 0.909 = \$36.36$$
$$PV \text{ in year } 0 = \$36.36 \times 0.909 = \$33.05.$$

We have already noted that the discount factors (DFs) do not have to be calculated from our formulae each time we want to perform a calculation, as they are usually available in Discount Tables, which give discount factors for different discount rates (interest rates) and years (see Appendix 2, p 340). Table 3.1 shows the DFs for 10% and 15% rates of discount (interest) to three decimal places:

Table 3.1 Discount Factors for 10% and 15% Discount Rates

Year	1	2	3	4	5	6	7	8	9	10
10%	0.909	0.826	0.751	0.683	0.621	0.565	0.513	0.467	0.424	0.386
15%	0.870	0.756	0.658	0.572	0.497	0.432	0.376	0.327	0.284	0.247

The present value of $100 accruing in 10 years' time, assuming a 10% discount rate, is found arithmetically by: $100 × 0.386, where 0.386 is the discount factor for year 10 at a 10% discount rate, and obtained from the above Table. This discounting technique can now be used to discount the whole net cash flow (NCF) of a project to obtain its discounted net cash flow. In order to obtain this, one simply multiplies the net benefit (or cost) in each year by the respective DF, given a particular discount rate. To illustrate this, the NCF of a hypothetical project is discounted in the following example.

Example 3.2: Calculating Discounted Net Cash Flow

Table 3.2 Discounted Net Cash Flow for a Hypothetical Project ($ millions)

Year	0	1	2	3	4	5
1 NCF	−1000	200	300	400	500	600
2 DF_{10}	1.000	0.909	0.826	0.751	0.683	0.621
3 Discounted NCF (1x2)	−1000.0	181.8	247.9	300.5	341.5	372.5

To obtain row (3) we simply multiplied row (1) by row (2). Note that for year 0 the DF is always 1: this is so, irrespective of what the discount rate is, because $DF_0 = 1/(1+r)^0$. From the Discounted Net Cash Flow we then derive the Net Present Value (NPV):

$$NPV_{0.10} = -\$1000.0 + \$1444.2 = \$444.2 \text{ million.}$$

Using Annuity Tables

We also saw in the previous Chapter that when an investment project produces a cash flow with a regular or constant amount in each year it is possible to calculate the present value of this stream more easily using an **Annuity Table**. For example, consider the following cash flow and discount factors for 10%:

Year	0	1	2	3	4
NCF	−100	35	35	35	35
DF	1.0	0.909	0.826	0.751	0.683

We could calculate the PV of net benefits by multiplying each year's cash flow by its respective DF and then summing these up. Alternatively, because each year's cash flow from year 1 onwards is the same, we can simply add up the DFs and then multiply the *cumulative DF* by the constant amount: $(0.909+0.826+0.751+0.683) \times \$35 = 3.169 \times \$35 = \$110.92$

In fact, there is an even quicker method. Annuity Tables (see Appendix 2, p. 341) provide us with the values of the cumulative discount factors for all discount rates and years. We simply look up year 4 in the 10% column and read off the *annuity factor* (AF) of 3.170.

Example 3.3: Using the Annuity Table
Find the NPV of an investment with an initial cost of $1000 and an annual return of $500 for three years, when the discount rate is 4%.

$$NPV(A)_{0.04} = -1000 + 500(0.962) + 500(0.925) + 500(0.889)$$
$$= -1000 + 500(2.776)$$

From the Annuity Table, year 3 at 4% gives the annuity factor 2.775. The value 2.775 is the annuity factor (AF) for a 3 year annuity at a 4% discount rate, and it is obtained from Annuity Tables in the same way as obtaining the DF for a given year and discount rate. (The slight difference is due to rounding.)

Note that the Annuity Tables can be used to calculate the PV of a stream of equal annual net benefits occurring over a subset of consecutive years during a project's life. For example, a project may have equal NCF for years, say, 5 to 10 of its life, and different NCF in other years. In this case Annuity Tables can be used for years 5 to 10, and Discount Tables for other years. The AF for years 5 to 10 is simply found by subtraction of the AF for year 4 from the AF for year 10, i.e.

$$AF_{5 \text{ to } 10} = AF_{10} - AF_4$$
$$= 6.145 - 3.179$$
$$= 2.975 \text{ (at 10\% rate of discount)}$$

In general if you want to find the AF for years X to Y, then use the following rule (where $Y > X$):

$$AF_{x \text{ to } y} = AF_y - AF_{x-1}$$

i.e. the appropriate AF between any pair of years is the AF for the larger numbered year minus the AF for the year prior to the smaller numbered year. (When performing these sorts of calculations be careful to use all four digits of the calendar year if the period defined by the two years spans the year 2000.)

It is also possible to convert a given present value into an annuity; i.e. into an equivalent annual amount for a given number of years. For example, if we have a present sum of say $3000 and wish to know what constant annual amount for 6 years at 10% discount rate would have the same present value we simply divide $3000 by the AF. In this case, $3000/4.354 = $689.02. This calculation comes in handy when you want to annualize any given fixed amount, such as working out the annual (or monthly) repayments necessary on a loan, or, for calculating economic depreciation as discussed in Chapter 2.

It is also sometimes necessary to know what the present value of a perpetual annual sum is. The Annuity Tables do not show what the annuity factor is for an infinite number of years. As noted earlier in Chapter 2, this can be calculated using the formula: $AF = 1/r$, where r is the discount rate. In other words, $100 per annum for an infinite number of years has a present value of $100 \times 1/r = $100 \times 10 = 1000, if r = 10%; or, $100 \times 20 = 2000 if r = 5%, and so on.

Using Investment Decision-Making Criteria

We have already seen that there are a number of variants of DCF decision-rules that are used to appraise or evaluate investment projects. Among these decision-rules the most well known are the **net present value** (NPV) criterion, the **internal rate of return** (IRR), and **benefit/cost ratio** (BCR). In the sections that follow we shall examine each of these criteria and their usefulness in the different project decision-making situations.

The Net Present Value (NPV) Criterion

The NPV of a project simply expresses the *difference between* the discounted present value of future benefits and the discounted present value of future costs: NPV = PV (Benefits) – PV (Costs). A positive NPV value for a given project tells us that the project benefits are greater than its costs, and *vice versa*. When we compare the project's total discounted costs and discounted benefits, we derive the NPV:

Example 3.4: Comparison of Projects A and B using Net Present Value

Project A:

Year	0	1	2	3
(1) Cash Flow	−100	+50	+40	+30
(2) Discount Factor (at 10%)	1.00	0.909	0.826	0.751
(3) Discounted cash flow (=1x2)	−100.00	45.45	33.04	22.53

$$NPV(A)_{0.1} = -\$100(1.0) + \$50(0.909) + \$40(0.826) + \$30(0.751)$$
$$= \$101.02 - 100.00$$
$$= \$1.02$$

As NPV(A) > 0, accept the project (when cost of capital = 10%).

Project B:

Year	0	1	2	3
(1) Cash Flow	−100	+30	+45	+50
(2) Discount Factor (at 10%)	1.00	0.909	0.826	0.751
(3) Discounted cash flow (=1×2)	−100.00	45.45	33.04	22.53

$$
\begin{aligned}
\text{NPV(B)}_{0.1} &= -\$100(1.0) + \$30(0.909) + \$45(0.826) + \$50(0.751) \\
&= -\$100.00 + \$27.27 + \$37.17 + \$37.55 \\
&= \$101.99 - \$100 \\
&= \$1.99
\end{aligned}
$$

As NPV(B) is positive, project B can also be accepted.

Which project is preferred: A or B?

As NPV(B) > NPV(A), B would be preferred to A (at 10% discount rate).

The Effect of Changing the Discount Rate

We have been assuming a 10% discount rate so far. What happens to the NPV if we:
(i) increase the discount rate to 20%?
(ii) decrease the discount rate to 5%?

Consider Project A at a discount rate of 20%:

$$
\begin{aligned}
\text{NPV(A)}_{0.2} &= -100 + 50(1/1.2) + 40[1/(1.2)^2] + 30[1/(1.2)^3 \\
&= -100(1.00) + 50(0.83) + 40(0.69) + 30(0.58) \\
&= -100.0 + 41.5 + 27.6 + 17.4 \\
&= -100.0 + 86.5 \\
&= -\$13.5
\end{aligned}
$$

Note that NPV(A) has decreased, and even become negative. Therefore: if the discount rate is 20%, *reject* project A. We leave it as an exercise to show that the NPV rises when the discount rate falls to 5%.

Example 3.5: Comparing Project NPVs under Assumptions about the Discount Rate
In Example 3.2 used earlier, the NPV = $444.2 at a discount rate of 10%. Using the NPV decision-rule, we should accept this project. If we were to increase the discount rate from 10% to 15%, would this investment still be worthwhile? To determine this we can recalculate the NPV as follows:

$$
\begin{aligned}
\text{NPV} &= -1000(1.0) + 200(0.870) + 300(0.756) + 400(0.658) + 500(0.571) + 600(0.497) \\
&= -1000 + 174.0 + 226.8 + 263.2 + 285.5 + 298.2 \\
&= \$247.7
\end{aligned}
$$

Clearly the NPV of the project is still positive. Thus if the appropriate discount rate was 15% we would still accept it. It should be noted however, that the NPV at 15% is much lower than the NPV at 10%. This stands to reason, as the project's net benefits accrue in the future whereas the net costs are all at the beginning. The higher the rate of discount, the lower will be the present value of the future benefits and, therefore, the NPV. We noted earlier that typical investments of this sort have a downward sloping NPV curve. Can you derive the NPV schedule and plot the NPV curve for this project? (You should derive the NPV for at least 3 discount rates, including 0%. See Figure 2.8 in Chapter 2 for an illustration of an NPV curve.)

From the NPV schedule it is evident that when the discount rate rises above 23%, the NPV for the project described in Table 3.2 becomes zero. At 25%, the NPV is clearly negative. In other words, if we were to use a discount rate that is 23% or less, the project would be acceptable; if we were to use any rate above that the viability of the project becomes questionable.

Summary of NPV Decision-Rules

(1) For accept or reject decisions:

$$\text{if NPV} \geq 0, \text{ accept}$$
$$\text{if NPV} < 0, \text{ reject}$$

(2) When choosing or ranking alternatives:

$$\text{if NPV(A)} > \text{NPV(B), choose A}$$
$$\text{if NPV(B)} > \text{NPV(A), choose B}$$

At this stage we should point out that no mention has been made of the size of the available investment budget. The *implicit* assumption is that there is no budget constraint. As we shall see later, in situations of a budget constraint, other decision-rules are needed to rank projects.

Benefit-Cost Ratio Decision-Rule

Another form of the NPV decision-rule is called the **Benefit-Cost Ratio** (or BCR) decision-rule, which is, in effect, another way of comparing the present value of a project's costs with the present value of its benefits. Instead of calculating the NPV by *subtracting* the PV of Costs from the PV of Benefits, we *divide* the PV of Costs into the PV of Benefits, i.e.

$$BCR = \frac{PV \text{ (Benefits)}}{PV \text{ (Costs)}}$$

(It should be noted that the denominator of the BCR includes the present value of all project costs, not just the capital costs. Later on we discuss a variant of this rule that includes only the capital costs in the denominator.)

If this ratio is equal to or greater than unity, then accept the project. If it is less than unity, then reject the project. It should be clear that when:

$$\text{NPV} \geq 0, \text{ then BCR} \geq 1$$
$$\text{and,} \quad \text{NPV} < 0, \text{ then BCR} < 1$$

However, when it comes to *comparing or ranking* two or more projects, again assuming no budget constraint, the BCR decision-rule can give incorrect results. For instance, if two projects A and B are being compared, where:

	PV Benefits	PV Costs	NPV	BCR
Project A	$100	$60	$40	1.67
Project B	$80	$45	$35	1.78

using the BCR to rank these projects would place B (BCR=1.78) above A (BCR=1.67). Using the NPV decision-rule would place A (NPV=$40) above B (NPV=$35). In this situation the NPV decision-rule would be the correct one to use for ranking purposes, unless there is a budget constraint, when another variant of the BCR rule needs to be used. (This is discussed below.)

The Internal Rate of Return (IRR) Criterion

We have seen that in the case of "normal" or "well behaved" investment cash flows the NPV curve slopes downwards from left to right. At some point the curve intersects the horizontal axis. That is, it becomes "0". The discount rate at which the NPV becomes "0" is called the **Internal Rate of Return** (IRR). In Example 3.5, the IRR was found to lie between 20 and 25%, approximately 23%. Once we know the IRR of an investment we can compare this with the cost of financing our project. Let us say, in this case, the cost of financing the project is 15%. Now, as the rate of return, the IRR, is *greater than* the cost of financing the project, we should accept the investment. In fact, in the case of this investment, we would accept the investment at any cost of finance that is below 23%. When the IRR is *less than* the cost of finance, the project should be rejected. We can summarize this decision-rule as:

$$\text{when IRR} \geq r, \text{ then accept}$$
$$\text{and} \quad \text{when IRR} < r, \text{ then reject}$$
$$\text{where } r = \text{the interest rate (cost of financing the project)}$$

When considering an individual project, the IRR decision-rule will always give exactly the same result as the NPV decision-rule: from the NPV curve in Figure 2.5 it can be seen that when the discount rate (cost of capital) is less than IRR, the NPV will be positive, and *vice versa*. For instance, provided the discount rate we used to calculate the NPV (i.e. the cost of financing the project) was less than 23%, the NPV would be *positive* and the project *accepted*. Similarly, using the IRR decision-rule, we saw that once we knew what the IRR was (i.e. 23%), we would compare it with the given cost of finance, and so long as the latter was *lower*, we would *accept* the project. These two decision-rules amount to exactly the same thing in such a situation.

Therefore: NPV and IRR give identical results *for accept* vs. *reject* decisions when considering an individual project. As discussed later in this Chapter, this may not be the case when a choice has to be made between two or more projects.

A Note on Calculating the IRR

Today we are generally more fortunate than our predecessors, as financial calculators and electronic spreadsheets used on PCs have built-in algorithms for calculating the IRR. In the absence of a spreadsheet or programmable calculator with a built-in IRR formula, there are two ways of approaching the IRR calculation. Which of the two is used depends on the type of cash flow the project has:

(i)   When the cash flow is not regular in the sense that there is not an identical value every year after the initial (year 0) investment, it must be estimated by trial and error; "iteration" and "interpolation".

(ii) When the cash flow is regular the easiest method is to use Annuity Tables, as discussed earlier.

Interpolation

The IRR of an investment can be approximated using a process of *interpolation*. In Example 3.2, the NPV is positive at a 15% discount rate, so we should try a higher rate, say 20%, which again gives a positive NPV, so we should try a yet higher rate – say 25% – which gives a negative NPV. Since the NPV is positive at 20% and negative at 25%, the IRR must lie somewhere between these two rates. The actual IRR is found by interpolation:

$$\text{IRR} = 20 + 5 \left[\frac{88.73}{88.73 + 41.79} \right] = 23.4$$

i.e. the rule for interpolation is:

$$\text{IRR} = \begin{bmatrix} lower \\ discount \\ rate \end{bmatrix} + \begin{bmatrix} difference\ between \\ the\ two\ discount \\ rates \end{bmatrix} \times \left[\frac{NPV\ at\ the\ lower\ discount\ rate}{sum\ of\ the\ absolute\ values\ of\ the\ NPVs} \right]$$

Note that the difference between the two discount rates (the range) should be as small as convenient. This is because the larger this range, the more inaccurate the interpolation will be. However, although there is no hard and fast rule about this, a range of 5% will usually reduce the amount of work involved and give a reasonable estimate of IRR.

Use of Annuity Tables

It should also be noted that when there is a constant or regular cash flow it becomes very easy to calculate the IRR using the Annuity Tables. Using the Example 3.3, we proceed as follows: noting that the IRR is given by that discount rate which yields an NPV = 0, we write the NPV as:

$$NPV = -1000(1.0) + 500(AF_3) = 0, \text{ which implies that,}$$
$$1000 = 500(AF_3)$$

or, solving for AF_3 , when $\dfrac{1000}{500}$, $AF_3 = 2$.

In other words, all we need to do now is find out at what discount rate the annuity factor for year 3 has a value equal to 2.0. To determine this we simply refer to our Annuity Tables and look along the row for year 3 until we find an AF that is approximately equal to 2.0. This occurs when the discount rate is just above 23%. We can therefore conclude that the IRR is approximately 23%.

Example 3.6: Using Annuity Tables to Calculate the IRR
Find the IRR for an investment (B) of $2362 that generates an annual net return of $1000 for 3 years.

$$NPV(B) = -2362(1.0) + 1000(df_1) + 1000(df_2) + 1000(df_3)$$
$$= -2362 + 1000(df_1 + df_2 + df_3)$$
$$= -2362 + 1000(AF_3)$$

Remember, IRR gives NPV = 0

Therefore, $AF_3 = 2362/1000$
                   $= 2.362$

From Annuity Tables, see year 3 and look for the row in which AF = 2.362. This entry appears in the row corresponding to a discount rate of 13%. Therefore, IRR(B) = 13%.

Problems with the IRR Decision Criterion

Selecting among Mutually Exclusive Projects

In the previous sections we have been examining investment decision-rules in situations in which a decision must be made whether or not to accept a given investment. In these situations we saw that the NPV and IRR decision-rules gave identical results.

In other situations this need not necessarily hold true. In particular, when faced with the choice between mutually exclusive projects, that is, in situations where one has to choose *one* of two or more alternatives (and where the acceptance of one automatically eliminates the other project), the NPV and IRR decision-rules can yield conflicting results. One could think of a road project for example where one is considering two or more alternative designs or types of road. Once one of these is accepted, the other potential projects are automatically rejected.

Let us consider Example 3.7 with two mutually exclusive road projects, A and B.

Example 3.7: Choosing between Mutually Exclusive Projects

Net Cash Flows for Two Mutually Exclusive Road Projects ($ thousands)

Year	0	1	2	3	IRR
A	−1000	475	475	475	20%
B	−500	256	256	256	25%

We are given a cost of financing the project of 10% per annum. Using the IRR decision-rule it would appear that Project B is preferable to Project A given that the IRR is 25% for B as opposed to 20% for A. However, if we were, instead, to use the NPV decision-rule we would discount the future net benefits of each investment at 10% and obtain:

$$NPV(A) = \$181.3$$
$$NPV(B) = \$136.6$$

Using the NPV decision-rule we would naturally prefer A to B, the exact opposite of the ranking using the IRR rule! Which of the two is correct? Why do the two decision-rules conflict? In such situations, the NPV decision-rule will always give the correct ranking, so it would make sense to use it in preference to the IRR. The reason for the conflicting result is due to a phenomenon referred to as "switching". Switching occurs when the NPV curves of the two projects intersect one another as illustrated in Figure 3.1. The NPV curves of the two projects cross over at 15%. In other words at a discount rate of 15%, the NPV of A is equal to the NPV of B. At all discount rates below 15%, the NPV of A is greater than the NPV of B, and at all discount rates above 15%, the NPV of A is less than the NPV of B. Thus, with these two projects, their ranking changes or *switches* as the discount rate changes, hence the concept of "switching". In conclusion, because of the possibility of switching, it is always safer to use the NPV decision-rule when selecting from among mutually exclusive alternatives.

However, there is a way in which the IRR rule could still be used to choose between mutually exclusive projects. Consider the *incremental project* where this is defined as the *difference between* cash flows of projects A and B. We first compute the cash flow of a hypothetical project "A–B". We then calculate the IRR of that cash flow. If the IRR of the incremental project is equal to or greater than the cost of capital, we choose project A. If it is less we choose project B.

Year	0	1	2	3
Project (A–B) IRR (A–B) = 15%	–500	219	219	219

In other words, if the cost of capital is less than 15% then we should accept A rather than B. Note that project A is larger than project B in the sense that it has a larger initial investment cost, of $1000 compared with $500. In effect what we are doing is asking whether it makes sense to invest the *additional* $500 in project A; i.e. project A's cash flow is made up of the

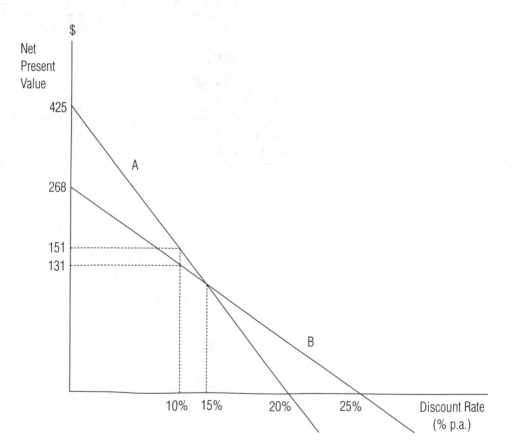

Figure 3.1 Switching

equivalent of project B's cash flow plus the incremental cash flow we have labeled "A–B". If the IRR is greater than the cost of capital then it does make sense to invest the extra amount in project A.

It should also be noted that the IRR of the incremental cash flow (A–B) is also the discount rate at the switching point shown in Figure 3.1. We can see from the figure that at the switching point the NPV of project A is equal to the NPV of project B. In other words, NPV(A) *minus* NPV(B) is zero. If the NPV of (A–B) is zero at some rate of discount, then that discount rate must also be the IRR of (A–B). Therefore, when we find the IRR of an incremental cash flow as in the case of (A–B) we are also identifying the switching point of the two NPV curves for projects A and B.

Example 3.8: Interpreting the IRR of an Incremental Cash Flow

	($ millions)				IRR	NPV	
	0	1	2	3		4%	10%
A	−1000	500	500	500	23%	387	243
B	−2362	1000	1000	1000	13%	413	125

Which project should be chosen, A or B ? (assume they are mutually exclusive)
Assume the cost of capital is: (i) 4%
(ii) 10%
As can be seen from the example, IRR(A) > IRR(B), which suggests A is preferred to B both at 4% and 10% discount rates, but

$NPV(A)_{0.04} < NPV(B)_{0.04}$, therefore accept B if the discount rate is 4%
$NPV(A)_{0.1} > NPV(B)_{0.1}$, therefore accept A if the discount rate is 10%.

Which is the correct decision? Try also using the IRR of the incremental cash flow (B–A) as a decision-rule in this example.

Problems with the NPV Decision Criterion

While the NPV decision-rule performs better than the IRR in choosing between mutually exclusive projects, it is not problem-free. There are essentially two investment decision-making situations in which the NPV rule, as described above, needs to be modified: namely, under a capital rationing situation in which the objective is to finance the combination of investment projects from a given, constrained budget, in such a way as to obtain the highest overall NPV; and, when comparing two or more investment projects that do *not* have equal lives.

Under Capital Rationing

The problem in this situation is that it may be better to accept a combination of smaller projects that are less profitable in terms of the size of their individual NPVs, but which allow for a higher overall NPV from the available budget than to accept those with the highest individual NPVs. A simple example will serve to illustrate this case. Suppose that we have a budget of $800 thousand and we have five potential investment projects (Table 3.3), where PV(K) = Present value of initial investment outlay, PV(B) = Present value of net benefits, and $\frac{B}{K}$ = Ratio of PV(B) over PV(K).

Example 3.9: Ranking of Projects where there is Capital Rationing

Table 3.3 Ranking of Projects by NPV and Profitability Ratio ($ thousands)

Project	PV(K)	PV(B)	NPV (rank)	$\frac{B}{K}$ (rank)
A	100	130	30 (5)	1.30 (2)
B	400	433	33 (4)	1.08 (5)
C	200	303	103 (1)	1.52 (1)
D	400	494	94 (2)	1.24 (3)
E	500	558	58 (3)	1.11 (4)

As we can see, all five projects have positive NPVs and all would be acceptable if there were enough funds available to finance them all. However, as the budget is limited to $800 thousand, we must rank them and select only the best combination. Using the NPV rule, we would rank them in the sequence C, D, E, B, A. With the available budget we would only be able to fund C and D, which would use up $600 thousand. With the remaining $200 thousand we would also finance part of E (40% of it) assuming it is a divisible investment. The total NPV obtained from this package would be $220 thousand ($103 + $94 + 0.4*$58 thousand).

If instead, we now calculated the ratio of the present value of each project's net cash inflows (NPV(B)) to the initial investment necessary to fund the project (NPV(K)), we could then rank the projects according to their *profitability ratios* $\left[\frac{B}{K}\right]$, i.e. the present value of the net benefits generated *per $ of investment*. This is also referred to as the **Net Benefit Investment Ratio** (NBIR). It is very similar to the Benefit-Cost Ratio (BCR) discussed earlier, but should not be confused with this. (The important difference is that the NBIR shows the value of the project's discounted *benefits net of operating costs*, per $ of (discounted) investment costs whereas the BCR shows the value of the project's discounted *gross* benefits per $ of (discounted) *total* costs, both investment and operating.)

Note that using the NBIR changes the project ranking to C, A, D, E, B. With the $800 thousand budget we would then finance projects C, A, D, and 20 percent of E. This would yield a total NPV of $239 thousand ($103 + $30 + $94 + 0.2*$58 thousand), which is higher than the NPV obtained from the projects selected according to the NPV rule. Using the NBIRs is clearly a better way of ranking potential investments in situations of capital rationing, in comparison with ranking according to NPVs.

A further complication arises if the projects cannot be partially undertaken because of their so-called "lumpiness". In this situation it is possible that two smaller projects which have lower profitability ratios but which exhaust the total investment budget generate a higher overall NPV than, say, one more profitable investment which leaves part of the budget unused. Example 3.10 illustrates this case.

Example 3.10: Ranking Indivisible Projects with Capital Rationing

Table 3.4 Ranking Lumpy Projects ($ thousands)

Project	PV(K)	PV(B)	$\dfrac{B}{K}$
A	125	162.5	1.30 (2)
B	175	189	1.08 (4)
C	200	304	1.52 (1)
D	400	496	1.24 (3)

If we were to follow the NBIR decision-rule we would rank the projects in the sequence C, A, D and B. Now assuming an available investment budget of $300 thousand, and assuming all projects are indivisible or "lumpy", the NBIR decision-rule would tell us to finance project C, which would yield an NPV of $104 thousand (plus $100 thousand of investible funds which would remain unutilized by the agency concerned). However, if we look at the other projects we see that it would have been possible to finance A and B instead of C. Even though these have lower NBIRs, we would utilize the full budget ($125 + $175 thousand), and generate a higher *overall* NPV of $351.5 thousand ($162.5 + $189 thousand). Before we come to a final conclusion we would need to consider the net benefits of any alternative allocation of the portion of the budget not used by the agency.

In conclusion, in situations of **capital rationing** where funds are constrained and potential investments must be ranked, we should use the *profitability ratio* (NBIR) rather than the absolute size of the NPV. However, when investments cannot be divided into smaller parts (lumpy investments), we should give consideration to whether or not our selection utilizes the full budget available; and, if not, to whether accepting a combination of lower ranking, smaller projects would generate a higher overall NPV.

Comparing Projects with Different Lives

Another instance in which it would be incorrect to use the NPV decision-rule as presented above is when we compare two or more projects that have different lives. For example, an infrastructure project such as an irrigation network could have a number of possible designs, with varying durability, and hence, longevity. This is illustrated in Example 3.11.

Example 3.11: Comparing Projects with Different Lives

Table 3.5 Two Investments with Different Lives

Project	Initial Cost	Annual Net Costs	Life (Years)
A	$40,000	$2,800	4
B	$28,000	$4,400	3

Assuming a discount rate of 10 percent per annum:

$$\text{PV of Costs (A)} = -40,000(1.0) - 2,800(3.17) = -48,876$$
$$\text{PV of Costs (B)} = -28,000(1.0) - 4,400(2.49) = -38,956$$

The present values of the projects' costs indicates that B has lower net costs. However, we should note that project A has a longer life. It provides an irrigation network that lasts one year longer than that of project B. How then should we decide between A and B? One solution is to renew each project so that they cover the same total number of years. In the above example, a period of 12 years would be common to both projects if A was renewed 3 times over, and B was renewed 4 times over. The cash flows then appear as follows (Table 3.6):

Table 3.6 Establishing Equal Project Lives

Project	0	1	2	3	4	5	6	7	8	9	10	11	12
A	−40.0	−2.8	−2.8	−2.8	−2.8 −40.0	−2.8	−2.8	−2.8	−2.8 −40.0	−2.8	−2.8	−2.8	−2.8
B	−28.0	−4.4	−4.4	−4.4 −28.0	−4.4	−4.4	−4.4 −28.0	−4.4	−4.4	−4.4 −28.0	−4.4	−4.4	−4.4

Using a 10% discount rate:

$$
\begin{aligned}
\text{PV of Costs (A)} \;&= -40(1.0) - 40(0.683) - 40(0.467) - 2.8(6.814) \\
&= -40.00 - 27.32 - 18.68 - 19.08 \\
&= -105.08 \\
\text{PV of Costs (B)} \;&= -28(1.0) - 28(0.751) - 28(0.564) - 28(0.424) - 4.4(6.814) \\
&= -28.00 - 21.03 - 15.79 - 11.87 - 29.98 \\
&= -106.67
\end{aligned}
$$

This shows that if we compare the present value of costs of the two alternatives *over identical life spans* project A is indeed less costly than project B. The rule in this situation, therefore, is that the NPV decision criterion should only be used in project selection once we have constructed cash flows of equal lives for our potential investment projects.

The identical life spans comparison might be easy to do in cases like the one above, where the lowest common denominator (the LCM) of the projects' lives is a relatively low figure, such as 12 years in Example 3.11. But, what would we do if one project had a life of, say, 5 years and the other 7 years? We would need to construct a 35-year cash flow for each project. And, what if we wanted to compare these with another alternative that had a 9-year life? We would need to extend each cash flow to 315 years! Aside from the computational problem, we would be dealing with benefit and cost flows in a future period beyond our ability to predict.

For this reason, we use another decision-rule when comparing projects of different life spans. It is called the **Annual Equivalent Cost** (or Benefit) method, which is based on a Present Value (PV) calculation. The rationale of this method is to convert the actual stream of costs (or benefits) of a project into an equivalent stream of *constant* costs (or benefits). In other words, we take the cash flow of project A and ask: what fixed annual sum incurred over the same 4-year period would give us the same PV? We then repeat this for project B over a 3-year period and compare the two annual equivalent costs (or benefits).

To derive the annual equivalent costs we follow two steps:
(i)   we compute the PV of costs for each project *for its own life*; and,
(ii) we convert the PV of costs for each project into an annuity by dividing the PV derived in step (i) by the corresponding annuity factor for that life.

Example 3.12: Using the Annual Equivalent Cost Method of Project Comparison

We illustrate the annual equivalent cost method using the data in Table 3.6, and again using a 10 percent discount rate. Returning to Table 3.6 above, we find:

$$\text{PV of Costs (A)} = -\$48{,}876$$
$$\text{PV of Costs (B)} = -\$38{,}956$$

A has a 4-year life and B has a 3-year life. The annuity factor, at 10 percent, is: 3.17 for 4 years, and 2.49 for 3 years. The Annual Equivalent Cost (AEC) is therefore:

$$\text{AEC(A)} = \frac{\$48876}{3.17} = \$15418$$

$$\text{AEC(B)} = \frac{\$38956}{2.49} = \$15645$$

Thus project A is less costly than project B.

In conclusion, when projects of unequal lives are being compared, one must *not* simply compare their NPVs. We need to convert the cash flows into an **Annual Equivalent** by dividing the PV of costs (or benefits) by the annuity factor corresponding to the life of the project.

Using Electronic Spreadsheets

In this section we review some simple operations of electronic spreadsheets, using NPV and IRR calculations as illustrations. The reader who is familiar with the use of spreadsheets in financial analysis may wish to skip this section.

Consider Figure 3.2 which illustrates a simple NPV calculation using an *Excel*© spreadsheet. For the reader who is not already familiar with a spreadsheet, the best way to understand what a spreadsheet is is to think of it as nothing more than a very large calculator that is organised in rows (1, 2, 3 ... etc.) and columns (A, B, C, ... etc), forming a matrix of *cells*, each with its own address (A1, B3, X75, ... etc). One important difference between a calculator and a spreadsheet is that you can use any given cell in a spreadsheet for a variety of operations. For instance you could use it to enter plain text. In cell A1 we have written the text *Example 1(a)*. We could have entered a whole sentence as with a word processor.

In this spreadsheet we have also set up the cash flow of two projects used as examples earlier in this Chapter in the section on Discounting and the Time Value of Money: Project A and Project B. You will notice that column A contains a set of *labels*. In other cells we have

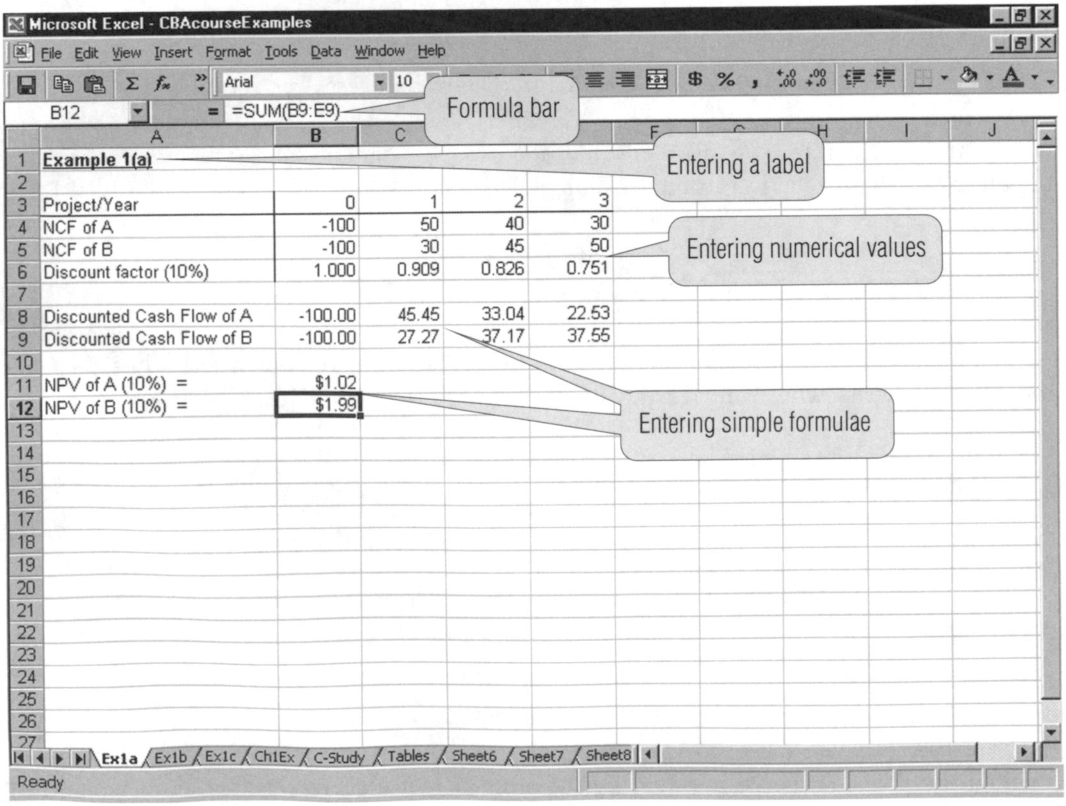

Figure 3.2 Spreadsheet Presentation of DCF Calculation

entered *numbers*. In row 3 we have numbered the years: year 0 in B3, year 1 in C3, etc. In row 4 we have entered the net cash flow for project A: –100 in B4, 50 in C4, and so on. In row 5 we have entered the NCF for project B. (Note that we have chosen to set up the cash flows in rows running from left to right rather than in columns from top to bottom. Either method will work but we believe, from our own practical experience, that setting-up a spreadsheet in rows makes it easier to handle the more complicated sorts of analyses we will be doing later.)

Having set up the two cash flows like this we are now ready to compute their NPVs. To do this we use another function of the spreadsheet cell: we enter a formula into a cell. You can enter almost any formula into a cell. For instance, you could simply instruct the spreadsheet to add together, say, "50" and "30" by entering the formula "=50+30". (*Note that when using Excel© we always begin with the "=" sign (or some other operator such as a "+" sign) when entering a formula. This is to distinguish the entry of a formula from the entry of a label.*)

Alternatively, instead of using actual *values* in the formula, you could instruct the spreadsheet to add together the contents of two cells, by giving their reference addresses. For example, if we entered the formula "=C3+C4" into cell G6, then the amount "80" would appear in that cell; i.e. 50+30=80. Although you do not see the formula you have entered in the cell itself, you can see what it is by placing the cursor on the cell and looking in the "window" or *Formula Bar* near the top of the spreadsheet. In the spreadsheet shown in Figure 3.2 the cursor is positioned on cell B12, so the formula in that cell appears in the *Formula Bar*.

In this simple example we have also entered the discount factors (at a 10% discount rate) for each project year in row 6. To derive the NPV for each project we firstly calculate the *discounted* cash flow by multiplying each year's cash flow by the corresponding discount factor. This is shown in rows 8 and 9 for projects A and B respectively. For instance, in cell C8 we have entered the formula "=C4*C6": i.e. 50 × 0.909. The result displayed in C8 is "45.45". If we do this for each cell of the cash flow we can then find the NPV by adding up the values in each cell. To do this we place another formula in cells B11 and B12 instructing the spreadsheet to add up the cells B8, C8, D8 and E8 to get the NPV of A, and B9 through to E9 for project B. The solutions are shown in cells B11 and B12: +$1.02 and +$1.99 respectively.

Note that there are two types of formula we could have used in cells B11 and B12: a "self-made" formula or a "built-in formula". If we had used a self-made formula we would have written into cell B11, "=B8+C8+D8+E8". (*Note that the symbol " * " is used as the multiplication sign, " / " is used as the division sign, and " ^ " is used as the exponent sign.*) When there are a lot of cells to add up this becomes a laborious exercise and one that is prone to careless error. The alternative is to use one of the built-in formulae. In this case we use the "SUM" formula which is displayed in the *Formula Bar* at the top of the spreadsheet. This tells us that in cell B12 we have entered the formula "=SUM(B9:E9)" where the colon sign indicates that all other cells in between B8 and E8 are to be included in the summation. With built-in formulae the spreadsheet is programmed to know what functions to perform when it reads certain words. In this instance, the word "SUM" instructs it to add-up. Similarly, "AVERAGE" would instruct it to find the mean; "STDEV" would instruct it to find the standard deviation, and so on. Information about the range of formulae available and their operation can be found in the "Help" section of the spreadsheet program.

What we have just done demonstrates the use of some of the very basic functions of a

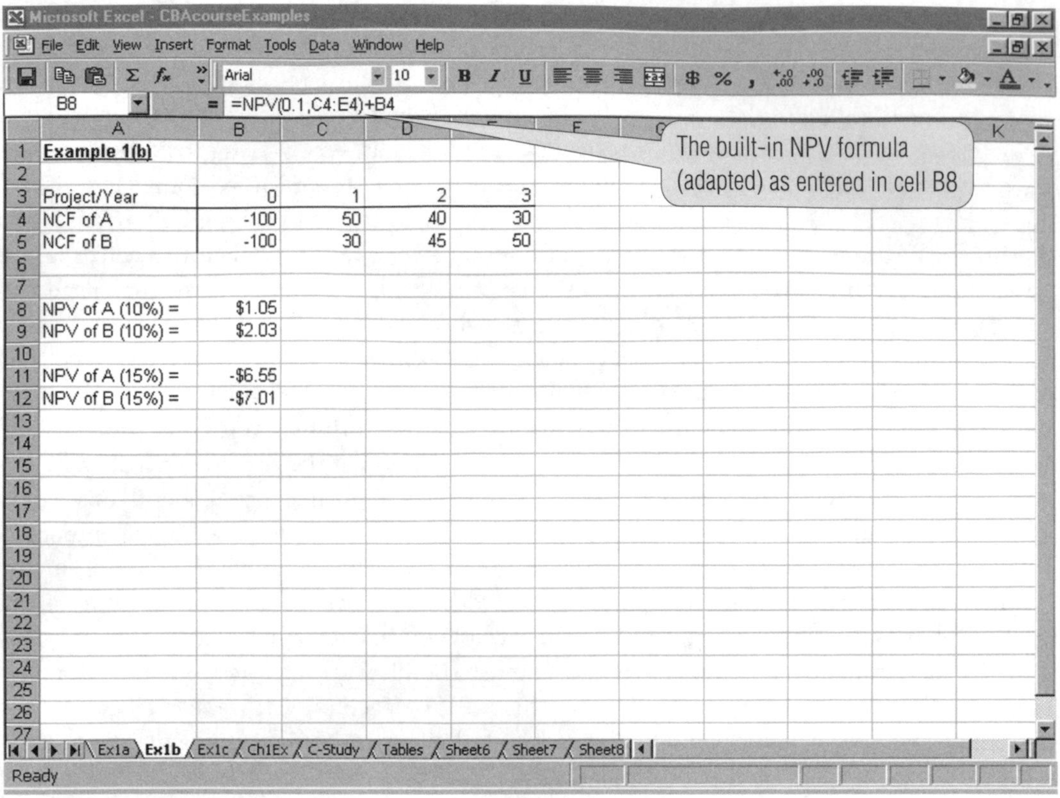

Figure 3.3 Using Built-in Spreadsheet Formulae

spreadsheet. In practice you would not need to enter in the discount factors as we have done in row 6. We could have written our own formulae for the discount factor instead and let the spreadsheet calculate the actual figure, but even this is unnecessary because the spreadsheet has built-in formulae for all the DCF calculations you need to use, including the NPV and IRR formulae.

To demonstrate the use of the built-in NPV formula, look at Figure 3.3 where we show the same NPV calculations as before, but using the built-in formula. Note that we do not have a row of discount factors or a row showing the discounted cash flow of each project. Instead we simply enter one formula into cells B8 and B9 to calculate the NPVs for projects A and B respectively. The first thing you will notice is that the answers are not exactly the same as those shown in Figure 3.2. The reason is due to rounding differences. When we entered the discount factors into the spreadsheet in Figure 3.2, we rounded them off to three decimal places. As the spreadsheet is capable of using very many more decimal places in its computations, the solutions in Figure 3.3 are more precise.

The first part of the formula for the NPV calculation entered into cell B8 is shown in the *Formula Bar* at the top of the spreadsheet: "=NPV(0.1,C4:E4)+B4". The "0.1" tells the program to use a 10% discount rate, then follows a comma, and then "C4:E4" tells it to discount the contents of cell C4 (year 1) through to cell E4 (year 3). Note that we have to include "+B4" in the formula to instruct it to include the *undiscounted* year 0 amount of –$100. The reason we have to do this is that the spreadsheet does not use the same convention that we do when numbering project years. Our convention is to treat all project costs and benefits accruing in the initial year as *year 0*, which therefore remain *undiscounted* in our NPV calculations. The spreadsheet, on the other hand, is programmed to treat the earliest year of the cash flow as accruing one year later and therefore will always discount the initial year of the cash flow. For this reason we have to adapt the formula by adding back the year zero cash flow on an undiscounted basis, and beginning the NPV computation for our project in year 1.

If we change the discount rate in the NPV formula, the solution in the corresponding cell will automatically change. In cells B11 and B12 we have entered the identical formula as in B8 and B9 except we have set the discount rate at 15%: e.g. "=NPV(0.15,C4:E4)+B4". It should be noted that all entries in column A of the spreadsheet are labels. We have typed into cell A8, for example, "NPV of A (10%) =". This is not a formula! It is only there for the user's convenience. If a label were accidentally used in performing a calculation, the spreadsheet will treat it as a zero. This also applies where numbers have been entered as part of a label as in the case of "10%" in cells A8 and A9.

The discount rate is a variable in most benefit-cost analysis as the analyst will generally want to see how the NPV of a project changes with different discount rates. To construct an NPV curve you will need to recalculate a project's NPV at several discount rates. To simplify undertaking this sort of *sensitivity analysis* there is another "trick" we use when designing a spreadsheet. Instead of entering the actual values in the NPV formula we can enter a reference to another cell somewhere else in the spreadsheet. This cell might contain the discount rate, for example, so, whenever we change the value of the discount rate in that cell, the value of the NPV will change *wherever in the spreadsheet there is an NPV formula that refers to that cell for the discount rate*. For instance, if we placed the discount rate in cell B10 and then entered the value "0.1" into that cell, we could then change the formulae in cells B8 and B9 to read "=NPV(+B10,C4:E4)+B4" and "=NPV(+B10,C5:E5)+B5" respectively. The results will be the same as we have in Figure 3.3 but if we were to change the value in cell B10 to 0.15, the NPVs of projects A and B, in cells B8 and B9 respectively, would immediately change to the values already computed in cells B11 and B12.

Similarly, what we enter into the net cash flows in rows 4 and 5 could also be *references* to other cells in the spreadsheet rather than actual values. For instance, the net cash flow in each year is likely to be derived from other calculations consisting perhaps of a number of different costs and benefits. These calculations can be performed elsewhere in the same spreadsheet, and then, instead of re-entering the values derived from these calculations we would simply refer to the cells in which the solutions to these "working calculations" appear. An example of this is shown in Figure 3.4 where we have inserted a "working table" in the spreadsheet, still using the same example as previously. In the working table, rows 21 and 22 contain simple arithmetic formulae that derive the net cash flows for projects A and B from the raw data in the rows above. (These values could themselves be based on calculations elsewhere in the spreadsheet.) In the final table in the upper part of Figure 3.4, that we now label "Net Cash Flow", we no longer have any values in any of the cells. The cells in that table

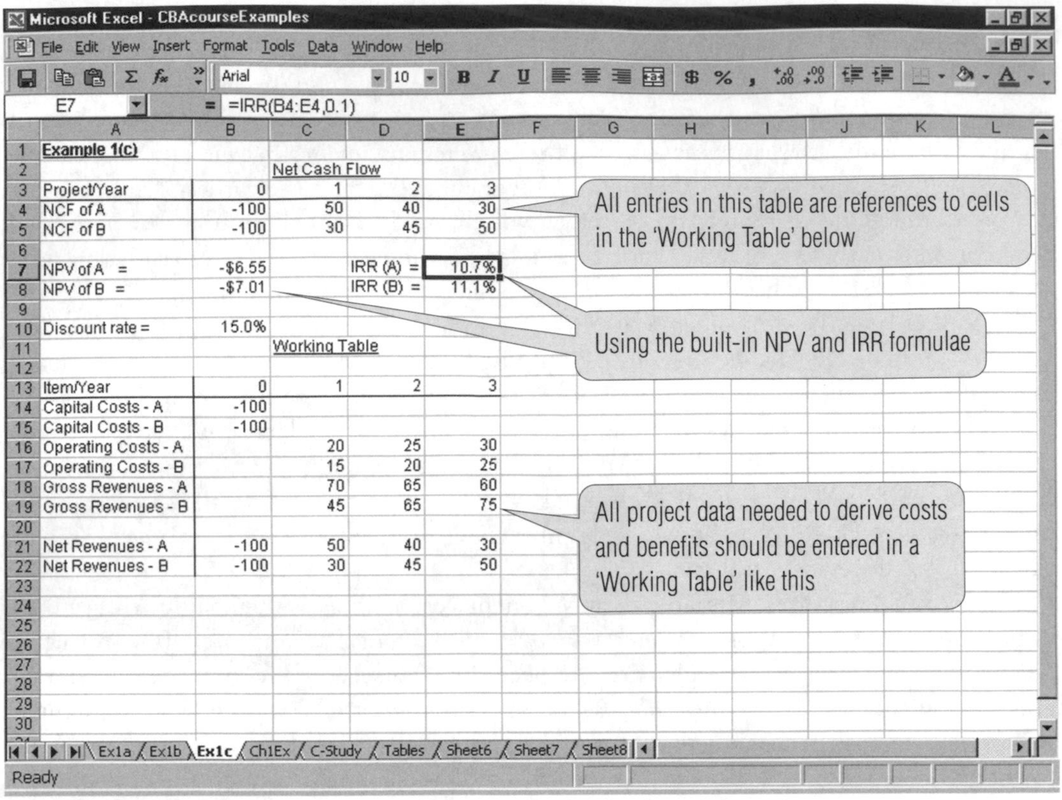

Microsoft Excel - CBAcourseExamples

E7 = =IRR(B4:E4,0.1)

	A	B	C	D	E
1	Example 1(c)				
2			Net Cash Flow		
3	Project/Year	0	1	2	3
4	NCF of A	-100	50	40	30
5	NCF of B	-100	30	45	50
6					
7	NPV of A =	-$6.55		IRR (A) =	10.7%
8	NPV of B =	-$7.01		IRR (B) =	11.1%
9					
10	Discount rate =	15.0%			
11			Working Table		
12					
13	Item/Year	0	1	2	3
14	Capital Costs - A	-100			
15	Capital Costs - B	-100			
16	Operating Costs - A		20	25	30
17	Operating Costs - B		15	20	25
18	Gross Revenues - A		70	65	60
19	Gross Revenues - B		45	65	75
20					
21	Net Revenues - A	-100	50	40	30
22	Net Revenues - B	-100	30	45	50

Figure 3.4 Referencing within the Spreadsheet

contain only references to cells in the working table. Similarly, the NPV formulae in cells B7 and B8 contain a reference to cell B10 where we have entered "15%". (Remember, the rest of the NPV formula is also in the form of references to the appropriate rows in the "Net Cash Flow" table above.)

Finally, spreadsheets also contain built-in formulae for the IRR. In cells E7 and E8 we have entered the formulae for the IRR of projects A and B respectively. The IRR formula for project A is displayed in the *Formula Bar* at the top of the screen in Figure 3.4, as "=IRR(B4:E4,0.1)". Notice two things here. First, there is no need to leave out of the formula the cash flow in year zero and then add it back in as we had to with the NPV formula. Second, we have had to include a "trial" or "prompt" discount rate in the formula. The program needs this to know where it should begin the iteration process to derive the IRR (this process was illustrated in Figure 2.7 of Chapter 2). In this case it makes no difference what rate we enter. You can try changing it yourself to, say, 5% or 20% and you will always get the same answer, because, as we learned earlier, a cash flow with only one change in sign, as we have here, has only one IRR. There are exceptions however where there is more than one solution, as seen in Chapter 2. In this case entering a different "trial" discount rate in the formula could produce a

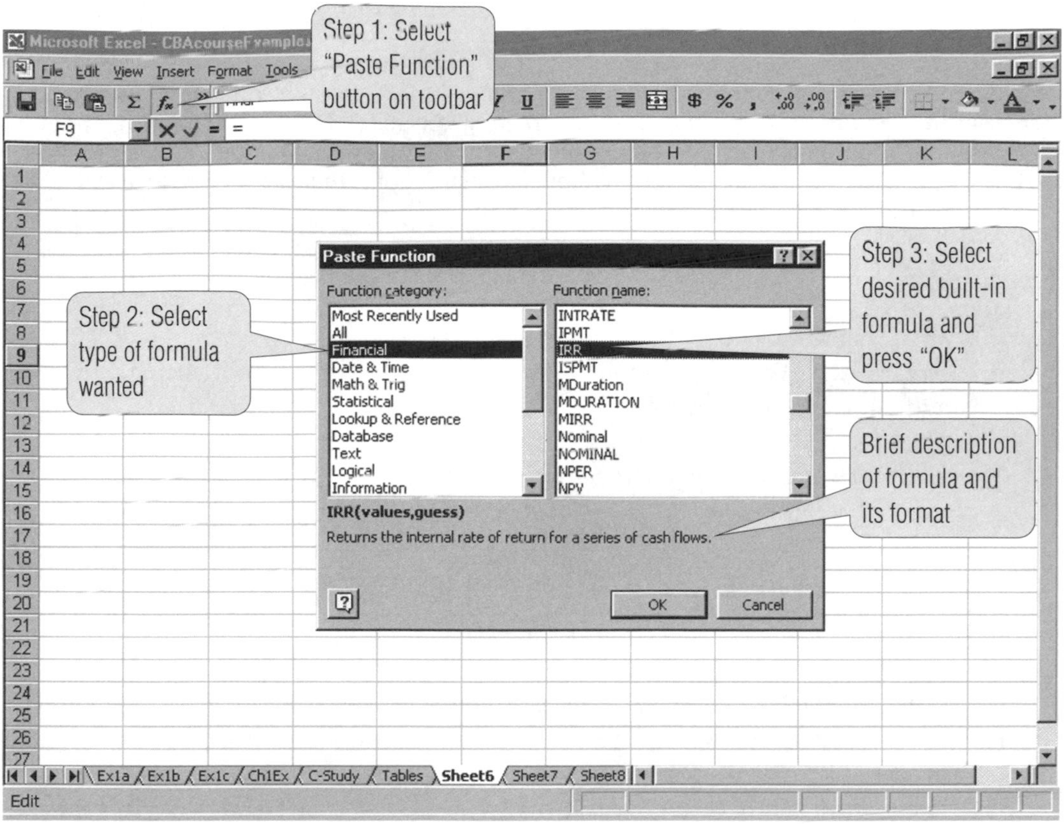

Figure 3.5 Selecting and Pasting a Built-in Formula

different IRR. (Note that some spreadsheets are programmed to report an error when an attempt is made to use the IRR formula when there is more than one positive IRR.)

Until now, when using the built-in formulae such as "NPV" and "IRR", we have needed to type out the formulae and enter the appropriate parentheses, values, cell references, commas, etc. for the spreadsheet to perform the desired calculation. The spreadsheet contains very many formulae that are extremely useful and time saving for the project analyst. These include numerous financial formulae for performing other commonly used calculations in financial analysis, such as interest and repayments on loans or depreciation allowances, as well as statistical formulae and others. It is not necessary to have to memorize or even look up the appropriate words and format for all these formulae so that each time a function is to be used you may enter the details correctly. In the spreadsheet's main toolbar at the top of the screen there is a function button (fx) which, when entered, displays all available formulae. Once you have selected the one you wish to use, this can be pasted into the appropriate cell in the spreadsheet. These processes are illustrated in Figure 3.5 for the built-in IRR formula.

Further Reading

One example of a book containing discussion of investment decision-rules is H. Bierman and S. Smidt, *The Capital Budgeting Decision* (Macmillan, 1971). Further information about the operation of spreadsheets can be obtained from the relevant manual, such as Microsoft Excel *User's Guide*. See also Boardman et al., *Cost-Benefit Analysis: Concepts and Practice* (Prentice Hall, 2001), Ch. 6.

Exercises

1. (a) What is meant by the term "mutually exclusive projects"?
   (b) Explain why the IRR decision-rule could give the wrong result when comparing mutually exclusive projects.

2. The following net cash flows relate to two projects:

NET CASH FLOWS (IN $1,000)

YEAR	0	1	2	3	4	5	6
PROJECT A	–60	20	20	20	20	20	20
PROJECT B	–72	45	22	20	13	13	13

   (i) Calculate the NPVs for each project, assuming 10% cost of capital.
   (ii) Assuming that the two projects are independent, would you accept them if the cost of capital is 15%?
   (iii) What is the IRR of each project?
   (iv) Which of the two projects would you prefer if they are mutually exclusive, given a 15% discount rate?

3. Using a spreadsheet generate your own set of Discount and Annuity Tables for, say, all discount rates between 1% and 20% (at 1 percentage point intervals) and for time periods 1 to 30 (at one time-period intervals), as well as time periods 50 and 100. You should generate these tables by inserting the numbers for the time periods in the first column of each row and the discount rates in the first row of each column, and then inserting the appropriate formula into one cell of the Table – year 1 at 1% – and then copying it to all other cells in the matrix. (Hint: Do not forget to anchor the references to periods and discount rates using the "$" symbol.)

4. A firm has a capital budget of $100 which must be spent on one of two projects, each requiring a present outlay of $100. Project A yields a return of $120 after one year, whereas Project B yields $201.14 after 5 years. Calculate:
   (i) the NPV of each project using a discount rate of 10%;
   (ii) the IRR of each project.
   What are the project rankings on the basis of these two investment decision-rules?
   (iii) Suppose that you are told that the firm's reinvestment rate is 12%, which project should the firm choose?

5. A firm has a capital budget of $100 which must be spent on one of two projects, with any unspent balance being placed in a bank deposit earning 15%. Project A involves a present outlay of $100 and yields $321.76 after 5 years. Project B involves a present outlay of $40 and yields $92 after one year. Calculate:
    (i)   the IRR of each project;
    (ii) the B/C ratio of each project, using a 15% discount rate.
    What are the project rankings on the basis of these investment decision-rules?
    (iii) Suppose that if Project B is undertaken its benefit can be reinvested at 17%; what project should the firm choose? Show your calculations (spreadsheet printout is acceptable as long as entries are clearly labelled).

6. A firm has a capital budget of $30,000 and is considering three possible independent projects. Project A has a present outlay of $12,000 and yields $4, 281 per annum for 5 years. Project B has a present outlay of $10,000 and yields $4,184 per annum for 5 years. Project C has a present outlay of $17,000 and yields $5,802 per annum for 10 years. Funds which are not allocated to one of the projects can be placed in a bank deposit where they will earn 15% (the discount rate for the project).
    (a) Identify six combinations of project investments and a bank deposit which exhaust the budget.
    (b) Which of the above combinations should the firm choose:
         (i)   when the reinvestment rate is 15%?
         (ii) when the reinvestment rate is 20%?

    Explain your answer and show your calculations (spreadsheet printout is acceptable as long as entries are clearly labeled).

7. A public decision-maker has a budget of $100 which must be spent in the current year. Three projects are proposed, each of which is indivisible (it is not possible to undertake less than the whole project) and non-reproducible (it is not possible to construct two versions of the same project). The discount rate is 10% per annum. The project benefits and costs are summarized in the following Table:

Project	Cost ($)	Benefits ($)	
	Year 0	Year 1	Year 2
A	30	40	0
B	30	0	50
C	70	0	100

    (i)   Work out the Net Present Value (NPV), Internal Rate of Return (IRR) and Benefit-Cost Ratio (BCR) for each project;
    (ii) Rank the projects according to the NPV, IRR and BCR investment criteria;
    (iii) Which projects should be undertaken to spend the budget:
          (a) if the reinvestment rate is 12% per annum;
          (b) if the reinvestment rate is 18% per annum?

4
Private Benefit-Cost Analysis: Financial Analysis

Introduction

As noted in Chapter 1, social benefit-cost analysis takes a wide, "social" perspective in the context of investment appraisal – it measures and compares the costs and benefits experienced by all members of "society". In contrast, when a project is being evaluated by a private or public enterprise from a purely commercial or "private" perspective, account is taken only of the benefits and costs of the project that accrue to the enterprise itself and that affect its profitability. The project may have wider implications – environmental and employment effects, for example – but if these do not affect the enterprise's commercial profitability, they are omitted from the *private* analysis.

It is to be expected that the private enterprise would already have undertaken a *private* investment analysis of the project and will be basing its investment decision on the results of that analysis. However these results may not be available to the public sector decision-maker, and the social benefit-cost analysis, using discounted cash flow techniques very similar to those used in private benefit-cost analysis, and incorporating a private analysis, may be important in helping the public decision-maker decide what incentives are required in the form of tax concessions, for example, to induce the firm to undertake the project. For this reason the appraisal of a proposed project from a purely *private* viewpoint is often an integral part of a social benefit-cost analysis undertaken by the project analyst. This Chapter focuses on the methodology of *private* benefit-cost analysis, using *discounted cash flow (DCF) analysis*.

It can be noted that, in the case of a public project, similar considerations of revenue and cost flows to those addressed in the private analysis may be relevant in determining whether the government department decides to undertake the project or not. However, issues relating to government expenditure and tax flows are dealt with in the *referent group analysis* discussed in Chapter 6, and in the part of Chapter 10 dealing with the opportunity cost of public funds. The present Chapter considers only private sector projects.

Cash flows

Cash flows play a central role in the development and appraisal of almost any investment project: they are a summary presentation of the various costs and benefits expected to accrue over the project's life. As we saw in the previous Chapter, it is these cash flows that provide the main basis for deciding whether a project is "worthwhile" (are benefits greater than costs?), and/or which of a number of project variants or alternatives is the "best" (shows the greatest net benefits).

In this first part of the Chapter we shall focus on the *derivation of cash flows*, i.e. how to build up cash flow estimates from the basic technical, economic and social information that is collected and analysed in the course of preparing a project proposal or performing a project appraisal.

In the previous Chapter we considered the cash flows of a number of hypothetical projects. We saw how a project's net cash flow shows the difference between benefits and costs for each year of the project's life. The net cash flow of an investment normally has a very distinctive time profile, being negative in the earlier years when the project is under construction, and becoming positive only after the project has been completed and has started to produce the goods or services for which it was designed. We deliberately simplified the analysis by using projects with a relatively short life and uncomplicated cash flow profile. In practice cash flows are not so simple. There are a number of ways in which actual project cash flows might deviate from the profile of the hypothetical examples we have used until now. For instance:

- Cash flows of projects usually cover a relatively large number of years: anything from 10 to 20 years is quite normal, while certain projects have even longer lives (up to 50 years or more), depending on the nature of the project and the useful life of its main assets. The total number of years covered by a project's cash flow we usually call the length of a project's life or "lifetime", though some authors also use the word "planning horizon" or "time horizon".

- Although the net cash flows of investment projects have a distinct time profile, the exact shape and dimensions will differ from one project to another; there can be large variations in project life and in the "gestation period", i.e. the period before a project starts to yield positive net benefits. Moreover, some projects have high initial benefits that gradually taper off towards the end of their life; others (e.g. tree crop projects) require much more time before they reach their maximum net benefits but then maintain these for a relatively long time.

- In the previous Chapter we also saw how a project's costs are usually divided into: (a) investment costs, e.g. the cost of construction and installation of a project's physical assets, the cost of building up stocks of materials and spare parts needed to operate the project and the cost of training the staff; and, (b) operating costs, i.e. the costs of the materials, labour etc. used to operate and maintain the project. In our simple examples we always assumed that the entire investment cost occurred at the very beginning of the project: in year 0. In practice, although most investment costs are concentrated in the early years of the project (the initial investment), there is usually also a need for regular replacement investments when certain shorter-lived assets (machinery, transport equipment) reach the end of their useful life. Some projects even require a large outlay at the end of their life, such as mining projects where the owners are required to rehabilitate the landscape after the mine closes down.

- The relative importance of investment and operating costs can vary from one type of project to another. In the case of infrastructure projects (e.g. roads), a very large part of the total costs consists of the initial investment, while operating cost consists only of maintenance cost. In other projects (e.g. for crop production) the operating cost (land preparation, sowing, cultivation, costs of seeds, fertilizers, etc.) will be much more important relative to the initial investment.

- Project benefits consist mainly of the value of the output (the goods or services) produced by a project. In addition there may be incidental benefits such as the scrap value of equipment replaced during the project's life. At the end of the project's life the scrap or rest value (also called salvage or terminal value) of a project's assets is included as a benefit, though in certain cases this value may be negative, e.g. when a project site has to be brought back to its original condition upon termination of the project.

- Project benefits and project costs do not always result in cash receipts and cash outlays. An obvious example is the benefits of public roads, which are made available to the general public free of direct charge and which, therefore, do not result in revenues for the entity undertaking the investment (the national or regional government or local council). In such cases, which are very common when appraising public investment projects, it would be more correct to use the expression "flow of benefits and costs" and "net benefit flow" instead of "cash flow" and "net cash flow". In reality many textbooks and manuals continue to use the term (net) *cash* flow even in those cases where the net cash flow contains many non-cash benefits and costs. In this Chapter we shall do the same, i.e. use net cash flow and net benefit flow as synonyms.

- We also noted in the previous Chapter that the accounting period used in cash flow accounting is normally a year, but project years do not necessarily (and in reality hardly ever do) correspond to calendar years, and, although costs and benefits normally accrue throughout the year the standard convention in all cash flow accounting is to assume that all costs and benefits are concentrated (accrue as one single outflow or inflow) at the end of each project year.

In this Chapter we also deal with a number of other important issues to do with the derivation of cash flows, including: the treatment of incremental (or relative) cash flows; how to account for inflation; depreciation; how we should deal with flows of funds relating to the financing of a project; and, calculating profits taxes and the after-tax net cash flow. We should also note at this stage that the procedures that have to be followed may vary from case to case, depending on, among other factors, the point of view taken by the analyst when appraising a specific investment proposal. In this Chapter, however, we will begin by considering the cash flows of projects from the relatively narrow perspective of the individual investor.

Inflation and Relative Prices

Most countries experience *inflation*, i.e. an increase in the general price level. A dollar today will buy less than it did one, five or ten years ago. Rates of inflation – the percentage increases in the general price level per annum – differ widely between countries. At best the rate of inflation will be 1–2% per annum, but in many countries rates of 10–15% per annum have been regularly experienced. At the other end of the spectrum we find always some countries have experienced "hyper-inflation" – up to 100% per annum or sometimes more.

The question that arises is how to deal with inflation in preparing our cash flow estimates. We have seen that the cash flows of development projects might cover anything between 10 and 50 years. We need to make the distinction again between project *appraisal* when we are looking into the future, and project *evaluation* when we are looking back. In appraisal, do we have to forecast inflation that far ahead in order to be able to value our flows of inputs and outputs in a correct way? The answer is luckily "no", since there is no one who would be able to provide us with such estimates. As inflation is an increase in the *general* price level, we can safely ignore it for purposes of *appraisal*. In effect, we are assuming that it affects all costs and benefits in the same way, and therefore will not affect the relative returns on different projects in any real sense (recall the discussion of discounting and inflation in Chapter 2). What we do in practice is to assume that there is *no* inflation, i.e. we estimate all costs and benefits throughout the project's life at the price level obtaining at the time of appraisal (or as near to it as is possible).

In project *evaluation* when we are looking at a project's performance in retrospect, we can deflate actual prices by an appropriate deflator such as the CPI (consumer price index), GDP (Gross Domestic Product) deflator, or wholesale price index, to convert nominal cash flows to real values. We then compare the project IRR with the real cost of capital. Alternatively, we could leave all cash flows in nominal terms and then calculate a *nominal* IRR which we would compare with a *nominal* cost of capital, or which we convert to a real IRR by subtracting from it the rate of inflation. As discussed in Chapter 2, in NPV analysis we would have to be careful to use a *nominal* discount rate to discount a nominal cash flow. A simple example is shown in Table 4.1

Table 4.1 Nominal *vs.* Real Cash Flows

Year		0	1	2	3
1	Net Cash Flow (current prices)	−$100	42.0	44.1	46.3
2	Net Cash Flow (constant year 0 prices)	−$100	40.0	40.0	40.0

Inflation rate = 5% per annum
IRR(nominal) = 15%
IRR(real) = 10%
Cost of Capital = 6% (real)
   or = 11% (nominal, 6%+5%)
NPV (row 1 @ 11%) = $7.5
NPV (row 2 @ 6%) = $6.9

In this example we have a nominal cash flow (row 1) where each year's net cash flow is in current prices. When we calculate the IRR on this cash flow we arrive at a rate of 15% per annum; but, this is the *nominal* IRR which includes the effects of inflation on the cash flow. If we know the inflation rate for each year we can convert this to a real cash flow (row 2) by converting the nominal values to constant (base year) prices. If we assume that the inflation rate in each year is 5%, and taking year 0 as the base year, we derive the real cash flow shown in row 2. If we then calculate the IRR we arrive at a rate of 10% per annum. This is the *real* rate of return. Note, that the difference between the real and nominal rate is equal to the inflation rate: 15% minus 10% equals 5%.

If we were interested in knowing the NPV at a given cost of capital, again we have two options. If the *real* cost of capital is given as 6% per annum, we would need to discount the *nominal* cash flow (row 1) using a *nominal* discount rate of 11% (6% real plus the 5% inflation rate). The NPV is $7.50. Alternatively, we can discount the *real* cash flow (row 2) using the *real* cost of capital (6%). Here the NPV is $6.90. There is a slight difference between the NPVs which is due to the fact that when we discount in one stage (by 11%) this is not precisely equivalent to discounting in two stages, first by 5% (to convert nominal to real values) and then by 6%. You can check this by looking at the Discount Tables. Take year 3 discount rates as an example. The discount factor for 5% is 0.86 and for 6% is 0.84. Multiplying the two we get 0.72. Yet, when we look up the discount rate for 11% we see it is 0.73. The reason for this discrepancy was discussed in more detail in Chapter 2.

However, it is also true that in periods of inflation not all prices increase at the same rate. There may be goods and, in particular, services, whose prices increase at a much faster rate than the general price level. There are also, on the other hand, goods – for example consumer durables – the prices of which increase much less than the overall rate of inflation, or which even show nominal price decreases (e.g. consumer electronics, personal computers and pocket calculators). These price changes, which are changes in *relative* prices, should not be ignored in project appraisal and therefore should be incorporated into our cash flow estimates. The point to remember, however, is that relative price changes would also occur in a world without general price inflation. Relative price changes are not the result of inflation, but occur alongside inflation, because of changes in demand, technological developments (e.g. development of synthetic materials and improved inputs), exhaustion of natural resources, and destruction of the environment. They should, in principle, always – even in the absence of inflation – be taken into account when preparing cash flow estimates.

While it is clear that, in principle, cash flow estimates should be based on *projected* changes in relative prices of inputs and outputs over the project's life, this is easier said than done, and, in most studies, it is *not* done – so that cost and benefit estimates tend to be based on the assumption of a constant price level *and* unchanged relative prices. What can be done, however, and is often done as standard practice, is to apply some form of risk or sensitivity analysis, which is discussed in Chapter 9. At this stage all that we need note is that a sensitivity analysis would identify those prices (and other parameters) on which the overall result of the project is most dependent, and calculate the net benefits of a project making a range of assumptions about possible price movements. This does not yield a clear answer, however, but it shows how project decisions depend on certain assumptions. Risk analysis takes this a step further, in the sense that it attempts to place probabilities on each price scenario and possible project outcome.

Incremental or Relative Cash Flows

The concept of incremental cash flow is relevant for all types of investment projects. Its meaning and importance can be most easily explained, however, with reference to investments that aim at the improvement of existing schemes. Examples of these are abundant and may range from the simple replacement of an outdated piece of machinery by a more modern model to the complete rehabilitation of a factory or agricultural scheme, such as an irrigation project.

In such instances it is assumed that there is already a cash flow from the existing project and that the main objective of a proposed additional investment is to improve the net cash flow, either by decreasing cost, or by increasing benefits, or by doing both of these at the same time. Such an improvement in the net cash flow we call the *incremental cash flow* (or incremental net benefit flow). Generally defined it is the difference between the net benefit flow *with* the new investment and the net benefit flow *without* this investment.

If one wants to find out if an improvement or rehabilitation is worthwhile one should, in principle, look at the incremental cash flow, and the same holds true if one wants to find out which of two alternatives is better; e.g. the rehabilitation of existing irrigation facilities or the construction of an entirely new irrigation scheme. The answer to these questions will often turn out to be in favour of rehabilitation. In many cases relatively small investments, if used to improve weak components (or remove bottlenecks) in a much larger system, can have relatively large returns.

At the same time, however, there are pitfalls in appraising or evaluating investments of the above type on the basis of incremental cash flows where we consider only the *with* and *without* rehabilitation scenarios. The main points can best be explained by means of a few simple hypothetical examples (Examples 1, 2 and 3 shown in Table 4.2 below). In the first two examples we show the net cash flow *with* rehabilitation (line 1), the net cash flow *without* rehabilitation (line 2) and the resulting incremental cash flow (line 3). It will be noted that in both cases rehabilitation yields the same improvement (the same incremental cash flow), but in Example 1 the starting position (the without cash flow) is much better than in Example 2 where it is negative and remains negative even with rehabilitation. In Example 2 rehabilitation does improve things but it merely cuts losses and does not convert these into positive net benefits. The question that arises, of course, is if we should undertake rehabilitation in the event that the scheme concerned continues to yield negative returns even with the rehabilitation carried out. The answer is "no", assuming of course that the rehabilitation proposed is the best that can be done under the circumstances, and that the unrehabilitated project can be terminated.

That the answer should be "no" may be further demonstrated with the help of Example 3, which starts from the same assumptions as case 2 (it has the same net cash flow without rehabilitation). In Example 3 we compare the "without" cash flow with the alternative of completely abandoning the scheme (closing down the factory or whatever the example may be). Line 1 is now the cash flow if the scheme is abandoned (liquidated). We assume it to be zero but it might be positive in year 0 (because of a positive salvage value). The incremental cash flow (line 3) is now the improvement in the cash flow that results from abandoning (closing down) the scheme completely. If we compare this incremental cash flow with the one resulting from rehabilitation (Example 2), it shows, of course, that liquidating the scheme is the better alternative.

Table 4.2 Incremental Cash Flows

EXAMPLE 1		0	1	2	3		10
1	Net Cash Flow With Rehabilitation	−1500	750	750	750	—	750
2	Net Cash Flow Without Rehabilitation		500	500	500	—	500
3	Incremental Cash Flow (1–2)	−1500	250	250	250	—	250
EXAMPLE 2							
1	Net Cash Flow With Rehabilitation	−1500	−250	−250	−250	—	−250
2	Net Cash Flow Without Rehabilitation		−500	−500	−500	—	−500
3	Incremental Cash Flow (1–2)	−1500	250	250	250	—	250
EXAMPLE 3							
1	Net Cash Flow With Closure	0	0	0	0	—	0
2	Net Cash Flow Without Closure		−500	−500	−500		−500
3	Incremental Cash Flow (1–2)		500	500	500	—	500

This example illustrates the danger of basing a rehabilitation decision simply on the resulting incremental cash flow – taking as a basis only two alternatives: the scheme *with* and the scheme *without* rehabilitation. The examples above show that it is necessary to consider at least one more alternative – that of liquidating the scheme.

A further look at these examples will also show that there is an alternative to incremental cash flow analysis. Instead of comparing *with* and *without* flows and calculating an incremental (or relative) flow, one could look at the *with* and *without* flows themselves (the absolute flow) and use DCF appraisal techniques to decide which is the better of the two: the *with* or the *without* flow and, at the same time, see if the *with* flow yields sufficiently large net benefits to make it worthwhile to continue (instead of liquidating).

The question that arises is why introduce the incremental cash flow at all or even – as in the case of certain textbooks – lay down the rule that all projects should be appraised on the basis of incremental cash flows? The answer is that in the case of many projects it is extremely difficult to establish the full *with* and *without* situation and that the only feasible alternative may be directly to estimate the improvement (the incremental cash flow) expected to result from the project. Many investments aim at introducing marginal and gradual improvements to existing projects, where it may be more practical to estimate directly the net benefits resulting from the improvements instead of having to compare the complete benefit and cost information in the area of operations affected by the improvements.

Capital Costs and the Treatment of Depreciation

As a rule, there will usually be two forms of investment or capital cost: *fixed investment* and *working capital*. In this section we discuss issues relating to these two types of capital investment, including replacement investment, salvage or terminal values, and depreciation.

Fixed Investment

Fixed investment, as the term suggests, usually refers to all those capital goods such as land, buildings, plant and machinery that effectively remain intact during the production process, apart from the usual wear-and-tear. Investment in fixed capital is usually concentrated in the first year or years of a project's life, but, as different types of fixed investment have different life spans, replacement investment will also occur in various years during a project's life. These costs will, of course, appear as negative items in the cash flow. It is also conceivable that at the end of the project period at least part of the fixed investment will be intact: almost certainly the land (unless this has been destroyed, environmentally, by the project), buildings, equipment, vehicles, etc. As these can be sold off, it is usual for there to be a positive amount (inflow of cash) in the last year of the project representing scrap, salvage or terminal value of the project's fixed assets. In some instances, however, additional investment-related costs could be incurred. For instance, some types of projects are costly to close down, such as nuclear power plants. Mining investments, too, will often have a negative cash flow in the final year if environmental regulations in the country require that the mine developers restore the natural environment to its "original" (or at least, pre-mining) state. Of course, not all investments require that the investor purchases physical capital goods. In the case of investment in human capital by an individual, for instance, the "fixed" investment is in the form of an initial outlay on education and training and the benefits are the stream of additional income flows in the future.

What about depreciation charges? In the financial statements of an enterprise's operations there will always be a "cost" item labelled "depreciation". Should this also be entered as a capital cost? If it is included in the accountant's profit and loss statement as an item of expenditure should we leave it in when calculating the project's operating costs? The answer to both questions is "NO!".

A "golden rule" in discounted cash flow analysis is that all investment costs should be recorded in the cash flow only in the year in which the investment cost was actually incurred. This represents a departure from standard bookkeeping practices where an accountant will apportion investment costs over a number of years in the firm's profit and loss statements. This is an accounting convention and is done for purposes of calculating an operation's *taxable profits*, which, we are going to see later on, are not necessarily the same thing as net operating revenues in discounted cash flow (DCF) analysis. Although the project accountant will always include *depreciation* of capital equipment as a cost in preparing a profit and loss (or income and expenditure) statement for the project, depreciation is not like other project expenses or costs in the sense that it does not actually involve a *cash transaction*.

Depreciation is purely a bookkeeping device – it amounts to setting aside some part of the project's income or benefits each year in order to finance capital (investment) expenditure in the future. In practice, the amount set aside as depreciation in any one year is based on some percentage of the value of the capital equipment already installed. Let us say, for example, that we have a project with an investment in buildings, machinery and transport equipment worth $100,000. Of this, $50,000 is the value of the project building with an estimated life of 50 years; $30,000 is the value of machinery with an estimated life of 10 years, and $20,000 is the value of transport equipment with an estimated life of 5 years.

One method of calculating the annual depreciation allowance is the straight-line method, where we spread the depreciation evenly over the life of the investment. Applying this method to the above example would give us the results shown in Table 4.3:

Table 4.3 Calculating Depreciation Using the Straight–Line Method

ITEM	INITIAL COST	LIFE	%ANNUAL DEPRECIATION	ANNUAL DEPRECIATION ALLOWANCE
BUILDINGS	$50,000	50	2%	$1,000
MACHINERY	$30,000	10	10%	$3,000
TRANSPORT EQUIP.	$20,000	5	20%	$4,000
TOTAL	$100,000	—	—	$8,000

In other words, the project accountant would enter $8,000 as a "cost" or "expenditure" each year when calculating the project's taxable profits. The sum of the depreciation allowance set aside in this manner each year would, in principle, and ignoring any interest which might be earned on a capital reserve, permit the project to finance the replacement of each item of capital equipment at the end of its expected life.

However, from the point of view of the project analyst, who is interested in deriving the net cash flow of the project, depreciation should not be treated as a project cost. If we were to include depreciation as a cost, we would be double-counting the project's investment cost and therefore undervaluing the project's net benefit. The reason for this is simple. If we look at the examples in Chapters 2 and 3, we will be reminded that the investment costs of the various projects we looked at were recorded as costs as and when they were actually incurred, i.e. usually at the beginning of the project's life, and then again when various items of equipment were replaced. If we were now to include depreciation allowances as an annual "cost", we would, in fact, be recording our investment costs twice – once at the beginning of the project's life and then again as a series of annual costs. For this reason, project analysts do not treat depreciation as a cost in calculating a net cash flow. Therefore, if the project accountant provides us with a net income (or net cost) figure that includes depreciation as a cost, we should be careful to add this amount back in (i.e. as a "benefit" to our annual cash flow).

Working Capital

In addition to fixed investment, it is normally necessary for an operation to have some working capital as part of its operations. Working capital refers essentially to stocks of goods that the business or project needs to hold in order to operate. A manufacturer who is engaged in the production of goods using raw materials will need to hold stocks of raw materials to offset possible interruptions to supply. The producer will also want to hold stocks of finished goods to meet orders without delay. If the producer uses machines, equipment, vehicles, etc. it may also be necessary to maintain a reasonable stock of spare parts, and perhaps fuel, if these are not close on hand from nearby suppliers. At any point in time, a project will be carrying such stocks. As existing stocks are used up they need to be replaced with new stocks, so the actual components of working capital will be changing during the course of the year, and it is possible that their total value will change from one year to the next. The most important point to note about working capital is that it is only a change in the level of working capital that should be treated as investment in cash flow analysis.

When a project is first established and the stocks of working capital are first set up, the full amount of the initial working capital will be recorded as an investment cost (cash outflow, or negative cash flow). If the total value of working capital then remains constant, even though its actual composition may change, there is no additional investment cost. If the stock of working capital were to decrease, i.e. a lower value of the total stocks at the end of the year than at the beginning, then investment has fallen and this must be recorded in the cash flow as an inflow. This will normally happen in the final year of the project's life. The project will either run down or sell off all its stocks of working capital completely. An example is illustrated in Table 4.4.

Table 4.4 Investment in Working Capital

Item/Year	0	1	2	3	4	5
Total Working Capital	$0	$50	$100	$100	$100	$0
Investment in W/Capital	$0	–$50	–$50	$0	$0	+$100

In setting up the cash flow the lower row entitled "Investment in Working Capital" will be added to the cash flow for fixed investment to arrive at a total investment cash flow. Note that a positive investment in working capital appears as a *negative* cash flow and *vice versa*, because investment is always treated as a negative value in cash flow analysis, reflecting its status as a cost.

Interest Charges, Financing Flows and Cash Flow on Equity

Another item of "capital cost" that the accountant will have included in the project's profit and loss statement is interest paid on money borrowed, perhaps to finance the initial capital investment. Again, we must ask the same questions. Should interest be included as part of investment cost, or, if it has been included as part of the operating costs, should it be left in our cash flow statement when undertaking DCF analysis? Again the answer is "NO", but, we should qualify this by stating that interest charges should not be included in the cash flow *in the initial instance when we are interested in the project's total profitability – we call this the "project" appraisal.* At subsequent stages, when we are interested in calculating the project's profitability *from the standpoint of the owners' equity capital – we call this the "private" appraisal –* then *all* cash inflows and outflows relating to the debt financing of the project, including the disbursements and repayments of the loan itself, need to be incorporated into the cash flow. Furthermore, as with depreciation, interest charges are a legitimate tax deductible cost, so when we come to calculate taxes and the net cash flow *after tax*, we will need to include interest as a project cost. We return to this point in the next section.

The cash flows of the projects that were discussed in Chapter 3, for example, were indeed all *project* cash flows; i.e. *before* financing. The cash flow used in most benefit-cost analysis (BCA) is usually the project cash flow. This shows the financial flows expected to result from the project itself and contains no information about the way the project might be financed. Any given project can, in theory at least, be financed in many different ways, involving different possible combinations of debt and equity finance, and, within the debt finance category, many different possible loan arrangements and terms. Different loan terms, involving, say, different rates of interest and/or different maturities will generate different profiles of financing inflows and outflows for the project's owners or *equity* holders. It is therefore important that we are able to consider any given project's profitability *independently* of the terms on which its debt finance is arranged – *project* appraisal using our terminology. If we were to ignore this, it is conceivable that a "bad" project is made to look good, simply by virtue of its sponsors having access to concessional funding on terms much more favourable than what the financial markets offer. Conversely, a potentially "good" project may look "bad" only because its sponsor is unable to secure (or is unaware of) more favourable loan conditions available elsewhere in the market.

Does the foregoing imply that in appraising a project and coming to a decision about its profitability without considering the cost of funding we are effectively ignoring the "cost of capital"? The answer is "NO!" This is precisely what we are doing when we apply DCF analysis to a project's cash flow, whether we use the NPV or IRR decision-rule as discussed in Chapter 3. When we discount a cash flow we use a discount rate that we believe to be a good indication of the opportunity cost of funds to the party concerned, as determined by the capital market.

As noted above, the project analyst's interest in a project's overall cash flow (ignoring the manner in which the project is to be financed) should not be interpreted as implying that we are not interested in knowing the financial arrangements or terms of the debt finance for any particular project under consideration. Indeed, it is a very important part of the appraisal process also to derive the cash flows showing the inflows and outflows of debt finance, and then to derive a separate net cash flow for the project *after debt finance*. In our terminology, this is the *private* appraisal.

The two questions immediately arising in this connection are: (a) What is shown by such a cash flow *after* financing? and, (b) How can such a cash flow be used in the investment appraisal process?

These two questions can best be answered with the help of a simple, hypothetical example, shown in Table 4.5, illustrating the case of a small-scale farmer participating in a large publicly supported agricultural scheme. Farmers participating in the scheme are expected to make a number of investments from their own funds at the farm level, perhaps for a tractor, some simple machinery and tools, irrigation equipment, and so on, and will also be provided under the scheme with certain inputs (e.g. irrigation water) against payment of a certain fee. All these investments, plus the farm-gate value of the crops produced are reflected in the net cash flow *before* financing (the investment cash flow at the farm level), shown in Table 4.5 (*line 1*). The *investment cash flow* shows an initial investment of $5,000 in year 0, to be undertaken by the farmer, followed by a stream of net benefits of $1,000 per annum for 10 years. Farmers participating in the scheme will also qualify for a loan covering part of the required investment and carrying an interest rate of 7% per annum. It has to be repaid in 10 years. The flows connected to this loan are shown in *line 2* of the Table. They constitute the *financing flow* (or in the terminology used in corporate accounting, the *debt finance flow*). The financing flow shows that the farmer receives a loan of $3,512 in year 0, while the servicing cost of the loan (amortization plus interest) will be $500 per annum for 10 years (when you consult your Annuity Tables you will find that an annuity of $500 per year for 10 years is just sufficient to service a loan of $3,512 at an interest rate of 7%).

Note that the profile of a debt finance flow is the mirror image of that of an investment flow. An investment flow starts negative and then turns positive, if everything goes well. A debt finance flow starts positive and then turns negative, from the standpoint of the borrowing party.

The net cash flow *after* financing, shown in *line 3*, is the sum of the investment cash flow (line 1) and the debt finance flow (line 2). If we examine the Table we notice that the net cash flow *after* financing shows us two things: (a) which part of the investment has to be financed from the farmer's own funds ($1,488); and (b) the net return she can expect ($500 per annum) after meeting the servicing cost of the loan. While the net cash flow *before* financing shows us the return to the *project* investment at the farm level, the net cash flow *after* financing shows us the return on that part of the investment financed from the farmer's *own funds*: in the terminology used in corporate accounting this is called the return on *equity*. In our terminology, it is called the *private* return.

Table 4.5 Deriving the Private Cash Flow on Farmer's Equity

Year	0	1	2	3	4	5	6	7	8	9	10
1 Net cash flow before financing	−5000	1000	1000	–	–	–	–	–	–	–	1000
2 Debt finance flow	3512	−500	−500	–	–	–	–	–	–	–	−500
3 Net cash flow after financing (1+2)	−1488	500	500	–	–	–	–	–	–	–	500

This still leaves us with the question of why this return is calculated and why we do not stick to the general rule of using the cash flows before financing. The answer to the last part of the question is easier. We are in fact not departing from the rule, as the farm level cash flow after financing is not used for purposes of decision-making about the scheme as a whole. The decision to carry out the scheme will be based on the aggregate cash flow of the scheme of which the net cash flow before financing to all the farms in the scheme forms an important component. The cash flow after financing is only calculated because it determines whether farmers will be willing to participate in the scheme on the conditions offered to them. What farmers will be interested in is primarily the net returns accruing to them after having met their financial obligations. If these are too low (or perhaps zero in case all net benefits generated at the farm level go towards servicing the loan) farmers will not be interested in participating.

Returns to farmers may be too low for a number of reasons. One reason may be that the potential returns on the scheme *as a whole* are not high enough. That would mean that the scheme should not be carried out or should be revised. If the aggregate costs and benefits of the scheme show that it is potentially attractive then too low returns to farmers will mainly be a reflection of the distribution of net benefits between farmers and other parties in the scheme (the public authority running the scheme and general government). It is an indication that the incentives to farmers (the conditions on which they can participate) may have to be reviewed.

We noted above that the profile of the debt financing flow, from the perspective of the borrower – in this case the farmer – was *positive* in the initial, investment period and then *negative* over the repayment period. Of course, from the standpoint of the lender, this debt cash flow has the opposite signs: negative followed by positive. It may be useful to consider the same project example we used previously (Table 4.5), where we now show the two components of the financing flows, debt and equity, from the perspective of the funding sources: *lenders* and *owners* (or, *equity holders*). Their respective financing flows are shown in Table 4.6, rows 2 and 3.

Table 4.6 Project Cash Flows Equal Debt Plus Equity (Private) Cash Flows

	0	1	2	3	4	5	6	7	8	9	10
1 *Project* Net cash flow	−5000	1000	1000	–	–	–	–	–	–	–	1000
2 Debt finance flow	−3512	500	500	–	–	–	–	–	–	–	500
3 Equity finance flow	−1488	500	500	–	–	–	–	–	–	–	500

Notice that the two parts of the project's financing flows add up to exactly the same amount as the overall *project* cash flow. This is true by definition, for that part of the investment that is not funded by the lender (debt) must come from the investor's own funds (equity). Conversely, that part of the positive net cash flow that is not paid out to (received by) the lender (interest plus principal repayments) is left over as profit to the equity holder. This cash flow on equity (the *private* cash flow in our terminology) is, in effect, derived as the residual cash flow as we saw previously.

Calculating the Return on Total Investment, Cost of Debt Finance and Return on Equity: An Example

We have seen that financing inflows and outflows are of two broad types: *debt* (loans, long or short term, trade credit, etc.), and *own funds* (equity, shares, etc.). A project can be funded entirely by debt, entirely by own funds or by a combination of these. The latter is most common; i.e. the investor finances part of the project from borrowed funds and the remainder from "own funds" (whether it be an independent producer, private company or state enterprise).

The point to remember is that the total (or net) inflow and outflow of *finance* must, by definition, correspond exactly with the net inflow and outflow of the project's costs and benefits over the life of the project. A useful exercise is to calculate the following from Table 4.6 above:
(a) the IRR on the total investment made at the farm level: the *project* IRR (line 1)
(b) the rate of interest implied in the debt finance flow (line 2)
(c) the rate of return on the farmer's own investment: the *private* IRR (line 3).
If it is then also assumed that, given the alternatives open to farmers, full participation in the scheme will only be attractive to them if they could secure a return on their own (equity) investment of 20% per annum, we can then ask, what flow of annual net benefits *before* financing would be required to give farmers that minimum return? The initial investment would still be $5,000 and the amount of debt finance and the conditions on which it can be obtained (line 2) are also unchanged. We can also work out what IRR on total investment at the farm level is required to give farmers the minimum return of 20% on their own investment. Given the nature of the cash and financing flows, the quickest way to compute your answers is by making use of the annuity factor:

(a) To calculate the IRR on the project's Net Cash Flow before financing, we follow the simple procedure shown in Chapter 3, using the Annuity Tables:
$$\text{if NPV} = 0$$
$$-5000 \ (1.0) + 1000(AF_{10}) = 0$$
$$AF_{10} = 5000/1000$$
$$= 5$$
$$\text{IRR} = 15\%$$
(b) Assuming we did not already know what the annual rate of interest was on the loan, we can determine this by calculating the IRR on line 2, the "Debt Finance Flow":
$$\text{if NPV} = 0$$
$$3512(1.0) - 500(AF_{10}) = 0$$
$$AF_{10} = 3512/500$$
$$= 7.024$$
$$\text{IRR} = 7\%$$

(c) From the residual cash flow (line 3), we derive the IRR on the farmer's own funds:

$$\text{if NPV} = 0$$
$$-1488(1.0) + 500(AF_{10}) = 0$$
$$AF_{10} = 1488/500$$
$$= 2.976$$
$$\text{IRR} = 31\%$$

From the results of these calculations we see that although the IRR on the project as a whole is only 15%, the farmers themselves can expect a return of 31% on their own investment, due to the availability of loans at only a 7% interest rate. We can also ascertain what minimum cash flow on the project would be needed to ensure that farmers earned a 20% rate of return on their own investment. Again, using the Annuity Tables:

$$\text{For IRR of 20\% on farmer's investment}$$
$$\text{NPV} = -1488(1.0) + X(AF_{10/0.20}) = 0$$
$$\text{Where } X = \text{Farmer's annual net benefit after financing.}$$
$$X(AF_{10/0.20}) = 1488/X$$
$$= 1488/4.1925$$
$$= 354.9$$

This shows us that annual net benefit required to yield a 20% return for farmers after financing is $354.9. As the loan is repaid at $500 per annum the required annual net benefit before financing will be $354.9 plus $500 = $854.9. We can then calculate what the IRR on this is:

$$\text{IRR on New Cash Flow before financing:}$$
$$\text{if NPV} = 0$$
$$-5000(1.0) + 854.9(AF_{10}) = 0$$
$$AF_{10} = 5000/854.9$$
$$= 5.849$$
$$\text{IRR} = 11\%$$

In other words, if farmers are to earn 20% on their investment, the project as a whole must yield a return of 11% per annum.

Taxation and After-Tax Net Cash Flows

Up until now all the examples we have considered ignore company or profits tax. When a private investor appraises a project, she will want to know what return to expect on an after-tax basis. From a private investor's standpoint, taxes paid to government are, like any other costs, to be deducted in deriving a net cash flow. (In Chapters 5 and 6 we will see that in social benefit-cost analysis, when a project is appraised from the standpoint of society as a whole, taxes should *not* be treated as a project cost.) Tax laws vary considerably from one country to the next. These laws will determine what can and cannot be treated as a legitimate, tax deductible expense, what rate of taxation will apply to different types of project, and so on. It is not the purpose of this section to consider the implications for cash flow analysis of the tax laws of any country in particular. The main point that needs to be stressed here is that the analyst should be aware that there are certain components of project cost that we, as investment analysts, do not consider as "costs" in DCF analysis, but which are considered as costs from a taxation perspective. In other words, these items of project cost may not enter into our derivation of a project's cash flow *directly*, but they will affect the net cash flow *indirectly* through their effect on the project's *taxable profits*.

We refer here to two items dealt with at some length in the preceding sections: *depreciation* and *interest*. We saw that neither of these should be treated as components of project cost when considering the overall project. We saw that depreciation is an accounting device, and as the project analyst includes investment costs in the cash flow as and when they are incurred, to also include depreciation would involve double-counting. Similarly, interest charges on borrowed capital are not treated as *project* costs *per se* as these relate to the financing of the project, and the process of discounting in DCF analysis uses the discount rate as the opportunity cost of capital. To include interest costs would again amount to double-counting. But, as both depreciation and interest charges appear in the accountant's profit and loss statements for the project, and therefore affect the project's declared or taxable profits, we need to perform a "side" calculation of the project's taxable profit, applying the same conventions used by the accountant.

In effect, all that this amounts to is setting up an additional "cash flow" that includes all the same items of operating costs and revenues as in our DCF analysis, to which we must:
(i)   add back in depreciation and interest charges;
(ii) exclude capital costs (and subsequent inflows of salvage or terminal values, unless it is stipulated that these are to be treated as incomes or losses for taxation purposes).
Having derived a taxable income cash flow we then apply the appropriate tax rate to that stream to obtain a "taxation due" cash flow. *It is only this "taxation due" line that should be added to our main cash flow table in order to derive the after-tax net cash flow.*

One issue that is likely to arise is the treatment of *losses* in any year. This will depend on the laws of the country in question, but, by and large it would normally be reasonable to assume that losses incurred in one project could be offset by the enterprise against profits it earns elsewhere, or, that losses in one year may be offset against profits in subsequent years. In the first case, you would then need to calculate the *decrease* in overall tax liability resulting from the loss and treat this as a *positive* value in deriving the *after-tax* cash flow. In the second case you would need to reduce the subsequent year(s) taxable profits by the magnitude of the loss, which again would imply a positive impact on the *after-tax* cash flow in the subsequent year(s).

The Discount Rate

In calculating net present values a range of discount rates, incorporating both the domestic government bond rate and the firm's required rate of return on equity capital, should be used. The private analysis will be used to assess whether the project is attractive from a private point of view, and this will be determined by comparing the private IRR with the required rate of return, or by considering the NPV calculated at a rate of discount approximately equal to the required rate of return. However, where the private firm is a member of the referent group the private analysis may also be used to assess some of the implications of the project for the referent group in the social benefit-cost analysis, and, as argued below, the government bond rate is appropriate for discounting referent group net benefits. The firm's required rate of return on equity may be unknown and the range of discount rates chosen should be wide enough to include any reasonable estimate. If no attempt is made to inflate benefits or costs, a real rate of interest is required as the discount rate, and, as noted in Chapters 2 and 3, the use of a real rate of interest involves the implicit assumption that all prices change at the general rate of inflation. The real domestic bond rate can be approximated by the money rate less the current rate of inflation (which acts as a proxy for the expected rate). The real required rate of return on equity capital is approximated by the money rate less the expected rate of inflation. There are also considerations of risk which are deferred until Chapter 9.

In summary, a range of discount rates is used for several reasons: first, in the private analysis, the firm's required rate of return on equity capital may not be known; second, as to be discussed in Chapter 10, there may be valid reasons why the market rate of interest should be replaced by a shadow (or social) discount rate in the efficiency or referent group analysis, and we don't know what that rate should be; and, third, we want to see how sensitive the NPV is to the choice of discount rate (if it is very sensitive this compounds the difficulty posed by the uncertainty about the appropriate discount rate).

Derivation of Project Private Cash Flows Using Spreadsheets

In this section, using a hypothetical case study, we illustrate, step-by-step, how to derive a project's (private) net cash flow from basic information about the project's costs, revenues and financing. In doing this we also recommend a method for designing and setting up the spreadsheet in such a way that it is readily amenable to subsequent revisions or refinements, whether these be for purposes of social benefit-cost analysis, referent group analysis, or sensitivity and risk analysis. *The underlying principle we adhere to in setting up a spreadsheet is that any project data or variable (or potential variable) should be entered into the spreadsheet only once. Any subsequent use of those data should be in the form of a reference to the address of the cell into which the value was first entered.*

Worked Example: National Fruit Growers (NFG) Project

In the year 2000 NFG is considering a potential project to grow apples, peaches and pears in Black Valley. The current market prices are: apples, $1,000 per tonne; peaches, $1,250 per tonne; and pears, $1,500 per tonne. Once the project is at full production, the company expects to grow and sell 100 tonnes of apples, 90 tonnes of peaches and 75 tonnes of pears per annum.

To set up the project NFG plans to rent 100 hectares of land, currently planted with fruit trees, at an annual rent of $30 per ha. The contract will be for 20 years and the company will begin paying rent in 2001. NFG will purchase the capital equipment immediately (year 2000) consisting of: (i) 4 units of farm equipment at $100,000 each; (ii) 3 vehicles at $30,000 each; (iii) 250 m^2 of storage units at $1,000 per m^2. For depreciation purposes the equipment has a book life of 10 years; vehicles 5 years; and buildings 20 years. (In practice the company plans to maintain these for the full duration of the investment without replacement and at the end of the project it anticipates a salvage value of 10% of the initial cost of all investment items.)

NFG will also need to invest in various items of working capital in 2001. These are: (i) 2 tonnes of fertilizer stocks at $500 per ton; 2,500 litres of insecticide at $30 per litre; 10 months supply of spare parts for equipment and vehicles at $1,000 per month; 500 litres of fuel at $0.70 per litre. The items included in annual operating costs are summarized in Table 4.7 below:

Table 4.7 NFG's Annual Operating Costs

ITEM	NO. OF UNITS	COST/UNIT ($)
Rent on land (Ha)	100	30
Fuel (lt)	2,500	0.70
Seeds/plants (kg)	250	20
Fertilizer (Tonnes)	3	500
Insecticides (lt)	3,000	30
Water (ML)	900	20
Spares & maintenance	12	1000
Casual labor (days)	100	60
Administration (per month)	12	1,000
Insurance[1]	1	8,263.5
Management salary	12	3,000
Miscellaneous (p.a.)		7,700

[1] Representing 1% of total investment cost, i.e. fixed investment plus working capital.

NFG expects operations to begin in 2001, initially at 25% of capacity, increasing to 50% in 2002, 75% in 2003 and to full capacity in 2004. All operating costs and revenues in the years 2001 to 2003 are assumed to be the same proportion of full-scale costs and revenues as output is of the full-scale level. The project is to be terminated after 20 years of operation.

To finance the project NFG intends to secure an agricultural loan for $700,000 in 2000, carrying an interest rate of 3.5% per annum, repayable over 10 years. NFG will also take out a bank overdraft in 2001 for $40,000, at 5%, which it intends to repay after 4 years. The balance of the required funding will be met from NFG's own funds (equity). The current tax rate on agricultural profits is 25%, payable annually after deducting depreciation allowances and interest on debt. NFG's accountant informs us that any losses incurred in this operation may be deducted, for taxation purposes, from profits the company earns in other agricultural projects, in the same year.

You have been asked to assist NFG by calculating the following:
(i)   the IRR and NPV (at 5%,10%, and 15%) for the project, before tax and financing;
(ii) the private IRR and NPV (at 5%,10%, and 15%) on NFG's own equity, before *and* after tax.

   To qualify for the subsidies on its inputs, NFG may have to satisfy the government that this project is in the broader public interest – is socially worthwhile. It is also conceivable that NFG will want to consider variations of this project in some form of scenario and sensitivity analysis in the future. You should therefore be careful to set up your spreadsheet for the project and private analysis in such a way that it is readily amenable to changes in the values of key variables at a later stage, and to further development to calculate efficiency and social benefits and costs. (The cash flow entries should be in thousands of dollars.)

Step 1: Setting up the "Key Variables" Table

As we will be using most of the variables at a number of different places in the spreadsheet it is important that we enter all the "Key Variables" in one dedicated section of the spreadsheet. We suggest that this section is created at the top of the spreadsheet as a table, in the format shown in Figure 4.1.

Table 1: Key Variables		Project			Operating Costs	No.	Price	Cost (Project)
Investment Costs	No.	Price	Cost					
(i) Fixed Investment	(units)	($)			Rent on land (Ha)	100	30	3,000
Farm equipment (units	4	100,000	400,000		Fuel (litres)	2,500	0.7	1,750
Vehicles (units)	3	30,000	90,000		Seeds (Kg)	250	20	5,000
Buildings (m2)	250	1,000	250,000		Fertilizers (tonnes)	3	500	1,500
TOTAL			$740,000		Insecticides (litres)	3,000	30	90,000
(ii) Working Capital					Water (ML)	900	20	18,000
Fertilizer Stocks (tons	2	500	1,000		Spares	12	1,000	12,000
Insecticide stocks (Lit	2500	30	75,000		Casual labor (days)	100	60	6,000
Equipment spare part:	10	1,000	10,000		Administration (/month	12	1000	12,000
Fuel stocks (Litres)	500	0.7	350		Insurance (p.a.)	1	8,263.5	8,263
TOTAL			$86,350.0		Management (/month)	12	3,000	36,000
(iii) Salvage Value	10%		$74,000		Miscellaneous	1	7,700	7,700
					TOTAL (Market prices)			$201,213
Depreciation	Life(yrs)	Amount p.a.			Revenues			
	Equipmr	10	40,000		Apples (tons)	100	1,000	100,000
	Vehicles	5	18,000		Peaches (tons)	90	1,250	112,500
	Building	20	12,500		Pears (tons)	75	1,500	112,500
Financing	Amount	Interest	Life (yrs)		TOTAL			$325,000
Loan	$700,000	3.5%	10					
Overdraft	$40,000	5.0%	4		Capacity Output			
Discount rate =	5.0%	10.0%	15.0%	Year	2001	2002	2003	2004+
Tax rate on profits =	25.0%			%	25%	50%	75%	100%

Tabs: Ex1a / Ex1b / Ex1c / Ch1Ex \ **Variables** / ProjectBCA / PrivateBCA / EfficiencyBCA

Figure 4.1 NFG Case Study: Key Variables Table

Notice that all the information contained in the preceding paragraphs about the project has been arranged systematically under the headings "Investment Costs", "Operating Costs", "Revenues". We have also provided the relevant information about other important variables including: depreciation rates for each type of fixed investment; the expected salvage value of investment; the details of the loans for financing the project; the rate of taxation; the percentage of full capacity output; and the discount rates. Later on we may wish to add further variables for the purpose of undertaking the social or efficiency BCA and sensitivity and risk analysis. Notice that in the sub-sections of Table 2 (Figure 4.2) we have used the data in Table 1 (together with formulae) to derive sub-totals for each of the main categories of the cash flow: i.e. Fixed Investment Costs, Working Capital, Operating Costs, and Revenues.

Step 2: Setting up the Project's Cash Flow

To set up the main *project* cash flow table we have listed the categories of cost and benefit in the left hand column as shown in Figure 4.2, while the project years (from year 2000 through to 2020) are listed across the columns, so that the cash flow runs from left to right rather than from the top down. We recommend this format for reasons of convenience when working with a number of additional working tables in the same spreadsheet. It should also be noted that we

ITEM/YEAR	0	1	2	3	4	5	6	7	8	9	10	11	12	13	14	15	16	17	18	19	20
Investment costs																					
Fixed Investment	-740.0																				74.0
Working Capital		-86.4																			86.4
Total Investment	-740.0	-86.4	0.0	0.0	0.0	0.0	0.0	0.0	0.0	0.0	0.0	0.0	0.0	0.0	0.0	0.0	0.0	0.0	0.0	0.0	160.3
Operating Costs		-50.3	-100.6	-150.9	-201.2	-201.2	-201.2	-201.2	-201.2	-201.2	-201.2	-201.2	-201.2	-201.2	-201.2	-201.2	-201.2	-201.2	-201.2	-201.2	-201.2
Revenues		81.3	162.5	243.8	325.0	325.0	325.0	325.0	325.0	325.0	325.0	325.0	325.0	325.0	325.0	325.0	325.0	325.0	325.0	325.0	325.0
Net Cash Flow	-740.0	-55.4	61.9	92.8	123.8	123.8	123.8	123.8	123.8	123.8	123.8	123.8	123.8	123.8	123.8	123.8	123.8	123.8	123.8	123.8	284.1

(Before Financing & Tax)

	5%	10%	15%
NPV=	$609.6	$100.4	-$178.3
IRR =	11.5%		

TABLE 2: PROJECT NET CASH FLOW

Figure 4.2 NFG Case Study: Project Cash Flow Table

have chosen, in this instance, to have a single line for major components of the cash flow, such as Operating Costs and Revenues. In some instances, where you may want to have more detail on the composition of these categories, it might make sense to include sub-categories of cash flow components in the main cash-flow table: it is essentially a matter of stylistic choice and what you as the analyst consider more user-friendly. For convenience, all entries in Table 2 (see Figure 4.2), and subsequent tables, are in thousands of dollars.

The main point to note, however, is that every cell in this part of the spreadsheet is based on a reference back to Table 1 in the spreadsheet (see Figure 4.1) containing the key variables. Once the categories of the cash flow have been entered we can set up the Net Cash Flow (row 14) which contains the simple arithmetic formula subtracting all project costs (rows 8 and 10) from the revenues (row 12). We then insert the appropriate NPV and IRR built-in formulae (rows 17 and 18). We see from the results that the project has an IRR of 11.5%, and that the NPV is therefore negative at a 15% discount rate. If we were to change any of the key variables in Table 1, so too would the cash flows and NPV and IRR results change. The cash flow will be updated and the results will be recalculated automatically.

Notice also that, at this stage, we have set up the cash flow for the project as a whole – the *project* BCA – ignoring how it is financed. To ascertain the profitability of the project from NFG's *private* (or "equity") standpoint, after tax, we need to incorporate the relevant details of debt financing and taxation.

Step 3: Setting up the Cash Flow for the Financing of the Project

The Key Variables table (see Table 1 in Figure 4.1) also contains details of the loan and bank overdraft NFG intends to use to finance the project. We are informed that NFG will take out a loan of $700,000 in year 2000, that this will carry interest at 3.5% per annum, and will be repaid over 10 years. For the purpose of this exercise we assume that this is 3.5% in real terms; i.e. there is no inflation incorporated in any of the values included in the table. We need to calculate what the annual repayments and interest charges will be on this loan, assuming it takes the form of an annuity: equal annual instalments of interest and principal repayment. However, we must also anticipate that we will need to know what the interest component of the annual annuity is in order to calculate NFG's taxable profits, as interest charges are tax-deductible costs. We use two of the spreadsheet's built-in formulae for this purpose. The annual principal repayments are calculated using the "PPMT" formula in row 8 of the spreadsheet, and the interest payments are calculated using the "IPMT" formula in row 11 in Figure 4.3.

Notice again that all the entries are references back to the Key Variables table in Figure 4.1. Also notice that we present these cash flows from the standpoint of the lenders, so the signs are the opposite to what they would be from the borrower's perspective. The sum of each year's interest and principal repayment comes to the same constant amount of $84.2 thousand. The cash flow for the bank overdraft is shown in rows 9 and 12. The $40 thousand is borrowed in 2001 and repaid in 2004 (row 9). In each year interest of $2,000 (5% rate of interest) is paid (row 12). Adding these financing flows together gives us the Net Financing Flow shown in row 13. Subtracting this from the Project Net Cash Flow (row 14 in Figure 4.2) gives the Net Cash Flow (on equity, before tax) (row 15 in Figure 4.3). Now we need to calculate what tax NFG will need to pay on the profits earned from this project.

File Edit View Insert Format Tools Data Window He

Callout: *Use the "PPMT" and "IPMT" formulae to calculate debt payments*

Callout: *Depreciation and interest payments are included in the calculation of taxable profits*

Callout: *The private cash flow is derived by subtracting debt financing flows and profits taxes from the project cash flow in Table 2 (row 12)*

TABLE 3: PRIVATE NET CASH FLOW

ITEM/YEAR	0	1	2	3	4	5	6	7	8	9	10	11	12	13	14	15	16	17	18	19	20
(i) Financing																					
Principal																					
Loan	-700.0	59.7	61.8	63.9	66.2	68.5	70.9	73.3	75.9	78.6	81.3										
Overdraft	-40.0					40.0															
Interest																					
Loan		24.5	22.4	20.3	18.0	15.7	13.3	10.8	8.3	5.6	2.8										
Overdraft			2.0	2.0	2.0	2.0															
Net Financing Flows	-700.0	44.2	86.2	86.2	86.2	126.2	84.2	84.2	84.2	84.2	84.2										
NCF(equity, pre-tax)	-40.0	-99.6	-24.3	6.7	37.6	-2.4	39.6	39.6	39.6	39.6	39.6	123.8	123.8	123.8	123.8	123.8	123.8	123.8	123.8	123.8	284.1
(ii) Taxes																					
Revenues		81.3	162.5	243.8	325.0	325.0	325.0	325.0	325.0	325.0	325.0	325.0	325.0	325.0	325.0	325.0	325.0	325.0	325.0	325.0	325.0
Operating Costs		-50.3	-100.6	-150.9	-201.2	-201.2	-201.2	-201.2	-201.2	-201.2	-201.2	-201.2	-201.2	-201.2	-201.2	-201.2	-201.2	-201.2	-201.2	-201.2	-201.2
Depreciation		-70.5	-70.5	-70.5	-70.5	-70.5	-52.5	-52.5	-52.5	-52.5	-12.5	-12.5	-12.5	-12.5	-12.5	-12.5	-12.5	-12.5	-12.5	-12.5	-12.5
Interest on loans		-24.5	-24.4	-22.3	-20.0	-17.7	-13.3	-10.8	-8.3	-5.6	-2.8	0.0	0.0	0.0	0.0	0.0	0.0	0.0	0.0	0.0	0.0
Profits (before tax)		-64.1	-33.0	0.1	33.3	35.6	58.0	60.5	63.0	65.7	68.4	111.3	111.3	111.3	111.3	111.3	111.3	111.3	111.3	111.3	111.3
Taxes Liable		-16.0	-8.3	0.0	8.3	8.9	14.5	15.1	15.8	16.4	17.1	27.8	27.8	27.8	27.8	27.8	27.8	27.8	27.8	27.8	27.8
(iii) Equity (after tax)																					
Private Cash Flow	-40.0	-83.6	-16.0	6.6	29.3	-11.3	25.1	24.5	23.9	23.2	22.5	96.0	96.0	96.0	96.0	96.0	96.0	96.0	96.0	96.0	256.3

	5%	10%	15%
NPV =	$483.3	$196.4	$59.6
IRR =	19.1%		

Sheet tabs: Ex1a / Ex1b / Ex1c / Ch1Ex / Variables / ProjectBCA / **PrivateBCA** / EfficiencyBCA

Figure 4.3 NFG Case Study: Private Net Benefits Table

Step 4: Calculating Taxes and After-Tax Cash Flows

To calculate taxable profits we need to set up a separate working table within Table 3, as shown in Figure 4.3 entitled *(ii) Taxes* (see rows 17–23). There is an important reason why we calculate tax separately rather than in the main cash flow table itself: taxable profits are not the same as net cash flow. You will recall from earlier sections of this Chapter that for the purpose of calculating taxes, a private investor is allowed to include depreciation and interest charges (not principal repayments) as project costs. By the same token, investment costs (both fixed and working capital) are not included in the calculation of taxable profits, and salvage value from the sale of assets at the end of the project's life is also excluded. Depreciation is calculated (row 20) from the information provided in the Key Variables table in Figure 4.1, while interest on loans is taken from the first part of Table 3 (rows 11 and 12). From these rows we derive taxable profits (row 22) from which Taxes Liable (row 23) are derived, using the tax rate of 25% given in the Key Variables table. Note that in the first three years (2001 to 2003), taxable profits and taxes liable are negative, as the project is running at a loss. As NFG is entitled to deduct these losses from profits it earns in other projects, we should still include these "negative taxes" in deriving the after-tax net cash flow.

Step 5: Deriving the Private (After-Tax) Net Cash Flow

It is now a simple matter to derive the after-tax net cash flow by subtracting the Taxes Liable row (row 23) from the Net Cash Flow (before tax) in row 15 of Table 3 (see Figure 4.3). The results for the *private* NPV and IRR after tax are then derived by inserting the appropriate NPV and IRR formulae as shown in rows 29 and 30 in Figure 4.3. We see from these results that the after-tax return on NFG's equity is 19.1%, and that the NPV of the investment is $59.6 thousand at a 15% discount rate.

This completes the private analysis of NFG's proposed project. In later chapters of this book we return to this case study to demonstrate how we would extend this analysis to include the calculation of *efficiency* and *referent group* net benefits. We also extend the scope of the spreadsheet analysis to consider the treatment of risk.

APPENDIX TO CHAPTER 4:
Case Study "International Cloth Products"

This Appendix discusses and commences the appraisal of the proposed *International Cloth Products Ltd** project using an *Excel* spreadsheet. An appraisal of this project can be undertaken as an exercise and the results compared with the solution tables in the appendices to Chapters 4–10.

Imagine that you are in the Projects and Policy Division of the Ministry of Industry in Thailand. Using the information which follows and which relates to the activities and plans of a wholly owned subsidiary of a foreign company, called International Cloth Products Limited (ICP), you are asked to answer the following questions:

(i)   Should the Government support the proposed yarn-spinning project of ICP in Central Thailand by granting a concession as requested by ICP?

(ii) Should the Government induce ICP to locate in the less-developed region of Southern Thailand? If so, should the Government be willing to give the incentives requested to bring this about?

What additional information would you like to have? How would you go about getting such information? What conditions, if any, would you wish to impose on the investment if approval is given?

The project analyst is required to calculate the returns on the investment (i) to the private sector, ICP and, (ii) to Thailand, under each of seven different scenarios. There are two possible locations, Bangkok and Southern Thailand, and at each of these, there are three possible cases; (i) no concessions at all, or (ii) no import duties to be paid by ICP on cotton imports; or (iii) ICP enjoys a tax holiday on profits taxes. Finally, the analyst should consider the case where ICP enjoys *both* concessions at the alternative location in Southern Thailand.

---

* This case study is hypothetical and not based on the activities of any actual company. Any similarity with regard to the activities or name of an actual company is unintended.

It is also suggested that there should be a written report that:
(i)   starts with an executive summary;
(ii) briefly discusses method of analysis, significant assumptions and the choice of key variables;
(iii) indicates the best scenario for ICP and Thailand, and the extent to which each party stands to gain or lose from the different concession;
(iv) calculates IRRs and provides a sensitivity analysis showing how the NPVs will vary at different discount rates between 0% and 20%;
(v)   is supported by summary tables.

The Project

You will find it useful as a first stage to analyse the profitability of the project to ICP, but do keep the analysis as simple as possible and round off all figures to one decimal place of a million *Baht*. Assume, for simplicity, that all payments and receipts are made and received at the end of each year.

1. Introduction

Values are expressed either in terms of local currency units or in foreign exchange. The *Thai Baht* (Bt.) exchanges with the US dollar at Bt.44 = US$1.00. International Cloth Products Ltd (ICP) is a foreign-owned textile firm that manufactures cloth products in the Bangkok area of Central Thailand, including both unfinished and finished cloth for sale to other textile and garment manufacturers, as well as textile prints for the domestic and export market. At present it imports cotton yarn, but it is thinking of investing at the end of 1999 in Central Thailand in a spinning mill with sufficient capacity to not only supply its own demand for yarn (10 million lbs for the foreseeable future), but also to supply about 5 million lbs for sale to other textile firms in Thailand.

2. The Market

A study of the textile industry shows that Thailand has the capacity to weave 125 million linear yards of cloth. Existing and planned spinning mills, except for ICP's proposed mill, are expected to be capable of producing enough yarn for 75 million linear yards of cloth; leaving a deficit of yarn for 50 million yards to be imported. One yard of cloth requires 0.33 lbs of yarn so that the domestic market for ICP's output seems to be reasonably assured. The Thai Government has no plans to change the duties on imported yarn. At present the landed c.i.f. price of yarn is $0.58/lb and this is expected to remain constant in real terms in the future. There is an import duty of Bt.2.1/lb, and customs handling charges of Bt.0.3/lb. This determines the Bangkok factory-gate price that ICP is paying for its own imported yarn and also the price at which it expects to be able to sell yarn to other firms in Thailand.

3. Investment Costs

ICP plans to purchase 40,000 spindles and related equipment (blowing machine, air conditioning and so on) capable of processing 16.2 million lbs of cotton into 15 million lbs of yarn each year. The equipment is expected to last for 10 years (including the start-up year), and technical consultants have given a satisfactory report on the company's investment plans. The estimated investment costs and their expected date of payment are listed in Table A4.1.

During 2000, ICP hopes to produce at about one-half of full capacity, reaching full capacity in the following year. In 2000 it expects water, power and raw material costs to be 50%, all other costs to be 100%, and output to be 50% of full-time operational levels.

4. Raw Materials

A total of 16.2 million lbs (3,240 bales) of imported cotton will be required to produce 15 million lbs of yarn (1.08 lbs of cotton/lb of yarn). The raw material requirement is expected to be strictly proportional to the output of yarn. The current price of cotton, expected to remain unchanged, is $0.30/lb c.i.f. Bangkok, and the import duty is 10% *ad valorem*.

Table A4.1 Investment Costs: Yarn-Spinning Project: ICP

Item	Cost		Date of payment
	$'000	Bt.'000	
Spindles	4,000[a]		1999
Ancillary equipment	850[a]		"
Installation	100[b]		"
Construction of buildings		36,000[c]	"
Start-up costs		18,000[b]	"
Working capital			
(i) raw materials (3 months' requirements at cif value)	1,200[d]		2000
(ii) spare parts (1 year's use)	243[a]		"

[a] Plus import duty at 5% of c.i.f. value
[b] Consisting of a mixture of traded goods at c.i.f. value and skilled labour
[c] All unskilled labour costs
[d] Plus import duty at 10% of c.i.f. value

5. Direct Labour Force (see Table A4.2)

In addition to the labour employed on the investment phases of the project, the mill will employ about 1,600 workers in spinning and associated operations. All workers will be recruited from the Bangkok area and paid the going market rate for their labour. But there is considerable unemployment in the area and the shadow-cost of unskilled labour recruited in the Bangkok area is assumed by the Government to be 50% of the market cost. For the less-developed areas of the country, the Government uses a shadow-cost for unskilled labour of zero. However, all skilled labour is valued, in efficiency terms, at its market cost regardless of its place of employment.

Table A4.2 Employment: Yarn-Spinning Project: ICP

	No. employed and date of first payment	Average wage salary (Bt. p.a.)	Total annual wage/salary bill (Bt.'000)
Supervisors and technicians	100 (during 2000)	150,000	15,000
Other skilled workers	1,000 (during 2000)	22,500	22,500
Unskilled workers	500 (during 2000)	1,200	6,000
Total	1,600		43,500

6. Fuel, Water, Spare Parts

Water and electricity each costs Bt.480,000 per million lbs of yarn produced. Power will be supplied from a hydro-power plant at a nearby dam using transmission lines already in place. The variable cost to the Electricity Corporation of Thailand of supplying power to ICP for the spinning mill is about 50% of the standard rate charged in Bangkok. The majority of this cost consists of traded goods, such as oil, valued at c.i.f. prices. ICP expects to import and use spare parts (in addition to those reported as investment costs) costing 10% of the c.i.f. cost of equipment in each year after the first (that is from 2000 onwards). The duty on spare parts is 5%. The labour costs of maintenance are already included in Table A4.2.

7. Insurance and Rent

The cost of insurance and rent are each estimated as Bt.3 million p.a. from 2000 onwards (it can be assumed that the insurance risk is widely spread so that the social cost of risk is zero). The spinning mill's share of overheads (already being incurred) is estimated to be Bt.7.5 million p.a.

8. Financing

ICP intends to finance imported spindles and equipment under the foreign supplier's credit for 75% of the c.i.f. value in 1999. The credit carries an interest rate of 8% p.a. and is repayable from 2000 in five equal annual instalments. In addition, once the plant is in operation, ICP expects to finance Bt.60 million of the working capital reported in Table A4.1 from a bank overdraft borrowed from local banks in 2000 and carrying a 10% p.a. interest rate payable from 2001 onwards. The bank overdraft will be repaid at the end of the project (year 2009). Interest payable on the bank overdraft and supplier's credit is allowable against profits tax. The remainder of the investment will be financed from ICP's own sources, but the company expects to be able to (and intends to) remit all profits as and when they are made.

9. Taxes and Incentives

ICP claims that this investment is not sufficiently profitable to induce them to invest, at the present profits tax of 50%. (The profits tax is levied on the profits calculated after allowing depreciation to be charged at 10% of the initial cost of spindles, equipment, installation and construction.)

The depreciation charge can be claimed from 2000 onwards. Losses made by the yarn-spinning project are assumed to be offset against ICP's profits from the existing cloth-producing operations. ICP says that it is unlikely to invest unless they are given some concession; *either* in the form of duty-free entry of cotton *or* exemption for ten years from profit taxes.

10. Location in "Deprived Areas"

ICP wants to locate its spinning mill (if it goes ahead with the investment at all) in the Bangkok area, adjacent to its existing plant. But the Government has a policy of dispersing industries to the "deprived areas". The Government would like to see the spinning mill located in Southern Thailand some distance to the south of Bangkok, but ICP has said that it will only locate the spinning mill there if it is given *both* duty-free entry of cotton *and* a ten-year tax holiday. ICP has provided a table showing the estimated additional costs of locating in Southern Thailand (see Table A4.3).

Table A4.3 Additional Cost of Locating in Southern Thailand

Item	Additional costs (Bt.'000)
1 Additional capital costs to be incurred at end 1999;	
– construction (more factory buildings, workers' housing, site preparation)	30,000[a]
– transportation and handling equipment	6,000[b]
– total additional capital outlay	36,000
2 Changes in recurrent costs (at full capacity)	
– transport of raw materials from Bangkok (about 100 miles at Bt.0.27/ton mile)	1,950
– transport costs for yarn to TFL's cloth factory and warehouse at Bangkok (100 miles at Bt.0.27/ton mile)	1,800
– 20% reduction in wages of unskilled workers	1,200
– cost of additional supervisors	450
– total additional recurrent costs	3,000

[a]   All unskilled labour costs
[b]   Plus import duty at 5% of c.i.f. value

Some Solution Spreadsheet Tables for the ICP Case Study

This section shows the set-up of the spreadsheet tables for the first part of the case study. This consists of three Tables linked together in one spreadsheet, but presented here in three separate Figures, showing: the Basic Data table (Fig. A4.1); the Project Cash Flow (Fig. A4.2) and the Private Cash Flow (Fig. A4.3). (Also linked to these tables are the Efficiency Cash Flow and the Referent Group Cash Flow, presented as appendices at the end of Chapters 5 and 6 respectively.)

ICP PROJECT: 1999-2009

TABLE 1 — KEY INPUT VARIABLES

VARIABLES		INVESTMENT COSTS	000 $'	000 BT'	RUNNING COSTS		MATERIAL FLOWS		FINANCE	
EXCHANGE RATE	44	SPINDLES	4000		WATER BT PER MN LBS	480000	COTTON MN LBS	16.2	SUPPLIERS CREDIT	75%
TARIFF A	5%	EQUIPMENT	850		POWER BT PER MN LBS	480000	YARN MN LBS	15	OVERDRAFT	60
TARIFF B	10%	INSTALLATION	100		SPARE PARTS (%)	10%	LABOUR 1	100	CREDIT REPAY YEARS	5
PROFITS TAX	50%	CONSTRUCTION		36000	INSURANCE&RENT BT MN	6	LABOUR 2	1000		
DEPRECIATION	10%	START-UP COSTS		18000	OVERHEADS	0	LABOUR 3	500		
PRICE YARN CIF US$	0.58	WORKING CAPITAL							DISCOUNT RATES	4%
YARN TARIFF BT	2.1	RAW MATERIALS	1200							8%
HANDLING BT	0.3	SPARE PARTS	243							12%
TARIFF C	10%									16%
PRICE COTTON CIF US$	0.3									
WAGE 1 BT PA	150000									
WAGE 2 BT PA	22500									
WAGE 3 BT PA	12000									
INTEREST RATE 1	8%									
INTEREST RATE 2	10%									

> All basic data for the project and private cash flow calculations are entered in one table

Figure A4.1 ICP Project Solution: Key Input Variables

> Investment costs can be shown in both US$ and Bht

TABLE 2 — PROJECT CALCULATION

YEAR	1999 '000 US$	1999 MN BT	2000 MN BT	2001 MN BT	2002 MN BT	2003	2004	2005	2006	2007	2008 MN BT	2009 MN BT
INVESTMENT COSTS												
SPINDLES	-4200.000	-184.800										
EQUIPMENT	-892.500	-39.270										
INSTALLATION	-100.000	-4.400										
CONSTRUCTION		-36.000										
START-UP COSTS		-18.000										
RAW MATERIALS		-58.080										58.080
SPARE PARTS		-11.227										11.227
TOTAL	-282.470	-69.307	0.000	0.000	0.000	0.000	0.000	0.000	0.000	0.000	0.000	69.307
RUNNING COSTS												
WATER			-3.600	-7.200	-7.200	-7.200	-7.200	-7.200	-7.200	-7.200	-7.200	-7.200
POWER			-3.600	-7.200	-7.200	-7.200	-7.200	-7.200	-7.200	-7.200	-7.200	-7.200
SPARE PARTS			-22.407	-22.407	-22.407	-22.407	-22.407	-22.407	-22.407	-22.407	-22.407	-22.407
RAW MATERIALS			-117.612	-235.224	-235.224	-235.224	-235.224	-235.224	-235.224	-235.224	-235.224	-235.224
INSURANCE			-6.000	-6.000	-6.000	-6.000	-6.000	-6.000	-6.000	-6.000	-6.000	-6.000
LABOUR			-43.500	-43.500	-43.500	-43.500	-43.500	-43.500	-43.500	-43.500	-43.500	-43.500
TOTAL			-196.719	-321.531	-321.531	-321.531	-321.531	-321.531	-321.531	-321.531	-321.531	-321.531
REVENUES												
SALE OF YARN			209.400	418.800	418.800	418.800	418.800	418.800	418.800	418.800	418.800	418.800
NCF (Project)		-282.470	-56.626	97.269	97.269	97.269	97.269	97.269	97.269	97.269	97.269	166.576

> Working capital appears at start (−ve) and end (+ve) of project

NPV	$(Mn)	IRR (%)
4%	405.3	20.6%
8%	259.8	
12%	152.0	
16%	70.7	
0%	605.6	

> All entries in cash flow tables are references to cells in 'Basic Data' table above, or are formula drawing on these data and other cells in this table

> NPV and IRRs shown in box

Figure A4.2 ICP Project Solution: The Project Cash Flow

> This table shows how the firm calculates its taxable profits. Depreciation and interest payments are included as 'costs' only for the purpose of calculating taxable income.

TABLE 3 PRIVATE CALCULATION

YEAR	1999 '000 US$	1999 MN BT	2000 MN BT	2001 MN BT								
FINANCIAL FLOWS												
DEPRECIATION			-26.447	-26.447	-26.447	-26.447	-26.447	.447	-26.447	-26.447	-26.447	-26.447
INTEREST												
SUPPLIERS CREDIT	3637.500	160.050	-12.804	-10.621	-8.264	-5.719	-2.969					
REPAYMENT			-27.282	-29.464	-31.821	-34.367	-37.116					
BANK OVERDRAFT			60.000	-6.000	-6.000	-6.000	-6.000	-6.000	-6.000	-6.000	-6.000	-6.000
REPAYMENT												-60.000
NET OPERATING REVENUE			12.681	97.269	97.269	97.269	97.269	.269	97.269	97.269	97.269	97.269
TAXABLE PROFIT			-26.570	54.201	56.558	59.103	61.853	6..2	64.822	64.822	64.822	64.822
PROFIT TAX			13.285	-27.100	-28.279	-29.552	-30.926	-32	-32.411	-32.411	-32.411	-32.411
FLOW OF OWN FUNDS		-122.420	-23.426	24.083	22.905	21.632	20.257	58.8	58.858	58.858	58.858	68.165

NPV	$(Mn)	IRR (%)
4%	154.5	16.7%
8%	88.7	
12%	40.8	
16%	5.4	
0%	246.6	

> Inflows and outflows on loans and profits taxes are then deducted from the 'Project' cash flow to derive cash flow on the firm's own funds or 'equity'

> The IRR and NPVs show the profitability from the firm's private viewpoint

Figure A4.3 ICP Project Solution: The Private Cash Flow

Further Reading

Most corporate finance texts cover the issues discussed in this chapter in more detail. An example is J. C. Van Horne, *Financial Management and Policy* (Prentice Hall, 1980). This book is also available in more recent editions with a country-specific focus, e.g. J. C. Van Horne, R. Nicol and K. Wright, *Financial Management and Policy in Australia* (Prentice Hall, 1995).

Exercises

1. A project's net cash flow, valued at constant (year 0) prices, is given by:

Year	0	1	2	3	4	5
Net Cash Flow ($):	−1000	250	250	250	250	250

    (a) The nominal or money rate of interest is 8% and the anticipated rate of general price inflation over the next five years is 3%. Calculate the NPV of the net cash flow:
    (i) using the real rate of interest as the discount rate;
    (ii) using the nominal rate of interest as the discount rate.
    (b) Suppose that you are told that the above project net cash flow in years 1–5 is expected to rise at 5% per annum. Recalculate the NPV of the net cash flow:
    (i) using the real rate of interest as the discount rate;
    (ii) using the nominal rate of interest as the discount rate.

2. The dam currently providing irrigation water to farmers in Happy Valley cost $100 million to build, and the valley currently produces 15 million kilos of sugar per annum which sells at the world price of $1 per kilo. The height of the dam can be raised at a cost of $8 million in order to provide more irrigation water to farmers. It is estimated that, as a result of the extra water supplied in this way, sugar production would rise to 15.5 million kilos per annum in perpetuity (i.e. forever), without any increase in the levels of other inputs such as fertilizer, labour, equipment, etc. Using a 10% rate of discount, what is the net present value, as indicated by the project benefit-cost analysis, of raising the height of the dam?

3. If a project involving an initial investment of $20 million is funded partly by debt (75%) and partly by equity capital (25%) and the internal rate of return on the overall cash flow of the project is 15%, while the rate of interest on the debt capital is 10%, what is the rate of return on equity capital? (Make any additional assumptions explicit.)

4. Suppose that a firm has borrowed $1000 in the current year at a 10% interest rate, with a commitment to repay the loan (principal and interest) in equal annual instalments over the following five years. Calculate:
   (i) the amount of the annual repayment;
   (ii) the stream of interest payments which can be entered in the tax calculation of the private benefit-cost analysis.

5. A firm's stock of working capital at the end of each year in the life of a project was as follows:

Year	0	1	2	3	4	5
Working Capital ($)	0	50	75	70	30	20

Calculate the working capital cost stream which should be entered in the project analysis.

6. Explain why depreciation and interest should not be included as costs in a discounted cash flow (DCF) analysis of a project.

5
Efficiency Benefit-Cost Analysis

Introduction

In Chapter 1 it was suggested that the word "social" in "social benefit-cost analysis" has a rather restricted interpretation: it refers to the group whose costs and benefits are to be calculated and compared by means of the analysis. Often the referent group consists of all the residents of a country or State, but sometimes the definition is a narrower one. We have used the term "efficiency" cost-benefit analysis to refer to a study which calculates all the benefits and costs of a proposed project, irrespective of who gains or loses. A benefit-cost analysis from an efficiency perspective tells us whether the project is an efficient use of resources in the sense that the gainers from the project could, in principle, compensate the losers.

As noted in Chapter 1, a project makes a difference and the purpose of the benefit-cost analysis is to identify and measure that difference using the "with and without" approach. Each person who benefits from the project could, potentially, give up a sum of money so that she remains at the same level of economic welfare as she would have had without the project; these sums are money measures of the project benefits. Similarly, each person who bears a net cost as a result of the project could, potentially, be paid a sufficient sum to keep her at the same level of well-being as she would have had without the project; these sums are money measures of the project costs. If the sum of the monies which could notionally be collected from beneficiaries exceeds that required to compensate those who are affected adversely by the project then the project is an efficient allocation of resources according to an economic welfare criterion known as the **Kaldor–Hicks criterion**, as discussed in Chapter 1. We will return to this concept in Chapter 7, but for the moment we simply note that a project which has a positive NPV in an efficiency benefit-cost analysis is an efficient use of resources according to this welfare criterion.

Before we consider how to appraise a project from an efficiency perspective we need to remind ourselves that, while the efficiency analysis will ignore the distributional consequences of the project, these are important in the decision-making process. First, the fact that the decision-maker has specified a particular subset of the economy as the referent group tells us that some groups "matter" more than others in the comparison of benefits and costs. Secondly, even if a project is inefficient from an overall perspective it may still be undertaken because of its positive aggregate net benefits to the referent group; as noted in Chapter 1, we will find it convenient to calculate net benefits to the referent group indirectly – by subtracting non-referent group net benefits from efficiency net benefits – as well as directly. Thirdly, even if the social benefit-cost analysis indicates that the aggregate net benefits to the referent group are negative the decision-maker may still favour the project because it benefits a particular subset of the referent group. For example, an irrigation project in a low-income area may be undertaken to alleviate rural poverty even although the referent group as a whole incurs a negative NPV. The analyst needs to accept that some "efficient" projects will be rejected and some "inefficient" projects accepted on distributional grounds, and needs to feel comfortable with this outcome as long as the distributional consequences have been drawn to the attention of the decision-maker as clearly as is feasible in the analysis. The issue of income distribution is addressed in Chapter 11.

In principle an economic efficiency analysis is concerned with all aspects of the project which can affect economic welfare. In Chapter 1 the "with and without approach" to social benefit-cost analysis compared the value of project output with the value of output which the resources allocated to the project could produce in their best alternative use – their opportunity cost. In discussing this approach it was implicitly assumed that all project inputs and outputs were traded in markets and that market prices could be used to value them. Neither of these assumptions, however, is realistic: some project outputs (inputs), such as, for example, the services of national parks (waste disposal), may not be traded in markets; and some project outputs (inputs), such as irrigation water (services of labour) may be traded in imperfect markets. In the latter case, market prices are not an accurate measure of marginal benefit (cost) and must be adjusted for the purposes of efficiency benefit-cost analysis; the adjusted prices, used in the analysis, are termed shadow-prices. In the former case, non-market valuation techniques, which are the subject of Chapter 12, must be used to value project outputs or inputs. In the present Chapter we are concerned mainly with shadow-pricing – adjusting observed market prices to reflect social benefit or social cost.

In competitive equilibrium there is a single market price determined by the intersection of the market demand and supply curves. In contrast, however, as we shall shortly see, a feature of non-competitive equilibrium is that there are effectively two equilibrium prices – a supply price and a demand price. In undertaking an efficiency benefit-cost analysis a simple pricing rule must be followed: all project outputs and inputs must be valued at prices representing equilibrium points on demand or supply curves. It is tempting to conclude from this simple rule that a project output is always valued at a point on a demand curve, and a project input at a point on a supply curve. This is in fact correct when the project output adds to the total amount of the good or service consumed, or when the project input is an addition to the total

ITEM TO BE VALUED	VALUED AT EQUILIBRIUM POINT ON A:	
	DEMAND CURVE	SUPPLY CURVE
OUTPUT	SATISFIES ADDITIONAL DEMAND	SATISFIES EXISTING DEMAND FROM ALTERNATIVE SOURCE
INPUT	SOURCED FROM AN ALTERNATIVE MARKET USE	SOURCED FROM ADDITIONAL SUPPLY

Figure 5.1 The Efficiency Benefit-Cost Analysis Pricing Rule

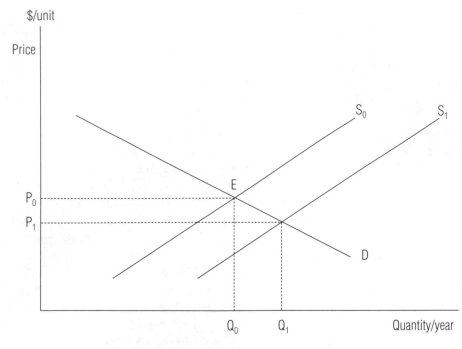

Figure 5.2 Competitive Market Equilibrium

supply of the input. However the possibility exists that the project output simply replaces an alternative source of supply of the product, without adding to the total amount consumed; in that case output should be valued at its supply price from the alternative source – a point on a supply curve. Similarly it is possible that a project input is not sourced from an addition to the total supply of that input, but is simply diverted from another use; in that case the cost of the input is its value in that other use, which is measured by a point on the demand curve for the input. Figure 5.1 summarizes the operation of the rule.

Underlying the simple pricing rule for efficiency benefit-cost analysis is the proposition that the competitive market system leads to an efficient allocation of scarce resources. Figure 5.2 illustrates a competitive market in equilibrium at point E, where the demand (D) and supply (S_0) curves for a product intersect (the analysis applies equally to the market for an input).

The demand curve tells us, at each level of output of the product, how much money someone is willing to pay for one extra unit of the product; the supply curve tells us, at each level of output, what an extra unit of the product will cost. The cost of producing an extra unit of the product is the market value of the extra factors of production which will be needed. However in a competitive market system factor prices are bid to a level where they are equal to the value of their contribution to additional output in their highest value use. In other words, the cost of an extra quantity of factors, as measured by the supply curve for a particular product, is equal to the value of what that extra quantity of factors could add to production in their best alternative use. This means that the supply curve measures, at each possible output level, the opportunity cost of producing an additional unit of the product.

Since the demand curve slopes downward it must be the case that the value of an extra unit of a product, its marginal benefit, declines as the level of output increases: this follows from the principle that the more of something you have, the less do you value an additional unit of it. Since the supply curve slopes upward it must be the case that the opportunity cost of producing an extra unit, the marginal cost of the product, increases as the level of output rises; this follows from the fact that producing more and more units of the product involves diverting scarce resources from progressively higher and higher value uses elsewhere in the economy. The equilibrium point E is efficient because at that point the last unit of the product supplied is worth exactly its opportunity cost of production; to the left of point E an additional unit is valued higher than its opportunity cost – the gain from producing it outweighs the loss, and hence producing more of it contributes to efficiency; to the right of point E the reverse holds.

A feature of equilibrium in a competitive and undistorted market is that the demand price (the amount buyers are willing to pay for an additional unit of output) equals the supply price (the opportunity cost of an additional unit of output). In this situation no question arises as to whether the demand or supply price should be used to value an extra quantity of an output because the two prices coincide. In a non-competitive or distorted market, on the other hand, the demand and supply prices are different in equilibrium and the benefit-cost analyst must apply the pricing rule to determine the appropriate valuation of the output. The same argument applies to the market for an input such as labour.

Returning to the competitive undistorted market, suppose that a large-scale public project is proposed which will cause a change in the price of an input or an output: for example, a large hydro-electric project shifts the supply curve of electricity to the right, as illustrated in Figure 5.2, from S_0 to S_1 and results in a fall in the market price from P_0 to P_1. Since the project adds to the total amount of electricity consumed, the pricing rule tells us to use a price which is an equilibrium point on a demand curve to value the output in an efficiency benefit-cost analysis. However there are two prices, P_0 and P_1, which are equilibrium points on the demand curve. Which price should be used to value the project output in an efficiency benefit-cost analysis? This question has a simple answer (use the average of the two prices) but involves some complicated issues which are postponed for discussion to Chapter 7. For the moment we will assume that we are dealing with a relatively small project which will have no effect on market prices of outputs or inputs – many projects are of this nature.

It was suggested in Chapter 1 that many markets in any actual economy are not perfectly competitive in the sense of being complete, undistorted and without any individual buyer or seller having the power to set or influence price. In imperfectly competitive markets, which lack at least one of these characteristics, the observed demand price may not represent the marginal value of an output and the observed supply price may not represent the marginal cost of an input. Indeed in some cases, such as, for example, the market for wilderness recreation, the market (and the price) may not exist at all. We will defer consideration of what to do in the case of missing markets until Chapter 12, and in the meantime focus on how to use the information provided by prices generated in imperfect markets in an analysis of efficiency.

The approach adopted is known as shadow-pricing: we adjust the observed imperfect market price to make it measure marginal benefit or marginal cost, and we use the adjusted price – the shadow-price – in the efficiency benefit-cost analysis. Shadow-prices are sometimes also referred to as "economic prices" or "accounting prices". It should be stressed that these prices are used for the purposes of project appraisal and evaluation only, and may not be prices at which project inputs or outputs are actually traded.

We now consider a series of examples of shadow-pricing dealing with market distortions in the form of regulations and taxation, and with imperfections involving market power over the price of an output or input. In this discussion we will be concerned only with efficiency and will ignore any distributional issues. The question of distribution – who benefits and who loses – will be the topic of Chapter 6 dealing with the net benefits to the referent group, and assessing the distributional implications will be discussed in Chapter 11. In Chapter 6 some of the following examples will be revisited to tease out their distributional implications. Finally, each of the examples raises the broad question of why departures from perfect competition are "allowed" to exist, given their effect in reducing the efficiency of resource allocation. This question is beyond the purview of the analyst who takes the world as she finds it: the relevant question is whether the proposed project improves resource allocation in an imperfect world.

Examples of Shadow-Pricing

Example 5.1: A Minimum Wage

A minimum wage sets a lower bound to the market price of labour. As illustrated in Figure 5.3 the effect of the market price being set at W_m is to result in the quantity of labour supplied, Q_s, to exceed the quantity demanded, Q_d: the difference between quantity supplied and quantity demanded is the amount of unemployed labour – labour hours that are offered for hire but not taken up by employers because the market value of the extra output that the labour could produce is less than the minimum wage.

Suppose that a public project involves hiring labour in such a market – public projects are often designed to provide work for the unemployed – at what wage should the labour be costed in the efficiency benefit-cost analysis? The relevant cost is the opportunity cost – the value of what the labour would produce in its alternative use. If the worker hired for the public project would otherwise be unemployed it is tempting to say that the opportunity cost is zero. However, in the case illustrated in Figure 5.3, where the labour supply elasticity exceeds zero, that is incorrect: an extra unit of labour has an opportunity cost of W_a – according to the efficiency pricing rule an equilibrium point on a supply curve of an input measures the opportunity cost of an extra unit of the input at that level of supply. W_a represents the value to the economy of the marginal hour of unemployed labour in its alternative occupation – work in the informal economy, such as gardening, or just plain leisure. Hence W_a is the appropriate wage at which to price the labour used in the project (remember that we are assuming that the project is not large enough to cause a change in the supply price of labour); in other words, W_a is the shadow-price of labour. *This is a direct application of the pricing rule*: the labour input is an addition to the current supply and hence is priced at the current equilibrium point on the supply curve, W_a.

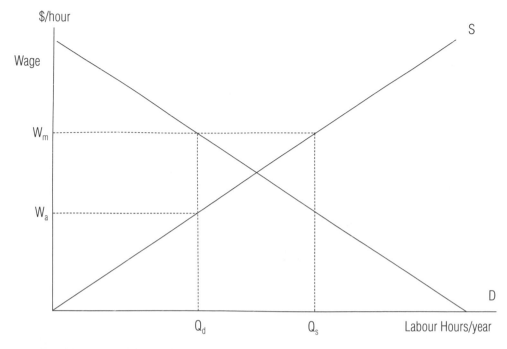

Figure 5.3 The Effect of a Minimum Wage

In developing economies the alternative to paid employment is sometimes subsistence agriculture, hunting or fishing. The value of such activity to the economy is often less than the value of the goods which the worker acquires as a result. The reason for this is that where resources, such as land or fishing grounds, are subject to open-access the total value of the output produced is effectively divided among the workers who exploit them. This means that each worker, on average, takes home goods equal in value to the value of the average product of labour in the occupation in question. Since labour applied to land or fisheries has a diminishing marginal productivity, the value of the average product of labour, which is the worker's "take-home pay", exceeds the value of the marginal product of labour, which is the value of the contribution of the worker's labour to the economy. In other words, even if W_a is what the worker could earn in a subsistence activity it will exceed the opportunity cost of labour. In such a case the opportunity cost could be zero, or close to zero.

It could be argued that the fact that unemployment exists in the economy does not necessarily mean that the labour hired to construct the project would have otherwise been unemployed – a worker could be hired from some other job which pays the minimum wage. In this case the relevant question is who would replace that worker? If the job is relatively unskilled it is reasonable to assume that it would be filled by someone from the ranks of the unemployed, in which case the opportunity cost of labour is still W_a, or less if the job is filled by a person who has been exploiting open-access resources. Alternatively if the worker hired is skilled it may be that there will be no one available to fill the vacancy she leaves behind her; this situation is known as structural unemployment – where the skill profile of the labour force does not match the skill profile of the job vacancies. In this case the opportunity cost of labour would be W_m – an equilibrium point on the demand curve for labour – because the previous employer was willing to pay W_m to secure the worker's services, implying that the worker would have added the amount W_m to the value of output in that use. Again *this is an application of the pricing rule*: if the project input is reallocated from another market use it should be priced at an equilibrium point on the demand curve, W_m.

In summary, the cost of an input is generally measured either by a point on the supply curve of the input or by a point on the demand curve at the current equilibrium: which of these points indicates the relevant price depends on the alternative use of the labour – the "without" part of the "with and without" analysis. If a project hires several workers – some of whom are replaceable in their current occupation or who are currently unemployed, and some who are not replaceable because of skill shortages – then the quantity of labour supplied by the former group needs to be shadow-priced at the supply price, W_a, while the quantity supplied by the latter group can be valued at the demand price, W_m. Generally this procedure is accomplished by differentiating between skilled and non-skilled workers and shadow-pricing the labour of the latter at the supply price. As noted above, the supply price tends to overstate the opportunity cost of subsistence activity, and labour diverted from that source can generally be shadow-priced at zero.

Example 5.2: The Value of Time

One kind of market imperfection can be termed the "all or nothing" situation. For example, one- or two-member households encounter this problem when they visit the supermarket to buy a couple of steaks for dinner and find that steaks come in packets of six. The choice is six steaks or none and neither alternative provides as much net benefit to the customer as their preferred amount. Another example is hours of work: a person might like to work 6 or 10 hours a day but they have a job which requires 8 hours. Figure 5.4 illustrates an individual's demand curve for leisure, D. The price of leisure is its opportunity cost – the hourly wage that could be earned, W. As can be seen from the intersection of the wage with the demand curve, this individual would ideally like to work 10 hours a day, but the employer has specified 8 hours (or nothing – no job). At this level of leisure (16 hours) an extra unit of leisure is worth W_L to the individual.

Now suppose that a public project is proposed which will reduce the time taken to travel to work. There will be many kinds of benefits – reduced vehicle wear and tear, reduced risk of an accident etc. – but one important benefit is a reduction in travel time resulting in an increase in time the individual can devote to other purposes. Since the individual is still required to work 8 hours, and no more, the travel time saved will be devoted to additional leisure – getting up 15 minutes later, for example. How is this time to be valued in an efficiency benefit-cost analysis? At the risk of oversimplifying a complicated issue, we can refer to Figure 5.4 and argue that W_L is the appropriate shadow-price. This is because the worker would prefer to be working more hours at the current wage, but the work is not available and hence the marginal value of leisure time is less than the market wage. The choice of W_L as the shadow-price of leisure is *an application of the efficiency pricing rule*: the project output satisfies an additional demand for leisure and hence should be priced at an equilibrium point on the demand curve.

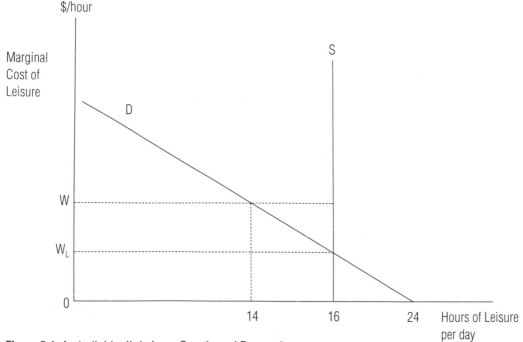

Figure 5.4 An Individual's Leisure Supply and Demand

Example 5.3: A Maximum Price – Rent Control

Suppose that a maximum value is set on the price which can be charged for an input or output. A common example is a maximum value set on an exchange rate – an official exchange rate, in terms of the number of units of the local currency per US dollar, which is lower than the equilibrium price. This issue is considered further in Chapter 8. Another example is rent control – the setting of a maximum price that can be charged for the services of a rental unit. The distorted rental market is illustrated in Figure 5.5 which shows the demand and supply curves for rental units; the supply curve illustrated is a short-run supply curve (S_S) – it is perfectly inelastic (vertical) to reflect the fact that in the short-run (the space of a few months) no additional units can be completed and offered for rent.

W_m is the maximum price – the level of the controlled rent. Suppose that a public project involves bringing some specialized workers into the area and accommodating them for a few months while they complete the project. What is the opportunity cost of the accommodation? An apartment occupied by one of the project workers is not available for rent to a local resident. We can see from the diagram that while a local resident could expect to rent an apartment for W_m, she actually places a value of W_a on it – at the current level of supply W_a is the marginal value of a month's accommodation in a rental unit if one were available. Hence in this case W_a is the relevant shadow-price of the input in an efficiency benefit-cost analysis. Again this is *a direct application of the pricing rule*: the input is diverted from an alternative market use and hence is priced at an equilibrium point on the demand curve.

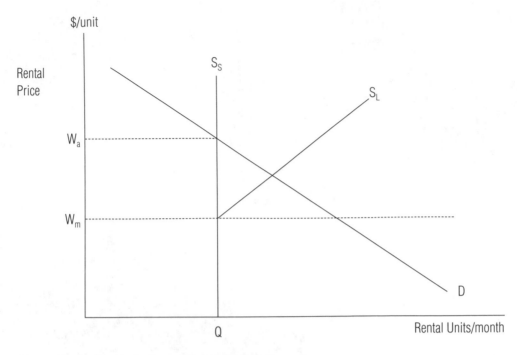

Figure 5.5 The Market for Rental Units with Rent Control

One of the features of a controlled housing market is that it is difficult to find a rental unit at the controlled price; since the marginal unit is worth more to the tenant than the rent which is actually paid, it tends to get handed on informally when the tenant leaves. Hence the above example begs the question of how the manager of the public project managed to secure some of these scarce units for her staff. While the example deals only with the short-run, it can be seen that a long-run analysis is irrelevant because of rent control. Suppose the long-run supply curve is S_L as illustrated in the diagram. This curve tells us that if the market rent rose, additional units would be supplied in the long-run because the higher rent would cover the extra costs involved in supplying the additional units. If an additional rental unit were to be produced for use in the project then the pricing rule would tell us to cost it at W_m: the project input is an addition to supply and is priced at the equilibrium point on the supply curve. Under effective rent control, however, rents cannot rise and hence quantity supplied will not increase.

Example 5.4: An Indirect Tax – a Tariff on Imports

Figure 5.6 illustrates a market for an imported good which is distorted by an import duty or tariff. The supply curve of imports, S, is perfectly elastic (horizontal) reflecting the assumption that the country in question can import any amount of the good without affecting the world price – this is referred to as the *small country assumption*. The supply curve of the domestic industry is represented by S_D, which is upward sloping, reflecting the fact that the opportunity cost of producing an extra unit rises as quantity supplied rises. The market price is the domestic price of the imported good (the world price plus tariff) since buyers will never pay more than this for the good, and sellers have no incentive to sell for less. The price of the imported good is a US dollar landed price (known as a c.i.f. price) converted to domestic currency by means of the official exchange rate (we will see later in Chapter 8 that a system of tariffs may result in a shadow-exchange rate different from the official rate, but we will ignore this problem for the present). It can be seen from Figure 5.6 that, in equilibrium, the price domestic buyers pay for the good, P_b, exceeds the world price P_w by the amount of the tariff. The tariff is either a specific tariff levied at (P_b-P_w) per unit of the good imported, or an *ad valorem* tariff, t, such that $P_b = P_w(1+t)$. The equilibrium quantity demanded is given by Q and the quantity supplied by the domestic industry is Q_D.

Suppose that the good is to be used as an input in a domestic investment project. An increase in demand for the good will not affect the domestic price, which is determined by the world price and the tariff, and hence will not affect domestic supply. The increase in demand will be met by additional imports at the world price. Our pricing rule tells us that, since the quantity of the input used in the project represents an addition to the total supply to the country, in an efficiency benefit-cost analysis the opportunity cost of the input is measured by the equilibrium point on its supply curve, in this case P_w, its price in international trade. Hence, *a direct application of the pricing rule* tells us that, in an efficiency benefit-cost analysis, the shadow-price of the input is P_w, which is less than its market price P_b.

Now suppose that the investment is an import-replacing project which produces the imported good as an output. Our pricing rule tells us that, since the project satisfies existing

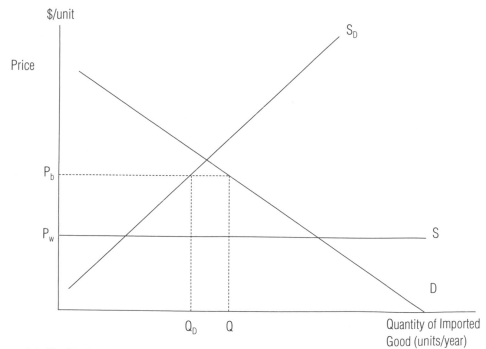

Figure 5.6 The Market for an Imported Good Subject to a Tariff

demand for the product from an alternative source, the value of the project output is given by its supply price – which is its price in international trade, P_w. From an efficiency perspective the good is worth only what it would cost from an alternative source – its net of tariff price P_w. We will return to the issue of internationally traded goods in more detail in Chapter 8.

Example 5.5: A Subsidy

Suppose that the government provides a subsidy on diesel fuel used in agricultural production. In Figure 5.7 the supply curve S represents the supply of fuel to the agricultural sector from the viewpoint of the oil industry; the supply curve is perfectly elastic because the rural sector is not a large enough part of the economy to influence the market price of diesel fuel – this is known as the *small industry assumption*. The price of fuel paid by farmers is P_s which equals the price received by fuel producers, P, less the specific subsidy. The supply curve S_s represents the supply of fuel from the viewpoint of farmers. The agricultural sector's demand for diesel fuel, D, is downward sloping, reflecting diminishing marginal productivity of the input in each farm's production process.

Suppose that a public project is proposed which will reduce the distance farmers have to truck their wheat – an expanded network of wheat silos, for example. One of the benefits of the project is a reduction in the quantity of diesel fuel used to truck wheat. At what price should this benefit be valued? From the farmer's point of view the benefit is P_s per unit because that is their unit cost of fuel. However in an efficiency benefit-cost analysis, if the industry supplying the fuel is competitive, it can be assumed that the price that producers receive, P per

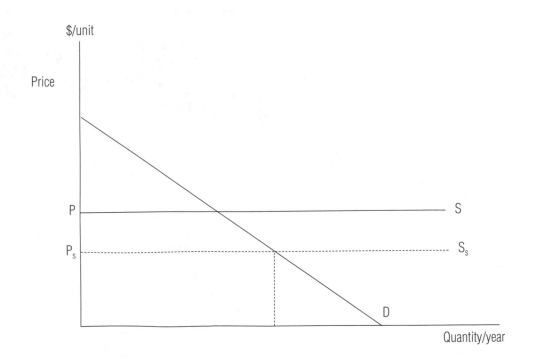

Figure 5.7 The Market for Diesel Fuel Subject to a Subsidy

unit, measures the opportunity cost of the scarce resources used to produce the marginal unit of fuel, and hence P would be the price used to value the fuel savings. This is another *application of the pricing rule*: the project results in a reduced quantity of an input which would have been sourced from additional supply; hence the saving in fuel use is valued at a point on the supply curve.

Example 5.6: A Regulated Utility

One of the features of electricity production is economies of scale over a wide range of plant output; this means that the average cost of production of power continues to fall as the chosen level of output increases until that level becomes quite large. Figure 5.8 illustrates the average (AC) and marginal (MC) costs of power production. Power plants come in discrete units: when the generation capacity has to be increased it usually involves construction of a large plant which has the capacity to provide more power than is currently demanded of it. This means that the plant may be operating on the declining portion of its average and marginal cost curves, as illustrated in Figure 5.8. Since the utility is a monopoly the government regulates the price of power at a level sufficient to cover the utility's costs – at price P. Needless to say, there is a substantial literature and debate in economics about this complicated issue which we will pass over.

From the viewpoint of the analyst, what is the appropriate price of electricity, used as a project input, in an efficiency benefit-cost analysis? If the small quantity of power used in the project will be in addition to the total supply it is valued at its supply price, or marginal

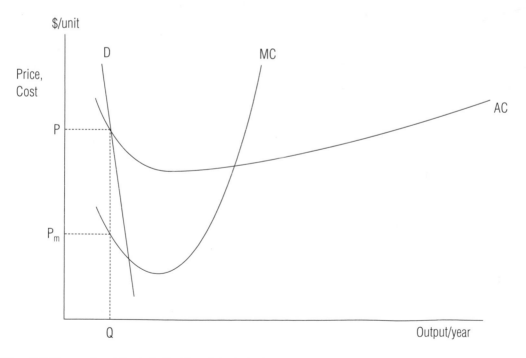

Figure 5.8 Demand and Costs in the Electricity Industry

cost – the value of the extra quantity of scarce resources required to produce the extra power. Hence power would be shadow-priced at the level of marginal cost – P_m in Figure 5.8. If, on the other hand, the utility is operating at capacity, the power used in the project will be diverted from some other use, and the electricity input to the project should be priced at its market price, P. This is a *direct application of the pricing rule*: if the input is diverted from use elsewhere in the economy, price it at a point on the demand curve; if it is an addition to total supply, price it at a point on the supply curve. Since the utility is a natural monopoly it does not have a supply curve as such, but it does have a marginal cost curve and marginal cost is the relevant information conveyed by a supply curve.

Now let us suppose that the electricity grid is operating at capacity and that the project being appraised is a power station which will add a small amount of capacity to the grid. Since the extra power produced meets a demand for extra power, and since consumers are willing to pay the current market price for the extra power, the project output would be valued at the price P in Figure 5.8. This is *consistent with the pricing rule*: when a project output meets additional demand, in efficiency benefit-cost analysis price it at a point on the demand curve.

Example 5.7: Monopoly Power

Suppose that a public project will hire labour away from a monopoly. A monopoly producer can influence the price of her product by varying the quantity supplied, and maximizes profit by restricting output to force up price. Like any other profit maximizing producer the monopoly will hire labour as long as the extra benefits of doing so exceed the extra costs. The extra cost of a unit of labour is the market wage, and the extra benefit is the additional profit generated by employing the labour. However in computing the extra profit the monopolist has to take into account the fact that hiring more labour and supplying more output will result in a fall in product price. The lower price will apply not only to the additional units of output, but also to all the current units as well. This means that the addition to revenue as a result of selling an extra unit is less than the price received for that unit.

Figure 5.9 illustrates the monopolist's demand curve for labour, the marginal revenue product curve, MRP. It is constructed by multiplying the marginal product of labour (MPL) – the quantity of extra output resulting from using an extra unit of labour input – by the marginal revenue (MR) – the addition to revenue as a result of lowering price and selling an extra unit of output. In contrast, a competitive firm cannot affect the market price of the product by selling an extra quantity of its product, and, consequently, its demand curve for labour is the value of the marginal product of labour curve, VMP, which is obtained by multiplying labour's marginal product by the output price.

At the market wage, W, the monopolist will hire L units of labour. Suppose that a public project hired labour away from the monopoly. In reality this would be accomplished by bidding up the market wage, thereby reducing the profit maximizing amount of labour for the monopolist to use and releasing labour to be hired for the public project. However, in this Chapter we are assuming that the public project is not large enough significantly to affect the market price of any input or output, and so we have to assume that any increase in market wage is so small as to be able to be ignored. When the monopolist releases a unit of labour her revenue falls by W, which equals the marginal revenue product of labour, but the value of

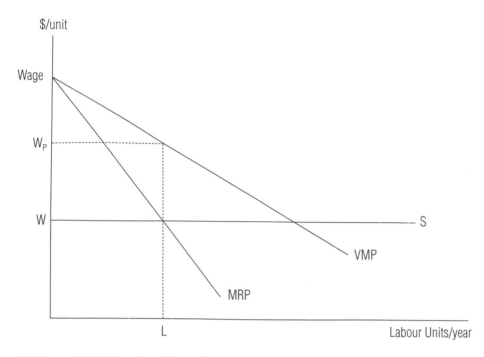

Figure 5.9 Demand for Labour by a Monopoly

output falls by W_p, the value of the marginal product of labour. The opportunity cost of the labour released from the monopoly is the value of the output forgone – the VMP measured by W_p in Figure 5.9 – and this would be the appropriate shadow-price to be used in an efficiency benefit-cost analysis.

In this case, since the input used in the project is not an addition to the total supply, but is reallocated from the monopoly to the project, the pricing rule tells us to value it at a point on the market demand curve. While the monopolist's demand curve for labour is the MRP schedule, the market demand curve for labour to be used in monopoly production is the derived demand curve represented by the VMP schedule. Consumers are willing to pay W_p for the additional quantity of monopoly output produced by an additional unit of labour, and hence this is the relevant equilibrium demand price of labour.

Example 5.8: Monopsony Power

A monopsonist is the sole buyer of a product or factor: for example, if a factory is the only or predominant employer of labour in a town it has monopsony power; similarly, if there is only one fish processing plant fishers can sell to, then that plant has monopsony power. A profit-maximizing monopsonist limits the quantity of the product she buys in order to drive down the price. Figure 5.10 shows the supply of labour, S, to a monopsonist.

The supply curve shows that if the monopsonist decided to hire more labour she would have to offer a higher wage, and that higher wage would apply to all hours of labour currently supplied as well as to the additional quantity. The result is that the marginal factor cost (MFC)

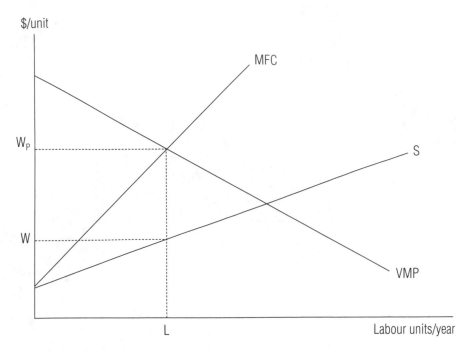

Figure 5.10 Supply of Labour to a Monopsony

– the increase in the wage bill as a result of hiring an extra hour of labour – exceeds the wage. Assuming that the monopsonist sells in a competitive product market, she maximizes profit by hiring labour up to the point at which the value of the marginal product of labour (VMP) – the amount an extra unit of labour adds to the value of output, and hence revenue – equals the MFC – the amount hiring the extra unit of labour adds to cost. It can be seen from Figure 5.10 that the profit maximizing monopsonist will hire L units of labour and pay a wage of W per unit.

Suppose that, in a similar way as that discussed in Example 5.7, a public project was going to hire a small quantity of labour away from the monopsonist. The public project would need to pay the wage, W, for a marginal unit of labour, but the opportunity cost would be W_p, the value of the marginal product of labour, and this would be the appropriate shadow-price in an efficiency benefit-cost analysis. Since the labour used in the project is reallocated from the monopsony, it is priced at the equilibrium price on a market demand curve. As in the previous example, the relevant market demand curve for labour is its VMP schedule in the monopsony production process.

In each of the above examples there is only a single imperfection in the market. What happens if a market suffers two or more distortions? We are now venturing into an area known as **the theory of second-best**. What it says, simply, is that where there are several imperfections in the market economy, such as market power, tax and regulatory distortions, and open-access to resources, removing one of these distortions will not necessarily result in a more efficient allocation of resources. The implication for efficiency benefit-cost analysis is that you need to take account of all the significant market distortions in order to construct the appropriate shadow-price for an input or an output. This point can be illustrated by the following example of a monopoly which is also receiving an output subsidy.

Example 5.9: A Subsidy on Monopoly Output

Figure 5.11 illustrates a monopoly producer who is receiving a subsidy on each unit of output produced. The marginal cost of production is represented by MC, and the marginal cost net of the subsidy is represented by MC_s. There are two imperfections in this monopoly market: the monopolist can influence market price – she faces a downward sloping demand curve for her product – and therefore has an incentive to limit production to drive up price; and the monopolist receives a subsidy on output which creates an incentive to increase production. In the absence of the subsidy the monopolist maximizes profit by producing output level Q_m, where marginal revenue (MR) – the increase in revenue as a result of selling an extra unit of output – equals marginal cost (MC). This involves charging price P_m. However the effect of the subsidy is to lower the effective marginal cost so that the profit maximizing level of output is Q_s which fetches a price of P per unit. The example has been contrived to make Q_s – the appropriate level of output from an efficiency viewpoint – the profit-maximizing output level for the monopolist.

Suppose that a public project is to use some of the monopoly output as an input. Let us first consider the application of the pricing rule in the absence of the subsidy. If the project input represents an additional supply, the pricing rule tells us to price it at a point on the supply curve, or, in the case of an imperfectly competitive industry which does not have a

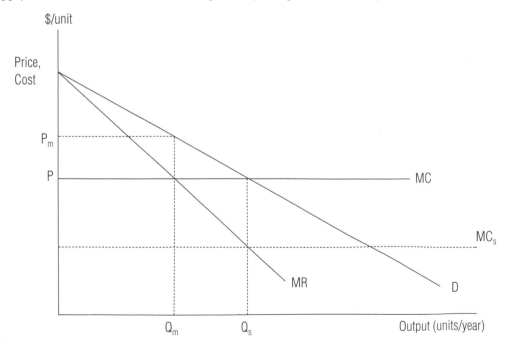

Figure 5.11 Monopoly Output with and without a Subsidy

supply curve, at a point on the marginal cost curve. In this case the project input would be shadow-priced at the true marginal cost, P. If, on the other hand, the project input is diverted from other uses it would be priced at the market price, P_m.

Now consider the application of the pricing rule when monopoly output is subsidized, as illustrated in Figure 5.11. If the project input is an addition to total supply our shadow-pricing rule tells us to price it at an equilibrium price on a supply, or marginal cost curve, P. If the project input is diverted from another use the pricing rule tells us to price it at a point on a demand curve, again P. In the case of the subsidy, the pricing rule gives the same answer whether the input being valued is an addition to supply or diverted from other uses in the economy.

The above example shows that "two wrongs can make a right". The two distortions in the example offset one another so that the competitive outcome of price equal to marginal cost is achieved. As discussed earlier, when price equals marginal cost there is no need to shadow-price the input: its opportunity cost is measured by its market price whether the input is an addition to supply or diverted from use elsewhere. The theory of second-best tells us that we can only be sure that the removal of a market imperfection will improve the efficiency of the allocation of resources if the imperfection in question is the only one in the economy. For example, we cannot automatically assume that the removal of a subsidy will improve efficiency: in Example 5.9 it is clear that removal of the output subsidy reduces the efficiency of resource allocation since a quantity of output $(Q_s - Q_m)$, which is valued by consumers at prices higher than the marginal cost of production, is forgone. At the market equilibrium in the absence of the subsidy, market price, P_m, exceeds marginal cost of production, MC, and hence an increase in the level of output would increase economic welfare.

The Treatment of Taxes in the Efficiency Benefit-Cost Analysis Pricing Rule

The pricing rule illustrated in Figure 5.1 told us to use the demand curve to determine the appropriate price when the item to be valued is an output which satisfies additional demand, or an input which is sourced from an alternative market use; and it told us to use the supply curve when the item is an output which supplies existing demand from an alternative source, or an input which is sourced from additional supply. We now consider whether those prices should be net or gross of tax. The simple answer is that, in the presence of distortionary taxes, when a demand curve is used to determine the appropriate price, the price should be measured gross of tax, and when a supply curve is used, the price should be measured net of tax.

Let us go back to Example 5.1 which dealt with shadow-pricing labour. It was argued that if the labour is sourced from an alternative market use it should be priced at the market wage. We are now arguing that the appropriate wage is the before-tax wage. The reason for this is that, referring to Figure 5.3, the opportunity cost of labour is W_m, the value of its marginal product in its alternative use. Because labour has to pay tax on income earned, the marginal unit of labour employed in the alternative occupation does not receive the full benefit of its contribution to the value of output in that sector of the economy; instead this contribution is shared between labour (the after-tax wage) and the government (the income tax). If we were to price labour at the after-tax wage we would be understating its opportunity cost to the economy by the amount of the tax.

Now consider an addition to labour supply, and suppose that unemployed labour receives an unemployment benefit. This payment is effectively a subsidy (a negative tax) on leisure which has the effect of reducing the supply of labour at all wage levels, and reducing the level of unemployment. Again referring to Figure 5.3, it will be left to the reader to draw the new supply curve of labour, S_t, to the left of the original supply curve, S, and to locate the gross of subsidy return to the unemployed, W_{at}. There are now two opportunity costs of otherwise unemployed labour in market equilibrium: the opportunity cost to the economy is the value, Wa, measured by the supply curve S, as before; and the opportunity cost to the unemployed person is the gross of subsidy value, W_{at}, measured on the new supply curve, S_t. The private opportunity cost per unit of labour is the value of leisure time, W_a, plus the unemployment benefit ($W_{at} - W_a$), which the person will forgo if she accepts a job. However, in determining social opportunity cost, we must set the gain to government in the form of the reduction in unemployment benefit against the corresponding cost to the individual. In other words, the unemployment benefit is a transfer which nets out in the efficiency benefit-cost analysis. The opportunity cost of labour is the value of output forgone as a result of employing the person on the project, which remains W_a as before.

These two examples provide an instructive lesson on the treatment of transfers. In the case of the subsidy on leisure the unemployment benefit netted out of the efficiency analysis.

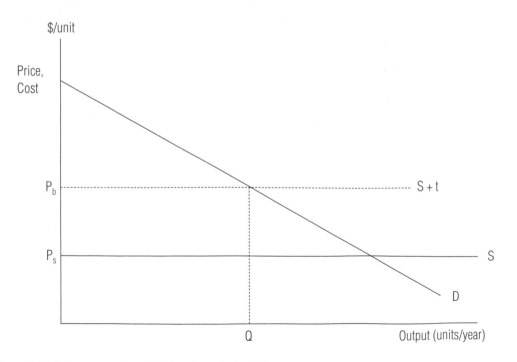

Figure 5.12 A Consumer Good Subject to an Indirect Tax

However the income tax is also a transfer, so why does it not net out of the efficiency calculation as well? Since the employer pays the before-tax wage, Wm, that wage level measures the contribution of the marginal unit of labour to the value of output, labour's value of the marginal product (VMP). The effect of the income tax is to share out the VMP between labour and the government; in other words, the income tax transfers a real benefit from labour to government. Contrast this with the unemployment benefit which is not matched by any output in the real economy. To put it in a colloquial way: the unemployment benefit represents a redistribution of the national cake, with no corresponding increase in its size; whereas a tax levied on earned income, while it also redistributes the cake, is part of the increase in the size of the cake resulting from work.

We now consider taxes levied on the sale of output. Figure 5.12 illustrates the supply and demand for a consumer good subject to an indirect tax. At the market equilibrium quantity traded P_b is the price paid by buyers and P_s the price received by sellers; the difference $(P_b - P_s)$ is the amount of the tax per unit of the good. Suppose that a project were to provide a small addition to the total supply of the good (but not enough to have an observable effect on market price). Since the output of the project satisfies additional demand, in social benefit-cost analysis it should be valued at an equilibrium point on a demand curve, which is the gross of tax price, P_b.

Suppose now that the additional project output replaces supply from an alternative source such as imports. As already argued in the discussion of Example 5.4, project output in this instance should be valued at its net of tax price.

In each of the above two cases the value of the project output to consumers is measured by the demand price. However, in the case of the import-replacing project, part of the benefit measured by the demand price is offset by the reduction in tariff revenue experienced by the government, so that the net benefit is the supply price. Put another way, the net benefit to the economy of the output of an import-replacing project is the saving in cost resulting from the reduction in imports, which is measured by the supply price of imports. In the case of the domestically supplied good, there is no corresponding reduction in sales tax revenue, in fact quite the reverse, since sales tax revenues increase. The increase in sales tax revenues represents a transfer of some of the gross benefit derived from the project output from consumers to the government. Since we want to measure the total amount of the gross benefit, we price the output at the gross of tax price.

In summary, the implications of indirect taxes and subsidies for the efficiency pricing rule described in Figure 5.1 are as follows: when a project output satisfies additional demand, or an input is sourced from an alternative use, a gross of tax (net of subsidy) price is used to measure benefit or opportunity cost; on the other hand, when an output replaces existing supply, or an input is in addition to existing supply, a net of tax (gross of subsidy) price is used. These conclusions are based on the assumption that indirect taxes and subsidies distort otherwise efficient markets. However an alternative possibility is that indirect taxes and subsidies play a corrective role – that they contribute to rather than detract from meeting the goal of efficient allocation of resources. We now consider the implications of corrective taxes for benefit-cost analysis.

Corrective Taxation

To this point in our discussion of the treatment of taxes in social benefit-cost analysis we have been implicitly assuming that the purpose of indirect taxes is to raise public revenue. However another possible role for indirect taxes or subsidies is to discourage or encourage consumption of certain goods and services, or use of certain inputs in production. For example, is the tax on tobacco aimed at raising revenue or discouraging smoking? Because the demand for tobacco is very inelastic, many commentators have concluded that the primary aim of taxation of tobacco is raising revenue. Suppose, however, that the aim of the tax was to discourage smoking because of the cost of its adverse health effects; some of these costs are borne by the smoker, but some are borne by the general community through the health care system. The latter category of cost is termed an external cost – in this case a cost of consumption not borne by the consumer of the good.

Economic efficiency requires that each good or service should be consumed to the point where its marginal benefit equals its marginal cost. We supposedly can rely on the smoker to balance his own health costs against the satisfaction obtained from smoking in determining his marginal benefit. However we cannot rely on him taking the external cost of smoking into account unless we incorporate it into the price of a packet of cigarettes. If the tobacco tax is set at a level equal to the marginal external health cost of smoking, the price of a packet of cigarettes to the consumer will equal the marginal cost of producing the cigarettes plus the marginal external health cost. An indirect tax set at this rate, in effect, forces the smoker to take the marginal external health cost into account in choosing his level of consumption. Setting the rates of indirect taxes in this way is termed *corrective taxation*.

If we assume that the tax on tobacco is a corrective tax, set at the efficient level, what are the implications for valuing the output of tobacco in a social benefit-cost analysis? Suppose that the market illustrated by Figure 5.12 is that for tobacco. It was argued that the output of a project producing a small additional quantity of the product to satisfy additional demand should be valued at P_b, the gross of tax price. However the gross of tax price, P_b, measures only the marginal benefit to the smoker. The additional output of tobacco will impose an additional health care cost on the community, measured by the indirect tax $(P_b - P_s)$. This means that the net benefit to the community of the additional output of tobacco is measured by P_s per unit of output. In other words, where the indirect tax is a corrective tax the output of the project should be valued at the net of tax price.

An alternative way of dealing with the negative externality of smoking in an efficiency analysis is to value the project output at the price the smoker pays (the gross of tax price) and to enter the externality as a separate cost category in the efficiency cash flow table. If the corrective tax is set at an optimal level the external cost per unit is measured by the supply price of cigarettes multiplied by the *ad valorem* tax. The net benefit per unit of project output is measured by the supply price as before.

Let us now consider an example dealing with a subsidy. Consider Figure 5.7 which illustrates the market for a subsidized good. Suppose that the good in question was a flu vaccination. The reason for the subsidy is that the person who pays for and takes the vaccination not only protects himself but also protects others who might have caught the infection from him. The subsidized price measures the benefit of the vaccination to the private individual, and the subsidy measures the marginal external benefit to the community as a whole. If a project were to produce additional flu vaccinations, which price should be used to value them? Marginal benefit to society of an additional vaccination is measured by the unsubsidized price, P, which is the sum of the marginal private benefit plus the marginal external benefit.

The above two examples deal with valuing outputs which satisfy additional demand, and are subject to corrective taxes or subsidies. It was concluded that the appropriate price is a net of tax price, or a gross of subsidy price. In the case of inputs which are in addition to existing supply, and subject to corrective taxes or subsidies, this conclusion is reversed: the appropriate price is gross of tax and net of subsidy. For example, if coal were subject to a carbon tax, the price that measures the cost of using an additional unit of coal is the marginal cost of production plus the marginal external cost, i.e. the supply price plus the tax. If air pollution abatement devices are subsidized, the marginal cost of employing one is its supply price less the subsidy which measures the marginal external benefit of the cleaner air which results from the use of the input.

When a project output satisfies existing demand from an alternative source, and the output is subject to a corrective tax (subsidy), the output should be valued at the net of tax (gross of subsidy) price since that value measures the savings in production cost as a result of the alternative source of supply of the good. When a project input is diverted from an alternative use, and the input is subject to a corrective tax (subsidy), the input should be costed at the gross of tax (net of subsidy) price, since that price measures the value of its marginal product in the alternative use, and there is no change in the overall level of the negative (positive) externality as a result of reallocating the input.

In summary, when indirect taxes or subsidies play a corrective role, the efficiency pricing rule described in the previous section of this Chapter needs to be amended. We need to distinguish between those situations in which the level of the external effect associated with the project output or input changes, and those in which it does not. In the former case, the project output (input) satisfies (is sourced from) additional demand (supply), and a net of tax/gross of subsidy (gross of tax/net of subsidy) price must be used so that the increase in the level of the external effect is costed or valued, along with the extra amount of the output (input) consumed (used) as a result of the project. In the latter case, there is no change in the level of the external effect, since existing demand (supply) is met from alternative sources and no adjustment to the efficiency pricing rule is required.

How is the analyst to determine whether indirect taxes or subsidies play a corrective role? Unlike income taxes or general sales taxes, corrective taxes are targeted at particular consumption goods, such as alcohol or tobacco, or, particular inputs, such as, perhaps, brown coal or pesticides. It must be left to the analyst's judgement, however, to determine how to treat indirect taxes or subsidies in any given benefit-cost analysis.

The Discount Rate

The choice of discount rate to be used in calculating net present values is of critical importance in determining the outcome of the social benefit-cost analysis. This raises the question of whether a market rate of interest should be used as the discount rate or whether the market rate needs to be shadow-priced because of market imperfections. As noted in Chapter 2, if no attempt is made to inflate benefits or costs a real rate of interest is required as the discount rate, and the use of a real rate of interest involves the implicit assumption that all prices change at the general rate of inflation. The real market rate of interest is the real domestic government bond rate, approximated by the money rate less the current rate of inflation (which acts as a proxy for the expected rate). In choosing a money rate of interest to represent the market rate it is sensible to choose a government security with roughly the same time to maturity as the life of the project; for example, choose the 10 year bond rate for a project with a 10 year life.

The real rate of return on government bonds reflects the willingness of individual members of society to trade present for future consumption goods, which is what is contemplated in considering a proposed investment project. Hence the real government bond rate would be a good candidate for choice of discount rate in an efficiency benefit-cost analysis. However there may be situations in which wider considerations than the choices of individuals in the market place are relevant, suggesting the need for an adjustment to the market rate of discount, and these are considered in Chapter 10. Because of these wider considerations a range of discount rates, incorporating the domestic government bond rate, should be used in calculating the net present value of efficiency benefits.

Non-Marketed Inputs and Outputs

It was argued earlier that all project outputs or inputs which affect economic welfare are relevant to the efficiency analysis, whether these outputs or inputs are marketed or not. For example a public transport project may reduce air pollution, and an electricity generating project may increase air pollution. A change in the level of air pollution affects economic welfare in a variety of ways: for example, an increase in the level of air pollution is unpleasant, has health effects, and may result in faster depreciation of material assets such as buildings and equipment. Where these effects are significant they should be accounted for in the social benefit-cost analysis. Various approaches to valuing non-marketed benefits and costs are discussed in Chapter 12, and are not pursued further here.

Worked Example: Efficiency Analysis of National Fruit Growers (NFG) Project

Economists from the University of Kingsland have undertaken an efficiency BCA of the NFG project presented in Chapter 4. Their research has revealed that the opportunity cost of the land is zero, and the opportunity cost of labour is 20% of the market wage. It is also found that the market prices of a number of the project's inputs are affected by indirect taxes or subsidies as indicated in Table 5.1. Apart from the need to shadow-price some of NFG's internal costs, we learn that this project also generates some external costs for downstream users. Nutrient, chemical and sediment run-off from NFG's orchard is polluting the adjacent Kingsland River and will all but destroy the local commercial and recreational fishery. From this additional information it is possible to re-estimate the project's net benefits using efficiency prices instead of the actual market prices paid by NFG. In this analysis it is assumed that all inputs to the project represent additional quantities supplied rather than reallocations from other uses and all indirect taxes and subsidies are distortionary.

Table 5.1 Indirect Taxes or Subsidies on NFG Project Inputs

Input Item	
Opportunity cost	
– labour	20%
Tax on fuel	10%
Subsidies – seeds	25%
– fertilizer	30%
– insecticides	20%
– water	40%
Import duties – equipment	10%
– vehicles	20%
– spares	15%

On the right hand side of the Key Variables Table (Table 1 of Figure 5.13) the details of the adjustments to the project's operating costs are entered as shown in columns P to T. In row 4 the opportunity cost of land is entered as zero; cells R5 to R9 provide details of *ad valorem* taxes and subsidies on various inputs; cell R10 provides details of the duties on spares; and, cell R11 shows that labour has an opportunity cost equal to 20% of its market price. To value these inputs, the efficiency prices (column S) are multiplied by the respective quantities (column M) to arrive at the efficiency cost (column T). Where there is a tax or import duty on the input, the price in column N is divided by $(1+t)$ to derive the efficiency price (in column S), where t is the tax rate or rate of import duty. For subsidies, the efficiency price is derived by dividing the market price by $(1-s)$ where s is the rate of subsidy. It is assumed that the efficiency prices of the remaining components of operating cost – insurance, management fees and miscellaneous costs – are the same as their respective market prices, so the same values are carried across (from column N to column S).

Investment costs also need to be shadow-priced as shown in columns G and H in Table 1 of Figure 5.13. Equipment and vehicle costs are recalculated using the information on import duties in cells S21 and S22. We price buildings at their market price and arrive at an efficiency cost for total fixed investment of $688,636 (cell H8). Note that the salvage value of fixed investment is also recalculated at 10% of its efficiency cost (cell H15). This assumes that used equipment is a potential import carrying the same import duty as the new equipment. Finally, components of working capital need to be shadow priced taking import duties and subsidies into account. The same duty and subsidy rates shown in Column R are used to derive the efficiency costs for working capital ($104,192) as shown in cell H14.

File Edit View Insert Format Tools Data Window Help													
Table 1: Key Variables		Project		Efficiency				Project			Efficiency Pricing		
Investment Costs	No.	Price	Cost	Price	Cost	Operating Costs	No.	Price	Cost		%	Price	Cost
(i) Fixed Investment	(units)	($)		($)		Rent on land (Ha)	100	30	3,000	Rent op. cost	0%	0.00	0
Farm equipment (units)	4	100,000	400,000	90,909	363,636	Fuel (litres)	2,500	0.7	1,750	Fuel tax	10%	0.64	1,591
Vehicles (units)	3	30,000	90,000	25,000	75,000	Seeds (Kg)	250	20	5,000	Seed subsidy	25%	26.67	6,667
Buildings (m2)	250	1,000	250,000	1,000	250,000	Fertilizers (tonnes)	3	500	1,500	Fertilizer Subsi	30%	714.29	2,143
TOTAL			$740,000		$688,636	Insecticides (litres)	3,000	30	90,000	Insecticide sub	20%	37.50	112,500
(ii) Working Capital						Water (ML)	900	20	18,000	Water subsidy	40%	33.33	30,000
Fertilizer Stocks (tons)	2	500	1,000	714.29	1,429	Spares	12	1,000	12,000	Spares -duty	15%	869.57	10,435
Insecticide stocks (Litr	2500	30	75,000	37.50	93,750	Casual labor (days)	100	60	6,000	Labour op. cos	20%	12.00	1,200
Equipment spare parts	10	1,000	10,000	870	8,696	Administration (/month)	12	1000	12,000	Administration (/month)			12,000
Fuel stocks (Litres)	500	0.7	350	0.64	318	Insurance (p.a.)	1	8,263.5	8,263	Insurance (p.a.)		8,263.5	8,263
TOTAL			$86,350.0		$104,192	Management (/month)	12	3,000	36,000	Management		3,000	36,000
(iii) Salvage Value	10%		$74,000		$68,864	Miscellaneous	1	7,700	7,700	Miscellaneous		7,700	7,700
						TOTAL (Market prices)			$201,213	TOTAL (Efficiency Prices)			$228,499
Depreciation	Life(yrs)	Amount p.a.				Revenues							
	Equipmr	10	40,000			Apples (tons)	100	1,000	100,000	External Costs			$10,000
	Vehicles	5	18,000			Peaches (tons)	90	1,250	112,500				
	Building	20	12,500			Pears (tons)	75	1,500	112,500	Import duties			
Financing	Amount	Interest	Life (yrs)			TOTAL			$325,000	Equipment	10%		
Loan	$700,000	3.5%	10							Vehicles	20%		
Overdraft	$40,000	5.0%	4			Capacity Output							
Discount rate =	5.0%	10.0%	15.0%			Year	2001	2002	2003	2004+			
Tax rate on profits	25.0%					%	25%	50%	75%	100%			

Ex1a / Ex1b / Ex1c / Ch1Ex \ **Variables** / ProjectBCA / PrivateBCA / EfficiencyBCA

Figure 5.13 NFG Case Study: Key Variables Table with Efficiency Prices

Economists from the local University of Kingsland have estimated the resulting reduction in value of the fish catch at $10,000 per annum from year 2 onwards (see cell T18), and that there will be no corresponding reduction in fishing costs. To take this external cost into account when undertaking an efficiency BCA, an additional row (Row 11, Figure 5.14) is added to the cost section of the efficiency cash flow.

NFG's fruit output is valued at its market price as we assume that it satisfies additional demand, rather than being an alternative way of meeting existing demand.

We are now ready to undertake the Efficiency analysis as shown in Table 4 of Figure 5.14. This Table is identical to the Project cash flow that we derived in Chapter 4 (Figure 4.2), except that we now use efficiency prices instead of actual market prices to value inputs and outputs, and we have added an extra row showing the external costs to the downstream fishers (Row 14). Note that when we calculate the return on this project at efficiency prices, it is much lower than the value obtained from the project analysis. The IRR is now only 7.8%, which also means that the NPV is negative at 10%. At a cost of capital above 7.8% the project would not be worthwhile from an overall efficiency perspective.

Why is the proposed NFG project less attractive from an efficiency viewpoint than from the perspective of the private market? By comparing the information in Table 4 of Figure 5.14 with that reported in Figure 4.2, Chapter 4, it can be seen that the net effect of shadow-pricing

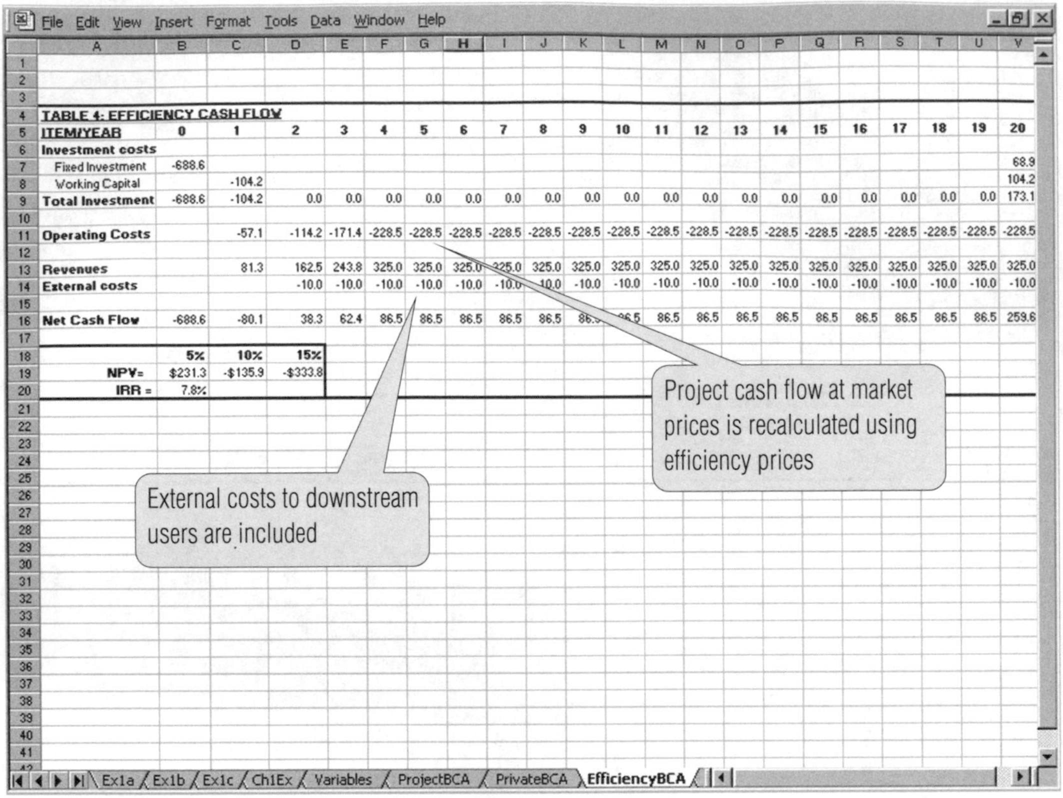

Figure 5.14 NFG Case Study: Efficiency Cash Flow Table

TABLE 4: EFFICIENCY CASH FLOW

ITEM/YEAR	0	1	2	3	4	5	6	7	8	9	10	11	12	13	14	15	16	17	18	19	20
Investment costs																					
Fixed Investment	-688.6																				68.9
Working Capital		-104.2																			104.2
Total Investment	-688.6	-104.2	0.0	0.0	0.0	0.0	0.0	0.0	0.0	0.0	0.0	0.0	0.0	0.0	0.0	0.0	0.0	0.0	0.0	0.0	173.1
Operating Costs		-57.1	-114.2	-171.4	-228.5	-228.5	-228.5	-228.5	-228.5	-228.5	-228.5	-228.5	-228.5	-228.5	-228.5	-228.5	-228.5	-228.5	-228.5	-228.5	-228.5
Revenues		81.3	162.5	243.8	325.0	325.0	325.0	325.0	325.0	325.0	325.0	325.0	325.0	325.0	325.0	325.0	325.0	325.0	325.0	325.0	325.0
External costs			-10.0	-10.0	-10.0	-10.0	-10.0	-10.0	-10.0	-10.0	-10.0	-10.0	-10.0	-10.0	-10.0	-10.0	-10.0	-10.0	-10.0	-10.0	-10.0
Net Cash Flow	-688.6	-80.1	38.3	62.4	86.5	86.5	86.5	86.5	86.5	86.5	86.5	86.5	86.5	86.5	86.5	86.5	86.5	86.5	86.5	86.5	259.6

	5%	10%	15%
NPV=	$231.3	-$135.9	-$333.8
IRR =	7.8%		

External costs to downstream users are included

Project cash flow at market prices is recalculated using efficiency prices

various inputs to the project is to increase the estimate of annual operating cost and investment costs, while annual revenues are unchanged. The main reason for the increase in the cost estimate is the existence of subsidies on inputs of seed, fertilizer, insecticides and water. An additional cost, in the form of an environmental cost, is also included in the efficiency analysis of Figure 5.14. Hence, with the same revenues, but higher costs, the NFG project is less attractive from an efficiency perspective.

The efficiency analysis includes the benefits and costs to all individuals affected by the project, irrespective of whether they form part of the defined referent group or not. The decision as to whether the project should be supported or not will depend on the net benefits to the referent group. The calculation of these for the NFG project is shown in the following Chapter.

Allowing for Changes in Indirect Taxes and Subsidies

Before completing this section, one important adjustment to the Key Variables Table in Figure 5.13 is necessary. When the market prices of the various inputs were initially entered we had no information about the indirect taxes and subsidies applicable to each. When we derived the efficiency prices we applied conversion factors to the market prices (in Columns E and N), generating the efficiency prices in Columns G and S respectively. However, it would be inadvisable to leave the efficiency price cells in this form. If we were to change the tax rate, rate of subsidy, or import duty, the market prices in Columns E and N would not change, but the efficiency prices would. This would be incorrect as indirect taxes and subsidies affect market prices, not efficiency prices. To set this up correctly, the efficiency prices in Columns G and S should be entered as given values (not as formulae). The market prices in Columns E and N should then be entered as formulae. Where there is a tax or duty, the market price (P_b) is equal to the efficiency price (P_s) plus the tax or duty (t), i.e. $P_b = P_s(1+t)$. Where there is a subsidy, $P_b = P_s(1-s)$.

APPENDIX TO CHAPTER 5:
Economic Efficiency Analysis in the ICP Case Study

We are now in a position to undertake an efficiency benefit-cost analysis of the proposed ICP textile project which we analysed from a private viewpoint in the Appendix to Chapter 4. Since our focus is on efficiency we will ignore all distributional aspects of the project: this means ignoring its tax implications for the government and the firm, ignoring the project's financial structure and its implications for equity holders, ignoring the distributional effects on various other groups such as public utilities, domestic financial and insurance agencies, and suppliers of labour, and ignoring the distributional effects among countries.

The efficiency cash flow for the ICP project is based on the project cash flow which we set up in Chapter 4, Figure 4.2, and is shown in Figure A5.1. We start by enumerating the "real" aspects of the project. It involves employing a range of inputs – land, capital goods, labour, water, electricity, raw materials – and using them to produce an output – yarn. The costs of the project are the opportunity costs of the inputs, and the benefits are the value of the output. Since the project is an extension of an existing factory involving the use of vacant land which will otherwise remain vacant, it will be assumed that the land used in the project has no opportunity cost, even though the firm pays a nominal rent on the land. (Similarly, we should ignore the overhead cost that the firm chooses to allocate to the project for its own internal accounting purposes.) The remaining inputs need to be shadow-priced because of various market imperfections, and we consider each input in turn. It should be noted that all input data relating to the calculation of efficiency prices are drawn from Key Input Variables section (Table 1) of the spreadsheet as shown in Figure A4.1 in Chapter 4. Adhering to this convention ensures that all cell entries in Table 4 (in Figure A5.1) are formulae or references to the preceding tables, and therefore also, that any subsequent changes to the values of the input variables will result in automatic changes to the respective cash flows.

Cost of Capital Goods

Capital goods need to be imported at various times to provide equipment and inventories for the project. These goods are purchased using foreign exchange obtained at the official exchange rate. Since we are assuming for the moment that the official rate represents the opportunity cost of foreign exchange, we can convert the US dollar price of capital goods to

YEAR	1999 '000 US$	1999 MN BT	2000 MN BT	2001 MN BT	2002 MN BT	2003 MN BT	2004 MN BT	2005 MN BT	2006 MN BT	2007 MN BT	2008 MN BT	2009 MN BT
TABLE 4 — EFFICIENCY CALCULATION												
INVESTMENT COSTS												
SPINDLES	-4000.000	-176.000										
EQUIPMENT	-850.000	-37.400										
INSTALLATION	-100.000	-4.400										
CONSTRUCTION		-18.000										
START-UP COSTS		-18.000										
RAW MATERIALS			-52.800									52.800
SPARE PARTS			-10.692									10.692
TOTAL		-253.800	-63.492	0.000	0.000	0.000	0.000	0.000	0.000	0.000	0.000	63.492
RUNNING COSTS												
WATER			-3.600	-7.200	-7.200	-7.200	-7.200	-7.200	-7.200	-7.200	-7.200	-7.200
POWER			-1.800	-3.600	-3.600	-3.600	-3.600	-3.600	-3.600	-3.600	-3.600	-3.600
SPARE PARTS			-21.340	-21.340	-21.340	-21.340	-21.340	-21.340	-21.340	-21.340	-21.340	-21.340
RAW MATERIALS			-106.920	-213.840	-213.840	-213.840	-213.840	-213.840	-213.840	-213.840	-213.840	-213.840
INSURANCE & RENT			0.000	0.000	0.000	0.000	0.000	0.000	0.000	0.000	0.000	0.000
LABOUR			-40.500	-40.500	-40.500	-40.500	-40.500	-40.500	-40.500	-40.500	-40.500	-40.500
TOTAL			-174.160	-286.480	-286.480	-286.480	-286.480	-286.480	-286.480	-286.480	-286.480	-286.480
REVENUES												
SALE OF YARN			191.400	382.800	382.800	382.800	382.800	382.800	382.800	382.800	382.800	382.800
NET EFFICIENCY BENEFIT		-253.800	-46.252	96.320	96.320	96.320	96.320	96.320	96.320	96.320	96.320	159.812

NPV	$ (MN)	IRR (%)
4%	433.2	23.4%
8%	289.9	
12%	183.6	
16%	103.2	
0%	630.3	

Callouts:
- All imported goods valued at c.i.f. prices
- Power is valued at its marginal cost
- Unskilled labour is valued at 50% of wage cost
- Yarn is valued at its world price

Figure A5.1 ICP Project Solution: The Efficiency Cash Flow

domestic currency using this exchange rate. The US dollar prices of imported goods landed in the country are what are termed "c.i.f." prices – including cost, insurance and freight; this means that the US dollar price is the price of the good at the country's border. Once that price is converted to domestic currency a tariff is applied – the price to domestic buyers is raised by some percentage above the border price in domestic currency. A tariff is an indirect tax as illustrated in Example 5.3. The opportunity cost of the imported capital good is its supply price which is net of the tariff. Hence, while the price the firm pays for the inputs is the gross of tariff price (the c.i.f. price plus tariff), we use the net of tariff price (the c.i.f. price) as the shadow-price in the efficiency benefit-cost analysis. The capital goods are an addition to total supply to the country and, hence, are valued at the supply price.

Cost of Labour

The project uses skilled, semi-skilled and unskilled workers in both its construction and operations phases. The unskilled labour market exhibits significant unemployment and the Ministry of Industry suggests that a shadow-price of 50% of the unskilled wage be used as the shadow-price. What is the basis of this figure? It could be that the Ministry is assuming, or has information to the effect that half of the unskilled workers engaged in the project would otherwise be unemployed (with a zero value placed on their non-market activities) and that the other half are hired away from jobs in which they cannot be replaced. The pricing rule would tell us to value the former at their supply price (zero) and the latter at the demand price (the market wage). Alternatively, and more likely, the assumption could be that all unskilled workers are effectively drawn from the ranks of the unemployed (an addition to the current supply) and that the unit value of the non-market activities of those workers (the supply price) is assumed to be 50% of the wage. In either case, and perhaps after some discussion with officials, the analyst adopts a shadow-price for unskilled labour of 50% of the unskilled wage. This means that only half of the unskilled labour costs incurred by the firm are counted as an opportunity cost in the efficiency social benefit-cost analysis of the project.

Utilities

Water and electricity are supplied by state-owned public utilities. We are informed by Ministry officials that the additional electricity required by the project can be produced at a lower unit cost than the price charged to customers. This is the kind of situation discussed in Example 5.5. The opportunity cost of an input, the supply of which is to be increased, is measured by an equilibrium point on its supply or marginal cost curve. The marginal cost of electricity is reckoned to be 50% of the price paid by the firm, and hence only 50% of the firm's power bill will be included as an opportunity cost in the efficiency benefit-cost analysis. A similar situation may exist with water supply, but it appears that after discussion with officials it has been concluded that the firm's additional water bill does in fact represent the cost of the additional supply, or, alternatively, that the water will be diverted from another use. Hence the water input is valued at the market price, and all of the extra water bill is included as an opportunity cost.

Cotton and Yarn Inputs and Outputs

The final input to be considered is raw materials. As in the case of capital goods, and for the same reasons, the appropriate shadow-price is the c.i.f. dollar price converted to domestic currency by means of the official exchange rate. We now turn to the output of the project – spinning yarn. When valuing output we look for an equilibrium point on a demand curve or a supply curve. In this case the project simply replaces an alternative source of supply – the world market which determines the equilibrium world price of yarn. The latter price is the US dollar c.i.f. price, converted to domestic currency by means of the official exchange rate. The pricing rule tells us that the output of an import-replacing project should be valued at this net of tariff world price.

The Efficiency Benefit-Cost Analysis

Now that we have decided upon the appropriate shadow-prices for the efficiency benefit-cost analysis, we need to enter the values in the spreadsheet and perform the NPV calculation which will tell us if the project is an efficient use of resources. It will be recalled from Chapter 4 that three sections of the spreadsheet have already been completed: Part 1 contains the data available to perform the analysis (which must now be augmented by the shadow-prices we have just computed); Part 2 contains the Project analysis; and Part 3 – the Private Benefit-Cost Account – contains the analysis from the point of view of the equity holders in the firm. We now open Part 4 of the spreadsheet – the Efficiency Benefit-Cost Account – by entering a set of rows containing the value of output and the opportunity costs of inputs as shown in Figure A5.1. These rows correspond to the categories of "real" output and inputs enumerated and discussed above. The efficiency benefit or cost represented by each category of output or input in each year is calculated by multiplying the quantity by the shadow-price. Each entry in this part of the analysis is a formula incorporating values contained in the first part of the spreadsheet as developed in Figures A4.1 to A4.3 in the previous chapter.

Once the various categories of efficiency benefits and costs have been valued in each year, the net benefit in each year is calculated by subtracting costs from benefits. This single row of net benefits will be negative in the early years of the project – the construction and development phase – and then generally positive in later years. The net benefit stream is discounted using a range of discount rates to yield a set of NPVs and the IRR is calculated where appropriate. The reason for using a range of discount rates is that there may be some dispute about the appropriate rate. This issue is discussed further in Chapter 10. For the moment, since we have not inflated the benefit and cost streams, we can use a real market rate of interest – the observed money rate less the observed current rate of inflation – as a reference point. Discount rates below and above this rate tell us how sensitive the NPV result is to the choice of discount rate.

The next task, to be taken up in Chapter 6, is to determine an aggregate measure of the net benefits, in each year, to members of the referent group, and then to determine, by a different process, a set of net benefits to each sub-group which, when aggregated, give the same answer as our aggregate measure.

Further Reading

The analysis of market equilibrium, indirect taxation, market regulation and market failure is included in most microeconomic theory texts. These issues, and their relevance to benefit-cost analysis, are also discussed in most works on public finance, such as, for example, R. W. Boadway and D. E. Wildasin, *Public Sector Economics* (Little, Brown and Coy., 1984). A dated but useful survey of shadow-pricing techniques is R. N. McKean, "The Use of Shadow Prices" in *Problems in Public Expenditure Analysis*, S. B. Chase (ed.) (Brookings Institution, 1968), pp. 33–77.

Exercises

1. Draw an upward sloping supply curve and a downward sloping demand curve for labour. Label the axes. Assuming that the labour market is distorted by a minimum wage (which is a binding constraint), draw in the level of the minimum wage, labelled W_m, and identify the quantity of labour demanded, labelled Q. On the supply curve of labour, identify the

level of the wage corresponding to Q units of labour supplied, and label it W_a.

(i)   State what the efficiency benefit-cost analysis rule tells us about valuing labour input in a benefit-cost analysis;

(ii) suppose that a project will use a small amount of labour drawn from the above market. Under what circumstances should the labour be costed in the efficiency benefit-cost analysis at:

(a) W_m per unit;

(b) W_a per unit?

2.   Suppose that the elasticity of demand for a monopolist's product is 1.5. Calculate the ratio of the value of the marginal product of labour to the marginal revenue product of labour. What is the opportunity cost of labour expressed as a multiple of the wage? What is the appropriate shadow-price of labour diverted from the monopoly's production process? [Hint: see Example 6.6 in Chapter 6.]

3.   For each of the 16 cases indicated in the following Table, state whether you would use the demand curve or the supply curve to determine the appropriate price for valuation purposes in an efficiency benefit-cost analysis, and state whether the appropriate price is gross or net of the tax or subsidy. In each case briefly justify your answer.

Item to be valued	Indirect Tax		Subsidy	
	Distorting	**Corrective**	**Distorting**	**Corrective**
Project Output – Satisfies additional demand	(i)	(ii)	(iii)	(iv)
– Satisfies existing demand from alternative source	(v)	(vi)	(vii)	(viii)
Project Input – From additional supply	(ix)	(x)	(xi)	(xii)
– Diverted from alternative use	(xiii)	(xiv)	(xv)	(xvi)

6
Calculating the Net Benefits to the Referent Group

Introduction

The referent group in a social benefit-cost analysis is unlikely to consist only of the equity holders of the private firm, at one extreme, or everyone affected by the project in the whole world, at the other extreme. The costs and benefits to the former group were analysed in Chapter 4, and those to the latter group in Chapter 5. In this Chapter we analyse the costs and benefits to the referent group. Our client will tell us what the referent group is, and she will normally nominate all groups affected by the project (sometimes referred to as "stakeholders") who are resident in her State or country, including effects on government receipts or payments: in the ICP Case Study discussed in the Appendices, "Thailand" is the referent group.

As noted in Chapter 1 it is sometimes easier to specify who is *not* a member of the referent group than to identify all the relevant sub-groups; in the ICP Case Study, of those groups who benefit or incur costs, the foreign equity holders in the firm and the foreign financial institution which lends to the project are not members of the referent group. This means that the aggregate net benefits to the referent group can be calculated by subtracting the net cash flows experienced by these two groups from the efficiency net benefits of the project discussed in Chapter 5. Thus we can open Part 5 of our spreadsheet – the Referent Group Benefit-Cost Account – by entering the efficiency net benefits row less the equity holder's and foreign financial institution's net benefit rows. (See Figure A6.2, Table 5, row 4, page 142.) We have now completed the aggregate referent group (or "social") BCA.

We also want a disaggregated analysis of the net benefits to the referent group for two reasons. The main reason is that our client will want information about the distribution of net benefits or costs among sub-groups because this will influence the project's attractiveness to the political decision-maker. The other reason is that if we enumerate all the sub-groups affected by the project, measure the net benefits to each, sum them and get the same answer as our aggregate measure, we can be fairly sure the analysis is correct, or, at least, is internally consistent. It is very common to omit some benefits or costs in the first run of the analysis and having a check of this kind is extremely useful.

How to Identify Referent Group Benefits in Practice

It is sometimes difficult to identify all the sub-groups within the referent group who are affected by the project, and it is not unusual for some group or category of net benefit to be omitted from the first draft of the Referent Group Benefit-Cost Account. Fortunately, as noted above, this kind of error can readily be detected within our project appraisal framework by the existence of a discrepancy between the measure of aggregate referent group net benefits computed by subtracting non-referent group benefits from the efficiency net benefits and the measure computed by aggregating the net benefits to various sub-groups within the referent group.

In principle there is a four-way classification of net benefits, illustrated by Table 6.1, distinguishing net benefits which accrue to the referent and non-referent groups respectively, and net benefits which either are, or are not properly measured by market prices.

Table 6.1 Classification of Net Benefits

	Net Benefits Accruing to:	
	Referent Group	**Non-Referent Group**
Net Benefits Measured by Market Prices	A	B
Net Benefits not Measured by Market Prices	C	D

Areas A, B and C correspond to the specific example illustrated by Figure 1.3 in Chapter 1. However, area D is a further potential category of net benefit which may be encountered in

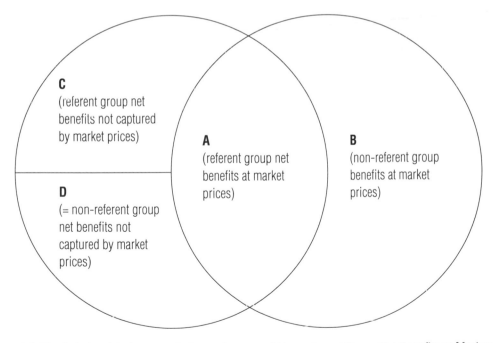

Figure 6.1 The Relationship between Referent Group and Non-referent Group Net Benefits at Market Prices and Efficiency Prices

general. Figure 1.3 can be updated to include this additional category, and the revised diagram is presented here as Figure 6.1.

The difference between Figures 6.1 and 1.3 is that **Area D** has been added. This allows for a situation where there are net benefits (costs) to non-referent group members arising because of divergences between market prices and efficiency prices. For example, if a negative externality, pollution, arising from a project is borne by stakeholders outside the referent group, perhaps across a state or international boundary, the cost of this should be included in the efficiency benefit-cost analysis (now defined as area A+B+C+D), but subtracted along with area B from the efficiency cash flow to derive the aggregate referent group cash flow (area A+C).

Table 6.1 and Figure 6.1 can be used to consider the categories of referent group and non-referent group net benefits in the ICP Case Study discussed in the Appendix. In this example:

- **Area A** contains the net benefits to the domestic financial institution and the government, which constitute the balance of the net benefits to referent group members identified by the project analysis at market prices.
- **Area B** contains the returns to foreign equity holders and foreign lenders, which constitute that part of the project net benefits, as measured by market prices, which accrues to non-referent group members.
- **Area C** contains referent group net benefits in the form of rents to the domestic insurance company, the electricity utility, and labour, which are external to the project. Since there are no non-market effects, such as increased pollution, referred to in the case study, this category is not included in the referent group analysis in this case. However, in general, non-marketed effects would be included in Area C or D of Figure 6.1.
- **Area D** is empty because, as noted above, in the case study there are no non-referent group net benefits not measured by market prices.

The scope for error in identifying referent group net benefits can be narrowed by following some simple guidelines as to where to expect to find referent group net benefits. There are two main ways of identifying referent group benefits: one way is to follow the tax and financing flows generated by the project, and the other is to examine the shadow-prices used in the analysis. Financial flows distribute the net benefits of a project among private sector stakeholders, and between the private and public sector. The public sector is normally part of the referent group, but some private sector agents, such as foreign firms, may be excluded. Shadow-prices identify differences between private and efficiency valuations of inputs or outputs, and the differences may represent benefits or costs to members of the referent group.

Consider first changes in tax or subsidy flows as a result of the project. The project may result in changes in direct tax revenues, such as income or company tax, and changes in indirect tax revenues, such as tariffs and sales taxes. When these tax revenue changes are transfers among members of the referent group they net out of the aggregate referent group net benefit calculation: in Example 5.4 in the previous chapter, for example, the project resulted in a reduction in diesel fuel consumption which provided a gain to government in the form of reduced fuel subsidies paid, and a loss to farmers in the form of reduced fuel subsidies received.

When changes in tax flows involve transfers between the referent group and the rest of the world, on the other hand, the referent group experiences a net gain or loss, depending on the direction of the flow. The net benefit is recorded as a gain or loss to the domestic government.

Now consider the private financing flows associated with the project. We have seen in Chapter 5 that these flows are not relevant to the efficiency benefit-cost analysis as they simply shift benefits and costs from one group to another. However they are relevant to the construction of the referent group benefit-cost account if they transfer net benefits between members and non-members of the referent group, or between members of the referent group, but are not relevant if they transfer net benefits among non-referent group members. An example of a financial flow which transfers net benefits between members and non-members of the referent group is provided by a domestic bank which lends money to a project to be undertaken by a foreign company. The bank advances a loan and then receives a series of interest payments and principal repayments. The initial loan is a cost to the domestic financial institutions section of the referent group benefit-cost account, while the interest and principal repayment flows are benefits. The present value of the net benefit to this sub-group will vary depending on the interest rate charged on the loan and the discount rate used in the social benefit-cost analysis.

Another clue to the existence of referent group net benefits lies in the rationale for shadow-pricing. Suppose that an input, such as labour, is assigned a shadow-price lower than its market price. This tells us that the wage exceeds the opportunity cost of labour, and, hence, that the labour employed on the project is receiving a net benefit. Since domestic labour is one of the sub-groups within the referent group, that net benefit should be recorded among the referent group net benefits. Now suppose that an input was assigned a shadow-price in excess of its market price. For example, labour to be diverted from a monopoly or monopsony to work on the project would be shadow-priced at the value of the marginal product of labour. The fact that the shadow-price of the input exceeds the market price tells us that the project is imposing a loss somewhere in the economy and this loss will generally be experienced by a member of the referent group. In the present example, there is a loss of profit to the domestic monopoly or monopsony which is part of the referent group.

We have considered cases where the shadow-pricing of inputs may help us identify categories of referent group net benefits. The same applies to the shadow-pricing of outputs. For example, suppose that a project produces an import-replacing good. Instead of valuing output at its market price, which is the border price plus the tariff, we shadow-price it at the border price. When a project output is shadow-priced at a lower price than the market price this generally indicates a loss to some members of the referent group. In the example of an import-replacing project, the loss is incurred by the government in the form of a reduction in tariff revenue. Now suppose that a project output is shadow-priced at a price above its market price. This will generally indicate a benefit to members of the referent group. An example is influenza vaccinations which may command a price in the market, but will have a social value in excess of the individual willingness to pay for them because, in addition to the benefit they confer on the buyer, they reduce the chance of others catching the disease. While it is difficult to place a dollar value on a non-marketed service of this nature, it is nevertheless clearly a referent group net benefit.

In summarizing the relationship between shadow-prices and referent group net benefits, we can conclude that where the market price of an input exceeds (is less than) its shadow-price, there are likely to be referent group benefits (costs); and where the market price of an output exceeds (is less than) its shadow-price, there are likely to be referent group costs (benefits). Table 6.2 summarizes this simple rule and provides an example of each of the four cases.

Table 6.2 Using Shadow-prices to Identify Referent Group Benefits and Costs

	INPUT	OUTPUT
MARKET PRICE GREATER THAN SHADOW-PRICE	BENEFIT TO OWNER OF THE INPUT e.g. Otherwise unemployed labour	COST TO GOVERNMENT OR PUBLIC e.g. Loss of tariff revenue, cost of pollution generated by use
MARKET PRICE LESS THAN SHADOW-PRICE	COST TO PREVIOUS USER OF THE INPUT e.g. Monopoly or monopsony firm	BENEFIT TO PUBLIC e.g. Value of vaccination to those other than the vaccinated

Some Examples of Referent Group Net Benefits

We now extend some of the examples considered in Chapter 5 to identify and measure benefits or costs to members of the referent group. We identify Project, Efficiency, Referent Group and Non-Referent Group net benefits. Private net benefits, reported in Table 3 of the benefit-cost analysis spreadsheet (see Figure 1.4 in Chapter 1), are a subset of project net benefits, and are not identified in the following discussion.

It will be seen in the following examples that government receipts and outlays sometimes appear in Area A, which includes that part of referent group net benefit which is captured by market prices, and sometimes in Area C, which includes referent group net benefits not captured by market prices. Market prices are gross of indirect taxes and net of subsidies, whereas as noted in Chapter 5, in the presence of distortionary taxes or subsidies, the analysis of efficiency benefits may be based on prices either gross or net of taxes or subsidies, depending on whether an output or an input is being valued, and depending on whether the commodity meets additional demand or satisfies existing demand from alternative sources, or whether the input is in addition to existing supply or is diverted from alternative uses. In consequence the project analysis at market prices will sometimes overvalue or undervalue outputs or inputs from an efficiency viewpoint and the required correction will be entered in Area C of Figure 6.1 showing the distribution of net benefits.

A further point to note is that when government enters the private market to commission production of goods and services, it does so because the private market in these goods and services is either non-existent or imperfect. This means that the revenue the firm receives from the government is related to the cost of production of the commissioned commodity, rather than to the value in use. Value in use is entered in Area C, along with any other non-market effects. To avoid double-counting of project benefits the government payment to the private firm is also entered in Area C. Thus it appears as a positive in Area A and a negative in Area C and cancels out in the efficiency analysis when Areas A and D are summed. The efficiency analysis then accounts for the project benefit in Area C and the project cost, measured at market prices, in Area A.

Example 6.1: A Minimum Wage (based on Example 5.1)

A domestic firm hires $100 worth of labour at the minimum wage and constructs a walking track for which it is paid $110 by the government. No fee is charged to access the track, and it has a present value of $120 to consumers. The labour would otherwise be unemployed and would be engaged in non-market activities valued at $50. The efficiency benefit-cost analysis tells us that the efficiency NPV of the project is $70: the present value of the output ($120) of the project less the present value of the opportunity cost ($100 worth of labour shadow-priced at 50% of the wage). We now enumerate the sub-groups comprising the referent group: the domestic firm; government; labour; and consumers. The net benefits to each group are, respectively, $10 (profit), –$110 (expenditure), $50 (labour rent), and $120 (use value). The aggregate net benefits sum to $70 which corresponds to the result of the efficiency analysis.

The example illustrates the simple premise on which the disaggregated analysis is based: if a project has an aggregate net benefit of $70 some groups, whether referent or not, must be receiving the benefits and incurring the costs of that project; the sum of the net benefits to all groups must equal the aggregate net benefit. In the example above, all groups affected by the project are members of the referent group, and hence the sum of referent group net benefits equals the aggregate net benefit.

Using the categories and symbols presented in Table 6.1, this example can be summarised as follows:

Project net benefit (A+B) = $10
Efficiency net benefit (A+B+C+D) = $70
Referent Group net benefit (A+C or (A+B+C+D) – (B+D)) = $70
Non-referent Group net benefit (B+D) = $0

Distribution of Net Benefits

A=$10	B=$0
Profits to firm	None
($110 – 100 = $10)	
C=$60	**D=$0**
Rent to labour ($100 – 50 = $50)	None
Benefits to Users ($120)	
Loss to Government (–$110)	

Example 6.2: A Maximum Price (based on Example 5.3)

The State Government hires a computer programmer from another State for a month, at a cost of $200, which is $50 more than she would normally expect to earn, and pays $100 for the accommodation of the programmer in a rent-controlled apartment with a market value of $125. The programmer revises some of the government's programs leading to a cost saving of $400. The referent group is defined as the residents of the State. The efficiency benefit is $400 and the opportunity cost is $275 – the wage forgone by the programmer plus the market value of the apartment – so that the efficiency net benefit is $125. The net benefits to the referent group are the efficiency net benefits less the net benefits to the non-referent group; in this case the programmer is not part of the referent group and her net benefit of $50 is subtracted from efficiency net benefits to give $75. Two sub-groups within the referent group are affected by the project: the government has a net benefit of $100 and potential renters of the rent-controlled apartment lose $25. The sum of these disaggregated referent group benefits ($75) equals the aggregate measure as required.

Using the categories and symbols presented in Table 6.1, this example can be summarized as follows:

Project net benefit (A+B) = $100
Efficiency net benefit (A+B+C+D) = $125
Referent Group net benefit (A+C or (A+B+C+D) – (B+D)) = $75
Non-referent Group net benefit (B+D) = $50

Distribution of Net Benefits

A=$100 Net Benefits to Government Department [$400 – (200+100) = $100]	B=$0 None
C= –$25 Loss of Rent to potential renters ($25)	D=$50 Rent to labour ($200 – 150 = $50)

Example 6.3: An Indirect Tax – a Tariff on Imports (based on Example 5.4)

A domestic firm proposes to import $100 worth of gadgets for use in a manufacturing project. The $100 includes the c.i.f. (landed) value of the imported goods of $75 plus $25 in tariffs. Other costs are $200 for skilled labour, and the resulting output will sell on the domestic market for $400. The efficiency net benefit is given by the value of the output less the opportunity costs of the inputs – $75 worth of imports and $200 worth of skilled labour – giving a net value of $125. In this example there are no non-referent group net benefits. The members of the referent group are the government, gaining $25 in tariff revenue, and the firm, gaining a profit of $100.

Let us alter this project to one which produces a good which is currently imported – an import-replacing project. Suppose that the project uses $200 worth of skilled labour to produce output valued on the domestic market at $400. Domestic consumers could obtain that same quantity of output from abroad at a cost of $300 c.i.f. plus $100 tariff. The efficiency net benefits are the value of the output at the c.i.f. price, $300, less the opportunity cost of the skilled labour, giving a net value of $100. Two sub-groups of the referent group are affected: the firm makes a profit of $200 and the government loses tariff revenue of $100 because of the import replacement. Since there are no non-referent group beneficiaries, the sum of referent group net benefits ($100) equals the total efficiency net benefit.

Using the categories and symbols presented in Table 6.1, this latter example can be summarized as follows:

Project net benefit (A+B) = $200
Efficiency net benefit (A+B+C+D) = $100
Referent Group net benefit (A+C or (A+B+C+D) – (B+D)) = $100
Non-referent Group net benefit (B+D) = $0

Distribution of Net Benefits

A=$200 Net Profits to Firm ($400 – 200= $200)	B=$0 None
C= –$100 Tariff Loss to Government ($100)	D=$0 None

Example 6.4: A Subsidy (based on Example 5.5)

The government spends $100 on constructing wheat silos, the services of which are supplied free to users, which results in farmers saving $75 worth of diesel fuel at the subsidized price. The subsidy paid on that quantity of fuel amounts to $25. In an efficiency net benefit analysis the saving in fuel is valued at its unsubsidized cost, reflecting the opportunity cost of the inputs required to produce it, so the efficiency net benefit is zero. In terms of referent group benefits, the farmers benefit by $75 and the government incurs costs of $100, but benefits by $25 in reduced fuel subsidies. The sum of the referent group net benefits ($0) equals the total efficiency net benefit.

Using the categories and symbols presented in Table 6.1, this example can be summarized as follows:

Project net benefit (A+B) = –$25
Efficiency net benefit (A+B+C+D) = $0
Referent Group net benefit (A+C or (A+B+C+D) – (B+D)) = $0
Non-referent Group net benefit (B+D) = $0

Distribution of Net Benefits

A= –$25	B=$0
Net Benefits to Farmers	None
($75)	
Project Cost to Government	
(–$100)	
C= $25	**D=$0**
Government's saving on subsidies	
($25)	None

Example 6.5: A Regulated Utility (based on Example 5.6)

A foreign company proposes to construct a smelter at a cost of $100 which will use $50 worth of power at the current price. The output of the smelter will be worth $400 on the world market and the company will pay $100 in tax. The cost of producing the extra power is $30. The efficiency net benefits are given by the value of output, $400, less the opportunity cost of inputs – $100 construction cost plus $30 power cost – giving a net value of $270. The net benefits of the referent group, which excludes the foreign firm, are the efficiency net benefits less the firm's after-tax profit of $150, giving a total of $120. The government and the power producer are the only referent group members affected, and their net benefits consist of $100 tax and $20 profit respectively.

Using the categories and symbols presented in Table 6.1, this example can be summarized as follows:

Project net benefit (A+B) = $250
Efficiency net benefit (A+B+C+D) = $270
Referent Group net benefit (A+C or (A+B+C+D) – (B+D)) = $120
Non-referent Group net benefit (B+D) = $150

Distribution of Net Benefits

A= $100	B=$150
Taxes paid to Government	Profit to Foreign Company
($100)	($400 – 150 – 100=$150)
C= $20	**D=$0**
Profit on power supplies	None
($50 – $30)	

Example 6.6: Monopoly Power (based on Example 5.7)

A domestic company has been appointed the country's sole supplier of cellular phones, which require skilled labour to produce. The government is considering establishing a factory to produce computers, which require the same type of skilled labour. Domestic skilled labour resources are fully employed, and skilled labour cannot be imported. As a monopoly the phone producer maximizes profit by hiring labour to the point at which its marginal revenue product equals the wage. However the value of the marginal product of labour (its opportunity cost) is higher than this; in fact, it can be shown that the VMP = MRP[1/(1 − 1/e)], where VMP is the value of the marginal product of labour, MRP is the marginal revenue product and e is the elasticity of demand for the product, expressed as a positive number, at the current level of output of phones.

Suppose that, under the proposed computer project, the demand elasticity is 1.5 (we know it must exceed 1 since marginal revenue falls to zero as demand elasticity declines to 1); this means that an additional $100 worth of skilled labour used in phone production results in an extra $300 worth of output. Suppose that the proposed computer plant would employ $100 worth of skilled labour and produce $300 worth of computers. In the efficiency benefit-cost analysis we cost the labour at $300 because, under the assumption of full employment, the labour is diverted from phone production and $300 is the value of its marginal product in that activity, and we find that the net value of the project is zero. In terms of disaggregated referent group net benefits, the proposed computer operation earns a profit of $200, but this is offset by a $200 fall in the profits of the phone company.

Using the categories and symbols presented in Table 6.1, this example can be summarized as follows:

  Project net benefit (A+B) = $200
  Efficiency net benefit (A+B+C+D) = $0
  Referent Group net benefit (A+C or (A+B+C+D) − (B+D)) = $0
  Non-referent Group net benefit (B+D) = $0

Distribution of Net Benefits

A= $200	B=$0
Profits to Computer Firm	None
($300 − 100=$200)	
C= −$200	D=$0
Losses to Telephone Company	None
(−$200)	

Example 6.7: Monopsony Power (based on Example 5.8)

A domestic company which produces fabricated metal for the export market is the main employer in a remote town. Because the company has monopsony power in the labour market, it maximizes profit by restricting its hiring to drive down the market wage: it hires labour to the point at which the marginal factor cost (the addition to cost as a result of hiring an extra unit of labour) equals the value of the marginal product of labour (the addition to revenue as a result of selling the extra output on the world market). It can be shown that the marginal factor cost, MFC = W(1+1/e), where W is the market wage and e is the elasticity of supply of labour at the current level of employment. Suppose that the labour supply elasticity is 1 (it can generally take any positive value) then $100 worth of extra labour adds $200 to the value of output. Suppose that the government proposes establishing a factory which will use $100 worth of local labour to produce output of some other good valued at $300. In the efficiency benefit-cost analysis the labour is costed at $200, on the assumption that it is diverted from the monopsony's workforce, and the net value of the project is found to be $100. In terms of referent group net benefits, the proposed factory earns a profit of $200 which is partially offset by a $100 reduction in profit to the company already operating in the town.

Using the categories and symbols presented in Table 6.1, this example can be summarized as follows:

Project net benefit (A+B) = $200
Efficiency net benefit (A+B+C+D) = $100
Referent Group net benefit (A+C or (A+B+C+D) – (B+D)) = $100
Non-referent Group net benefit (B+D) = $0

Distribution of Net Benefits

A= $200 Profits to new company ($300 – 100)		B=$0 None
C= –$100 Losses to existing company (–$100)		D=$0 None

Further Examples

To complete the discussion of possible combinations of categories of project net benefits, two further examples follow.

Example 6.8: Where the Project and Efficiency Net Benefits are the Same

A local firm engages a foreign contractor to assist with the upgrade of an existing plant. The foreign contractor is paid a management fee at the going international rate of $300. The firm spends a further $500 on new technology, purchased abroad at the current world price. The result is an increase in the firm's output of exports, sold at the going world price, equal in value to $1200. The firm pays $100 additional taxes to government and shares the remaining profit 50:50 with the foreign contractor, who is not considered as part of the referent group. In this case the project net benefit is $400, and the private net benefit to the local firm after tax and profit sharing is $150. As all market prices relevant to the project reflect opportunity costs, and there are no non-marketed effects, the efficiency net benefit is also $400. The aggregate referent group benefits are $250: government receives $100 in taxes and the local firm's equity holders receive $150:

Project net benefit (A+B) = $400
Efficiency net benefit (A+B+C+D) = $400

Referent Group net benefit $(A+C$ or $(A+B+C+D) - (B+D)) = \$250$
Non-referent Group net benefit $(B+D) = \$150$

Distribution of Net Benefits

A=$250	B=$150
Profits to local firm	Profits to foreign contractor
($1200 – 800 – 150 – 100)	[50% x ($1200 – 800 – 100)]
Taxes to Government	
($100)	
C= $0	D=$0
	None

Example 6.9: Where there are Market and Non-Market Non-Referent Group Net Benefits

A farmer invests $400 in an irrigation project, including a new pump from an inter-state supplier on credit for $200. He employs some local casual labour for $100, and an inter-state irrigation consultant for $150. The value of his output of fruit at domestic prices increases by $800, but the project causes $10 in lost output due to reduced water flow to downstream users. He repays the credit to the pump supplier with $20 interest, and pays another $30 in taxes. The opportunity cost of the local labour is $50 and the opportunity cost of the inter-state consultant is $100. The value of the farmer's increased output at world prices is $750, which is the value at domestic prices less the tariff on imports of fruit. Assuming that all inter-state parties are non-referent group members, and that his additional output of fruit replaces imports, the calculation of net benefits is as follows:

Project net benefit $(A+B) = \$150$
Efficiency net benefit $(A+B+C+D) = \$190$
Referent Group net benefit $(A+C$ or $(A+B+C+D) - (B+D)) = \$120$
Non-referent Group net benefit $(B+D) = \$70$

Distribution of Efficiency Net Benefits

A= $130	B=$20
Profits to Farmer	Interest to inter-state supplier
($800 – 400 – 100 – 150 – 20 – 30=$100)	($20)
Taxes to Government	
($30)	
C= –$10	D=$50
Rent to local labour	Rent to inter-state consultant
($100 – 50=$50)	($150 – 100= $50)
Losses to downstream users	
(–$10)	
Loss of tariffs to government	
($750 – 800= –$50)	

Lessons from the Examples

What these examples show is that a proposed project can have two sorts of effects: efficiency effects resulting from the reallocation of scarce resources; and distributional effects determined by property rights as well as market imperfections, government interventions and distortions. The efficiency benefit-cost analysis measures only the efficiency effects of a project, whereas the referent group benefit-cost account measures the distribution of benefits among the referent group (and non-referent group) members. Leaving aside non-marketed effects for the present, members of the referent group experience benefits and costs mainly through changes in the levels of tax/transfer payments or private rents (the difference between the private and social perspective on rent is examined later in the discussion of the case study in the Appendix to this Chapter).

A rent is a payment made to a factor of production in excess of the payment required to keep it in its current use: economic profit and wages in excess of opportunity cost are examples of rents. The net benefits of a project – the value of its output less its opportunity cost – are shared out in the form of changes in rents or taxes: the sum of the changes (whether positive or negative) in the levels of the various kinds of rent and taxes equals the net value of the project from an efficiency perspective. However, not all those affected by changes in levels of rent or taxes are members of the referent group and an important role of the Referent Group Benefit-Cost Account is to detail changes in the levels of these payments accruing to that group.

The term "transfer" is often used to refer to changes in the levels of rents or tax receipts: the reason is that these changes simply transfer the real net benefits of the project among various groups. While the changes in these receipts or payments are very real to those affected, from the point of view of the economy as a whole they are purely pecuniary: in other words, their sole function is to distribute the project's marketed net benefits. No matter how complicated and involved the set of transfer payments is, the sum total of the net benefits to all the groups affected must equal the net benefits of the project as a whole.

Worked Example: Referent Group Analysis of National Fruit Growers' (NFG) Project

In Chapter 5 it was found that NFG's orchard project was unlikely to be considered worthwhile from an overall economic efficiency perspective. However, this does not necessarily mean that the project is not worthwhile from the perspective of the relevant Referent Group – the people of Black Valley where NFG's orchard is located. Indeed, you now learn that NFG is not a locally owned company. It is based in another State across the Kingsland River, in Goldsville. It is expected that NFG will remit all its after-tax earnings there. Furthermore, the money borrowed for the project and NFG's overdraft facility are both with the Goldwealth Bank based in Goldsville. As you are required to appraise this project from the perspective of the people of Black Valley, you would not include NFG or the Goldwealth Bank as part of the referent group.

The Referent Group consists of all project beneficiaries and losers other than those identified above. It will be assumed that the labour employed by NFG, the landowners who rent the land to NFG, and the fishers whose catches will be affected by the project all live in Black Valley. Thus, in summary, the Referent Group, in this example, consists of:

i.   the government who receives the taxes and duties and pays the subsidies;
ii.   the landowners who rent out their land to NFG;
iii.   the labour NFG employs who earn wages;
iv.   the downstream fishers who lose some income because of the run-off from the orchard.

The next step in the analysis of the NFG project is to calculate the total Referent Group net benefits. We can do this in two ways. We can simply subtract the net benefits to non-referent group members from the efficiency net benefit estimate; in the example this is done by subtracting the cash flows on NFG's equity after tax (Private Cash Flow) and on bank debt (see Figure 4.3 in Chapter 4) from the total Efficiency Cash Flow (Figure 5.14 in Chapter 5). However, this will provide us with only the aggregate Referent Group net benefit, which is insufficient if we want to know how part of the project's benefits and costs is distributed among the different sub-groups within the Referent Group. The alternative method is to calculate the benefits and costs to each of the four sub-groups identified above and to add these up. As a consistency check, the two methods should provide the same aggregate net benefit stream. This is demonstrated in Figure 6.2.

In Figure 6.2 row 4 derives the aggregate Referent Group cash flow as a residual by subtracting from the Efficiency Cash Flow the cash flows of the two non-referent groups: NFG and Goldwealth Bank. The rest of the spreadsheet derives the respective referent group benefits and costs from the key input data in Figure 5.13, where information on taxes, subsidies, duties, opportunity cost and external cost is provided. Note that rent to landowners is calculated by subtracting the opportunity cost (zero) from the amount paid, and similarly, rent to labour is found by subtracting labour's opportunity cost (20% of the wage) from the wage actually paid. Also note that import duties on imported machinery, vehicles and spare parts as part of fixed and working capital are included as revenues to government when the project is undertaken. Import duties forgone on the used equipment and working capital in year 20 are treated as a reduction in benefits to government.

What then is the bottom line? It might appear from the IRR (Cell C18) that the Referent Group does very well – the IRR is 66%. However care is required in interpreting this estimate; note also that the Referent Group NPVs are all *negative*! Why is this the case? The reason is that the signs of the Referent Group's cash flow are reversed in this instance as compared with those of a normal investment project; the cash flow begins with a positive sign in year 0 and thereafter is negative, with the exception of the last value. This corresponds to a situation of a loan from the borrower's perspective. In this case it is as if the Referent Group receives an initial cash inflow (loan) of $51.4 thousand in year 0, and then makes a series of cash payments (loan repayments) starting off at $40.7 thousand in year 1 and levelling off at $9.5 thousand over the latter years. In this instance the cost of the "loan" is 66% per annum.

The only reason why the project is seen as being profitable from a private investor's standpoint (as was shown in Chapter 4) is because it is heavily subsidized and the costs

File Edit View Insert Format Tools Data Window Help

	A	B	C	D	E	F	G	H	I	J	K	L	M	N	O	P	Q	R	S	T	U	V
1	TABLE 5: REFERENT GROUP CASH FLOW																					
2	ITEM/YEAR	0	1	2	3	4	5	6	7	8	9	10	11	12	13	14	15	16	17	18	19	20
3	Efficiency-Non ReferentCroup Cash Flow(NFG+Banks)																					
4	Total Ref. Gp.	51.4	-40.7	-31.9	-30.4	-29.0	-28.4	-22.8	-22.2	-21.5	-20.9	-20.2	-9.5	-9.5	-9.5	-9.5	-9.5	-9.5	-9.5	-9.5	-9.5	3.2
5	Distribution by Group																					
6	Total Govt.	51.4	-42.6	-25.8	-26.3	-26.8	-26.2	-20.6	-20.0	-19.3	-18.7	-18.0	-7.3	-7.3	-7.3	-7.3	-7.3	-7.3	-7.3	-7.3	-7.3	5.4
7	- imp. duties	51.4	0.4	0.8	1.2	1.6	1.6	1.6	1.6	1.6	1.6	1.6	1.6	1.6	1.6	1.6	1.6	1.6	1.6	1.6	1.6	-3.8
8	- indirect taxes		0.0	0.1	0.1	0.2	0.2	0.2	0.2	0.2	0.2	0.2	0.2	0.2	0.2	0.2	0.2	0.2	0.2	0.2	0.2	0.2
9	- susidies		-27.0	-18.4	-27.6	-36.8	-36.8	-36.8	-36.8	-36.8	-36.8	-36.8	-36.8	-36.8	-36.8	-36.8	-36.8	-36.8	-36.8	-36.8	-36.8	-19.0
10	- company taxes		-16.0	-8.3	0.0	8.3	8.9	14.5	15.1	15.8	16.4	17.1	27.8	27.8	27.8	27.8	27.8	27.8	27.8	27.8	27.8	27.8
11	Landowners' rent		0.8	1.5	2.3	3.0	3.0	3.0	3.0	3.0	3.0	3.0	3.0	3.0	3.0	3.0	3.0	3.0	3.0	3.0	3.0	3.0
12	Labour rent		1.2	2.4	3.6	4.8	4.8	4.8	4.8	4.8	4.8	4.8	4.8	4.8	4.8	4.8	4.8	4.8	4.8	4.8	4.8	4.8
13	Downstream users		0.0	-10.0	-10.0	-10.0	-10.0	-10.0	-10.0	-10.0	-10.0	-10.0	-10.0	-10.0	-10.0	-10.0	-10.0	-10.0	-10.0	-10.0	-10.0	-10.0
14	Referent Group	51.4	-40.7	-31.9	-30.4	-29.0	-28.4	-22.8	-22.2	-21.5	-20.9	-20.2	-9.5	-9.5	-9.5	-9.5	-9.5	-9.5	-9.5	-9.5	-9.5	3.2
15																						
16			5%	10%	15%																	
17	Net Present Value =		-$201.9	-$143.7	-$105.9																	
18	IRR =		66.0%																			
19	Disaggregated Net Benefits																					
20			5%	10%	15%																	
21	Government		-173.2	-124.1	-91.5																	
22	Landowners' rent		33.2	21.7	15.2																	
23	Labour rent		53.2	34.7	24.3																	
24	Downstream users		-115.1	-76.0	-53.9																	
25	Total Referent Gp		-$201.9	-$143.7	-$105.9																	
26	Non-Referent Gp		$433.3	$7.8	-$227.9																	

Callout boxes:
- Individual RG net benefits sum-up to aggregate RG net benefits
- Aggregate RG net benefits calculated as a residual (A+B+C+D) – (B+D)
- PV of net benefits to each RG stakeholder

Sheet tabs: Ex1c / Ch1Ex / Variables / ProjectBCA / PrivateBCA / EfficiencyBCA / RGBCA / Table

Figure 6.2 NFG Case Study: Referent Group Analysis Table

imposed on the fishing industry are not borne by the investor, NFG. The people of Black Valley would be unlikely to support this project given the availability of loans at lower interest rates than 66% per annum.

The left hand bottom corner of the spreadsheet shows the distribution of the project's net benefits among the Referent Group stakeholders (and the non-Referent Group). At a discount rate of 10% we see that the two major losers are: the government ($124.1 thousand); and the downstream fishers ($76 thousand). The gainers are: the landowners ($21.7 thousand); and labour ($34.7 thousand). If each dollar's worth of gains or losses to each stakeholder group is valued equally, the losses clearly outweigh the gains and the government will not support the project: NFG will not qualify for the subsidies. If the government does support it, the implication is that it values the interests of the gainers much more highly than the interests of the losers. The important question of the distribution of a project's gains and losses is dealt with in Chapter 11.

To summarize the results of the whole analysis it is useful to return to the multiple-account framework introduced in Chapter 1, and developed further in this Chapter, showing how any project's efficiency net benefits can be allocated among the four categories as shown in Figure 6.3. Note from Figure 6.3 that the direct tax flow is captured in the measure of project

A (+$92.6) Government (Direct taxes)	**B (+$7.8)** +$196.4 NFG −$188.6 Bank
C (−$236.3) −$216.7 Govt. (Ind. taxes) −$76 Downstream fishers +$21.7 Landowners +$34.7 Labour	**D ($0)** None

Figure 6.3 Distribution of Efficiency Net Benefits ($ thousands, @ 10% discount rate)

net benefit (A+B), but that some of the indirect tax and subsidy flows relating to inputs are not. The reason for this is that project net benefit is calculated on the basis of market prices which are gross of indirect taxes and subsidies on inputs, i.e. the price to the firm is the market price. This is why input tax and subsidy flows appear under Category C in Figure 6.3.

In this example there are no output taxes or subsidies. Since the project analysis is based on market prices, which are gross of output tax or net of subsidy, the price to the firm is lower or higher than the market price of output, depending on whether an output tax or subsidy is being considered. In this case the output tax or subsidy flows would not be included in Category B but would be included in the project analysis summarized by Categories A and B. Hence they would have to be included in Category A in Figure 6.3 in the same way as direct taxes.

To recap:

- Category A shows the Referent Group net benefits that are captured by market prices
- Category B shows the Non-Referent Group net benefits captured by market prices
- Category C shows the Referent Group net benefits that are *not* captured by market prices
- Category D shows the Non-Referent Group net benefits that are *not* captured by market prices
- Categories A+B+C+D = Aggregate Efficiency Net Benefits (−$135.9 NPV at 10% discount rate) as calculated in Chapter 5, Figure 5.14
- Categories A+B = Project Net Benefits (market prices) (+$100.4) as calculated in Chapter 4, Figure 4.2
- Categories A+C = Referent Group Net Benefits (−$143.7) as calculated in Chapter 6, Figure 6.2

APPENDIX TO CHAPTER 6:
Referent Group Net Benefits in the ICP Case Study

Let us now turn to the analysis of the referent group net benefits in the case study. The first step is to enumerate those groups likely to be affected. Following the procedure outlined above, we first calculate the total referent group net benefit by subtracting the flows of funds on ICP's equity and the foreign credit to derive the cash flow for Total Referent Group as shown in the top row of the spreadsheet in Figure A6.1.

We then need to identify and quantify the various components of the referent group net benefit, beginning with tax flows: government will be affected through changes in various kinds of tax revenues (business income taxes and tariffs in this case). We then consider inputs or outputs which have been shadow-priced: labour will be affected through provision of jobs for people who would otherwise be unemployed; public utilities will be affected through sale of extra power at a price exceeding production cost; and the domestic insurance sector is affected by charging in excess of cost for an insurance policy. Finally, we examine financial flows: domestic financial institutions will be affected through provision of a loan.

Each of these sub-groups should be represented by a sub-section in Part 5 of the spreadsheet analysis as shown in Figure A6.1. For example, in the government sub-section we enter rows representing each category of input or output which has consequences for government tariff revenue: for example, forgone tariff revenue as a result of import replacement, and additional tariff revenues as a result of imports of various kinds of capital goods and raw materials; and we also enter a row reporting changes in business income tax revenues. We also need a row representing domestic labour and one representing the electricity utility. In the financial institutions sub-section we need a row representing the domestic bank and another row representing the domestic insurance company. As the various categories of referent group net benefits are calculated, it can be seen that what is recorded as a cost in one part of the benefit-cost analysis can appear as a benefit in another. For example, the wage bill is a cost to the firm, but a portion of the wage bill is a net benefit to domestic labour; taxes and tariffs are costs to the firm but benefits to the government; and the power bill is a cost to the firm, but a portion of it is a net benefit to the domestic utility. The loan received from the domestic bank is a benefit to the firm but a cost to the bank, and the interest and loan repayments are costs to the firm but benefits to the bank.

We now proceed to fill in the rows we have provided for the various referent group benefits and costs over the life of the project. As in the case of Parts 2 to 4 (Figures A4.2, A4.3 and A5.1) of the spreadsheet, all entries are cell addresses taken from the data reported in Part 1 (Figure A4.1). Tariff revenues obtained when the project imports an input, or forgone when the project output replaces an import, are entered in their various categories. Business tax revenues forgone when project costs are written off against other company income, or obtained when the project makes a profit are entered for each year. Similarly, half of the firm's power bill is entered as a benefit as it represents extra profit for the electricity utility. The amounts advanced by the domestic bank are entered as costs, and the interest and principal repayments are entered as benefits. Finally, the amount paid to the domestic insurance company is entered as a benefit.

The merits of treating the full amount of the insurance premium as a referent group benefit can be debated: we are treating the payment as if it were a straight transfer but of

> Total referent group net benefits are derived by subtracting flows on ICP's equity and the foreign loan from the efficiency cash flow

> Import duties gained and lost on all imported goods, including working capital, must be included

YEAR	1999 '000 US$	1999 MN BT	2000 MN BT	2001 MN BT	2002 MN BT	2003 MN BT	2004 MN BT	2005 MN BT	2006 MN BT	2007 MN BT	2008 MN BT	2009 MN BT
TOTAL REFERENT GROUP	28.670	-62.911	32.151	33.330	34.603	35.977	37.462	37.462	37.462	37.462	37.462	91.647
- IMPORT DUTIES												
YARN			-18.000	-36.000	-36.000	-36.000	-36.000	-36.000	-36.000	-36.000	-36.000	-36.000
COTTON			10.692	21.384	21.384	21.384	21.384	21.384	21.384	21.384	21.384	21.384
EQUIPMENT	1.870											
SPINDLES	8.800											
MATERIALS INVENTORY			5.280									-5.280
SPARES INVENTORY			0.535									-0.535
SPARES			1.067	1.067	1.067	1.067	1.067	1.067	1.067	1.067	1.067	1.067
- TAXES			-13.285	27.100	28.279	29.552	30.926	32.411	32.411	32.411	32.411	32.411
(i) TOTAL GOVERNMENT	10.670		13.711	13.551	14.730	16.003	17.377	18.862	18.862	18.862	18.862	13.047
(ii) POWER SUPPLIER			1.800	3.600	3.600	3.600	3.600	3.600	3.600	3.600	3.600	3.600
(iii) LABOUR	18.000		3.000	3.000	3.000	3.000	3.000	3.000	3.000	3.000	3.000	3.000
(iv) DOMESTIC BANK			-60.000	6.000	6.000	6.000	6.000	6.000	6.000	6.000	6.000	66.000
(v) INSURANCE			6.000	6.000	6.000	6.000	6.000	6.000	6.000	6.000	6.000	6.000
TOTAL REFERENT GROUP	28.670	-62.911	32.151	33.330	34.603	35.977	37.462	37.462	37.462	37.462	37.462	91.647

NPV ($mn)	Total	Govt.	Power Co.	Labour	Dom. Bank	Insur. Co.
4%	260.4	116.2	27.5	42.3	25.7	48.7
8%	201.3	93.4	22.5	38.1	6.9	40.3
12%	158.3	76.5	18.7	35.0	-5.7	33.9
16%	126.6	63.6	15.8	32.5	-14.3	29.0
0%	343.3	147.1	34.2	48.0	54.0	60.0

> Unskilled labour 'gains' half of what it earns

> The power company 'gains' half of what it charges

Figure A6.1 ICP Project Solution: The Referent Group Cash Flow

course the firm is also shifting some of its risk to the domestic insurance company and this must represent a cost to the latter. An alternative approach is to assume that the cost of risk exactly matches the insurance premium, in which case there is no net benefit to the insurance company. If this approach is taken, then the insurance premium has to be included as a cost in the efficiency benefit-cost analysis. In reality the true nature of the payment is somewhere between these two extremes: a part of it represents the cost of extra risk borne by the insurance company, and a part is simply a contribution to overhead costs or profits.

It was argued that unskilled labour would be paid twice the value of what it could otherwise earn, so half of the unskilled labour wage bill in each year is entered as a net benefit to labour. In the case study we assume that the value of what labour could otherwise earn is also the value of what it could otherwise produce. However, as discussed in Chapter 5, the value of what labour can earn in subsistence agriculture may be different from the value of the extra production it generates because of the open-access, or communal nature of some land and water resources. Under open-access it is usually a safe assumption that extra labour applied to these resources adds nothing to the value of total output. In that case the labour would be shadow-priced at zero in the efficiency benefit-cost analysis, thereby increasing the aggregate net benefit of the project.

This example illustrates the difference between the private and social perspectives on rents. When a worker leaves subsistence activity for a more rewarding job in the city, the rent generated from a private perspective is measured by the difference between the wage earned in the city and the value of the worker's share in the output of the subsistence activity (we are ignoring any non-monetary net benefits such as improved living conditions). From a social or economy-wide point of view, if the value of the worker's marginal product is zero in the subsistence activity, the rent generated by the move from subsistence activity to participation in the labour market is measured by the whole of the worker's wage in the city. The reason for this is that there is no cost to the economy, in the form of reduced output, as a result of a worker leaving the subsistence activity. In summary, while the worker's private net benefit is the difference between her remuneration in the two activities, the social or economy-wide net benefit is the value of the additional output in the market activity.

How would this difference between private and social rents show up in the referent group analysis? We have already assigned the difference between the wage and the value of what the workers would have taken home as the result of subsistence agriculture as a net benefit to unskilled workers on the project. If withdrawing these workers from subsistence activities has no effect on the value of total output of such activities, the remaining subsistence workers experience an increase in the quantity and value of the produce they take home: in effect the "subsistence cake" is divided among fewer participants and each gets a slightly larger share. If subsistence workers are part of the referent group then we would need to add a new row in the spreadsheet to record the value of this net benefit.

Assuming that the total value of subsistence output has not changed as a result of some workers quitting subsistence activity to work on the project, the amount of the transfer to subsistence workers is measured by the share of subsistence output which would have been received by the workers who left to participate in the ICP project. When we add this amount to referent group net benefits, it turns out that, while the wage bill is a cost to the firm, it is a net benefit to the referent group, some of which goes to workers employed on the project, and the balance to those who remain in subsistence activity. In the efficiency analysis the zero opportunity cost of a marginal amount of subsistence labour would be recognized by shadow-pricing the labour at zero, thereby increasing the efficiency net benefits by the amount paid to unskilled labour, as compared with the situation in which project labour is diverted from market activity.

Once the various rows representing referent sub-group benefits and costs have been filled in, the rows can be aggregated to give a summary statement of the net benefits to the referent group as a whole. The row representing this aggregate value should be identical in every year to the Total Referent Group net benefits we obtained in the top row of Figure A6.1 by subtracting non-referent group net benefits from the efficiency net benefits of the project. If an error has occurred it can usually be readily identified: if the two net benefit streams are different in each and every year then a whole category of net benefits may have been omitted or an inappropriate shadow-price adopted. On the other hand if the difference is in one year only there may be some problem with costing capital or with some other irregular payment or receipt. In their first attempt at the case study the authors noted a discrepancy in the last year of the project: they forgot to allow for the import-replacing effect on tariff revenues of running down inventory, thereby replacing some annual imports of materials and spare parts.

Once the net benefit stream to the referent group has been calculated, a summary figure is normally obtained by calculating a net present value (NPV), or, sometimes but infrequently, an internal rate of return (IRR). The net benefits to sub-groups within the referent group can also be summarized in this way, although it should be noted that for some groups, such as domestic labour, there may be no project costs and hence no IRR to be computed. The NPV is the appropriate measure at this level of disaggregation, and it has the advantage of corresponding to the notional sums specified under the potential Pareto improvement criterion to be taken from beneficiaries or paid to those who bear the costs in order to maintain pre-existing levels of economic welfare.

We have now completed the basic benefit-cost analysis of the ICP Case Study. Figure A6.2 assembles Tables 1–5, which were derived in Chapters 4–6, in the form of a single spreadsheet. As discussed below this spreadsheet can be used for various types of sensitivity analysis. It will also serve as a basis for comparison when we consider more advanced topics in Chapters 7–10. At the end of each of these Chapters an amended version of Figure A6.2 incorporating an additional feature of a benefit-cost analysis will be presented to illustrate how some advanced concepts are accounted for in practical analysis. In each case the reader will be invited to compare the amended Figure with the base case described by Figure A6.2.

The Discount Rate

In calculating net present values a range of discount rates, incorporating the domestic government bond rate, should be used. Since no attempt was made in the case study to inflate benefits or costs, a real rate of interest is required and the use of a single real rate of interest involves the implicit assumption that all prices change at the general rate of inflation. We use a range of discount rates in the analysis for two reasons: first, as to be discussed in Chapter 10, there may be valid arguments why the market rate of interest should be replaced by a shadow (or social) discount rate, and we may not know at this stage what that rate should be; and, second, we want to see how sensitive the NPV is to the choice of discount rate (if it is very sensitive this compounds the difficulty posed by the uncertainty about the appropriate discount rate). Sensitivity of the NPV to the values of other key variables, such as the exchange rate, can also be ascertained at this stage. Because of the way we have constructed the spreadsheet, with all entries in Parts 2 to 5 being composed of cell addresses in Part 1, all we have to do is to change the value of a variable, such as the exchange rate, in Part 1 to have the spreadsheet recalculate the NPV.

Comparing Alternative Scenarios

In addition to seeing how sensitive the project NPV is to the choice of discount rate and other key variables, we want to see how sensitive it is to the project design. This is part of the benefit-cost analyst's pro-active role in helping to design the best project from the client's point of view. We have just completed the analysis of the basic project, but in discussions with the client we asked a whole series of questions: what about varying the location of the project; what about varying the tax regime – offering various types of concessions to make the project more attractive to the foreign firm. We can take the base case analysis just completed and edit

ICP PROJECT: 1999-2009

TABLE 1 — KEY INPUT VARIABLES

VARIABLES		INVESTMENT C(	000 $'	000 BT'	INNING COSTS		MATERIAL FLOWS		FINANCE	
EXCHANGE RATE	44	SPINDLES	4000		WATER BT I	480000	COTTON MN	16.2	SUPPLIERS	75%
TARIFF A	5%	EQUIPMEN	850		POWER BT I	480000	YARN MN LB	15	OVERDRAF	60
TARIFF B	10%	INSTALLA	100		SPARE PAR	10%	LABOUR 1	100	CREDIT RE	5
PROFITS TAX	50%	CONSTRUCTION	36000	INSURANCE	6	LABOUR 2	1000		
DEPRECIATION	10%	START-UP COSTS	18000	OVERHEAD!	0	LABOUR 3	500		
PRICE YARN CIF US$	0.58	WORKING CAPITAL							DISCOUNT	4%
YARN TARIFF BT	2.1	RAW MAT	1200							8%
HANDLING BT	0.3	SPARE PAI	243							12%
TARIFF C	10%									16%
PRICE COTTON CIF US!	0.3									
WAGE 1 BT PA	150000									
WAGE 2 BT PA	22500									
WAGE 3 BT PA	12000									
INTEREST RATE 1	8%									
INTEREST RATE 2	10%									

TABLE 2 — PROJECT CALCULATION

YEAR	1999 '000 US$	1999 MN BT	2000 MN BT	2001 MN BT	2002 MN BT	2003 MN BT	2004 MN BT	2005 MN BT	2006 MN BT	2007 MN BT	2008 MN BT	2009 MN BT
INVESTMENT COSTS												
SPINDLES	-4200.000	-184.800										
EQUIPMENT	-892.500	-39.270										
INSTALLATION	-100.000	-4.400										
CONSTRUCTION		-36.000										
START-UP COSTS		-18.000										
RAW MATERIALS			-58.080									58.080
SPARE PARTS			-11.227									11.227
TOTAL	-282.470	-69.307	0.000	0.000	0.000	0.000	0.000	0.000	0.000	0.000	0.000	69.307
RUNNING COSTS												
WATER			-3.600	-7.200	-7.200	-7.200	-7.200	-7.200	-7.200	-7.200	-7.200	-7.200
POWER			-3.600	-7.200	-7.200	-7.200	-7.200	-7.200	-7.200	-7.200	-7.200	-7.200
SPARE PARTS			-22.407	-22.407	-22.407	-22.407	-22.407	-22.407	-22.407	-22.407	-22.407	-22.407
RAW MATERIALS			-117.612	-235.224	-235.224	-235.224	-235.224	-235.224	-235.224	-235.224	-235.224	-235.224
INSURANCE			-6.000	-6.000	-6.000	-6.000	-6.000	-6.000	-6.000	-6.000	-6.000	-6.000
LABOUR			-43.500	-43.500	-43.500	-43.500	-43.500	-43.500	-43.500	-43.500	-43.500	-43.500
TOTAL			-196.719	-321.531	-321.531	-321.531	-321.531	-321.531	-321.531	-321.531	-321.531	-321.531
REVENUES												
SALE OF YARN			209.400	418.800	418.800	418.800	418.800	418.800	418.800	418.800	418.800	418.800
NCF (Project)	-282.470	-56.626	97.269	97.269	97.269	97.269	97.269	97.269	97.269	97.269	97.269	166.576

TABLE 3 — PRIVATE CALCULATION

YEAR	1999 '000 US$	1999 MN BT	2000 MN BT	2001 MN BT	2002 MN BT	2003 MN BT	2004 MN BT	2005 MN BT	2006 MN BT	2007 MN BT	2008 MN BT	2009 MN BT
FINANCIAL FLOWS												
DEPRECIATION			-26.447	-26.447	-26.447	-26.447	-26.447	-26.447	-26.447	-26.447	-26.447	-26.447
INTEREST												
SUPPLIERS CREDIT	3637.500	160.050	-12.804	-10.621	-8.264	-5.719	-2.969					
REPAYMENT			-27.282	-29.464	-31.821	-34.367	-37.116					
BANK OVERDRAFT			60.000	-6.000	-6.000	-6.000	-6.000	-6.000	-6.000	-6.000	-6.000	-6.000
REPAYMENT												-60.000
NET OPERATING REVENUE			12.681	97.269	97.269	97.269	97.269	97.269	97.269	97.269	97.269	97.269
TAXABLE PROFIT			-26.570	54.201	56.558	59.103	61.853	64.822	64.822	64.822	64.822	64.822
PROFIT TAX			13.285	-27.100	-28.279	-29.552	-30.926	-32.411	-32.411	-32.411	-32.411	-32.411
FLOW OF OWN FUNDS	-122.420	-23.426	24.083	22.905	21.632	20.257	58.858	58.858	58.858	58.858	68.165	

TABLE 4 — EFFICIENCY CALCULATION

YEAR	1999 '000 US$	1999 MN BT	2000 MN BT	2001 MN BT	2002 MN BT	2003 MN BT	2004 MN BT	2005 MN BT	2006 MN BT	2007 MN BT	2008 MN BT	2009 MN BT
INVESTMENT COSTS												
SPINDLES	-4000.000	-176.000										
EQUIPMENT	-850.000	-37.400										
INSTALLATION	-100.000	-4.400										
CONSTRUCTION		-18.000										
START-UP COSTS		-18.000										
RAW MATERIALS			-52.800									52.800
SPARE PARTS			-10.692									10.692
TOTAL	-253.800	-63.492	0.000	0.000	0.000	0.000	0.000	0.000	0.000	0.000	0.000	63.492
RUNNING COSTS												
WATER			-3.600	-7.200	-7.200	-7.200	-7.200	-7.200	-7.200	-7.200	-7.200	-7.200
POWER			-1.800	-3.600	-3.600	-3.600	-3.600	-3.600	-3.600	-3.600	-3.600	-3.600
SPARE PARTS			-21.340	-21.340	-21.340	-21.340	-21.340	-21.340	-21.340	-21.340	-21.340	-21.340
RAW MATERIALS			-106.920	-213.840	-213.840	-213.840	-213.840	-213.840	-213.840	-213.840	-213.840	-213.840
INSURANCE & RENT			0.000	0.000	0.000	0.000	0.000	0.000	0.000	0.000	0.000	0.000
LABOUR			-40.500	-40.500	-40.500	-40.500	-40.500	-40.500	-40.500	-40.500	-40.500	-40.500
TOTAL			-174.160	-286.480	-286.480	-286.480	-286.480	-286.480	-286.480	-286.480	-286.480	-286.480
REVENUES												
SALE OF YARN			191.400	382.800	382.800	382.800	382.800	382.800	382.800	382.800	382.800	382.800
NET EFFICIENCY BENEFIT	-253.800	-46.252	96.320	96.320	96.320	96.320	96.320	96.320	96.320	96.320	159.812	

TABLE 5 — REFERENT GROUP ANALYSIS

YEAR	1999 '000 US$	1999 MN BT	2000 MN BT	2001 MN BT	2002 MN BT	2003 MN BT	2004 MN BT	2005 MN BT	2006 MN BT	2007 MN BT	2008 MN BT	2009 MN BT
TOTAL REFERENT GROUP	28.670	-62.911	32.151	33.330	34.603	35.977	37.462	37.462	37.462	37.462	91.647	
- IMPORT DUTIES												
YARN			-18.000	-36.000	-36.000	-36.000	-36.000	-36.000	-36.000	-36.000	-36.000	-36.000
COTTON			10.692	21.384	21.384	21.384	21.384	21.384	21.384	21.384	21.384	21.384
EQUIPMENT		1.870										
SPINDLES		8.800										
MATERIALS INVENTORY			5.280									-5.280
SPARES INVENTORY			0.535									-0.535
SPARES			1.067	1.067	1.067	1.067	1.067	1.067	1.067	1.067	1.067	1.067
- TAXES			-13.285	27.100	28.279	29.552	30.926	32.411	32.411	32.411	32.411	32.411
(i) TOTAL GOVERNMENT	10.670	-13.711	13.551	14.730	16.003	17.377	18.862	18.862	18.862	18.862	13.047	
(ii) POWER SUPPLIER		1.800	3.600	3.600	3.600	3.600	3.600	3.600	3.600	3.600	3.600	3.600
(iii) LABOUR	18.000	3.000	3.000	3.000	3.000	3.000	3.000	3.000	3.000	3.000	3.000	
(iv) DOMESTIC BANK	0.000	-60.000	6.000	6.000	6.000	6.000	6.000	6.000	6.000	6.000	6.000	
												60.000
(v) INSURANCE	6.000	6.000	6.000	6.000	6.000	6.000	6.000	6.000	6.000	6.000		
TOTAL REFERENT GROUP	28.670	-62.911	32.151	33.330	34.603	35.977	37.462	37.462	37.462	37.462	91.647	

PROJECT		PRIVATE		EFFICIENCY		REFERENT GROUP			
NPV	$(Mn)	IRR (%)		$(Mn)	IRR(%)	NPV	$ (MN)	IRR (%)	NPV	$ (MN)	IRR (%)
4%	405.3	20.6%	4%	154.5	16.7%	4%	433.2	23.4%	4%	260.4	n/a
8%	259.8		8%	88.7		8%	289.9		8%	201.3	
12%	152.0		12%	40.8		12%	183.6		12%	158.3	
16%	70.7		16%	5.4		16%	103.2		16%	126.6	
0%	605.6		0%	246.6		0%	630.3		0%	343.3	

Figure A6.2 ICP Project Solutions: Consolidated Tables

it to analyse the project NPV and the referent group benefits under various alternative scenarios. For example, suppose that the firm was allowed to import raw materials free of import duty: we change the raw materials tariff rate in its cell entry in Part 1 to zero, save the spreadsheet as a new file, and we now have a complete set of results under this scenario. Suppose that the government insisted that the firm locate in a depressed area; this would involve additional costs which can be entered in Part 1 and edited into Parts 2 to 5 to give a set of results under this scenario, and so on.

It would also be possible to develop the basic analysis to determine the effects on the firm and the referent group of various ownership structures for the project. For example, the domestic government may acquire equity in the project, either by purchasing it or simply by being given it in return for allowing the project to proceed. The project might be developed as a joint venture with members of the referent group contributing both equity capital and management expertise, or the domestic government might acquire all of the equity in the project and obtain the foreign firm's expertise under a management contract.

While it is very easy to generate results for a range of scenarios identified to be of interest to the client, it is not so easy to present the results in a readily digestible way. There is a danger in swamping the client with detail so that the wood cannot be seen for the trees! While Chapter 14 discusses in detail the presentation of the results of a benefit-cost analysis, we consider some issues relevant to the case study here.

A useful way to proceed is to think in terms of trade-offs. Some scenarios will be more advantageous to the firm – those involving tax and tariff concessions, for example – and some will be more advantageous to the referent group – location of the plant in a depressed area, for example. A *Summary Table* can be prepared which shows how the net benefits to the various parties change as we move from one scenario to another. For example, scenarios could be ranked in descending order of referent group net benefits; this may correspond loosely to ascending order of foreign firm benefits. Project feasibility is established by some cut-off value for the net benefits of the private agent (the individual, the firm, the farm or whatever); scenarios ranked lower than this will simply not occur. This establishes the feasible set of scenarios from among which the client can elect to choose the project design offering the highest aggregate referent group net benefits, or perhaps the preferred distribution of net benefits among referent group members. While it is useful to think in terms of trade-offs – one group getting more at the expense of another group – there are "win–win" situations where the additional net benefits of a more efficient project can be shared to the benefit of all groups.

Where there are trade-offs among referent group members, the distribution of net benefits among stakeholder groups could be a criterion for comparing and ranking alternatives. This might be the case where the government is committed to raising the economic welfare of disadvantaged groups such as residents of deprived regions, or particular socio-economic classes. The disaggregated referent group analysis provides important information for assessing the distributional implications of the project. The issue of distribution objectives and how these can be incorporated explicitly into benefit-cost analysis is discussed further in Chapter 11.

Further Reading

The further reading suggested for Chapter 5 is also relevant for Chapter 6. The term "referent group" does not appear to be used much in contemporary studies of benefit-cost analysis. An early use of this term in discussion of the principles of benefit-cost analysis occurs in V. W. Loose (ed.), *Guidelines for Benefit-Cost Analysis* (British Columbia Environment and Land Use Secretariat, 1977).

Exercises

1. A local firm hires $150 of unskilled labour at the minimum wage and constructs a walking track, for which it is paid $180 by the State Government. The firm incurs no other cost, apart from the wage bill, in constructing the track. The government is to charge a fee to users of the track, and the present value of the fees paid is estimated to be $100. Consumers place a net present value (net of the fees and any other costs incurred) of $50 on the track's services. The labour employed to construct the track would otherwise be unemployed, and the value of its non-market activity is estimated to be $50.
   (i) calculate the net benefit of the project to each member of the referent group:
       (a) the firm
       (b) consumers
       (c) labour
       (d) the government;
   (ii) using the appropriate shadow-price of labour, calculate the efficiency net benefit of the project.

2. The State Government hires a computer programmer from another State for a month at a cost of $30,000, which is $10,000 more than she could earn during that period in her home State. The State Government also pays $1000 for accommodation in a rent-controlled apartment with a market value of $1200. The programmer edits some programs and saves the State Government $40,000. Assuming the referent group consists of residents of the State:
   (i) calculate the net benefit to the referent group
   (ii) using the appropriate shadow-prices, calculate the net benefit of the project according to an efficiency benefit-cost analysis.

3. A foreign firm is considering a project which has, at market prices, a present value of benefits of $200 and a present value of input costs of $130. If the project goes ahead, tax with a present value of $50 will be paid to the host country, domestic labour which would otherwise be unemployed will be paid wages with a present value of $50 for working on the project (the wage bill is included in the input costs referred to above), and pollution caused by the project will reduce the value of output elsewhere in the host country's

economy by $10. Assuming that the owners of the foreign firm are not part of the referent group, and that the opportunity cost of unemployed labour is 50% of the market wage, what are the net present values generated by:
(i)   the project benefit-cost analysis;
(ii) the private benefit-cost analysis;
(iii) the efficiency benefit-cost analysis;
(iv) the referent group benefit-cost analysis?

4. For the ICP Case Study prepare a summary table of net benefits (discounted at 8%) in the same format as Figure 6.3.

7

Consumer and Producer Surplus in Benefit-Cost Analysis

Introduction

So far in this book it has been assumed that undertaking a proposed project would have no effect on the market prices of goods and services. However, since the market economy consists of a complex network of inter-related output and input markets, it is possible, in principle, that undertaking the project will have wide-ranging effects on market prices. If the project's output or input quantities are small relative to the amounts traded in the markets for these goods and services, the effects on market prices will be small enough to be ignored, on the grounds that including them would have no bearing on the outcome of the analysis. While this "small project assumption" is a reasonable one for many of the projects which the analyst will encounter, it is necessary to be able to identify circumstances in which price changes are relevant, and to know how to deal with them in the benefit-cost analysis.

A project increases the aggregate supply of the output produced by the project, and increases the aggregate demand for the inputs used in the project. Significant changes in market supply or demand can result in changes in market prices. A significant change in supply or demand is one that is large relative to the quantity that would be bought and sold in the market in the absence of the project being undertaken. It is evident that there is little chance of such a change occurring where the output or input in question is traded on international markets, as will be discussed in Chapter 8. Few countries, let alone individual projects, have the capacity to alter world prices by changing their levels of supply of, or demand for, goods and services.

Where non-traded goods are concerned, a project can cause a change in the market price of its output or its inputs where the level of output or input is large relative to the total quantity exchanged in the domestic market. This is most likely to occur where the relevant market is local or regional, rather than national in extent. Examples are local markets in transport services or irrigation water, and regional labour markets. Such goods and services have, at a national level, some of the characteristics which make commodities non-tradeable at the international level – principally relatively high transportation costs.

If a project is large enough at the local or regional level to cause changes in the market prices of goods and services it produces as outputs, or consumes as inputs, these price changes may affect the prices of complementary or substitute products traded in other markets. For example, a project which provides a new route into the city through provision of a bridge may result in increased demand for apartments in the area served by the bridge. Given a relatively inelastic supply of apartments, the increase in demand for this service, which is complementary to the service provided by the bridge, will result in a price increase. Apartments which are not favourably located relative to the bridge offer substitute services, and demand for these may fall once the bridge is constructed, leading to a fall in market price. The analyst needs to be able to determine the relevance, if any, of such price changes to the benefit-cost analysis.

This Chapter illustrates the implications of price changes for the benefit-cost analysis by considering a number of examples. In the first set of examples, undertaking the project results in a significant increase in the supply of the good or service produced by the project. Three cases are considered: where the market supply curve of the good or service is horizontal (perfectly elastic), upward sloping (positive elasticity of supply), and vertical (perfectly inelastic). An urban transportation project is used to illustrate the first case; an investment in job training the second; and an increase in the supply of irrigation water the third. In each case the emphasis will be on measuring project benefits, with little attention paid to costs. Following these examples in which the price of the project output changes, a case in which undertaking the project causes a change in an input price is considered. This case is illustrated by a rural labour market which serves farms which benefit from an increased supply of irrigation water.

In considering the above examples we will assume that there are no market imperfections as described in Chapter 5. This means that there will be no need to shadow-price the market values discussed in the examples in order to calculate benefits from an efficiency viewpoint. In general, however, the procedures described in Chapter 5 can be applied to obtain the appropriate valuations in the presence of price changes.

Two concepts which will be important in the discussion are the difference between real and pecuniary effects, and the notion of surplus accruing to producers or consumers. We have already encountered the notion of pecuniary effects in our discussion of transfers in Chapter 6 and, along with the notion of surplus, it will feature significantly in the examples to be discussed below. We now review these concepts briefly before considering the examples.

Real *vs.* Pecuniary Effects

Efficiency benefit-cost analysis can be thought of as concerned with the "size of the cake": does the project provide a net addition to the value of goods and services available to the world economy? Changes to the quantities of goods and services available are termed "real" changes, in contrast to "pecuniary" changes which represent changes in entitlements to shares in a "cake" of given size. For example, suppose that the price of a commodity falls but the quantity produced and consumed remains constant, so that there is no real effect. However buyers of the commodity are better off, and suppliers worse off to the same extent. The gain to buyers and the loss to sellers are termed pecuniary effects and they have the characteristic that they net out of an efficiency analysis. Because pecuniary effects measure changes in entitlement to an existing flow of goods and services, they are referred to as transfers – they transfer benefits or costs from one group to another. While they are not relevant in efficiency analysis, they must, as we saw in Chapter 6, be accounted for in referent group analysis which is concerned with the benefits and costs of the project to a subset of agents in the world economy.

Consumer Surplus

A surplus is generated when a consumer is able to buy a unit of a good at a price lower than her willingness to pay for that unit, or when a producer is able to sell a unit of a good or factor of production at a price higher than that at which he would willingly part with that unit. The concept of consumer surplus can be explained by means of Figure 7.1, which illustrates an individual consumer's demand for a commodity: according to the diagram, the consumer is willing to pay $0E$ dollars for the first unit of the good she purchases, and lower amounts, as measured by the demand curve, labelled D in Figure 7.1, for subsequent units until she is just willing to pay the current market price P_0, and no more, for the last unit she purchases. The reason the consumer is not willing to purchase more than Q_0 units is that additional units are worth less, as measured by the height of the demand curve, than the market price. The consumer's total willingness to pay for $0Q_0$ units of the good is measured by the area EAQ_00, while the actual amount she pays is measured by P_0AQ_00. The difference between these two amounts is termed the consumer surplus – the value to the consumer of the quantity $0Q_0$ over and above what she actually has to pay – and it is measured by area EAP_0.

Now suppose that the market price of the commodity falls from P_0 to P_1, as illustrated in Figure 7.1. The consumer will increase the quantity of the commodity she purchases from Q_0 to Q_1, because, as indicated by her demand curve, some additional units of the commodity are worth more to her than the new price P_1. The area of consumer surplus at the new price and quantity demanded becomes ECP_1, representing an increase in consumer surplus of P_0ACP_1.

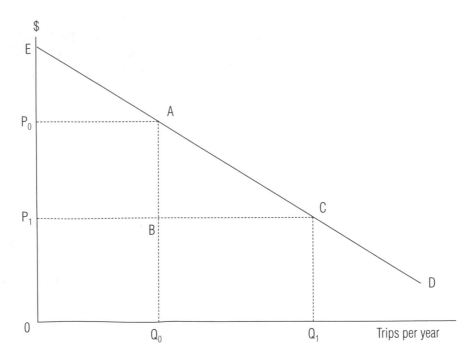

Figure 7.1 Consumer Surplus

The increase in the amount of consumer surplus can be regarded as a measure of the benefit the consumer has received as a result of the fall in the price of the commodity.

An intuitive explanation of why the area P_0ACP_1 measures the benefit of the price fall to the individual consumer runs as follows. When the price falls from P_0 to P_1 the consumer benefits by the amount $(P_0 - P_1)$ on each unit of the commodity she originally purchased, thereby saving her an amount measured by area P_0ABP_1. This amount is effectively extra "cash in hand" which can be used to purchase additional quantities of any commodities the consumer fancies. As an aside, it can be noted that, since we are concerned, at present, only with the benefit to this individual consumer it is not necessary for us to inquire whether the benefit is real or pecuniary as discussed above. When the price of the commodity falls from P_0 to P_1 the consumer purchases the additional quantity $(Q_1 - Q_0)$. The reason she increases the quantity purchased is that, as indicated by the demand curve, each of the extra units of the commodity is worth at least as much to her as the new market price. For example, the first additional unit she purchases is worth P_0 and the last additional unit is worth P_1. The extra consumer surplus obtained from the first additional unit purchased is measured by $(P_0 - P_1)$, and that from the last additional unit by $(P_1 - P_1)$, or zero. The total consumer surplus contributed by the additional quantity purchased is measured by area ACB. When this amount is added to the additional surplus obtained from the original quantity purchased, the total benefit is measured by area P_0ACP_1.

The Kaldor–Hicks Criterion

As noted in Chapter 1, a benefit-cost analysis is an attempt at implementing the Kaldor–Hicks (K–H) criterion for an improvement in economic welfare: the project contributes to an increase in welfare if the gainers from the project could, in principle, compensate the losers – in other words, if the project represents a potential Pareto improvement. The gain to an individual is measured by the sum of money which, if the project were undertaken, could be taken from her while still leaving her as well off as she would have been in the absence of the project. Conversely, a loss is measured as a sum of money which must be paid to an individual to compensate her for the effects of the project. We now consider what the relationship is between those sums of money, hypothetically to be paid to or received by a person affected by a project, and termed **compensating variations,** and the concept of consumer surplus. It is important to stress that these are hypothetical sums, and that benefit-cost analysis does not require that compensation is actually paid or received.

Consider first an individual's demand curve that is perfectly inelastic, as illustrated in Figure 7.2(a). When price falls from P_0 to P_1 the consumer receives a windfall gain amounting to area P_0AFP_1. This latter amount could be taken away from the consumer, following the fall in price, and she *could* still buy the same quantities of goods as she did before the fall in price, and *would*, in fact, still choose those quantities. In other words, if the price falls from P_0 to P_1 *and* the consumer was made to give up P_0AFP_1 dollars, she would be exactly as well off after the fall in price as she was before. Hence, in terms of the K–H criterion, P_0AFP_1 dollars measures the benefit of the price fall, and, conversely, measures the cost to the individual (the amount she would have to be paid in compensation) if price rose from P_1 to P_0.

Now consider an individual's elastic demand curve for a good as illustrated in Figure 7.2(b). If price fell from P_0 to P_1, and no sum of money was taken in compensation, the individual would increase quantity demanded as a result of two effects. First, when the price of a good falls the individual experiences an increase in purchasing power similar to that which would result from an increase in income. When income increases the individual will increase the quantity consumed of all normal goods, including, we assume, the good whose price has fallen. This type of increase in the quantity of the good consumed as a result of the fall in its price is termed the **income effect** of the price change. The second type of effect, termed the **substitution effect** of the price change, refers to the fact that when the price of a good falls, but purchasing power is held constant, an individual will be able to increase her economic welfare by purchasing more of the now relatively cheaper good, and less of other goods.

If the price of the good fell from P_0 to P_1 and the sum P_0AFP_1 dollars was taken from the individual in compensation, the income effect of the price change would be nullified, but the substitution effect would still occur. The individual *could* still buy the same quantities of goods as she did before the fall in price, but, because of the substitution effect, *would not* choose that bundle of goods. Instead she would elect to improve her economic welfare by consuming more of the now relatively cheaper good, and less of other goods. The net result is that, even if she had to surrender the sum P_0AFP_1 dollars, the individual would still be better off after the price fall because of the substitution effect. This means that, if we are to implement the K–H compensation criterion, we need, in principle, to take a little more money away from her, amounting to the area ACF in Figure 7.2(b). This area measures the gain resulting from the substitution effect – the difference between her willingness to pay for the extra quantity of the good and the amount she actually pays.

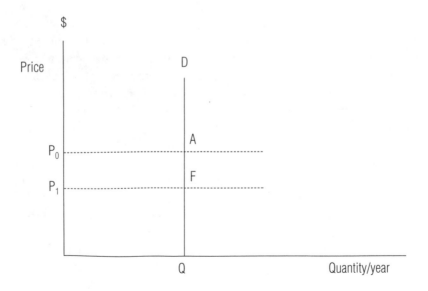

Figure 7.2(a) Consumer Surplus with Inelastic Demand

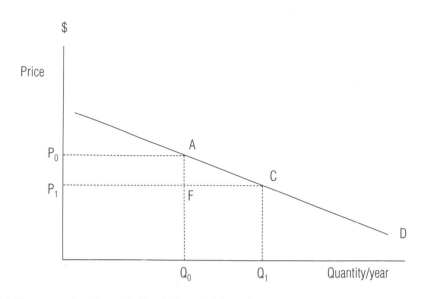

Figure 7.2(b) Consumer Surplus with Elastic Demand

It will be clear from the above discussion that, since we removed the income effect by extracting P_0AFP_1 dollars in compensation, the remaining amount ACF is measured under a consumer demand curve which takes account of the substitution effect only. Such a demand curve is termed a constant-utility or "Hicksian" demand curve. The Appendix to this Chapter discusses this concept in greater detail. However, at present it is sufficient to note that the difference between consumer surplus measured under a Hicksian demand curve, and that measured under an ordinary, or "Marshallian", demand curve is likely to be small since it arises from the income effect of the price change. The income effect of a change in price of a good is distributed among all goods the individual consumes and, hence, the effect on the level of consumption of the good whose change in price caused the income effect is likely to be small. This means that the Hicksian and Marshallian demand curves will be very similar, and that a change in consumer surplus measured under one will be similar to that measured under the other. Furthermore, in applied benefit-cost analysis the demand curve used to measure benefit or cost in the presence of a price change will be, at best, an approximation, and errors in estimating this curve are likely to dwarf the nice distinction between the two theoretical types of demand curves. In other words, for practical purposes consumer surplus measured under "the" demand curve will be adequate for implementing the K–H criterion.

Aggregating Consumer Surplus Measures

To this point we have been considering the measurement of the value of the gain or loss to an individual as a result of a change in market price. However a change in price will affect all consumers in the market and in efficiency analysis we want a measure of aggregate benefit or cost. Since the market demand curve for a private good is the lateral summation of the demand curves of all the individuals participating in the market, the area of consumer surplus change measured under the market demand curve is the aggregate of the changes which could be measured under the individual curves. This means that the area of consumer surplus identified by the market demand curve is the sum of the amounts hypothetically to be paid to (paid by) losers (gainers) to maintain each person's utility at the level it would be in the world without the project.

The Significance of Income Distribution

It should be noted that the size of the compensation hypothetically to be paid to or taken from an individual as a result of a price change (known as the compensating variation) depends on the position of her demand curve. Since an increase in income shifts the individual's demand curve for a normal good to the right, it is obvious that individuals with high incomes will have larger compensating variations than individuals with low incomes, in response to the same price change. A change in the distribution of income would change the positions of the individual demand curves, the individual compensation measures, and possibly the aggregate measure. This means that the measures used in a benefit-cost analysis are not value-neutral: they are based on, and tend to protect, the *status quo* in terms of income distribution. Furthermore potential and actual compensation are very different concepts, and since compensation is rarely paid or collected in practice, generally some individuals will be better off and some worse off as a result of the project. The issue of income distribution can be addressed in a benefit-cost analysis, but consideration of this question is deferred to Chapter 11.

Producer Surplus

The concept of producer surplus can be explained by Figure 7.10 (p. 166), which illustrates the supply of labour in a market serving the irrigation project described later in this Chapter: the first unit of labour can be drawn into the market at a wage of $0Z$ dollars, but subsequent units will present themselves only at higher wage rates. A wage rate of W_0 is required to induce the quantity supplied $0L_0$. While the total amount of wages paid to that quantity of labour is measured by area W_0UL_00, that quantity of labour could be hired for ZUL_00 if each unit was paid the minimum amount required to induce its supply. The difference between the wages actually paid and the minimum sum required to induce the number of units supplied is measured by area W_0UZ in Figure 7.10, and this amount is termed a *producer surplus*.

Benefits of Urban Transport Projects

Building a Bridge
Suppose that a municipality is considering building a bridge which will reduce trip length and travel time from the suburbs into the centre of the city. While the size of the reductions in

distance and time will vary from one suburb to another, the analysis can focus on the effects on the residents of an "average" suburb. If the bridge is built the cost of a trip into the city falls: a shorter distance results in savings in car running costs, and a shorter trip length confers a benefit by reducing the cost of travel time (in other words, releasing time for other purposes). Suppose that the value of these savings can be measured by means of the appropriate market and shadow-prices and expressed as a dollar amount per trip. Figure 7.3 can be interpreted as illustrating the aggregate demand for trips into the city by residents of the average suburb, and the fall in price per trip from P_0 to P_1 measures the reduction in average trip cost as a result of building the bridge. Because the demand curve for trips, labelled D in Figure 7.3, is downward sloping, the fall in price will result in a significant increase in the quantity of trips demanded from Q_0 to Q_1 per year. The costs of building, maintaining and operating the bridge will be ignored in this discussion which will focus on measuring consumer benefits.

Consider first the Q_0 annual trips which would be undertaken in the absence of the bridge. The consumers of each of those trips will experience a cost reduction of $P_0 - P_1$ if the bridge is built. The annual benefit to commuters undertaking these trips is measured by $(P_0 - P_1)Q_0$, which is represented by area P_0ABP_1 in Figure 7.3. Now consider the additional trips generated as a result of the reduced cost of travel. These trips were not considered worth undertaking at price P_0 because their gross value, measured by the relevant point on the demand curve, was lower than their price, making their net value to the consumer negative. However once the price falls to P_1 the trips from Q_0 to Q_1 begin to have a positive net value. The net value of the first additional trip above Q_0 is close to $(P_0 - P_1)$, and the net value of the

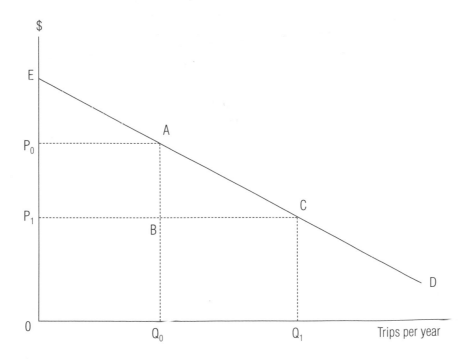

Figure 7.3 Benefits of a Bridge

last additional trip (the Q_1th) is close to zero. Assuming that the demand curve is a straight line, the average net value of the additional trips is $(P_0 - P_1)/2$, and hence the total annual value of these generated trips is given by $(P_0 - P_1)(Q_1 - Q_0)/2$, which is represented by area ACB in Figure 7.3. We now have an estimate of the approximate annual value derived by consumers as a result of building the bridge: it is area P_0ACP_1, or $(P_0 - P_1)Q_0 + (P_0 - P_1)$ $(Q_1 - Q_0)/2$. In other words, the annual benefit of the bridge consists of the sum of the cost savings on existing trips plus half of the cost savings on generated trips.

As discussed earlier, area P_0ACP_1 represents the increase in consumer surplus accruing to consumers as a result of the fall in the price of a trip. Consumer surplus measures the net value to consumers of the amount of the good that is consumed. Net value is the total amount consumers are willing to pay for the good less the amount that they actually pay. Total willingness to pay for a quantity of the good is measured by the area under the demand curve up to the point representing the current level of consumption; in Figure 7.3, total willingness to pay for Q_0 trips is measured by area EAQ_00. The logic underlying this measure is that someone is willing to pay OE for the first trip, and that person and others are willing to pay amounts measured by the height of the demand curve for subsequent additional trips until the Q_0th trip which is worth AQ_0.

Summing the values of all the trips from 0 to Q_0 gives total willingness to pay measured as the area under the demand curve from 0 to Q_0. Net willingness to pay for these trips is given by total willingness to pay less the amount actually paid for Q_0 trips, which in the initial equilibrium is measured by area P_0AQ_00. The initial amount of consumer surplus accruing to consumers is therefore measured by EAP_0. Applying a similar line of argument to the equilibrium after the fall in price from P_0 to P_1, consumer surplus in the new equilibrium is measured as ECP_1. Hence the increase in consumer surplus, measured by the new level less the initial level, is measured by area P_0ACP_1 which represents the annual benefit to consumers of access to the bridge.

Let us now suppose that the municipality decides to levy a toll from motorists using the bridge in order to recoup some of the construction and operating costs. The price of a trip, once the bridge is in operation, will be the travel cost, P_1, plus the toll, as illustrated by P_2 in Figure 7.4, where $(P_2 - P_1)$ is the amount of the toll. The rise in the price of a trip, as compared with the no-toll case, will reduce the number of trips demanded from Q_1 to Q_2. The annual benefit to consumers, measured by the increase in consumer surplus as compared with the no-bridge equilibrium, now becomes P_0AFP_2, which is less than if the bridge were provided toll-free. However, introducing a toll also provides a benefit to the municipality in the form of toll revenues, measured as P_2FGP_1 in Figure 7.4. The total annual benefit of providing a toll bridge (ignoring the cost) is measured by area P_0AFGP_1, consisting of P_0AFP_2 to users and P_2FGP_1 to the municipality.

Introducing a toll has had two effects: it has reduced the annual benefit derived from the bridge by the amount GFC; and it has redistributed some of the remaining benefit from consumers to the municipality. Despite the apparent reduction in aggregate benefit as a result of the toll, tolls may be justified on both efficiency and distributional grounds. From an efficiency point of view, in the absence of a toll additional funds would have to be provided through increased taxes or government borrowing and, as we will see in Chapter 10, there may be a

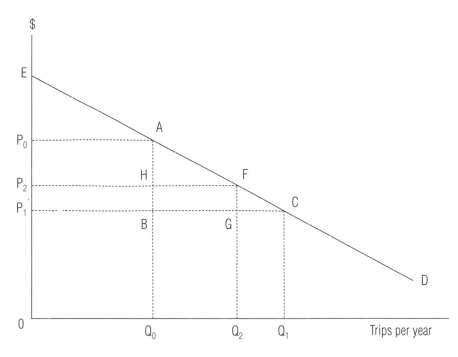

Figure 7.4 Effect of a Bridge Toll

premium on the opportunity cost of such funds which may exceed the inefficiency cost of tolls. And, from a distributional point of view, why should the general taxpayer meet all the costs of improving the access of suburban residents to the city centre?

An important issue, referred to earlier, and also discussed in the next section, is the distinction between **real** and **pecuniary** effects in an efficiency benefit-cost analysis. A pecuniary effect is a gain/loss to one group which is exactly offset by a loss/gain to another. When total gains and losses are summed to obtain an estimate of the net benefit of the project, pecuniary effects cancel out. Pecuniary effects are sometimes referred to as **transfers**, although this terminology can be misleading. In the case of the toll bridge, for example, it could be argued that the toll transfers some of the benefit of the bridge from motorists to the government. However, since, in the example, benefits to motorists have been measured net of tolls, both the toll revenues and the cost savings to motorists are real benefits of the project. When the gains and losses to all groups are summed, the tolls are not offset by a corresponding loss elsewhere in the calculation of net benefit.

It should be stressed that the above discussion has not dealt with many issues which would arise in the benefit-cost analysis of a proposal to build a bridge. Costs have not been considered, and some of the benefits are not incorporated in the measure of the reduced cost of a trip. For example, when traffic is diverted from existing routes to the bridge, congestion on these routes falls and people who continue to use them benefit as a result. On the other hand, there may be increased congestion costs in the city centre as a result of the increase in the number of trips. Since the new route is shorter and quicker one of the savings resulting from the provision of the bridge is lower fuel consumption. While the reduced fuel bill experienced by motorists is included in the fall in trip price from P_0 to P_1, the benefits of improved air quality experienced by all citizens are not.

Cutting Bus Fares

We now consider the example of a proposal to cut bus fares, which places a different interpretation on the relationships illustrated in Figure 7.4. Suppose that the municipality supplies bus services as illustrated in Figure 7.5: there is a downward sloping demand curve for bus services, D, and the supply curve, S, is perfectly elastic, reflecting the assumption that any number of additional bus trips can be supplied at the current unit cost. Suppose that the municipality proposes to lower the bus fare in order to encourage more trips: it may be argued that this will reduce traffic congestion and pollution. Obviously a benefit-cost analysis of the proposal would need to value the latter effects, and valuing this sort of non-marketed output is the topic of Chapter 12. However for the present we will ignore these third-party effects and concentrate on the benefits and costs of the proposal to bus users and the municipality. Lowering the bus fare below unit cost is in effect a subsidy to bus users. As illustrated in Figure 7.5, the effect of the lower fare is to encourage additional trips $(Q_1 - Q_0)$ as intended.

What are the efficiency net benefits of the proposal, ignoring the effect on congestion and pollution costs? The cost of the extra output of trips is given by area ACQ_1Q_0 in Figure 7.5: this area consists of $Q_1 - Q_0$ extra trips costing P_0 each. At the initial equilibrium, denoted by point A in Figure 7.5, an extra bus trip was valued by consumers at P_0. Since the bus fare

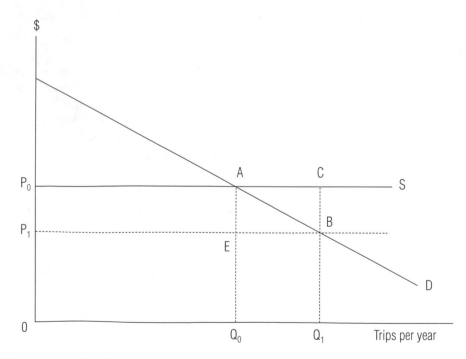

Figure 7.5 Subsidizing Bus Fares

was also P_0, consumers were not willing to undertake additional bus travel at that price: the value of an extra trip, as given by a point on the demand curve, was less than the cost to them of that trip, given by P_0. Once the bus fare is reduced to P_1 consumers are willing to take additional trips which, while they are worth less than P_0, are worth at least P_1, the new fare. As the number of trips rises from Q_0 to Q_1 the gross value of an additional trip falls from P_0 to P_1. On average the additional trips have a gross value of roughly $(P_0+P_1)/2$ each (this is an overestimate if the demand curve is convex to the origin, and an underestimate if it is concave, but we will ignore this complication).

It follows from this analysis that the gross value to bus users of the extra trips is an amount represented by area ABQ_1Q_0 in Figure 7.5. Ignoring the effects of the proposal on groups other than bus users and the municipality, the net efficiency benefit of the proposal is given by the benefits, area ABQ_1Q_0, less the costs, area ACQ_1Q_0, which amounts to a negative net benefit measured by area ACB. This is the annual amount which would have to be set against the benefits to other groups in terms of reduced congestion and pollution to determine whether the proposal involved an efficient use of scarce resources.

We now turn to the referent group benefits. Again we will assume that we are concerned only with the effects on two groups – bus users and the municipality. We have already seen that bus users value the extra trips at approximately area ABQ_1Q_0 in Figure 7.5. At the new fare they pay a total amount measured by area EBQ_1Q_0 for the extra trips. Hence the net benefit consumers derive from the extra trips is measured by area ABE. However this is not the total net benefit to consumers because they also experience a fall in the price of all trips they take, including the trips currently undertaken at the fare P_0. They now save $(P_0 - P_1)$ on each existing trip, with a total saving of P_0AEP_1. Thus the net benefit to bus users is a saving of P_0AEP_1 on existing trips plus a net benefit of ABE on the generated trips, giving a total net benefit of P_0ABP_1, which, as we saw earlier, is the increase in consumer surplus generated by the price reduction. The effect on the municipality is a change in its profit position: in the absence of the fare reduction it is breaking even on its bus service operation, with total revenue equal to total cost measured by area P_0AQ_00 in Figure 7.5. With the fare reduction total cost rises by ACQ_1Q_0 and total revenue changes by $EBQ_1Q_0 - P_0AEP_1$. The net effect on the municipality is to generate a loss of $ACQ_1Q_0 - (EBQ_1Q_0 - P_0AEP_1)$, equivalent to area P_0CBP_1.

Since, by assumption in this example, the referent group – bus users and the municipality – consists of all those affected by the proposal (we are ignoring benefits of reduced pollution and congestion in this discussion), the sum of referent group net benefits must equal the efficiency net benefit, a loss of ACB, and it can be verified that this is the case by reference to Figure 7.5. An important feature of the example is that the area P_0AEP_1 featured twice in the referent group analysis, but played no part in the efficiency benefit-cost analysis. The reason for this is that the fare reduction on existing trips is a **pecuniary effect** only: it is a **transfer** from the municipality to bus users in the sense that every dollar saved by consumers on the cost of the existing trips is lost revenue to the municipality. When these gains and losses are summed, together with the other effects of the proposal, over the referent group to give the efficiency net benefit position, they cancel out. In other words, as noted above, pecuniary effects net out of an efficiency benefit-cost analysis – one group's gain is another group's loss.

If pecuniary effects net out, why do we bother recording them? The answer is that we are interested in the distributional effects of the project – who benefits and who gains – as well as the efficiency effects, and we will return to the issue of distribution of benefits and costs in Chapter 11. For example, suppose that in the above illustration the bus company was foreign owned and hence not part of the referent group, and was obliged for some reason to cut the bus fare below cost: subtracting its (negative) net benefits resulting from the fare cut from the efficiency net benefits would give an estimate of the net benefit of the fare reduction to consumers. Continuing to ignore the congestion and pollution costs, the net benefit to the referent group is then given by area P_0ABP_1 in Figure 7.5, since the referent group now consists only of bus users.

It can be concluded from the above examples that price changes can sometimes be ignored in the efficiency benefit-cost analysis, and sometimes not! They can be ignored if they represent pecuniary effects, also termed transfers, although pecuniary effects will resurface in the referent group benefit-cost account. However if price changes represent real effects, as in the discussion of Figure 7.3, they must also be taken account of in the efficiency benefit-cost analysis. A price change which represents a **real effect** is matched by a cost change: this is a case where one person's gain (loss) is **not** another person's loss (gain).

In summary, when undertaking an efficiency benefit-cost analysis each price change predicted to result from the project must be classified as either a real or a pecuniary effect. If it is a pecuniary effect the predicted fall (rise) in price is matched by an equivalent rise (fall) in price somewhere else: one group's gain is another group's loss, and the effect of the price change is simply to transfer a benefit or cost from one group to another; when benefits and costs to all groups are summed in an efficiency benefit-cost analysis the pecuniary effects, or transfers, net out. If a price change is not identified as a pecuniary effect, then it is a real effect and it will have consequences for the aggregate net benefit outcome measured by an efficiency benefit-cost analysis.

Benefits of Job Training

Governments sometimes offer training programs which enhance the skills of people on low incomes and help them to get better paying jobs. The effect of the training program on the local labour market is to shift out the supply curve of skilled labour by the number of graduates from the training program. If we assume that the skilled labour market clears so that there is no involuntary unemployment, the effect of the increased supply of skilled labour is to lower its market wage. This situation is illustrated in Figure 7.6: the initial equilibrium involved L_0 units of skilled labour employed at wage W_0; when the supply of labour shifts out from S_0 to S_1 employment rises from L_0 to L_1 and the market wage falls from W_0 to W_1. We can use Figure 7.6 to measure the benefits of the training program which must be compared with the costs in assessing its economic efficiency. In the following discussion we will ignore the costs of the training program and concentrate on the benefits.

One group of beneficiaries of the program consists of firms which are able to employ more labour at a lower wage. Firms save W_0ACW_1 on the wage bill for the L_0 workers they

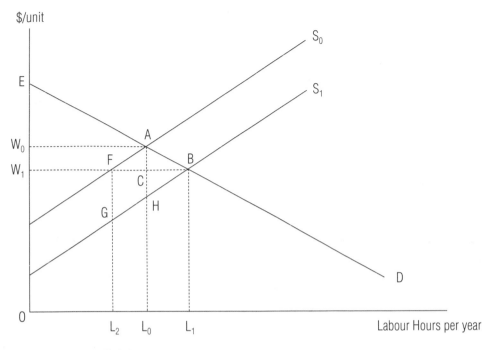

Figure 7.6 Effects of Worker Training

initially employed. They are also able to hire an additional L_0L_1 workers at a wage W_1 which is lower than the value of the marginal product of these workers as measured by the demand curve for labour. Area ABC measures the net benefit to firms of employing these additional workers: it is calculated by subtracting the cost of the extra labour, given by area CBL_1L_0, from the value of the resulting additional output, ABL_1L_0. The total benefit to firms is measured by the area of surplus W_0ABW_1 (to avoid confusion we have not termed this a consumer surplus even although the firm could be regarded as a consumer of labour services). The surplus will accrue to the firm as an increase in profit in the short-run, although in the long-run competition among firms might drive the market price of the product down, thereby transferring some of this benefit from the owners of firms to consumers.

We now consider why area ABL_1L_0 in Figure 7.6 measures the increase in value of output as a result of the increased labour input L_0L_1. The competitive firms' demand curve for labour, illustrated by the demand curve ED in Figure 7.6, is the value of the marginal product (VMP) of labour schedule. Given the firms' capital stocks – their buildings and machines etc. – and the levels of their variable inputs – energy, materials etc. – the VMP schedule shows what each successive unit of labour input will add to the value of output. This means that the total value of output is given by the area under the VMP schedule from the origin to the level of labour input demanded. Thus area $0EAL_0$ is the total value of the firms' output at input level L_0, and area $0EBL_1$ is the total value of output at labour input level L_1. The difference between these two values, ABL_1L_0 is the increase in the value of output as a result of the increase in labour input from L_0 to L_1.

When the market wage falls from W_0 to W_1 some of the workers originally employed in the skilled occupation leave to take other jobs; these are workers with the skills and opportunities to earn at least a wage of W_1 in other occupations. In Figure 7.6 the number of workers leaving the occupation is given by L_2L_0. However these departing workers are more than compensated for by the graduates of the training program who shift out the local supply curve of the skill by the amount L_2L_1, so that, as we saw above, there is a net increase in this type of employment of L_0L_1. Each worker who remains in the industry suffers a wage reduction from W_0 to W_1, while the workers who leave the industry find employment elsewhere at wages ranging from W_0 to W_1. The average loss to workers leaving the industry is $(W_0 - W_1)/2$. Thus the total net loss to the workers originally employed in the industry is measured by area W_0AFW_1, which represents a loss of producer surplus.

The graduates of the training program find employment at wage W_1 which is higher than the wage earned in their previous job, which is their best alternative employment. The latter wage, measuring the opportunity cost of the labour attracted to the training program, is given by the segment GB of the supply curve S_1: some workers have relatively low opportunity cost, measured by L_2G, whereas some have an opportunity cost close to W_1. The net benefit to the graduates of the training program is given by area FBG: this area measures the income earned by the graduates in the new occupation, FBL_1L_2, less the income which could have been earned in the absence of the training program, measured by GBL_1L_2. Area FBG is termed producer surplus – an amount paid to suppliers of a quantity of a good or service in excess of the minimum amount required to induce them to supply that quantity.

In summary, employers of labour benefit by an amount measured by the area of surplus W_0ABW_1 in Figure 7.6. Of this amount, W_0AFW_1 represents a transfer from previously employed labour to employers, and consequently nets out of the efficiency benefit-cost calculation. The graduates of the program benefit by an amount measured by the area of producer surplus FBG. The net benefits of the program, which must be compared with the cost of the training program, are measured by area FABG. While our main concern at present is with measuring the benefit of the program, it should be noted that the program costs include the opportunity cost of labour while training proceeds, as well as the costs of instructors, materials, and space.

As noted in Chapters 5 and 6, the sum of the net benefits of a project to each of the groups affected by it must equal the net efficiency benefit. In the case of the above example, the value of the extra output produced in the industry employing the trainees is measured by area ABL_1L_0. A quantity of labour previously employed in the industry, measured by L_2L_0, leaves to seek higher wages elsewhere and raises the value of output elsewhere by an amount measured by FAL_0L_2. Since these workers are replaced by the trainees there is no corresponding fall in the value of output in the industry in question. Thus the total increase in the value of output in the economy is measured by $FABL_1L_2$. Against this increase must be set the opportunity cost of the activities which would have been undertaken by the trainees in the absence of training, measured by area GBL_1L_2. The net efficiency benefit is then measured by area FABG, which is the sum of the net benefits to each group in the economy affected by the project.

The foregoing discussion was based on the assumption that the labour market cleared. However in practice there may be some sort of wage regulation which prevents wages falling to market-clearing levels, thereby resulting in involuntary unemployment in both the market for the skill provided by the training program, and in the alternative occupation for unskilled workers. In this situation there will be no change in the wage of labour, and the analysis of the benefits of a job training program would follow the principles outlined in Chapter 5, incorporating the appropriate shadow-prices of labour.

Producer Benefits from an Irrigation Project

We now turn to the example of a project which supplies additional irrigation water to farmers through raising the height of a dam. The opportunity cost of the resources used to raise the dam will not be considered in the discussion, which focuses on measuring the benefits of the project. Initially it will be assumed that the water authority sells irrigation water to farmers at whatever price the market will bear, and then subsequently it will be assumed that a regulated quantity of water is supplied at a regulated price.

Figure 7.7 illustrates the supply and demand for water in the region of the irrigation project. As in the case of a consumer demand curve, the demand curve for an input shows, at each level of quantity demanded, how much buyers are willing to pay for an extra unit of the input. Assuming that the agricultural industry in the region is competitive in the product market, buyers of the input will be willing to pay the value of the marginal product of water for an extra unit of water; in other words, they are willing to pay for an extra unit of water the value of the extra output that will result from using that extra unit of the input. The supply

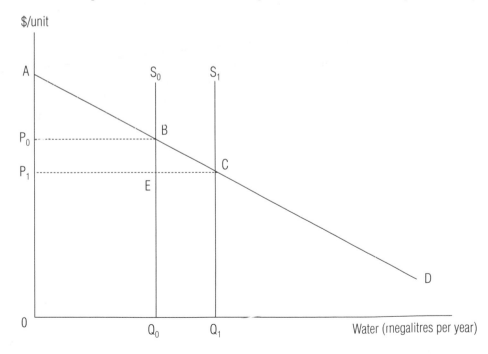

Figure 7.7 Benefits of an Irrigation Project

curve is drawn as perfectly inelastic reflecting the assumption that, leaving aside the variability of rainfall, a given infrastructure can only supply a particular quantity of irrigation water. In addition to the current supply curve, S_0, the curve S_1 is also drawn to reflect the effect of raising the level of the dam on the quantity of water supplied. Figure 7.7 is concerned only with analysing the benefits of the proposed project, and the opportunity cost will be ignored in the discussion.

As shown in Figure 7.7, the effect of increasing the quantity of water supplied is to lower the market price. The reason for this is summarized by the **law of diminishing marginal productivity**: when successive units of an input, such as water, are combined with a fixed quantity of the other input, such as land, then the increments in output resulting from the successive additional units of input (the marginal product of the input) become smaller and smaller (diminish). Since the value of the marginal product of water (the demand curve for water) consists of the price of output multiplied by the marginal physical product of water, the demand curve is downward sloping. In this analysis it is assumed that the price of output remains constant – the area affected by the proposed irrigation project is small relative to the total area involved in producing the product and hence can have no influence on the market price of the product.

Since the market price of water is predicted to fall as a result of the irrigation project the benefit-cost analyst has a choice of two prices, P_0 and P_1, with which to value the extra water produced by the project. As in the case of the transport examples, the initial price P_0 measures the value of the first extra unit of water to farmers, and the price P_1 measures the value of the last additional unit of water produced by the project; an average price, $(P_0 + P_1)/2$, multiplied by the extra quantity of water, Q_1Q_0 in Figure 7.7, will generally closely approximate the total value of the extra water, and will provide an exact measure when the demand curve for water is linear as shown in the figure.

Recalling that the demand curve for water shows at each level of input the value of the extra output that can be obtained by adding one extra unit of input of water, holding constant the input of the other factor (land), it can be seen that the area under the demand curve for the input equals the value of total output of food from the relevant area of land. In other words, area ABQ_00 measures the value of food produced by the region when the quantity Q_0 of water is used, and area ACQ_10 measures the value when the quantity Q_1 is used. This means that the value of the extra food produced as a result of using the extra quantity of water Q_1Q_0 is measured by area BCQ_1Q_0 in Figure 7.7. This is the area obtained by multiplying the additional quantity of water by the average of the prices before and after the project. In other words, the gross benefit, in an efficiency benefit-cost analysis, of raising the dam is the value of the extra food produced.

Let us now consider the referent group benefits. There are three groups that might be affected: consumers of food, the water authority, and landowners in the region. Since the price of food is assumed not to change as a result of the project, consumers receive no net benefit: they pay exactly what the extra food is worth to them. The water authority benefits by an amount measured by area $ECQ_1Q_0 - P_0BEP_1$, which is the change in water revenues; this amount could be positive or negative depending on the elasticity of the demand curve over the range BC (remember that in this discussion of project benefits we are ignoring the opportunity

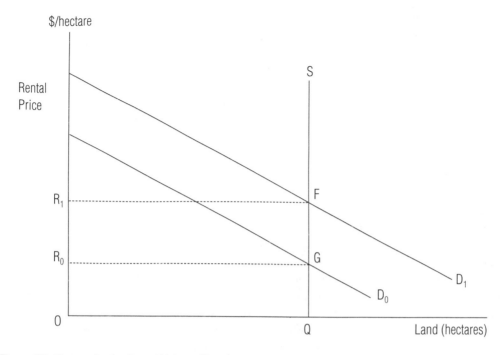

Figure 7.8 Change in the Rental Value of Land

cost of raising the dam which would presumably be borne by the water authority). To analyse the benefit to landowners we need the help of Figure 7.8 which illustrates the value of the marginal product schedule of land – the demand curve for land – together with the supply of land in the region, which is fixed at quantity Q. The demand curve for land shifts out from D_0 to D_1 as a result of the increased availability of water: potential farmers are willing to pay more rent per acre the lower is the price of irrigation water. The market rental value of the land rises from R_0 per acre to R_1 as a result of the demand shift, and the annual return to landowners rises by R_1FGR_0.

Assuming that the referent group consists of consumers (who receive a zero net benefit because the price of food is assumed not to change), the water authority and landowners, the aggregate net benefit of the project, ignoring the cost of raising the dam, is given by area $ECQ_1Q_0 - P_0BEP_1$ (in Figure 7.7) + R_1FGR_0 (in Figure 7.8), which should equal the benefit calculated by the efficiency benefit-cost analysis, and we now proceed to demonstrate that this is the case.

Recall that area ACQ_10 in Figure 7.7 measures the total value of food production in the region once the additional quantity of water is available. Note also that area P_1CQ_10 measures water authority revenues once the dam is raised. A simple rule in economics is that the value of output equals the value of the incomes generated in producing the output: in aggregate this rule is reflected in the equality of Gross National Expenditure (GNE) and Gross National Income (GNI) measures of Gross National Product (GNP); at a micro level the rule reflects the fact that the revenues earned by each firm are paid out as income to suppliers of inputs and to the owners of the firm. This means that area ACP_1 in Figure 7.7 must represent the income earned by landowners after the supply of water has increased; it represents the part of the revenue from food production that does not accrue to the water authority, and must therefore accrue to the owner of the other factor of production, land. Since area ABP_0 measures landowner income before the increase in availability of water, and area ACP_1 landowner income after the increase in the supply of water, the area P_0BCP_1 must represent the increase in income to landowners, which is also measured as R_1FGR_0 in Figure 7.8. If we now substitute P_0BCP_1 for R_1FGR_0 in the expression for the aggregate net benefits to the referent group derived in the previous paragraph, we find that it reduces to area BCQ_1Q_0 in Figure 7.7, which was the net benefit estimate obtained from the efficiency benefit-cost analysis.

In the above example a competitive market price was charged for water. Suppose that water is allocated to farms on the basis of some kind of formula, and that a nominal charge, lower than the competitive market price, is levied. Since the observed price of water no longer equals the value of its marginal product, the water price cannot be used to calculate the value of the extra food produced as a result of the extra water. Indeed, when water is allocated by some formula this usually means that the water levy or price is lower than the price of water in a competitive market. As an aside, it can be noted that if the allocation formula produces a different distribution of water among farms than would the competitive market outcome, the increase in the value of food production will be less than in the competitive outcome. In Figure 7.9 the supply of water is shown as increasing from Q_0 to Q_1, as a result of raising the level of the dam, but the extra water is sold at price P, yielding additional revenue of KLQ_1Q_0 to the water authority. Recalling that the area under the demand curve, or value of the marginal product schedule of water, measures the value of the output of food, it can be seen that the value of the extra food is measured by MNQ_1Q_0, which is the project benefit in an efficiency benefit-cost analysis.

How is the analyst to measure project benefit in the absence of a competitive market price for water? Since area MNQ_1Q_0 in Figure 7.9 represents the value of additional output, there must be an equivalent increase in income. The water authority's income rises by KLQ_1Q_0 so the income of the other factor of production, land, must rise by MNLK. In other words, as compared with the example in which the market price was charged for water, charging a lower price simply further increases land rent. This makes intuitive sense: the cheaper the water can be obtained, the more the land is worth. This suggests that there are two ways of measuring the project benefit: first, through studies of agricultural production, relating physical inputs to output, we can predict the effect of additional input of water on output; second, through studies of land values, relating land value to factors such as climate, soil and the availability of irrigation water, we can predict the effect of additional water on the capital value of land, and hence on the annual rental value; the sum of the increase in the annual rental value of land plus the additional revenues of the water authority is a measure of the annual value of the increased output of food.

Now suppose that other factors of production besides land and water are involved in food production. We can add as many factors as we like, but for simplicity assume that food is produced by combining land, labour and irrigation water. Just as an increase in the availability

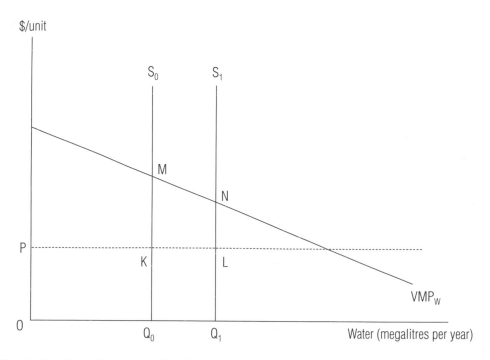

Figure 7.9 Irrigation Water Sold at Less than Market Value

of water increases the demand for land, so it also increases the demand for labour. For the moment assume that the extra workers are drawn from the labour force employed by farms in nearby regions, but that the impact of the project is not sufficiently large as to cause an increase in the wage. As before, the value of the extra output of food is equal to the sum of the values of the extra incomes to land, labour and the water authority. While there is no offsetting fall in production elsewhere as a result of the increased availability of water (ignoring the opportunity cost of the inputs used to raise the height of the dam) or the more intensive use of land, diverting labour from employment in other regions does have an opportunity cost. Assuming a competitive and undistorted labour market, the wage measures the opportunity cost of labour, and the extra wage bill must be subtracted from the increase in incomes generated by the project (measuring the value of the additional output of food) in order to calculate the project benefit in an efficiency benefit-cost analysis.

The referent group is now expanded to include labour as well as food consumers, landowners and the water authority, but, similar to food consumers, labour receives no net benefit since it continues to supply labour at the same wage. Hence the aggregate benefits of the referent group, consisting of the additional incomes to land and the water authority, sum to equal the project benefit in the efficiency analysis.

Other assumptions could be made about the labour market. For example, suppose that the extra labour would otherwise be unemployed. In the efficiency benefit-cost analysis we would then cost labour at its shadow-price as discussed in Chapter 5. Since the shadow-price is lower than the wage this will increase the estimate of the project benefit. This increase will be matched by an increase in referent group benefits to reflect the fact that the extra labour is receiving a wage higher than that required to induce it to work in the region.

Accounting for Input Price Changes

Now suppose that the labour market is competitive and undistorted but that the extra demand for labour in the region pushes up the market wage as illustrated in Figure 7.10. The first additional unit of labour hired has an opportunity cost of W_0, as shown in Figure 7.10, and the last extra unit hired has an opportunity cost of W_1. Multiplying the additional labour by an average of the two wages, $(W_0 + W_1)/2$, gives a rough measure of the opportunity cost of the total amount of extra labour (an exact measure if the supply curve of labour is linear as shown in Figure 7.10). This amount, given by area UVL_1L_0 in the figure, must be subtracted from the estimate of the value of the extra food to calculate project benefit in an efficiency benefit-cost analysis. Recall that the value of the extra food produced as a result of the irrigation project can be measured by the sum of the increases in income to the owners of the three factors of production involved – land, labour and water. To measure the efficiency benefit (i.e. the value of the extra food produced by the economy as a whole) we subtract from that sum the area UVL_1L_0 which represents the opportunity cost of the extra labour employed in the irrigation district. Labour still benefits by an amount measured by the increase in producer surplus W_1VUW_0 in Figure 7.10, and since this is a transfer from landowners the increase in income of the latter as a result of the project will be correspondingly lower.

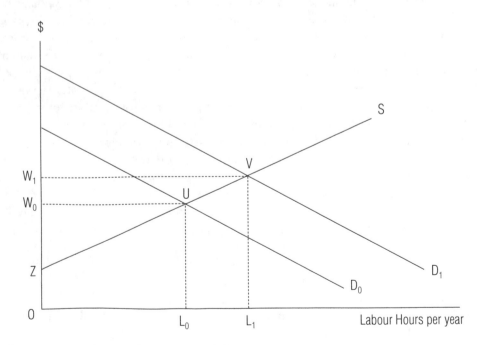

Figure 7.10 Effect of an Increase in Demand for Labour

When we turn to the referent group analysis, we find that total wages paid to labour in the region have risen by the amount $W_1VUW_0 + UVL_1L_0$ as illustrated in Figure 7.10. However the net benefit to labour is measured by area W_1VUW_0 since area UVL_1L_0 represents wages forgone in alternative employment. The net benefit to labour measured by area W_1VUW_0 is a pecuniary benefit since the benefit of the higher wage received by labour is offset by the cost of the higher wage paid by farms. In other words, as noted above, the area W_1VUW_0 is a transfer from employers in the region affected by the project to the regional labour force. Thus the amount represented by area W_1VUW_0 would appear as a benefit to labour and a cost to landowners in the referent group analysis and, in this example, would net out in both the aggregate referent group and efficiency benefit-cost analysis. If, on the other hand, the employers were foreign firms and not members of the referent group, the benefit to labour would not be offset by a cost to employers in the referent group analysis. However in the efficiency analysis pecuniary effects always net out.

The same argument as above would apply in the measurement of project cost if raising the dam involved a rise in the market wage as a result of the increased demand for labour. The opportunity cost of the labour, assuming it would be employed elsewhere, is approximated by the wage bill computed at an average of the initial and new equilibrium wage rates.

Price Changes in Other Markets

Suppose that a project results in a lower price for a good or service. It could be expected that the demand for a substitute (complementary) product would fall (rise). If this substitute or complementary product is in perfectly elastic supply there will be no change in its price. However, since the demand curve has shifted in (out), the area of consumer surplus measured under the demand curve appears to have fallen (risen). Should the apparent change in consumer surplus be measured and included in the analysis as a cost (benefit)? The answer is *no* because the shift in demand in the market for the substitute or complementary good is simply a reflection of consumers rearranging their expenditure to take advantage of the lower price of the good supplied by the project. The benefit of that lower price is fully measured by the consumer surplus change resulting from that lower price. A simple way to remember this point is to note that the benefit (cost) of a price change is measured by an area under a demand curve delineated by the original and the new price. If there is no price change, as in the case of a substitute or complementary good as considered above, then there is no benefit or cost to be measured in that market.

Suppose now that when the demand for a substitute (complementary) good falls (rises) there is a change in market price because of an upward sloping supply curve for the substitute (complementary) good. Now we have a benefit (cost) to consumers measured as the area under the new demand curve delineated by the difference between the original and new prices. While this area is a benefit (cost) to consumers, it is also a cost (benefit) to producers and nets out in the efficiency benefit-cost analysis. In other words, where price changes occur in other markets as a result of a project they may simply reflect transfers to (from) consumers from (to) producers.

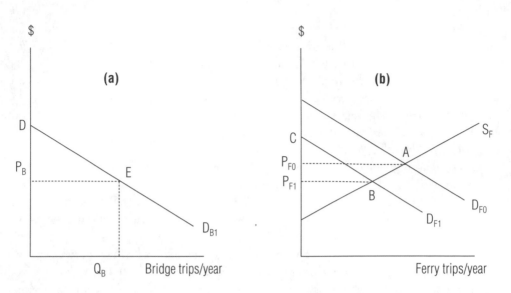

Figure 7.11 Effects of Building a Bridge on the Benefits from a Ferry

To illustrate the latter point, suppose that a bridge is to be built across a river which is already served by a ferry. Figure 7.11(a) shows the demand for bridge crossings, and Figure 7.11(b) shows the reduction in the demand for ferry crossings, from D_{F0} to D_{F1}, resulting from the provision of the bridge. Because the supply curve of ferry trips is upward sloping, the price of a ferry trip falls as a result of the reduction in demand for the services of the ferry. The area $P_{F0} AB P_{F1}$ in Figure 7.11(b) represents an annual benefit to ferry users in the form of a lower price, but a cost to the ferry operator in the form of a loss in producer surplus. Since it represents a transfer it can be ignored in efficiency benefit-cost analysis. Area DEP_B in Figure 7.11(a) measures the annual benefit to bridge users, net of the unit cost, P_B, of a bridge trip, given that the alternative of the ferry is available at price P_{F1}.

Now suppose that repair work is to be carried out on the ferry, putting it out of service for a year. In a benefit-cost analysis this is equivalent to raising the price of a ferry trip to a level which chokes off all demand. The annual cost to ferry users, as a result of its withdrawal from service, is measured by the area under the new demand curve for the ferry, D_{F1}, between the original and new price; in other words, the cost is the entire amount of consumer surplus, CBP_{F1}, generated annually by the ferry. Clearly this cost will be smaller than it would have been if the bridge had not been constructed, because the demand for ferry crossings has decreased, and if the repair work on the ferry was anticipated, this difference in cost could be considered as one of the benefits of constructing the bridge. When the ferry closes, demand for the bridge will increase, but in the absence of any price change in the market for bridge crossings there is no change in net benefit to be measured there.

Consider one final extension to the analysis. The price of bridge trips is a composite variable incorporating a variety of costs such as travel time and vehicle operating costs. Suppose that as the volume of traffic using the bridge increases, the cost of travel time rises because of increased congestion. This effect could be represented by an upward sloping supply curve of bridge trips. An increase in demand for bridge trips (not shown in Figure 7.11(a)), as a result of the closure of the ferry, would result in increased congestion and a higher price. This results in a loss to bridge users which would be measured by an area similar to area W_1VUW_0 in Figure 7.10. In that example the loss in consumer surplus suffered by farms was offset by an equivalent gain in producer surplus accruing to suppliers of labour, and the area netted out in the efficiency analysis. However in the present example the loss in consumer surplus due to increased congestion is a real, as opposed to a pecuniary effect. There is no offsetting gain to suppliers and hence the increased congestion cost would be deducted from the measure of consumer benefit in the efficiency benefit-cost analysis.

The ICP Case Study: Allowing for an Increase in the Skilled Wage

We now consider how to deal with price changes induced by the project in the spreadsheet framework. As noted earlier, the summary analysis of the ICP project reported in the Appendix to Chapter 6 serves as a basis for comparison with a series of spreadsheet analyses in Chapters 7–10, each amended to include an additional feature of benefit-cost analysis. The following discussion concerns how to deal with an anticipated increase in an input price as a result of a project's implementation.

As discussed at the beginning of Chapter 7, undertaking a project is unlikely to cause changes in the prices of tradeable inputs or outputs. However an example of a non-tradeable input whose price might be affected is skilled labour. Economies often experience skill shortages in particular areas of expertise which cannot be filled quickly because of the time required for training and the absence of alternative sources of supply resulting from migration restrictions.

Suppose that the International Cloth Products (ICP) project is predicted to drive up the wage of skilled labour from W_0 to W_1. How would this predicted effect be accounted for in the benefit-cost analysis? In the project and private accounts labour would be priced at the wage paid by ICP, W_1. As compared with the situation in which the wage remains at W_0, the net project and private benefits of the project decline by $(W_1 - W_0)$ per unit of skilled labour employed (converted to present value terms) as a consequence of the increase in wage.

In the efficiency analysis labour should be priced at its opportunity cost; the first unit of labour drawn into the project has an opportunity cost of W_0, while the last unit has an opportunity cost of W_1. As suggested earlier an average value for the opportunity cost of labour of $(W_0 + W_1)/2$ can be used in the efficiency analysis. As compared with the situation in which the wage remains at W_0, the annual efficiency net benefit falls by $(W_1 - W_0)/2$ per unit of skilled labour employed.

In the particular circumstances of the ICP Case Study, the aggregate referent group net benefit is obtained by subtracting the private net benefit, together with the net cash flow of the foreign financial institution, from the efficiency net benefit stream. Since the private net benefit has fallen by $(W_1 - W_0)$ per unit of skilled labour, and the efficiency net benefit has fallen by $(W_1 - W_0)/2$ per unit, the aggregate referent group net benefit has risen by $(W_1 - W_0)/2$. In terms of the disaggregated referent group net benefits, the increased skilled wage increases the producer surplus accruing to suppliers of skilled labour. As suggested earlier this

ICP PROJECT: 1999-2009

TABLE 1   KEY INPUT VARIABLES

VARIABLES		INVESTMENT C(	000 $'	000 BT'	INNING COSTS		MATERIAL FLOWS		FINANCE	
EXCHANGE RATE	44	SPINDLES	4000		WATER BT	480000	COTTON MN	16.2	SUPPLIERS	75%
TARIFF A	5%	EQUIPMEN	850		POWER BT	480000	YARN MN LB	15	OVERDRAF	60
TARIFF B	10%	INSTALLA	100		SPARE PAR	10%	LABOUR 1	100	CREDIT RE	5
PROFITS TAX	50%	CONSTRUCTION		36000	INSURANCE	6	LABOUR 2	1000		
DEPRECIATION	10%	START-UP COSTS		18000	OVERHEAD!	0	LABOUR 3	500		
PRICE YARN CIF US$	0.58	WORKING CAPITAL							DISCOUNT	4%
YARN TARIFF BT	2.1	RAW MAT	1200							8%
HANDLING BT	0.3	SPARE PA!	243							12%
TARIFF C	10%									16%
PRICE COTTON CIF US$	0.3									
WAGE 1 BT PA	150000	180000								
WAGE 2 BT PA	22500	27000								
WAGE 3 BT PA	12000									
INTEREST RATE 1	8%									
INTEREST RATE 2	10%									

TABLE 2   PROJECT CALCULATION

YEAR	1999	1999	2000	2001	2002	2003	2004	2005	2006	2007	2008	2009
	'000 US$	MN BT	MN BT	MN BT	MN BT	MN BT	MN BT	MN BT	MN BT	MN BT	MN BT	MN BT
INVESTMENT COSTS												
SPINDLES	-4200.000	-184.800										
EQUIPMENT	-892.500	-39.270										
INSTALLATION	-100.000	-4.400										
CONSTRUCTION		-36.000										
START-UP COSTS		-18.000										
RAW MATERIALS		-58.080										58.080
SPARE PARTS		-11.227										11.227
TOTAL	-282.470	-69.307	0.000	0.000	0.000	0.000	0.000	0.000	0.000	0.000	0.000	69.307
RUNNING COSTS												
WATER			-3.600	-7.200	-7.200	-7.200	-7.200	-7.200	-7.200	-7.200	-7.200	-7.200
POWER			-3.600	-7.200	-7.200	-7.200	-7.200	-7.200	-7.200	-7.200	-7.200	-7.200
SPARE PARTS			-22.407	-22.407	-22.407	-22.407	-22.407	-22.407	-22.407	-22.407	-22.407	-22.407
RAW MATERIALS			-117.612	-235.224	-235.224	-235.224	-235.224	-235.224	-235.224	-235.224	-235.224	-235.224
INSURANCE			-6.000	-6.000	-6.000	-6.000	-6.000	-6.000	-6.000	-6.000	-6.000	-6.000
LABOUR			-51.000	-51.000	-51.000	-51.000	-51.000	-51.000	-51.000	-51.000	-51.000	-51
TOTAL			-204.219	-329.031	-329.031	-329.031	-329.031	-329.031	-329.031	-329.031	-329.031	-329.031
REVENUES												
SALE OF YARN			209.400	418.800	418.800	418.800	418.800	418.800	418.800	418.800	418.800	418.800
NCF (Project)	-282.470	-64.126	89.769	89.769	89.769	89.769	89.769	89.769	89.769	89.769	89.769	159.076

TABLE 3 PRIVATE CALCULATION

YEAR	1999	1999	2000	2001	2002	2003	2004	2005	2006	2007	2008	2009
	'000 US$	MN BT	MN BT	MN BT	MN BT	MN BT	MN BT	MN BT	MN BT	MN BT	MN BT	MN BT
FINANCIAL FLOWS												
DEPRECIATION			-26.447	-26.447	-26.447	-26.447	-26.447	-26.447	-26.447	-26.447	-26.447	-26.447
INTEREST												
SUPPLIERS CREDIT	3637.500	160.050	-12.804	-10.621	-8.264	-5.719	-2.969					
REPAYMENT			-27.282	-29.464	-31.821	-34.367	-37.116					
BANK OVERDRAFT			60.000	-6.000	-6.000	-6.000	-6.000	-6.000	-6.000	-6.000	-6.000	-6.000
REPAYMENT												-60.000
NET OPERATING REVENUE			5.181	89.769	89.769	89.769	89.769	89.769	89.769	89.769	89.769	89.769
TAXABLE PROFIT			-34.070	46.701	49.058	51.603	54.353	57.322	57.322	57.322	57.322	57.322
PROFIT TAX			17.035	-23.350	-24.529	-25.802	-27.176	-28.661	-28.661	-28.661	-28.661	-28.661
FLOW OF OWN FUNDS		-122.420	-27.176	20.333	19.155	17.882	16.507	55.108	55.108	55.108	55.108	64.415

TABLE 4   EFFICIENCY CALCULATION

YEAR	1999	1999	2000	2001	2002	2003	2004	2005	2006	2007	2008	2009
	'000 US$	MN BT	MN BT	MN BT	MN BT	MN BT	MN BT	MN BT	MN BT	MN BT	MN BT	MN BT
INVESTMENT COSTS												
SPINDLES	-4000.000	-176.000										
EQUIPMENT	-850.000	-37.400										
INSTALLATION	-100.000	-4.400										
CONSTRUCTION		-18.000										
START-UP COSTS		-18.000										
RAW MATERIALS		-52.800										52.800
SPARE PARTS		-10.692										10.692
TOTAL	-253.800	-63.492	0.000	0.000	0.000	0.000	0.000	0.000	0.000	0.000	0.000	63.492
RUNNING COSTS												
WATER			-3.600	-7.200	-7.200	-7.200	-7.200	-7.200	-7.200	-7.200	-7.200	-7.200
POWER			-1.800	-3.600	-3.600	-3.600	-3.600	-3.600	-3.600	-3.600	-3.600	-3.600
SPARE PARTS			-21.340	-21.340	-21.340	-21.340	-21.340	-21.340	-21.340	-21.340	-21.340	-21.340
RAW MATERIALS			-106.920	-213.840	-213.840	-213.840	-213.840	-213.840	-213.840	-213.840	-213.840	-213.840
INSURANCE & RENT			0.000	0.000	0.000	0.000	0.000	0.000	0.000	0.000	0.000	0.000
LABOUR			-44.250	-44.250	-44.250	-44.250	-44.250	-44.250	-44.250	-44.250	-44.250	-44.25
TOTAL			-177.910	-290.230	-290.230	-290.230	-290.230	-290.230	-290.230	-290.230	-290.230	-290.230
REVENUES												
SALE OF YARN			191.400	382.800	382.800	382.800	382.800	382.800	382.800	382.800	382.800	382.800
NET EFFICIENCY BENEFIT	-253.800	-50.002	92.570	92.570	92.570	92.570	92.570	92.570	92.570	92.570	92.570	136.062

TABLE 5   REFERENT GROUP ANALYSIS

YEAR	1999	1999	2000	2001	2002	2003	2004	2005	2006	2007	2008	2009
	'000 US$	MN BT	MN BT	MN BT	MN BT	MN BT	MN BT	MN BT	MN BT	MN BT	MN BT	MN BT
TOTAL REFERENT GROUP	28.670	-62.911	32.151	33.330	34.603	35.977	37.462	37.462	37.462	37.462		91.647
- IMPORT DUTIES												
YARN			-18.000	-36.000	-36.000	-36.000	-36.000	-36.000	-36.000	-36.000	-36.000	-36.000
COTTON			10.692	21.384	21.384	21.384	21.384	21.384	21.384	21.384	21.384	21.384
EQUIPMENT		1.870										
SPINDLES		8.800										
MATERIALS INVENTORY			5.280									-5.280
SPARES INVENTORY			0.535									-0.535
SPARES			1.067	1.067	1.067	1.067	1.067	1.067	1.067	1.067	1.067	1.067
- TAXES			-17.035	23.350	24.529	25.802	27.176	28.661	28.661	28.661	28.661	28.661
(I) TOTAL GOVERNMENT	10.670		-17.461	9.801	10.980	12.253	13.627	15.112	15.112	15.112	15.112	9.297
(ii) POWER SUPPLIER			1.800	3.600	3.600	3.600	3.600	3.600	3.600	3.600	3.600	3.600
(iii) LABOUR		18.000	6.750	6.750	6.750	6.750	6.750	6.750	6.750	6.750	6.750	6.750
(iv) DOMESTIC BANK		0.000	-60.000	6.000	6.000	6.000	6.000	6.000	6.000	6.000	6.000	6.000
												60.000
(V) INSURANCE			6.000	6.000	6.000	6.000	6.000	6.000	6.000	6.000	6.000	6.000
TOTAL REFERENT GROUP	28.670	-62.911	32.151	33.330	34.603	35.977	37.462	37.462	37.462	37.462		91.647

	PROJECT		PRIVATE		EFFICIENCY		REFERENT GROUP	
NPV	$(Mn)	IRR (%)	$(Mn)	IRR (%)	NPV	$ (MN)	IRR (%)	NPV	$ (MN)	IRR (%)
4%	344.5	18.3%	4%	124.1	14.3%	4%	402.8	22.1%	4%	260.4	n/a
8%	209.5		8%	63.5		8%	264.8		8%	201.3	
12%	109.7		12%	19.6		12%	162.4		12%	158.3	
16%	34.4		16%	-12.7		16%	85.1		16%	126.6	
0%	530.6		0%	209.1		0%	592.8		0%	343.3	

Figure 7.12 ICP Project Solution: Higher Skilled Wages

increase in producer surplus can be measured by an area such as W_1VUW_0 in Figure 7.10. This area can be approximated by $(W_1 - W_0)/2$ multiplied by the amount of labour employed in the project. In other words the additional benefit to labour resulting from the wage increase caused by the project is measured by $(W_1 - W_0)/2$ per unit. When this value is entered in the disaggregated referent group benefit section the adding-up requirement for consistency of the benefit-cost analysis is satisfied.

If undertaking the project drives up the skilled wage from W_0 to W_1, skilled labour employed elsewhere in the economy will also benefit by $(W_1 - W_0)$ per unit. However employers of that labour will experience a cost of $(W_1 - W_0)$ per unit. In other words the increase in the skilled wage results in a transfer of benefit from employers to workers. As explained in Chapter 5, transfers net out and can be ignored in efficiency benefit-cost analysis. However the transfer could be relevant in the referent group analysis if skilled labour was mainly employed by foreign firms.

Figure 7.12 shows the case study spreadsheet of Chapter 6 revised to take account of a project-induced rise in the skilled wage rate. Referring to Table 1, Figure 7.12, the wage rates of supervisors and technicians and other skilled workers are assumed to increase by 20% because of the increased labour demand resulting from the project: the annual salary of individuals working as supervisors and technicians is assumed to increase from 150,000Bt. p.a. to 180,000Bt. p.a., and the annual salary of other skilled workers from 22,500Bt. p.a. to 27,000Bt. p.a.

By comparison with Figure 6.4 it can be seen that introducing this assumption has a number of effects. The higher running costs imply that both the project and private NPVs and IRRs are lower; the project IRR falls from 20.6% to 18.3% and the private IRR falls from 16.7% to 14.3%. Similarly the efficiency IRR falls from 23.4% to 22.1% due to the higher opportunity cost of skilled labour. Total referent group benefits are also lower. The reason for this is that the government's tax revenues from ICP decline as a result of ICP's profits being lower. In other words, the higher opportunity cost of skilled labour reduces the net benefit to both the non-referent group private investor and to government. As a consistency check to verify that the analyst has not made an error in making these adjustments the aggregate referent group benefits at the top of Table 5 (derived by subtracting ICP's cash flow and the overseas lender's cash flow from the efficiency cash flow) should be the same as those on the bottom line (derived by aggregating the sub-referent group members' net cash flows).

APPENDIX TO CHAPTER 7:
Compensating and Equivalent Variation

We saw that the project which led to the market price of the commodity falling from P_0 to P_1 generated a consumer surplus gain of P_0ACP_1 for the individual whose demand curve is illustrated by Figure 7.1. It was argued that the increase in consumer surplus is an approximate measure of what is called the compensating variation – the sum of money which could be taken from (paid to) a person who gains (loses) from the project, still leaving her as well off as in the absence of the project. We now consider this argument in more detail.

To investigate this issue we must digress to one of the more arcane corners of economic science in order to pursue the issue of compensation. Economics deals with "rational" consumers. One of the things a rational consumer exhibits is a preference ordering: offered a choice between two bundles of commodities she can tell us either which bundle she prefers, or that she is indifferent between the two bundles because they offer her the same amount of utility or satisfaction. From the individual consumer's point of view, we can consider the world with, and the world without the proposed project as alternative bundles of goods. In principle we could ask the consumer which bundle she prefers. If she chooses the "with" bundle, it means that she considers that she will be a gainer from the project, and if she chooses the "without" bundle she believes she will be a loser as a result of the project. In the former case (a gainer) we can obtain a money measure of the amount the consumer gains by attaching a money penalty to the "with" bundle, and successively increasing the amount of that penalty until she tells us she is indifferent between the "with" bundle, together with its attendant money penalty, and the "without" bundle. At that point the amount of the money penalty measures the compensating variation. In the latter case (a loser) a money premium must be attached to the "with" bundle to obtain, in a similar manner, the compensating variation measure of the loss.

A critical feature of the above conceptual experiment is the attainment of indifference – the amount of the money penalty or premium is altered until the individual tells us that she is indifferent between the "with" and "without" bundles. Indifference between these two hypothetical states of the world implies that the individual gets the same amount of utility or satisfaction from each. This means that if we want to measure the compensating variation by an area under a demand curve, the relevant demand curve is one which shows all price and quantity combinations which provide the same amount of utility as that yielded by the initial combination (P_0, Q_0). Ordinary, or Marshallian, demand curves do not have the property of holding utility constant as price falls and quantity demanded increases; as price falls, and the individual moves down the ordinary demand curve, utility increases.

To hold utility constant in the face of a fall (rise) in price we have to take some income away from (give some additional income to) the individual. The effect of taking or giving income in compensation for the price change is to offset the income effect of the price change. In the case of a *normal good* (defined as a good which the individual will purchase more of as income rises), the income effect is positive: the increase in income received as compensation for a price rise causes an increase in quantity of the good demanded, and the reduction in income as a result of having had to pay compensation for a fall in price causes a reduction in quantity demanded. This means that the utility-constant demand curve passing though the point A in Figure A7.1 is to the right of the observed demand curve for prices higher than P_0 (because compensation has been paid to the individual, thereby increasing quantity demanded, as compared with the ordinary demand curve) and to the left of it for prices lower than P_0 (because compensation has been taken from the individual, thereby reducing quantity demanded, as compared with the ordinary demand curve). In other words, the utility-constant demand curve passing through A is steeper than the observed demand curve, and this is true for all price quantity combinations on the ordinary demand curve. This is illustrated in Figure A7.1 where two utility-constant demand curves, denoted by D_{U0} and D_{U1} are drawn through points A and C on the ordinary demand curve, D_0.

If we start at price P_0 in Figure A7.1 and reduce price to P_1, the area P_0AFP_1, under the utility-constant demand curve D_{U0}, measures the amount we can take from the individual in compensation for the fall in price, while maintaining her original level of utility. This is the measure of the benefit of a price fall required under the Kaldor–Hicks criterion. If we start at price P_1 and raise price to P_0, the area P_0GCP_1, under the utility-constant demand curve D_{U1}, measures the amount we must pay the individual in compensation for the rise in price, to maintain her original level of utility. This is the measure of the cost of a price rise required under the Kaldor–Hicks criterion. It can be seen from Figure A7.1 that the area of consumer surplus measured under the observed demand curve (P_0ACP_1) overstates the measure of compensating variation for a price fall, and understates the measure for a price rise. However, since the extent of the shift in the individual's demand for a commodity in response to a relatively small increase in income is likely to be slight, the utility-constant demand curves are likely to be very similar to the ordinary demand curve (contrary to Figure A7.1 which is drawn for expositional purposes), and the size of the error is likely to be small.

The notion of compensation requires that money is paid to those who will lose as a result of a project, and taken from those who will gain (negative compensation). A related notion is that of equivalence: the equivalent variation is the sum of money to be paid to an individual to make her as well off in the absence of the project as she would have been if the project had gone ahead. In other words, the equivalent variation is a sum of money to be paid to (taken from) a potential gainer (loser) from a project *in lieu* of the project. In the example illustrated in Figure A7.1 the fall in price from P_0 to P_1 enables the consumer to increase her consumption of

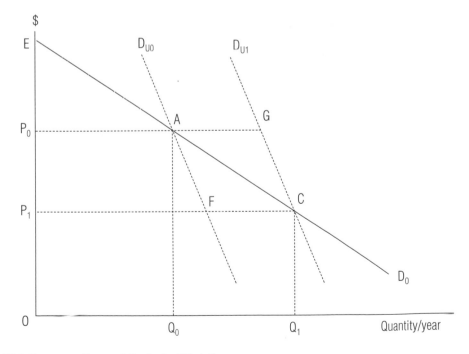

Figure A7.1 Compensating and Equivalent Variation

the commodity from Q_0 to Q_1. Suppose that the price had remained at P_0. Money would have had to have been paid to the individual to make her as well off as she would have been if the project had gone ahead. As she receives additional income her utility-constant demand curve shifts to the right of the original curve, D_{U0}, until it passes through the point (P_1,Q_1) where she is as well off as she would have been if the price of the commodity had fallen. The sum of money required to achieve this increase in utility, termed the equivalent variation, is measured by the increase in consumer surplus measured under the demand curve at the new level of utility between the prices P_0 and P_1, and is given by P_0GCP_1.

Now suppose that the original equilibrium is at (P_1,Q_1) in Figure A7.1 and that price rises from P_1 to P_0. We can measure the compensating variation associated with this change in price by the area of reduced consumer surplus between P_1 and P_0 under the utility constant demand curve passing through (P_1,Q_1), measured by area P_0GCP_1. This is a sum of money to be paid to the individual in compensation for a price increase. However, recalling the discussion in the previous paragraph, it is also the sum of money which is equivalent to the fall in price from P_0 to P_1 when the consumer is at the equilibrium point (P_0,Q_0). In other words, the compensating variation for a fall (rise) in price is the same as the equivalent variation for a rise (fall) in price over the same range.

It follows from the above discussion that, perhaps contrary to intuition, the compensating and equivalent variations for a given change in price are not equal in absolute value. For example, starting at the equilibrium (P_0,Q_0), the sum of money which must be taken from the individual to make her as well off when price falls to P_1 as she was in the initial equilibrium (the compensating variation for the price fall from P_0 to P_1) is smaller than the sum of money which must be paid to the individual to make her as well off as she would have been had the price fallen from P_0 to P_1 (the equivalent variation for the price fall from P_0 to P_1). Question 6 in the Exercises section of this Chapter illustrates this point.

Further Reading

The discussion of compensation in this Chapter has been simplified to bring out the essential points. A more technical summary is available in H. Mohring, "Alternative Welfare Gain and Loss Measures", *Western Economic Journal*, Vol. 9, 1971, pp. 349–368. A useful book on welfare economics which includes a diagrammatic exposition of the concepts of compensating and equivalent variation is D. M. Winch, *Analytical Welfare Economics* (Penguin Books, 1971). A paper by R. D. Willig, "Consumer Surplus without Apology", *American Economic Review*, Vol. 66, 1976, pp. 589–597, discusses the significance of income effects in measuring compensating variation in benefit-cost analysis. See also Boardman et al., *Cost-Benefit Analysis: Concepts and Practice* (Prentice Hall, 2001), Ch. 3.

Exercises

1. A new publicly financed bridge is expected to reduce the cost of auto travel between two areas by $1 per trip. This cost reduction to motorists consists of a reduction in travel time, auto depreciation and petrol expenses totalling $1.50 per trip, less the $0.50 bridge toll which the government will collect. Before the bridge was built there were 1 million trips per year between the two areas. Once the bridge is in operation it is estimated that there will be 1.5 million trips per year between the two areas.
   In terms of areas under the demand curve, what is the annual benefit of the bridge:
   (a) to motorists?
   (b) to the government?
   What other referent group benefits would need to be considered in a social benefit-cost analysis?

2. (a) Briefly outline the model and principles you would use to conduct a benefit-cost analysis of a highway project which will reduce the travel time between two cities (include the appropriate diagram showing the demand for trips in your explanation);
   (b) Using the above framework, together with the following information and any reasonable assumptions you need to make about the values of variables and the timing of benefit flows, work out a rough estimate of the present value of the benefit to users of an extension to the Pacific Motorway:
   Current usage rate: 85,000 trips per day
   Estimated future usage: 170,000 trips per day by 2020
   Estimated time saved per trip at current usage rate: 10 minutes;
   (c) The capital cost of the project is reported to have a present value of $850 million. Using this value, work out a rough estimate of the net present value of the project;
   (d) Briefly discuss the accuracy of your net present value estimate as a measure of the net social benefit of the project, taking account of any significant omissions from your analysis.

3. The Headless Valley Water Control Board (HVWCB) will undertake an irrigation project which will provide 10 million gallons of water annually to 100 wheat farms of 100 acres each. The HVWCB will charge $0.02 per gallon for the water, which will be distributed equally among the 100 farms. It is estimated that:
   (i) land rent in Headless Valley will rise by $70 per acre per annum;
   (ii) 50 farm labourers will be attracted to work on Headless Valley farms, at the market wage of $2000 per annum, from the vineyards of nearby Sunshine Valley;
   (iii) production of wheat on Headless Valley farms is subject to constant returns to scale.
   Assuming the referent group is the economy as a whole, work out the annual social benefit of the irrigation project in terms of areas defined by demand and supply curves for output or inputs. Explain your answer with specific reference to your assumptions about the labour market.

4. Comment critically on the following approaches to measuring project benefits:
   (a) an analyst measures the annual benefit of a bridge as the gain in consumer surplus to bridge users plus the increase in annual rental value of properties served by the bridge;
   (b) an analyst measures the annual benefit of an irrigation project by the increase in the value of food production, plus the increase in rental value of the land served by the project. He takes the present value of the annual benefit, calculated in this way, and adds the increase in capital value of the land to obtain an estimate of the present value of the benefit.

5. When a public project results in lowering the price of a particular commodity (Commodity A) it impacts on the markets for complementary or substitute commodities. Give some examples of this type of relationship. Choose one of the examples (call it Commodity B) and use it to explain in detail the relevance of the changes in the market for Commodity B for the benefit-cost analysis of the project which results in a lower price for Commodity A.

6. Ellsworth spends all of his income on two goods, x and y. He always consumes the same quantity of x as he does of y, $Q_x = Q_y$. Ellsworth's current weekly income is $150 and the price of x and the price of y are both $1 per unit. Ellsworth's boss is thinking of sending him to New York where the price of x is $1 and the price of y is $2. The boss offers no raise in pay, although he will pay the moving costs. Ellsworth says that although he doesn't mind moving for its own sake, and New York is just as pleasant as Boston, where he currently lives, he is concerned about the higher price of good y in New York: he says that having to move is as bad as a cut in weekly pay of $A. He also says he wouldn't mind moving if when he moved he got a raise of $B per week. What are the values of A and B?
   a   A = 50 B = 50.
   b   A = 75 B = 75.
   c   A = 75 B = 100.
   d   A = 50 B = 75.
   e   None of the above.
   Which is the compensating, and which the equivalent variation? Explain.
   (Hint: see the Appendix to Chapter 7).

8

Valuing Traded and Non-traded Commodities in Benefit-Cost Analysis

Introduction

A project undertaken in an open economy may result in changes in the flows of goods and services which are exported or imported. It is not important whether the actual output of the project is exported, or the actual inputs imported. If the output is a traded commodity (a commodity which the country exchanges in international trade) it may be exported or it may replace imports; similarly, if the inputs are traded commodities they may be imported or they may come from domestic sources which are replaced by increased imports or reduced exports. The changes in international trade flows resulting from the project need to be valued, and the prices which measure the benefit or cost to the economy of changes in exports or imports are international prices.

Projects which involve outputs or inputs of traded commodities are likely also to involve outputs and inputs of non-traded commodities (goods and services which are not involved in the country's international trade), and these non-traded commodities are valued at domestic prices. The benefit-cost analysis of such projects requires comparisons of values of traded and non-traded goods. This poses two problems: first, since traded good prices are denominated in foreign currency (often US$) and non-traded good prices are denominated in domestic currency, an exchange rate is required to convert from one to the other; and, second, the domestic price structure differs from the international price structure, and benefits and costs must be valued under the same price structure if they are to be compared.

Traded and Non-traded Goods

We start this discussion of the distinction between traded and non-traded goods by considering a broader distinction – that between tradeable and non-tradeable goods. A tradeable good or service is one that is *capable* of being traded in international markets. Many commodities are tradeable – steel, cement, wheat, consulting services etc. The main reason some commodities are non-tradeable is that they have high international transport costs relative to their production cost. For example, services such as haircuts are non-tradeable because no one is willing to pay the cost of travelling abroad to get a haircut; perishables such as fresh bread and milk are non-tradeable because of the high cost of keeping them fresh while they are being transported; and bulky commodities such as sand and gravel are non-tradeable because of high transport costs relative to their market prices. The fact that cost is the key factor in determining tradeability is illustrated by the recent example of a wealthy New Yorker paying for Vidal Sassoon to fly over from Paris to provide a hair style, thereby possibly removing haircuts as the time-honoured example of a non-tradeable service!

Where commodities do not currently enter into international trade for reasons of cost, either:

- the domestic price of the good is lower than the c.i.f. import price and hence no domestic customer wants to import the good; or
- the domestic price of the good is higher than the f.o.b. export price and hence no foreign customer wants to import the good (i.e. export it from the producing country).

The c.i.f. (cost, insurance and freight) price is the price of an imported good at the border, and the f.o.b. (free on board) price is the price of an exported good at the border. The basic condition for a commodity to be a non-tradeable commodity under current cost conditions is:

$$\text{f.o.b. price} < \text{domestic price} < \text{c.i.f. price}$$

Of course there are other trade-related costs, such as domestic handling, transport and storage costs and agents' fees, but we will ignore these in this discussion.

In considering the costs of international trade we have to decide how to treat tariffs. Tariffs are not a social cost in themselves, as they involve no real resources beyond those required to collect them. However they are a private cost and do inhibit the imports of the country which levies the tariff, and the exports of potential supplying countries. Suppose that a good is tradeable in the absence of a tariff, but is made prohibitively expensive as a result of the tariff. Should we treat it as a traded or non-traded good? This is a fundamental question as it forces us to choose between dealing with the world as it "ought to be" from the viewpoint of economic efficiency, and the world as it is. The former is the world of the economic planner, whereas, we argue, the latter is the world inhabited by the benefit-cost analyst. The benefit-cost analyst takes the world as it is, warts and all. The relevant distinction is not between tradeability and non-tradeability, but rather between commodities that are actually traded and commodities that are not. The basic condition for a commodity to be non-traded is:

$$\text{f.o.b. price less export tax} < \text{domestic price} < \text{c.i.f. price plus import duty}$$

If the commodity in question is not traded because of tariffs or other taxes, and if it will remain not traded once the project is undertaken, then we treat it as a non-traded good in the analysis.

Valuing Traded and Non-traded Commodities in Benefit-Cost Analysis

Once we introduce international trade into the benefit-cost framework we must take account of both traded and non-traded outputs and inputs. The value or cost to the economy of project output or inputs of traded goods is established in international markets. This is true irrespective of whether the particular units of output or inputs enter into international trade: for example, if a project produces a quantity of an importable good, it replaces that quantity of imports thereby avoiding the cost of imports measured at the c.i.f. price; if it uses a quantity of an importable good as an input, the economy incurs a cost measured by the value of that quantity at the c.i.f. price; if it produces a quantity of an exportable good, exports valued at the f.o.b. price per unit can be increased; and if it uses a quantity of an exportable good as an input, exports valued at the f.o.b. price per unit have to be curtailed.

While traded goods have to be valued at international prices and non-traded goods at domestic prices, values of traded and non-traded goods have to be compared in the benefit-cost analysis. In order to compare like with like it is necessary either to convert domestic prices to equivalent international prices, or to convert international prices to equivalent domestic prices. Furthermore, international prices are denominated in foreign currency (often US$) whereas domestic prices are denominated in domestic currency. An exchange rate is required to convert from one to another, and while there is normally only one official exchange rate, there is also a notional exchange rate devised by economists to take account of the effects of tariffs and other taxes or subsidies on domestic relative to international prices, and known as the **shadow-exchange rate**. The benefit-cost analyst has to decide which set of prices to use to value project inputs and outputs – world prices or domestic prices – and which rate of exchange to use in converting foreign currency prices to domestic currency or *vice versa*.

Domestic and International Price Structures: A Worked Example

Consider a simple example of how tariff protection can result in two sets of prices – domestic and international – and two exchange rates – the official rate and the shadow rate – and the implications for project evaluation. The example is first presented in real terms, without using domestic and foreign currencies to value outputs and inputs, in order to emphasize that the important issue is that of opportunity cost. Currencies and prices are then introduced to illustrate how benefit-cost analysis addresses this issue in practice.

Evaluation of an Import-replacing Project in Real Terms

Suppose a country has one factor of production, labour, which is non-traded and fully employed. Two traded goods are produced – food and clothing, and there is a 100% tariff on imported clothing. We can choose units of food and clothing such that the international price ratio is 1: for example, if a unit of clothing – thirty suits – costs the same as a unit of food – 1 tonne – then the ratio of the price of a unit of clothing to a unit of food is 1. On the domestic market, on the other hand, the price of a unit of clothing will be twice the price of a unit of food because of the tariff on clothing. This establishes the fact that there are two sets of relative prices – domestic and international. The international price is usually referred to as the **border price** – the price of exports f.o.b. or the price of imports c.i.f.

Now suppose that the domestic economy is competitive, with no tax distortions apart from the tariff on clothing. This means that labour transferred from food to clothing production would reduce the value of output of food by the same amount as it would increase the value of output of clothing, where both values are measured at current domestic prices. Since these values are equal at domestic prices, and since the domestic price of clothing is twice that of food, this means that if we choose the quantity of labour such that food production is reduced by one unit by the reallocation of labour, clothing production will increase by half a unit. What would be the efficiency net benefit of a project involving such a reallocation of labour?

The extra half unit of clothing produced domestically could be used to replace imports of half a unit of clothing. Since units of food and clothing trade on a 1:1 basis on world markets, exports of food could be reduced by half a unit. The net effect of the reallocation of labour in this case is a loss of half a unit of food – a reduction of one unit of domestic production partially offset by a reduction in exports by half a unit. Alternatively, exports of food could be reduced by one full unit, to keep the domestic supply of food constant, in which case imports of clothing would have to fall by one unit. The net loss to the economy would then be half a unit of clothing.

It is clear from the example that the country is worse off as a result of the proposed import-replacing project: the loss is some weighted average of half a unit of clothing and half a unit of food, with the weights depending on how the economy wishes to absorb the loss. If food and clothing are both normal goods (goods whose consumption rises/falls when income rises/falls) then consumers will opt for a reduction in consumption of both goods. In that case, if the proportion of the loss absorbed by reduced food consumption is denoted by the fraction a, then we can say that $0<a<1$, and that the reduction in food consumption is $a/2$ units, and the reduction in clothing consumption $(1-a)/2$ units.

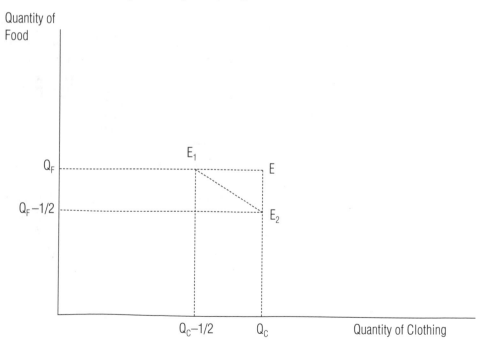

Figure 8.1 Consumption Opportunities with and without an Import-Replacing Project

Figure 8.1 illustrates the options available to consumers with and without the project: without the project the initial consumption bundle is denoted by point E; with the project a consumption bundle along E_1E_2 must be chosen. Clearly such a point will represent less of at least one of the goods, implying that undertaking the project makes the country worse off. However, as we shall see later, the project breaks even when evaluated at domestic prices without taking the tariff distortion into account.

In project evaluation we argue that the efficiency net benefit is given by the value of the extra clothing less the cost of the labour transferred to clothing production. At first sight, as noted above, the project appears to have a net benefit of zero: at domestic market prices the value of the extra clothing equals the cost of the extra labour in clothing production. However we are not comparing like with like: the value to the economy of traded goods such as food and clothing is expressed at international prices, whereas the cost of a non-traded good such as labour is expressed at domestic prices. We have to either convert the value of traded goods to equivalent domestic prices, or convert the value of the non-traded good to world prices to make an appropriate comparison.

Evaluation of an Import-replacing Project in Money Terms

Now let us attach some money prices to the quantities in the example. Suppose the tariff on clothing is 100% as before and that the project involves transferring 1000 Rupees worth of labour from food to clothing production. Suppose that the international prices of food and clothing are both $1000 per unit, and that the official rate of exchange (OER) is 1 Dollar = 1 Rupee. The exchange rate tells us the price of the domestic currency in terms of the foreign currency (US dollars), or, equivalently the price of US dollars in terms of the domestic currency.

In the example the exchange rate is unity whichever way the official rate is specified. In general, however, the price of domestic currency in terms of US dollars is the reciprocal of the price of US dollars in terms of domestic currency, and if we wish to convert US dollars to domestic currency we divide by the former and multiply by the latter. Because this can cause a lot of confusion in our discussion we will adopt the convention that the exchange rate is always expressed as the price of domestic currency in US dollars, which is the form in which it is usually quoted in the financial press. In working with exchange rates you may find it helpful to be explicit about the units involved: for example, OER ($/R) equals (1/OER) (R/$). In practical work it may sometimes be convenient to express the exchange rate in terms of domestic currency per US$ (for example, see Figure 8.5).

At domestic prices 1000 Rupees worth of labour is used to produce half a unit of clothing worth 1000 Rupees in the domestic market. Since the benefit appears to equal the cost the project seems to be a marginal one from the viewpoint of the economy. However we have already seen that undertaking the project makes consumers worse off. Clearly we need a way of evaluating the project that takes account of the distorting effect of the tariff and identifies the project as one that should be rejected on efficiency grounds.

We have seen that the project in the example results in a loss in the form of a weighted average of half a unit of food and half-a-unit of clothing: $a/2$ units of food plus $(1-a)/2$ units of clothing, where $0 < a < 1$, and a is the weight attached to food in the reduction of domestic consumption of food and clothing as a result of the project. The value, at world prices, of the reduced consumption of food is 1000a/2 Rupees and the value of the reduced consumption of clothing is 1000(1 – a)/2 Rupees; these values are obtained by taking the border prices of the goods in Dollars and converting to Rupees using the official exchange rate. However at domestic prices the values are 1000a/2 and 2000(1 – a)/2 Rupees respectively. This means that the ratio of domestic to international value of the consumption goods forgone is [a + 2(1 – a)] > 1. This ratio can be used, together with the official exchange rate, OER expressed in $/Rupee, to construct a shadow-exchange rate, also expressed in $/Rupee: SER = OER/[$a$ + 2(1 – a)], which can be used to convert values at international prices to values at domestic prices. In the example, the official exchange rate is $1/Rupee, but the shadow-exchange rate is $1/ [$a$ + 2(1 – a)] per Rupee.

Now let us consider how the shadow-exchange rate would be used in project evaluation to convert the border prices of food and clothing to domestic equivalent prices. The proposed project produces half a unit of clothing which is worth $500 at border prices. The $500 worth of clothing is converted to domestic prices using the shadow-exchange rate to give a value of 500/SER Rupees. Since we know that 0.5<SER< 1 in this case, because 0<a<1, we know that the value of the extra clothing at domestic prices is less than 1000 Rupees. Since the cost of the labour used to produce the extra clothing is 1000 Rupees, the project has a negative net efficiency benefit. For example, if a = 0.5, the SER = $0.67/ Rupee, the value of the project output is 750 Rupees, and the net efficiency benefit at domestic prices is –250 Rupees, or a loss of 250 Rupees.

Suppose that we decided to evaluate the project in terms of world rather than domestic prices. The output of half a unit of clothing could be valued at the border price of $500 and converted to 500 Rupees at the official exchange rate. However this value could not be compared with the 1000 Rupees labour cost since the latter is denominated in domestic prices. We need to work out the opportunity cost of labour at border prices: if the extra labour had been left in food production it would have produced an extra unit of food which could have been exported to earn foreign exchange. That quantity of foreign exchange could have been used to fund imports of quantities of food and clothing summing to one unit. The value of these imports at border prices is 1000a/2 + 1000(1 – a)/2 Dollars, where a is defined as above. The border value at Dollar prices can be converted to Rupees by dividing by the OER to give 1000[a/2 + (1 – a)/2] Rupees. At domestic prices, however, the imports are worth 1000[a/2 + 2(1 – a)/2] Rupees. Since the ratio of the opportunity cost of labour at domestic prices to its cost at border prices is [a + 2(1 – a)] we need to multiply the value of labour at domestic prices by the reciprocal of this amount to convert to a value in border prices. However we have already seen that 1/[a + 2(1 – a)] is the ratio SER/OER. Thus to convert from values at domestic prices to values at border prices, multiply by the ratio SER/OER. For example, if OER is 1 and SER is 0.67 the opportunity cost, at border prices, of the labour used in the project is 1000* 0.67/1 Rupees. This cost of 667 Rupees exceeds the value of the extra clothing output at border prices by 167 Rupees. Hence the net efficiency benefit is –167 Rupees, a negative net benefit, or, in other words, a net loss.

It can be seen that, while both approaches to measuring net efficiency benefit assign a negative net benefit to the project, they give different numerical results: at domestic prices the loss is 250 Rupees and at border prices it is 167 Rupees. However this difference is not surprising – different relative prices give different valuations. We can convert a value at domestic prices to a value at border prices by multiplying by SER/OER, or a value at border prices to a value at domestic prices by multiplying by OER/SER. Thus 250 Rupees multiplied by 0.67/1 equals 167, and 167 Rupees multiplied by 1/0.67 equals 250 Rupees.

Referent Group Net Benefits

In the above example the efficiency net benefit is the same as the sum of the net benefits to the referent group (foreigners are unaffected by what happens domestically as long as international prices do not change). There are four domestic groups which, it might be considered, could possibly be affected: producers, consumers, labour and government. However, as it turns out in this case, domestic producers of each product are unaffected because the change in revenue equals the change in cost; consumers are unaffected directly because the extra clothing is worth the same as the reduced food output on the domestic market; and as far as labour is concerned, the wage bill is unchanged. The only change directly experienced by the referent group is a reduction in tariff revenues because of the additional output of clothing, which replaces an equivalent amount of imports. In the example the reduction in tariff revenues is $1000(1 - a)/2$ Rupees which amounts to 250 Rupees when $a = 0.5$. This figure, which is the sum of the values of the changes experienced by all groups affected by the project, is the net efficiency benefit (a loss in this case) of the proposed project calculated at domestic prices, and it could be converted to a loss at border prices in the usual way. A loss in government tariff revenue will mean a reduction in provision of goods and services which implies that the project will affect domestic consumers indirectly.

Summary of the Two Approaches to Valuation: Border *vs.* Domestic Prices

In summary, once we recognize that markets may be distorted by regulation or tariffs, we can no longer rely on the official exchange rate to generate the appropriate relative valuation of traded and non-traded goods. There are two solutions to this problem: either convert domestic valuations of non-traded goods to world price equivalents, or convert world valuations of traded goods to domestic price equivalents. Under the former approach we use the OER to generate domestic currency prices of traded goods, and shadow-price domestic non-traded goods prices to account for trade and domestic market distortions; under the latter approach we convert the world prices of traded goods to equivalent domestic prices, using a shadow-exchange rate (SER), and shadow-price non-traded commodities to take account of distortions and imperfections in domestic markets only. As the above example demonstrated, the two approaches give the same result in terms of project ranking and selection, and we need to discuss why this is in general the case. However it should be emphasized that it is only a difference between the OER and the SER, arising from distortions in the commodities or foreign exchange markets, that distinguishes the two approaches. Distortions in the foreign exchange market and the calculation of the SER are discussed later in this Chapter. First we discuss the two approaches in general and demonstrate their equivalence.

The Equivalence of the Two Approaches

As noted above, the analyst has a choice of whether to use domestic prices or border prices to value benefits and costs. It is important to understand that what is at issue is not the currency in which values will be denominated – this will be the domestic currency in either case – but the set of prices which will be used. The two conventions described above are known as:

- the UNIDO approach, named after the United Nations International Development Organization guidelines, which advocates the use of non-traded goods (domestic) price equivalents (see United Nations *Guidelines for Project Evaluation*, New York, 1970);
- the LM approach, named after its authors Little and Mirrlees and adopted by the Organization for Economic Cooperation and Development (OECD), which advocates using traded goods price equivalents (border prices) (see OECD *Manual of Industrial Project Analysis in Developing Countries*, Paris, 1968). The LM approach was further developed by Squire and van der Tak (1975) and is sometimes referred to as the LMST approach.

It is important to understand that while these approaches generally yield different estimates of project NPV, a project which is accepted (NPV>0) by one method is always accepted by the other, provided that the same data are used in the calculation of the relevant shadow-prices and the shadow-exchange rate.

To recap, under the UNIDO approach non-traded commodities are valued at domestic prices (shadow-priced to reflect domestic market imperfections), and traded commodities are valued at international prices (US$) which are converted to domestic prices using the shadow-exchange rate (SER). Under the LM approach traded commodities are valued at international prices converted to domestic currency by means of the official exchange rate (OER), and non-traded commodities are shadow-priced to account for domestic market imperfections, and also adjusted for foreign exchange market distortions using the SER. The OER is either the fixed rate set by the government or the market rate established by the foreign exchange (FOREX) market. The best way to illustrate the way the two approaches operate is by the kind of example discussed above, but first we need to convince ourselves that they will always give the same result in terms of whether the project has a positive or negative NPV.

Suppose that a project uses imports, M, and a non-traded commodity such as unskilled domestic labour, N, to produce an exported good, X. The traded commodities X and M are denominated in US$ and the non-traded commodity is denominated in domestic currency. Suppose that there are two types of distortions in the domestic economy: tariffs, resulting in a divergence between the OER and the SER; and a minimum wage resulting in unemployment of unskilled labour. The two approaches to calculating project NPV in an efficiency benefit-cost analysis can be summarized as follows:

(i) $\qquad$ UNIDO: $NPV(1) = (1/SER)X - (1/SER)M - bN,$

where SER is the shadow-exchange rate (measured in US$ per unit of local currency, and discussed later in this Chapter) and b is the shadow-price of domestic labour which takes account of unemployment as described in Chapter 5;

(ii)   LM: NPV(2) = (1/OER)X – (1/OER)M – cN,

where OER is the official exchange rate (measured in US$ per unit of local currency), and c is the shadow-price of domestic labour which takes account of both unemployment and trade distortions.

To see the equivalence of the two approaches, multiply NPV(1) by the ratio of SER/OER:

(iii)   NPV(1)(SER/OER) = (1/OER)X – (1/OER)M – b(SER/OER)N.

It can be seen that expression (iii) is the same as expression (ii) if b(SER/OER) = c. Recall that the value b shadow-prices the non-traded input to account for domestic distortions only, whereas the value c shadow-prices for both domestic distortions and foreign exchange market distortions. It follows that the value b, shadow-priced by the ratio SER/OER to account for foreign exchange market distortions, must equal the value c. In other words, NPV(1) (SER/OER) = NPV(2): the NPV under the LM approach is the NPV under the UNIDO approach multiplied by the ratio of the shadow to the official exchange rate. Hence when NPV(1) is positive, NPV(2) must be positive. Of course if there are no imperfections (tariffs or regulations) in the traded goods or FOREX markets, OER = SER and the distinction between the two approaches collapses.

In the above example the input supplied locally was unskilled labour, a non-traded commodity. However, in the absence of the project, some of that portion of the unskilled labour which would have been employed elsewhere in the economy might have produced traded goods, and, consequently, should be treated as a traded good in the benefit-cost analysis. Furthermore, suppose that the input had been concrete blocks produced locally from imported cement and unskilled labour. In principle we would identify the share of the cost of the blocks represented by imported cement and treat it as a traded good in the benefit-cost analysis, with the labour cost share being treated as a non-traded good. In principle every commodity produced as an output by, or used as an input in, projects undertaken in the economy could be assigned its own shadow-price. Squire and van der Tak (1975) describe how these shadow-prices – termed accounting rates or conversion factors – can be computed. However these refinements to the analysis require some very detailed information about the structure of the domestic economy which may not always be readily available, and they are often ignored in practice.

What is the logic, under the LM approach, of shadow-pricing the non-traded good, domestic labour, to account for distortions in international markets as well as those in the domestic labour market? When we shadow-price to account for unemployment we convert the wage of labour to a measure of its opportunity cost in the domestic economy – the value of what it would produce in an alternative occupation. However under the LM approach the goods or services produced by domestic labour in an alternative occupation have to be valued at border (international) prices. The question is: what is the equivalent in domestic currency of the US$ value of what the labour could produce if it were not employed on the project? The domestic currency overstates the opportunity cost of labour if the currency is overvalued relative to the US$ (i.e. SER<OER) because of international market distortions. This problem can be solved by converting the measure of opportunity cost to US$ using the SER, to get an accurate measure of opportunity cost at world prices, and then converting the US$ figure back to domestic currency by means of the OER, so that the opportunity cost of labour is measured in the same currency as the other project costs and benefits. For example, suppose that unskilled labour is willing to work for 3 Kina per hour (its domestic shadow-price) and that the shadow-exchange rate is 1.5 Kina = 1US$. This suggests that an hour of unskilled labour can produce US$2.0 worth of goods at world prices. In common with other US$ values in the benefit-cost analysis this figure is converted to domestic currency by means of the OER, say 1.33 Kina to the US$, to give an opportunity cost of 2.66 Kina.

The UNIDO and LM approaches are summarized in Figure 8.2 which illustrates an example of a simple project in Papua New Guinea (PNG). The project uses US$1 of imports and 5 Kina's worth of domestic labour to produce US$6 worth of exports. Because of the high rate of unemployment in PNG, the opportunity cost of domestic labour, in terms of the value of forgone output at domestic prices, is assumed to be 60% of the market wage. It can be seen from Figure 8.2 that the two approaches give the same result in the sense that the project NPV is positive in both cases, but different results in terms of the actual value of the NPV. It can be verified from the data in Figure 8.2 that if the NPV under the LM approach is multiplied by the ratio of (OER/SER) the NPV under the UNIDO approach is obtained: 3.99K multiplied by 0.75/0.67 equals 4.47K.

UNIDO		LM	
Tradeables	**Non-Tradeables**	**Tradeables**	**Non-Tradeables**
Use border prices in US dollars converted to domestic currency using the SER	Use domestic prices in domestic currency shadow-priced for domestic distortions	Use border prices in US dollars converted to domestic currency using the OER	Use domestic prices in domestic currency shadow-priced for domestic distortions and adjusted for FOREX market distortions using SER/OER

Example: OER: $0.75/Kina, implying that 1.3333 Kina = 1US$
SER: $0.67/Kina, implying that 1.4925 Kina = 1US$
Shadow-price of labour: 60% of market wage

Exports	Imports	Labour	Exports	Imports	Labour
$6	$1	K5	$6	$1	K5
K8.96	K1.49	K3	K8.0	K1.33	K2.68
Net Benefit = K4.47			**Net Benefit = K3.99**		

Figure 8.2 The UNIDO and LM Approaches to Project Appraisal

The example can be further developed to identify and measure referent group benefits. The referent group generally consists of the domestic economy, or some subset of it. It is natural for members of the referent group to measure benefits and costs at domestic prices, and hence the UNIDO approach is more suitable for this purpose. Suppose that the referent group is PNG and that the firm is domestically owned. There are three sub-groups potentially affected by the project: the firm, domestic labour, and the government. If we assume, for simplicity, that there are no taxes or tariffs (the distortion in the FOREX market is a fixed exchange rate) government revenues will not be affected by the project. The firm reports a profit of 1.67 Kina (its revenue less its costs, with foreign exchange converted to Kina at the OER), and labour receives a rent of 2 Kina (the wage less what labour could earn in an alternative occupation). However, because of the distortion in the FOREX market, the sum of these two measures of referent group net benefits understates the aggregate net benefits of the project.

The project's net foreign exchange earnings of US$5 need to be adjusted upwards to reflect the fact that local residents are willing to pay 0.16 Kina above the OER for each US$ (a foreign exchange premium of 17%), implying a benefit in the form of a total foreign exchange premium valued at 0.81 Kina. The total benefit to the referent group is then 4.47 Kina which is the project NPV estimated under the UNIDO approach. The distribution of the foreign exchange premium depends on the rationing system used to allocate foreign exchange. For example, if the firm were able to sell its net earnings of foreign currency on the black market it would appropriate the 0.81 Kina of foreign exchange benefits under the UNIDO approach. On the other hand, if the firm is forced to sell the foreign currency to the Central Bank at the OER, the bank appropriates the benefit.

Determinants of the Shadow-Exchange Rate

We now analyse the factors which determine the SER. The need for an SER arises from imperfections in international markets which have two main sources: fixed exchange rates and tariffs, taxes and subsidies on exports and imports. We consider fixed exchange rates first.

Suppose that a country decides to regulate the rate at which its currency can (legally) be exchanged for foreign currency. For example, PNG until recently operated a fixed exchange rate: the Kina was set at an artificially high rate against the US$ so that foreign companies wishing to do business in PNG had to pay above market value for Kina. Figure 8.3 illustrates a foreign exchange market distorted by a fixed exchange rate (note the resemblance to Figure 5.3 which illustrated the effect of a minimum wage). The horizontal axis shows the quantity of foreign exchange (US$) traded, and the vertical axis shows the price in Kina/US$. Suppose the regulated price is 1.33 Kina per US$, which implies an OER of $0.75 per Kina, and which overvalues the Kina since the market equilibrium price in terms of Kina per US$ is higher than 1.33. In the distorted market equilibrium illustrated in Figure 8.3 an additional US$ is actually worth 1.5 Kina, implying an exchange rate of $0.67 per Kina. If there was a small unofficial market in foreign exchange this is the price that we would expect to observe: a tourist could get 1.5 Kina for every US$. In terms of the UNIDO and LM approaches, the OER is $0.75 and the SER is $0.67.

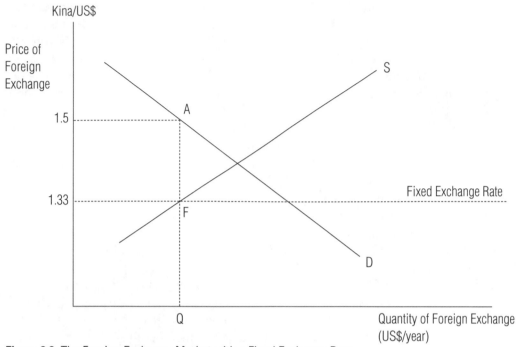

Figure 8.3 The Foreign Exchange Market with a Fixed Exchange Rate

Some foreign exchange markets are distorted by both fixed exchange rates and tariffs and subsidies. However to keep our diagrams simple we will now assume that there is a floating exchange rate, but that exports and imports are subject to taxes and subsidies. The effect of these taxes and subsidies is to shift the demand for imports and the supply of exports, and hence to shift the demand and supply curves for foreign exchange. In Figure 8.4, the demand and supply curves for foreign exchange in the absence of taxes and subsidies are denoted by D and S respectively, and those in the presence of the market distortions by D_t and S_t. It can be seen from Figure 8.4 that, in this example, the distortions have reduced the demand for foreign exchange – tariffs discourage imports – and increased the supply of foreign exchange – export subsidies promote exports.

Suppose that a proposed project involves importing some equipment. What value should be placed on the foreign exchange required to purchase the equipment? The effect of the project is to cause a small increase in the demand for foreign exchange, as illustrated by the demand curve D_p in Figure 8.4, and a small fall in the market exchange rate (the OER, measured in $/Kina) which we will disregard as being too small to measure. However this small fall in OER will reduce the quantity of foreign exchange demanded (because, for example, more Kina are required to buy each US$), and increase the quantity of foreign exchange supplied (because at the new OER foreigners get more Kina per US$). In this way the proposed project diverts some foreign exchange from the purchase of other imports, and draws in some foreign exchange earned through additional exports.

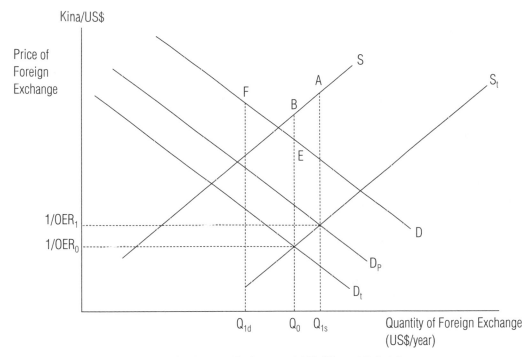

Figure 8.4 Supply and Demand for Foreign Exchange with Tariffs and Subsidies

To calculate the SER we need to value the foreign exchange used in the project at its opportunity cost. The opportunity cost of the quantity of foreign exchange $(Q_0 - Q_{1d})$, which is diverted from the purchase of imports, is given by FEQ_0Q_{1d} in Figure 8.4, while the opportunity cost of earning the additional quantity of foreign exchange $(Q_{1s} - Q_0)$ is given by $BAQ_{1s}Q_0$. The sum of these two areas is the opportunity cost, measured in domestic currency, of the foreign exchange to be used in the project. It can be seen that the opportunity cost in Kina of the foreign exchange is higher than the nominal cost as measured by the OER. To get a measure of the opportunity cost we convert the foreign exchange to Kina using the SER. Following our convention the SER is expressed in $/Kina and, in this example, is lower than the OER. When foreign exchange is converted to domestic currency by dividing by the SER, a higher value is obtained than if the OER were used.

The previous analysis can be developed in more detail to identify the effect of taxes and subsidies on the SER. Recall that the proposed project diverted some foreign exchange from imports (we will denote this quantity by d_{FEM}) and derived some from exports (denoted by d_{FEX}). To calculate the opportunity cost (denominated in domestic currency) to the economy of the additional foreign exchange we value d_{FEM} at the price given by the demand curve, D, and d_{FEX} at the price given by the supply curve, S, in Figure 8.4.

The demand curve D shows where the demand curve for foreign exchange to purchase imports would be if there were no tariffs. The effect of tariffs is to reduce the demand for foreign exchange and the price importers are willing to pay for it by an amount determined by the size of the tariff. In other words, the opportunity cost, in Kina, of d_{FEM} is $d_{FEM}(1+t)/OER$ where t is the tariff rate expressed as a proportion of the US$ c.i.f. price. The supply curve S shows where the supply curve of foreign exchange to purchase exports would be if there were no taxes or subsidies on exports. In Figure 8.4 S_t is to the right of S, suggesting that the net effect of taxes and subsidies on exports is to reduce their price to foreign purchasers, thereby increasing the quantity demanded, and hence increasing the supply of foreign exchange. The opportunity cost, in Kina, of d_{FEX} is given by $d_{FEX}(1+s-d)/OER$ where s is the proportional subsidy and d the proportional tax on exports. Since we are assuming that the net effect of the tax/subsidy regime is to lower the price of exports, s>d, and the opportunity cost of the foreign exchange derived from this source is therefore higher than its value at the OER.[1]

The SER is a notional or accounting exchange rate, as opposed to a market rate, measured in US$ per unit of local currency, which when divided into the amount of foreign exchange used in a project will give a measure of the opportunity cost, measured in units of local currency, of that foreign exchange. We have worked out an expression for the social opportunity cost of foreign exchange:

$$SOC = d_{FEM}.(1+t)/OER + d_{FEX}.(1+s-d)/OER.$$

Suppose that the amount of foreign exchange to be used in the project is represented by QF and that $d_{FEM} = b.QF$ and $d_{FEX} = (1 - b).QF$, i.e. that the foreign exchange is obtained from reduced imports and increased exports in the proportions b and $(1 - b)$ respectively. We can now rewrite our expression for SOC as:

$$SOC = \{b.(1+t) + (1-b).(1+s-d)\}.QF/OER.$$

This expression tells us that we can calculate the opportunity cost of a quantity of foreign exchange (US$) by dividing it by $OER/\{b.(1+t) + (1-b).(1+s-d)\}$. It follows that $OER/\{b.(1+t) + (1-b).(1+s-d)\}$ is the shadow-exchange rate, SER, because this is the exchange rate, in US$ per unit of local currency, which, when divided into the quantity of foreign exchange, converts it to a measure of opportunity cost in local currency. Since SER<OER, the effect of shadow-pricing foreign exchange, under the assumptions made here, is to raise the cost of foreign exchange above its value at the OER.

A reasonable assumption is that the proposed project diverts foreign exchange from the purchase of imports in the same proportion as imports are in total foreign trade: in other words, that $b = M/(X+M)$ where M and X are the values of total imports and exports respectively. On this basis we can rewrite the SER as:

$$SER = OER/\{(M/(X+M)).(1+t) + (X/(X+M)).(1+s-d)\},$$

where the expression $\{(M/(X+M)).(1+t) + (X/(X+M)).(1+s-d)\}$ is (1+FEP) where FEP is the foreign exchange premium. In the example of Figure 8.3, OER = $0.75, SER = $0.67 and (1+FEP) = (OER/SER) = 1.17, and FEP = 0.17.

---

1   In the case of exports the net subsidy is usually applied to the domestic price, P_d, so that $P_d(1-s+d) = P_w/OER$, where P_w is the world price in US$. The opportunity cost per unit of the exported good is $P_d = P_w/OER(1-s+d)$. However, in the literature the opportunity cost is usually expressed as the world price in domestic currency multiplied by $(1+s-d)$ and we have chosen to adhere to this convention. Since $1/(1-s+d)$ is approximately the same as $(1+s-d)$, the two approaches are equivalent.

Case Study: Shadow-Pricing Foreign Exchange in the ICP Project Evaluation

We now consider how to shadow-price foreign exchange in the benefit-cost analysis of the proposed International Cloth Products project. As noted above, we prefer to use the UNIDO approach as the focus is usually on referent group net benefits and it is more informative to measure these in domestic prices. Using the UNIDO approach implies that in efficiency benefit-cost analysis we will value tradeable goods at the SER rather than the OER. The other shadow-prices in the analysis will not be affected.

While we have no evidence that the Baht is overvalued on foreign exchange markets, we will assume for the sake of argument that the SER is 66Bt. per US$. The overvaluation has no effect on the project or private benefit-cost analyses which are based on market prices. However in the efficiency analysis the exchange rate of 44Bt. will be replaced with 66Bt wherever it occurs. Considering only the tradeable inputs and outputs of the project, benefits are higher relative to costs than is the case for the project as a whole. These changes are shown in the adjusted ICP spreadsheets in Figure 8.5 which should be compared with Figure 6.4 in Chapter 6. A new input is entered into Table 1 of the spreadsheet indicating that the SER is 66 Baht (see Figure 8.5).

It can be seen from Table 4 of Figure 8.5 that the net effect of introducing the shadow-price of foreign exchange is to increase the size of the net efficiency benefit. The efficiency IRR increases from 23.4% to 30.3% (see Figure 8.5). Since the aggregate referent group net benefit is calculated by subtracting the (unchanged) private and foreign financial institution net benefits from the efficiency net benefit, it is clear that net referent group net benefits will also increase.

The question which we now have to address is where the gain in net referent group benefit is experienced. There is no change in any of the referent group benefits which were reported in Table 5 of the spreadsheet in Figure 6.4. However, one additional line needs to be added to the calculation of *Total Government* net benefit. Each time the Central Bank sold a US dollar for imports it valued this at 44 Baht when its true opportunity cost was 66 Baht. Using the SER to calculate the efficiency cost of imported capital goods, spare parts and raw materials increases the efficiency costs as shown in Table 4 of Figure 8.5. Similarly, each time the Central Bank bought a US dollar saved as the result of the purchase of an import substitute (yarn) it valued it at 44 Baht when the true value to the economy was 66 Baht. Using the SER to calculate the efficiency benefits from the sale of yarn increases the project's gross benefits as shown in Table 4 of Figure 8.5. As the increase in gross efficiency benefits is greater than the increase in efficiency costs from this source, the net efficiency benefit is higher when the SER is used.

While this gain will not show up directly as an item in the Central Bank accounts (since changes in foreign exchange reserves are valued at the OER) it nevertheless represents a gain for the economy as a whole: individuals and firms who bought US$ from the Central Bank got them for less than their true value, and those who sold US$ received less than true value. The net effect in the example is a gain, and this is included as a benefit under the heading *Foreign Exchange* in an additional row under *Total Government* in the referent group benefits, as shown in Table 5 of Figure 8.5. This restores the equality in the spreadsheet between aggregate referent group benefits and the sum of net benefits to all members of the referent group.

ICP PROJECT: 1999-2009

TABLE 1 — KEY INPUT VARIABLES

VARIABLES		INVESTMENT C(	000 $'	000 BT'	INNING COSTS		MATERIAL FLOWS		FINANCE	
EXCHANGE RATE	44	SPINDLES	4000		WATER BT 1	480000	COTTON MN	16.2	SUPPLIERS	75%
TARIFF A	5%	EQUIPMEN	850		POWER BT 1	480000	YARN MN LE	15	OVERDRAF	60
TARIFF B	10%	INSTALLA	100		SPARE PAR	10%	LABOUR 1	100	CREDIT RE	5
PROFITS TAX	50%	CONSTRUCTION		36000	INSURANCE	6	LABOUR 2	1000		
DEPRECIATION	10%	START-UP COSTS		18000	OVERHEAD!	0	LABOUR 3	500		
PRICE YARN CIF US$	0.58	WORKING CAPITAL							DISCOUNT	4%
YARN TARIFF BT	2.1	RAW MAT	1200							8%
HANDLING BT	0.3	SPARE PA!	243							12%
TARIFF C	10%									16%
PRICE COTTON CIF US!	0.3	SER		66						
WAGE 1 BT PA	150000									
WAGE 2 BT PA	22500									
WAGE 3 BT PA	12000									
INTEREST RATE 1	8%									
INTEREST RATE 2	10%									

TABLE 2 — PROJECT CALCULATION

YEAR	1999 '000 US$	1999 MN BT	2000 MN BT	2001 MN BT	2002 MN BT	2003 MN BT	2004 MN BT	2005 MN BT	2006 MN BT	2007 MN BT	2008 MN BT	2009 MN BT
INVESTMENT COSTS												
SPINDLES	-4200.000	-184.800										
EQUIPMENT	-892.500	-39.270										
INSTALLATION	-100.000	-4.400										
CONSTRUCTION		-36.000										
START-UP COSTS		-18.000										
RAW MATERIALS		-58.080										58.080
SPARE PARTS		-11.227										11.227
TOTAL	-282.470	-69.307	0.000	0.000	0.000	0.000	0.000	0.000	0.000	0.000	0.000	69.307
RUNNING COSTS												
WATER			-3.600	-7.200	-7.200	-7.200	-7.200	-7.200	-7.200	-7.200	-7.200	-7.200
POWER			-3.600	-7.200	-7.200	-7.200	-7.200	-7.200	-7.200	-7.200	-7.200	-7.200
SPARE PARTS			-22.407	-22.407	-22.407	-22.407	-22.407	-22.407	-22.407	-22.407	-22.407	-22.407
RAW MATERIALS			-117.612	-235.224	-235.224	-235.224	-235.224	-235.224	-235.224	-235.224	-235.224	-235.224
INSURANCE			-6.000	-6.000	-6.000	-6.000	-6.000	-6.000	-6.000	-6.000	-6.000	-6.000
LABOUR			-43.500	-43.500	-43.500	-43.500	-43.500	-43.500	-43.500	-43.500	-43.500	-43.500
TOTAL			-196.719	-321.531	-321.531	-321.531	-321.531	-321.531	-321.531	-321.531	-321.531	-321.531
REVENUES												
SALE OF YARN			209.400	418.800	418.800	418.800	418.800	418.800	418.800	418.800	418.800	418.800
NCF (Project)	-282.470	-56.626	97.269	97.269	97.269	97.269	97.269	97.269	97.269	97.269	97.269	166.576

TABLE 3 — PRIVATE CALCULATION

YEAR	1999 '000 US$	1999 MN BT	2000 MN BT	2001 MN BT	2002 MN BT	2003 MN BT	2004 MN BT	2005 MN BT	2006 MN BT	2007 MN BT	2008 MN BT	2009 MN BT
FINANCIAL FLOWS												
DEPRECIATION			-26.447	-26.447	-26.447	-26.447	-26.447	-26.447	-26.447	-26.447	-26.447	-26.447
INTEREST												
SUPPLIERS CREDIT	3637.500	160.050	-12.804	-10.621	-8.264	-5.719	-2.969					
REPAYMENT			-27.282	-29.464	-31.821	-34.367	-37.116					
BANK OVERDRAFT			60.000	-6.000	-6.000	-6.000	-6.000	-6.000	-6.000	-6.000	-6.000	-6.000
REPAYMENT												-60.000
NET OPERATING REVENUE			12.681	97.269	97.269	97.269	97.269	97.269	97.269	97.269	97.269	97.269
TAXABLE PROFIT			-26.570	54.201	56.558	59.103	61.853	64.822	64.822	64.822	64.822	64.822
PROFIT TAX			13.285	-27.100	-28.279	-29.552	-30.926	-32.411	-32.411	-32.411	-32.411	-32.411
FLOW OF OWN FUNDS		-122.420	-23.426	24.083	22.905	21.632	20.257	58.858	58.858	58.858	58.858	68.165

TABLE 4 — EFFICIENCY CALCULATION

YEAR	1999 '000 US$	1999 MN BT	2000 MN BT	2001 MN BT	2002 MN BT	2003 MN BT	2004 MN BT	2005 MN BT	2006 MN BT	2007 MN BT	2008 MN BT	2009 MN BT
INVESTMENT COSTS												
SPINDLES	-4000.000	-264.000										
EQUIPMENT	-850.000	-56.100										
INSTALLATION	-100.000	-6.600										
CONSTRUCTION		-18.000										
START-UP COSTS		-18.000										
RAW MATERIALS		-79.200										79.200
SPARE PARTS		-16.038										16.038
TOTAL	-362.700	-95.238	0.000	0.000	0.000	0.000	0.000	0.000	0.000	0.000	0.000	95.238
RUNNING COSTS												
WATER			-3.600	-7.200	-7.200	-7.200	-7.200	-7.200	-7.200	-7.200	-7.200	-7.200
POWER			-1.800	-3.600	-3.600	-3.600	-3.600	-3.600	-3.600	-3.600	-3.600	-3.600
SPARE PARTS			-32.010	-32.010	-32.010	-32.010	-32.010	-32.010	-32.010	-32.010	-32.010	-32.010
RAW MATERIALS			-160.380	-320.760	-320.760	-320.760	-320.760	-320.760	-320.760	-320.760	-320.760	-320.760
INSURANCE & RENT			0.000	0.000	0.000	0.000	0.000	0.000	0.000	0.000	0.000	0.000
LABOUR			-40.500	-40.500	-40.500	-40.500	-40.500	-40.500	-40.500	-40.500	-40.500	-40.500
TOTAL			-238.290	-404.070	-404.070	-404.070	-404.070	-404.070	-404.070	-404.070	-404.070	-404.070
REVENUES												
SALE OF YARN			287.100	574.200	574.200	574.200	574.200	574.200	574.200	574.200	574.200	574.200
NET EFFICIENCY BENEFIT	-362.700	-46.428	170.130	170.130	170.130	170.130	170.130	170.130	170.130	170.130	170.130	265.368

TABLE 5 — REFERENT GROUP ANALYSIS

YEAR	1999 '000 US$	1999 MN BT	2000 MN BT	2001 MN BT	2002 MN BT	2003 MN BT	2004 MN BT	2005 MN BT	2006 MN BT	2007 MN BT	2008 MN BT	2009 MN BT
TOTAL REFERENT GROUP	-80.230	-63.087	105.961	107.140	108.413	109.787	111.272	111.272	111.272	111.272	197.203	
- IMPORT DUTIES												
YARN			-18.000	-36.000	-36.000	-36.000	-36.000	-36.000	-36.000	-36.000	-36.000	-36.000
COTTON			10.692	21.384	21.384	21.384	21.384	21.384	21.384	21.384	21.384	21.384
EQUIPMENT		1.870										
SPINDLES		8.800										
MATERIALS INVENTORY			5.280									-5.280
SPARES INVENTORY			0.535									-0.535
SPARES			1.601	1.601	1.601	1.601	1.601	1.601	1.601	1.601	1.601	1.601
- TAXES			-13.285	27.100	28.279	29.552	30.926	32.411	32.411	32.411	32.411	32.411
- FOREIGN EXCHANGE	-108.900		-0.710	73.276	73.276	73.276	73.276	73.276	73.276	73.276	73.276	105.023
(i) TOTAL GOVERNMENT	-98.230	-13.887	87.361	88.540	89.813	91.187	92.672	92.672	92.672	92.672	118.603
(ii) POWER SUPPLIER			1.800	3.600	3.600	3.600	3.600	3.600	3.600	3.600	3.600	3.600
(iii) LABOUR		18.000	3.000	3.000	3.000	3.000	3.000	3.000	3.000	3.000	3.000	3.000
(iv) DOMESTIC BANK		0.000	-60.000	6.000	6.000	6.000	6.000	6.000	6.000	6.000	6.000	6.000
												60.000
(v) INSURANCE			6.000	6.000	6.000	6.000	6.000	6.000	6.000	6.000	6.000	6.000
TOTAL REFERENT GROUP	-80.230	-63.087	105.961	107.140	108.413	109.787	111.272	111.272	111.272	111.272	197.203	

PROJECT			PRIVATE			EFFICIENCY			REFERENT GROUP		
NPV	$(Mn)	IRR (%)		$(Mn)	IRR (%)	NPV	$ (MN)	IRR (%)	NPV	$ (MN)	IRR (%)
4%	405.3	20.6%	4%	154.5	16.7%	4%	873.3	30.3%	4%	700.4	n/a
8%	259.8		8%	88.7		8%	622.5		8%	533.8	
12%	152.0		12%	40.8		12%	435.9		12%	410.6	
16%	70.7		16%	5.4		16%	294.5		16%	317.9	
0%	605.6		8%	246.6		0%	1217.3		0%	930.3	

Figure 8.5 ICP Project Solution with a Shadow Exchange Rate

In this example an SER makes a significant difference to the total Referent Group net benefits. Comparing Figures 6.4 and 8.5 shows that the net present value of aggregate referent group benefits, using a 4% discount rate, increases from 260.4 million to 700.4 million Baht. As a consistency check to verify that the analyst has not made an error in making these adjustments the aggregate referent group benefits at the top of Table 5 (derived by subtracting ICP's cash flow and the overseas lender's cash flow from the efficiency cash flow) should be the same as those on the bottom line (derived by aggregating the sub-referent group members' net cash flows).

While import-replacing projects have some adverse consequences for the efficiency of resource use, as discussed earlier in this Chapter, it was clear from Figure 6.4 that the proposed ICP project was of net benefit to Thailand. Since the project is a net earner of foreign exchange the measure of this net benefit is increased once it is recognized that there is a premium on foreign exchange.

Further Reading

The two approaches to project evaluation in developing economies are summarized in I. M. D. Little and J. A. Mirrlees, *Manual of Industrial Project Analysis in Developing Countries* (OECD, 1968) and P. Dasgupta, A. Sen and S. Marglin, *Guidelines for Project Evaluation* (United Nations, 1970). L. Squire and H. D. van der Tak, *Economic Analysis of Projects* (Johns Hopkins Press, 1975) further developed the Little and Mirrlees approach. For benefit-cost analysis texts specifically on developing countries, see Caroline Dinwiddy and Francis Teal, *Principles of Cost-Benefit Analysis for Developing Countries* (Cambridge, United Kingdom: Cambridge University Press, 1996); Robert J. Brent, *Cost-Benefit Analysis for Developing Countries* (Cheltenham, United Kingdom: Edward Elgar Publishing, 1998); and Steve Curry and John Weiss, *Project Analysis in Developing Countries* (London: Macmillan, 1993). See also Boardman et al., *Cost-Benefit Analysis: Concepts and Practice* (Prentice Hall, 2001), Ch. 16.

Exercises

1. A project in Bhutan uses $100 of imported goods, and 2000 Rupees worth of domestic labour, paid at the minimum wage, to produce exported goods worth $200 on world markets. The opportunity cost of labour in Bhutan is estimated to be 40% of the minimum wage. The official exchange rate is 15 Rupees = $1, and the shadow-exchange rate is 20 Rupees = $1.
   (i) Work out the NPV of the project:
        (a) using the UNIDO approach
        (b) using the LM approach.
   (ii) What is the relationship between the two values?

2. Suppose that the annual value of a country's imports is $1 million and the annual value of its exports is $750,000. It imposes a tariff of 20% on all imported goods, and exported goods receive a 10% subsidy. The official exchange rate is 1500 Crowns = $1. Work out the appropriate value for the shadow-exchange rate.

9
Incorporating Risk in Benefit-Cost Analysis

Introduction

If benefit-cost analysis is to assist in the decision-making process the analysis must be conducted in advance of the project being undertaken. This means that the value of none of the variables involved in the analysis can be observed, but rather has to be predicted. Risk and uncertainty are always associated with predictions about the future and should be taken into account in the benefit-cost analysis. Since risk and uncertainty impose costs on decision-makers, these costs need to be assessed and measures taken to reduce them if possible. One way of reducing risk and uncertainty is to acquire additional information – what a benefit-cost analysis does – and the value of information is briefly discussed in Chapter 10. The present Chapter discusses the related concepts of risk and uncertainty.

Risk and Uncertainty

In the preceding Chapters, exercises and case studies we have assumed that all costs and benefits to be included in a cash flow are known with *certainty*. While this assumption might be acceptable in the context of project evaluation where the analyst is undertaking an *ex post* assessment of what has already occurred, it is clearly an unrealistic assumption to make where the purpose of the analysis is to undertake an appraisal of proposed projects where one has to forecast future cost and benefit flows. The future is *uncertain*: we do not know with certainty what the future values of a project's costs and benefits will be.

Uncertainty arises either because of factors internal to the project – we do not know precisely what the future response will be to, say, some management decision or action taken today – or, because of factors external to the project – for instance, we do not know precisely what the world prices of the project's traded inputs and outputs will be. In brief, uncertainty implies that there is more than one possible value for any project's annual net benefits. The range of possible values a variable can take may vary considerably from one situation to another, with the two extremes being complete certainty, where there is one known value, to complete uncertainty where the variable could take on any value. Most situations lie somewhere between the two extremes.

Where it is believed that the range of possible values could have a significant impact on the project's profitability, a decision about the project will involve taking a *risk*. In most situations there will be some information on which to base an assessment of the probability of possible outcomes (or values) within the feasible range. If it is possible to estimate the probability or likelihood of the values that an outcome could take, the degree of risk can be quantified. In some situations the degree of risk can be *objectively* determined, for instance, when flipping a fair coin; there is a 50% chance it will be heads and a 50% chance it will be tails, about which there can be no disagreement.

On the other hand, estimating the probability of an *el Niño* effect next year involves some judgement being made on the part of the analyst on the basis of the current information available. There is not enough information for there to be an unequivocal answer, as with flipping a coin, but there is enough to place some estimate on the probability. In these situations estimating the probability of an event in order to quantify the element of risk involves *subjectivity*. In other words, it is something about which there can be disagreement; some may argue that there is a 20% chance of rain while others may argue, on the basis of the same information, that there is a 60% chance of rain. Neither forecast can be termed wrong *ex ante*, but *ex post* only one forecast will correspond to the actual outcome – rain or no rain.

Subjective risk characterizes most situations we will encounter in project appraisal. There will be some information which can be used to assign numerical probabilities, which can in turn be used to undertake a more rigorous analysis of possible project outcomes. As new information comes to hand we may revise our probability estimates accordingly.

The assignment of probabilities is one sense in which risk analysis is subjective. It is also the case that the extent to which an individual considers a situation to involve significant cost of risk will vary depending on the personal circumstances and attitude of the individual in question. For instance, poor and rich individuals are likely to have different perceptions of the significance of losing $1,000 on a wager. Moreover, individuals in the same income group might adopt a quite different attitude towards a 50% probability of losing or winning $1,000. In risk analysis these different forms of subjectivity need to be addressed, in:

- deciding what the degree of uncertainty or probability of an occurrence is;
- deciding whether or not the uncertainty constitutes a significant risk; and,
- deciding whether the risk is acceptable or not.

There are various ways in which the project analyst can incorporate the analysis of risk and uncertainty into the benefit-cost analysis. In this chapter we consider the two most commonly used approaches: sensitivity analysis and risk modeling.

Sensitivity Analysis

The term "sensitivity analysis" describes the simple process of establishing the extent to which the outcome of the benefit-cost analysis is sensitive to the assumed values of the inputs used in the analysis. In a number of the previous examples and exercises we calculated the NPV of a project over a range of discount rates. In performing these calculations we were, in effect, conducting a sensitivity analysis. In this case we were testing how sensitive the NPV of the project is to the choice of discount rate.

This kind of information can be very useful for the decision-maker in various ways. Performing a sensitivity analysis by varying only the discount rate constitutes one commonly used method of taking risk into account, which was discussed in Chapter 2, namely the use of a risk premium on the discount rate. Under this approach, if a project is believed to be more risky than usual, the analyst uses a higher discount rate than that which would be used in the absence of risk, the premium representing the analyst's perception of the degree of riskiness of the investment. As a higher discount rate implies a lower NPV, *ceteris paribus*, it will be more difficult for the project to pass the NPV decision criterion the higher is the risk premium. Providing the decision-maker with NPVs for a given project over a range of discount rates provides the information necessary to assess the significance of applying a risk premium, and deciding whether the project is marginal or not.

Using a risk premium on the discount rate, although common practice in private sector investment analysis, suffers a few important drawbacks:

• often the analyst will be relying on a totally subjective estimate of what value the risk premium should take, although it should be noted that inter-sectoral comparisons of rates of return are sometimes used to estimate sector-specific risk premia;

• by attaching a constant premium over the life of the investment it is being assumed that the further into the future the forecasted value, the more risky the outcome,[1] whereas it may be the case that it is the earliest years of an investment project that are the riskiest;

• applying the premium to the net cash flow effectively assumes that the forecasted cost and benefit streams are affected equally by the risk, whereas it is likely that each is subject to a different degree of riskiness.

Instead of (or in addition to) conducting a sensitivity analysis on the discount rate, the analyst can allow the values of particular key inputs to vary over the full range of their possible values. Let us assume that in relation to the construction of a road the engineers have indicated that the actual cost could vary by up to 25% above or below their "best guess" estimate. In this case the analyst may wish to calculate the present value of the road's costs or net benefits at each value – at 75%, 100% and 125% of the best guess value. The decision-maker is then provided with a range of possible outcomes corresponding to the range of possible input values.

It is likely that the analyst will want to test the significance of changes in the values of more than one of the project's inputs. Let us assume that there is uncertainty about both the construction costs and the future usage of the road. Again, there could be, say, three estimates of future usage: low; medium; and high, each corresponding to a different level of annual benefit. The analyst can again test the significance of changes in this variable independently of others – by calculating the net present value for each level of road usage – or in conjunction with others, for example by allowing both the capital costs and the road usage levels to vary simultaneously over their respective ranges. This case is illustrated schematically in Table 9.1 below.

---

1   Using the methodology discussed in Chapter 2 it can be seen that the discount factors $(1/(1+r+p))$ and $(1-p)/(1+r)$ are approximately the same. The former corresponds to adding the risk premium, p, to the discount rate, r, whereas the latter corresponds to incorporating the chance of project failure into the expected net present value calculation. To see this, suppose that there is a chance, p, of the project benefit stream terminating in any given year. The expected project benefit in year t is then $B(1-p)^t$ and the expected present value of this benefit is $B[(1-p)/(1+r)]^t$ which is approximately equal to $B/(1+r+p)^t$.

Table 9.1 Sensitivity Analysis Results: NPVs for Hypothetical Road Project
(\$ thousands at 10% discount rate)

		Construction Costs		
		75%	**100%**	**125%**
Road	**High**	\$50	\$40	\$30
Usage	**Medium**	\$47	\$36	\$25
Benefits	**Low**	\$43	\$32	\$20

Table 9.1 provides some useful information. We can see by how much the NPV varies (at a 10% discount rate) when we allow one or both input values to vary across their respective possible ranges. For instance, if we hold the level of road usage at its "best guess" or "Medium" level, we see that the NPV varies from \$25 to \$47 thousand, while, if road construction costs are held at their "best guess" level (100%), the NPV varies from \$32 to \$40 thousand. Clearly, the outcome is more sensitive to changes in assumed construction cost values than to road usage values, across their possible ranges as specified in Table 9.1. When we allow both input values to vary simultaneously, we see that NPV can vary from a minimum value of \$20 thousand – the most pessimistic scenario when road usage is assumed to be at its lowest and construction costs are at their highest level – to \$50 thousand – where road usage is at its highest and construction costs at their lowest level. This information may provide the decision-maker with sufficient information to incorporate risk in the decision-making process, provided that she is satisfied that these are the only two variables that can be considered "risky" and that all she is concerned about is knowing that even in the worst case scenario, the project's NPV is still positive at 10%.

However, what if the range of NPVs produced by the sensitivity analysis varies instead from, say, *negative* \$20 thousand to (positive) \$50 thousand? In other words, there are some scenarios under which the project would not be undertaken on the basis of the simple NPV decision criterion. Or what if the decision-maker was having to decide between a number of project alternatives where the range of possible NPV values was very large yet still positive in all instances? Unfortunately the main problem with sensitivity analysis is that the matrix of values as shown in Table 9.1 does not contain any information about the *likelihood* of the project NPV being positive or negative, or, in the case of choice among alternatives, of being higher than that of some other project.

Furthermore, it is conceivable that there will be other project inputs for which the forecasted values are also risky and which the analyst will want to include as variables in the sensitivity analysis. Adding one more input to the sensitivity analysis with, say, three possible levels will increase the number of scenarios to 27; adding three more inputs increases the number of scenarios to 81, and so on. Very soon we reach a situation of information overload where there is just too much raw information and far too many possible combinations for the decision-maker to use sensibly in reaching a decision.

Another issue concerns possible correlation between variations in levels of uncertain outputs and inputs. Sensitivity analysis assumes that the variables in question are all independent of one another. As we discuss in more detail below, it is likely that variations in some variables will be closely correlated with variations in others, such as, say, road usage and road maintenance costs. Allowing these to move in opposite directions could produce nonsensical results in the sensitivity analysis.

For these reasons sensitivity analysis should be used with care and discretion. It can be a useful first stage in determining:

- whether or not the project outcome is sensitive to the values of the variables used in the analysis; and,
- to which variables the project outcome appears to be most sensitive.

This preliminary stage can be useful for the analyst in deciding whether or not a more rigorous form of risk analysis is worth undertaking, and, if so, which forecasted variables are to be investigated further with a view to their inclusion in the more formal risk modeling exercise.

Risk Modeling

As discussed in the previous sections, the preliminary steps in risk analysis allow the analyst to determine whether or not the project outcome under consideration can be considered risky and, if so, whether a more detailed and rigorous form of risk analysis can be justified. Assuming the decision has been made to proceed further, the next stage is to identify and describe the nature of the uncertainty surrounding the project variables. To do this we use *probability distributions*. A probability distribution takes the description of uncertainty one level beyond that which we used in the sensitivity analysis. There we described a variable's uncertainty purely in terms of the range of possible values; e.g. high, medium, low; or, maximum, mean, minimum. A probability distribution does this, but it also describes the likelihood of occurrence of values within the given range. When only a finite number of values can occur the probability distribution is described as *discrete*, and when any value within the range can occur it is *continuous*. An example of the former type of distribution is the probabilities of heads or tails in the toss of a coin, and an example of the latter is the familiar normal distribution.

Use of Discrete Probability Distributions

An example of a discrete probability distribution for the road construction costs from Table 9.1 above is shown in Table 9.2:

Table 9.2 A Discrete Probability Distribution of Road Construction Costs ($ thousands)

	Road Construction Cost (C)	Probability (P)
Low	$50	20%
Best Guess	$100	60%
High	$125	20%

Once a probability distribution for a project input variable is given the analyst is able to calculate the *expected value* of the variable and to use this in the cash flow for the project rather than the *point estimate* that we would have used if uncertainty had been ignored. Table 9.3 provides a simple numerical example showing how the expected value of net road usage benefits is derived.

Table 9.3 Calculating the Expected Value from a Discrete Probability Distribution
($ thousands)

Road Construction Cost (C)		Probability (P)	E(C)=P x C	NPV	E(NPV)
Low	$50	20%	$10	$86	$17.2
Best Guess	$100	60%	$60	$36	$21.6
High	$125	20%	$25	$11	$2.2

The expected cost of road construction can be derived as E(C) = $10 + $60 + $25 = $95. Rather than using the point (best guess) estimate of $100 thousand, the analyst would use $95 thousand in the cash flow for the project. Moreover, it will also be possible to derive a probability distribution for the NPV of the project. If we assume for simplicity that this is the only uncertain variable, and that the net benefits exclusive of road construction costs are estimated at $136 thousand, we could derive the probability distribution for the project's NPV: a 20% probability of NPV = $86 thousand; 60% of $36 thousand; and 20% of $11 thousand. If we use these values to calculate the expected NPV, we get:

$$E(NPV) = 17.2 + 21.6 + 2.2 = \$41 \text{ thousand}$$

Joint Probability Distributions

In the previous example it was assumed that there was uncertainty about only one of the project's inputs, which made the task of deriving a probability distribution for the outcome – the NPV in this instance – a straightforward matter. More realistically however, the analyst will find that there is uncertainty about the level of more than one project input or output. The probability distribution for the outcome (NPV) will then depend on the aggregation of probability distributions for the individual variables into a joint probability distribution. In aggregating probability distributions we must first distinguish between *correlated* and *uncorrelated* variables. It will often be the case that we have two uncertain variables relevant to the project outcome that are closely correlated; for instance, if road usage increases so too do road maintenance costs. Modeling risk in this situation requires the analyst to take account of the dependence of possible variations in the level of one variable on the possible variations in the level of the other. The two variables cannot be assumed to vary independently of each other. In this situation deriving the joint probability distribution is quite easy as shown in Table 9.4. In this case there is a 20% chance of road maintenance costs being $50 thousand *and* road user benefits being $70 thousand, a 60% chance of road maintenance costs being $100 thousand *and* road user benefits being $125 thousand, and so on. The expected values are calculated in the usual way, and are reported in brackets in Table 9.4.

Table 9.4 Joint Probability Distribution: Correlated Variables
($ thousands)

	Probability (P)	Cost ($)	Benefits ($)	Net Benefits ($)
Low	20%	50(10)	70(14)	20(4)
Best Guess	60%	100(60)	125(75)	25(15)
High	20%	125(25)	205(41)	80(16)
(Expected value)		(95)	(130)	(35)

Where the variables are uncorrelated (can vary independently of each other) the situation becomes a lot more complicated. If we assume, for example, that the benefits of the project are determined exclusively by movements in international prices while the costs depend on domestic factors, there may no longer be any correlation between their probability distributions. In this situation it is necessary to consider all possible combinations of values for the costs and benefits on a pair-wise basis, and to calculate the value of net benefits for each combination. This will produce a whole range of possible values for the project's net benefits which then need to be ordered and arranged as a probability distribution. An example of this is shown in Table 9.5, in which all possible combinations such as Low Cost, High Benefit (LC–HB) are assigned joint probabilities.

Table 9.5 Joint Probability Distribution: Uncorrelated Variables
($ thousands)

Level	Probability (P)	Cost ($)	Benefits ($)
Low (L)	20%	50	70
Best Guess (M)	60%	100	125
High (H)	20%	125	205

Combination	Joint Probability	Net Benefit ($)
LC–HB	0.2 x 0.2 = 0.04	155(6.2)
LC–MB	0.2 x 0.6 = 0.12	75(9.0)
LC–LB	0.2 x 0.2 = 0.04	20(0.8)
MC–HB	0.6 x 0.2 = 0.12	105(12.6)
MC–MB	0.6 x 0.6 = 0.36	25(9.0)
MC–LB	0.6 x 0.2 = 0.12	30(3.6)
HC–HB	0.2 x 0.2 = 0.04	80(3.2)
HC–MB	0.2 x 0.6 = 0.12	0(0.0)
HC–LB	0.2 x 0.2 = 0.04	−55(−2.2)
		E(NPV) = 42.2

The upper panel of Table 9.5 shows the independent or uncorrelated probabilities for the costs and benefits respectively. The lower panel shows how the joint probability of each possible combination of cost and benefit is calculated; since some combination *must* occur, the joint probabilities sum to 1. The table also reports the estimated net benefit associated with each probability. From these net benefit estimates and joint probability values the expected values of the respective outcomes (net benefits) are then derived and reported in brackets. The expected or mean value is $42.2 thousand, which is the sum of the individual expected values associated with each event. The two extreme values are *negative* $55 thousand and *positive* $155 thousand, each with a probability of 4%.

Continuous Probability Distributions

A continuous probability distribution assigns some probability to the event that the outcome, the project NPV for example, lies in any particular segment within the range of the distribution; for example, the probability that NPV will be greater than zero, or less than $100. The continuous probability distribution familiar to most readers is the normal distribution which is represented as a bell-shaped curve. This distribution is completely described by two parameters – the *mean* and the *standard deviation*. Its *range* is the full extent of the real line, i.e. from minus infinity to plus infinity, implying that, in principle, *anything* is possible, but only events in the vicinity of the mean are likely. The degree of dispersion of the possible values around the mean is measured by the variance (s^2) or the square root of the variance – the *standard deviation* (s). When the standard deviation is divided by the mean we get the *coefficient of variation* which is a useful measure for comparing the degree of dispersion for different variables when their means differ. The degree of dispersion is a useful measure of the amount of risk: a high standard deviation implies a reasonable probability of the outcome being significantly higher or lower than the mean value, whereas a low standard deviation implies a relatively small range of likely outcomes in the vicinity of the mean.

The characteristics of the variable's probability distribution are important inputs into formal risk modeling using spreadsheet "add-ins" such as the *@RISK*© program that we use in this text. From analysis of relevant data, perhaps time series or cross-sectional data, the analyst must decide what type of probability distribution best describes the uncertain variable in question. Risk modeling programs like *@RISK*© offer the analyst a whole range of distributions to choose from, including: the linear distribution for which each value within the specified range is equally likely; the triangular distribution which assigns higher probabilities to values near some chosen point within the range, and lower probabilities to values near the boundaries of the range; and, of course, the familiar normal distribution. If the analyst has a reasonable set of past observations on the uncertain variable in question, but is unsure as to what type of probability distribution best describes that data, software add-ins such as *BestFit*© can be used to identify the most appropriate probability distribution.

Quite often, however, the analyst finds that there may be no reliable historical information about the variable in question and that he has no information beyond the range of values the variable could reasonably be expected to take, as described, for instance in the sensitivity analysis discussed previously. Here the analyst may still undertake a more formal risk modeling exercise than a sensitivity analysis by assuming what is called a triangular or "three-point" distribution, where the distribution is described by a high (H), low (L) and best-guess (B) estimate, which provide the maximum, minimum and modal values of the distribution respectively. Each event in the range between L and H is assigned some probability, with values in the range of B being most likely. The precise specification and statistics for the three-point distribution can vary, depending on how much weight the analyst wishes to give to the mode in

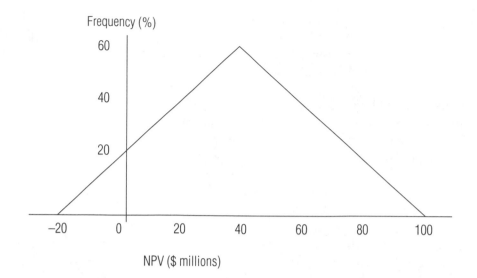

Figure 9.1 Triangular Probability Distribution

relation to the extreme point values. Clearly adopting a triangular distribution of this type is a "rough-and-ready" form of risk modeling and should only be used when insufficient information is available or resources prevent the obtaining of sufficient information to identify the characteristics of the uncertain variable's probability distribution more rigorously.

The triangular probability distribution can be represented graphically as shown in Figure 9.1. The decision-maker now knows not only the range of possible values the NPV could take, but can also see what the probability is of NPV lying within any particular range of possible values.

An alternative format for presenting this information is a *cumulative probability distribution*. Here, the vertical axis is scaled from 0 to 1 showing the cumulative probability up to the corresponding NPV value on the horizontal axis as shown in Figure 9.2. The cumulative distribution indicates what the probability is of the NPV lying below (or above) a certain value. For instance, in this example there is a 50% chance that the NPV will be below $28 million, and a 50% chance it will be above it. Similarly, it shows that there is an 80% chance that the NPV will be less than $48 million and a 20% chance that it will be more than this. At the opposite end, we can see that there is no chance that it will be less than negative $20 million, or, equivalently, a 100% chance that it will be greater than this value.

The advantage of presenting the results of a risk analysis in this way is that it provides the relevant information for the decision-maker in a user-friendly, and easy to interpret format. It is relatively easy for the decision-maker, unfamiliar with basic statistical concepts, to read from this the likelihood of the project achieving a given target NPV value, or, knowing what degree of risk she is willing to accept, what minimum expected value of the NPV is acceptable given the degree of risk. We discuss attitude to risk in more detail below.

Cumulative Frequency (%)

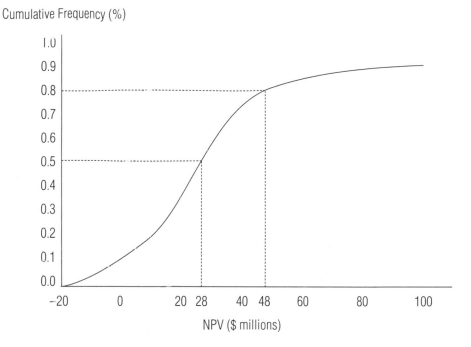

NPV ($ millions)

Figure 9.2 Cumulative Probability Distribution

To undertake these sorts of probability calculations manually, even with the aid of a spreadsheet, can become complicated and very time consuming, especially when a number of variables are uncertain. When one is working with a cash flow of say, 20 to 25 years, and where the value of a variable is allowed to vary randomly in each and every year of the project the task becomes unwieldy. But with add-ins such as @RISK© the process is relatively straightforward.

The use of @RISK© is illustrated with a simple example later in this Chapter. At this stage it needs to be noted that what such programs do is perform a simulation, known as a *Monte Carlo* analysis, whereby the NPV of the project, for example, is recalculated over and over again, each time using a different, randomly chosen, set of values for the input variables of the project's cash flow calculation. The random selection of values is based on the characteristics of each input variable's probability distribution, where this information, rather than a single point estimate, is entered into the relevant cell of the spreadsheet by the analyst. The program effectively instructs the spreadsheet to randomly sample values of the uncertain variables from their specified probability distributions, to calculate the project NPV using the sample values, to save the calculated value and to repeat this process many times over. The saved NPV calculations for all combinations of sampled values for the input variables can be used to develop a probability distribution of NPV. It is as if the analyst had run and saved thousands of NPV calculations by changing the input values across the full range of possible combinations implied by the probability distributions. The program then assembles all the saved results, presenting them as a probability distribution which can be displayed in numerical or graphical format.

Using Risk Analysis in Decision-Making

Producing a probability distribution for a project's range of possible outcomes is only part of the risk analysis process. As discussed at the beginning of this Chapter, the decision-maker needs to interpret this information and use it in the decision process. It must be emphasized that this necessarily involves the decision-maker revealing her subjective attitude towards risk. The same risk analysis results provided to a number of different individuals is likely to be interpreted differently and to result in different decisions being made. Figure 9.3 below illustrates this point.

In this figure the probability distributions for the NPVs of two projects, A and B, are shown. Project B has a higher expected NPV than project A. However, the dispersion of values around the mean is much wider in the case of project B than in A. Indeed, it can be seen that there is a (small) chance that the NPV of project B could be negative. Its maximum NPV is also very much higher than project A's. In other words, project B has a higher expected NPV (a good thing from the decision-maker's point of view) but has a higher variance or risk (a bad thing in the view of the risk averse decision-maker).

Which of the two should the decision-maker choose? There is no definitive answer to this. It will depend on the decision-maker's attitude towards risk. Even though B has a higher expected NPV, it is a riskier project than A. The final choice will depend on how much the decision-maker is *risk averse* or is a *risk taker*. If the decision-maker is a risk taker, then she may well prefer project B to project A. However a risk averse decision-maker will prefer a project with a lower variance of NPV, other things being the same. For example, if projects A and B

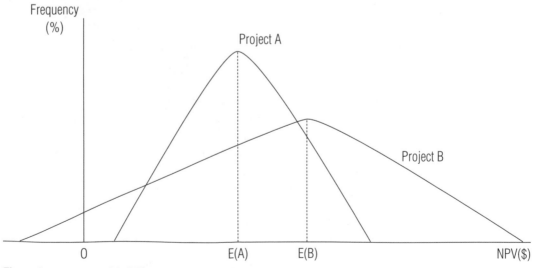

Figure 9.3 Projects with Different Degrees of Risk

had the same expected NPV then the project with the lower variance of NPV has a lower probability of failure – having a negative NPV. The probability of failure is measured by the area of the probability distribution to the left of the NPV = 0 point on the horizontal axis. The decision-maker might decide to accept a project that had a 95% probability of success, with only 5% chance of generating a negative NPV, but to reject any project with a lower probability of success.

The Theory of Risk Averse Behaviour

It is generally believed that individuals are risk averse when decisions involving large sums of money are being made. This is not necessarily inconsistent with the observed risk-loving behaviour of individuals at the race track where generally small sums of money are wagered in order to expose the bettor to risk.[2] Risk aversion follows from the proposition that the utility derived from wealth rises as wealth rises, but at a decreasing rate; at a low level of wealth an extra dollar can provide a significant amount of additional utility, whereas at a high level it may make little difference. It follows from this concept of *diminishing marginal utility of wealth* that taking a fair gamble will reduce the individual's level of utility. For example, if the individual bet $1000 on the toss of a fair coin the expected loss in utility if the call was incorrect would be greater in absolute terms than the expected gain in utility if the call were correct. This observation provides a useful characterization of risk averse behaviour – unwillingness to accept a fair gamble because the expected change in utility is negative.

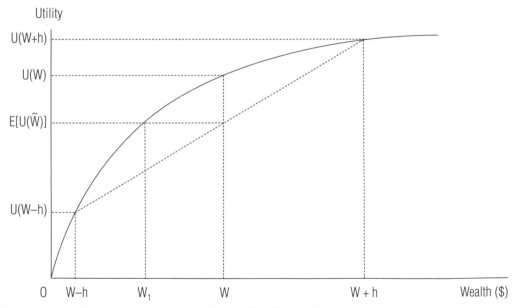

Figure 9.4 The Relationship between Utility and Wealth for a Risk Averse Individual

2   In *Investment, Interest and Capital* J. Hirschliefer discusses the Friedman-Savage utility of wealth function which implies risk aversion where large amounts of wealth are concerned, but incorporates a relatively small concave segment in the vicinity of the current wealth level which indicates a willingness to gamble small amounts on a fair bet.

Figure 9.4 illustrates the utility of wealth function of a risk averse individual. The current level of wealth is denoted by W, and we suppose that the individual has been offered a fair bet consisting of a 50% chance of winning $h and a 50% chance of losing $h. Since h is a random variable it follows that, if he accepts the bet, his level of wealth will also be a random variable, which we denote by $\widetilde{W}$. Since the bet is "fair" in the sense that the expected value of h, E(h), is zero, it follows that the expected value of the individual's wealth, if he accepted the bet, E($\widetilde{W}$), equals W. If he were to base his decision on the expected value of wealth he would be indifferent between accepting or not accepting the bet, since E($\widetilde{W}$) = W. However, under the *expected utility hypothesis*, we assume that he will choose the alternative that has the higher expected utility. As we will see from the discussion of Figure 9.4, the expected utility of the random variable is less than that of W with certainty: E[U($\widetilde{W}$)] < U(W).

In Figure 9.4 the utilities associated with the wealth levels W+h, W, and W–h are identified on the vertical axis. The expected utility of wealth if the bet is accepted, E[U($\widetilde{W}$)], is also identified on the vertical axis: since there is a 50% chance of winning and a 50% chance of losing, this value occurs exactly half-way between U(W+h) and U(W–h). It can be seen from the diagram that, because of diminishing marginal utility of wealth, E[U($\widetilde{W}$)] < U(W). From this we can conclude that the individual will choose not to accept the bet.

We can use Figure 9.4 to work out the cost of the risk associated with taking the bet. It can be seen from the diagram that the level of wealth with certainty that yields the same utility as the expected utility of wealth with the gamble is W_1: in other words, U(W_1) = E[U($\widetilde{W}$)]. It follows that the individual would be indifferent between giving up an amount of wealth (W – W_1) and accepting the bet. This means that the cost of risk associated with having to take the bet is (W – W_1), and that the individual would be willing to pay up to this amount to avoid the risk. It will be left to the reader to demonstrate that if the size of the bet is increased to $h_1 > h$, the cost of risk rises. When the bet is increased from h to h_1, with the odds unchanged, the amount of risk, measured by the variance of the random variable $\widetilde{W}$, increases, and hence the total cost of the risk rises.

It makes intuitive sense that, for a risk averse individual at a given level of wealth, the cost of risk rises as the amount of risk rises. But what happens to the cost of risk if the individual's wealth is increased? We cannot tell *a priori* because at a higher level of wealth both the increase in utility as a result of a win, and the fall in utility as a result of a loss, are reduced. However it seems to make sense that the higher the level of wealth, the lower the cost of risk to the individual: a rich person worries less about hazarding a given sum of money than does a poor person.[3] This means that the amount of additional expected wealth that would be

---

3   The cost of risk is calculated by equating E[U(W+ $\widetilde{h}$)] with U(W–p) and solving for p, where p is the cost of risk, and $\widetilde{h}$ is the standard normal random variable representing the risky prospect. Taking a first order Taylor Series approximation to U(W–p), and a second order approximation to U(W+ $\widetilde{h}$), to account for the randomness of $\widetilde{h}$, taking the expected value and then equating the resulting expressions, it can be shown that the cost of risk is approximately p = E(h^2)r(W)/2. In this expression E(h^2) is the variance of $\widetilde{h}$, the amount of risk, and r(W) is the Pratt measure of risk aversion: r(W) = –[U"(W)/U'(W)]. For the case in which utility is measured by the natural logarithm of wealth, U=lnW, the Pratt measure is 1/W. In other words, the cost of risk is the amount of risk, measured by the variance of the risky prospect, times the cost per unit of risk, measured by 1/2W. As can be seen from the formula, the cost of the risk falls, in this instance, as W increases.

required to compensate the individual for a given increase in the risk of his wealth portfolio falls as the expected value of the portfolio rises.

To illustrate a decision-maker's attitude to risk we construct what is known as an individual's *indifference map*, which treats the level of wealth as a random variable and shows the trade-offs the individual is willing to make between the expected value or mean value of wealth, and the variance of wealth, measuring the degree of risk. An example is shown in Figure 9.5. The expected value of the individual's wealth, $E(W)$, is measured on the vertical axis, and the degree of risk, as measured by the variance of wealth, $VAR(W)$, is shown on the horizontal axis. The indifference curves show the particular individual's attitude to risk. Each curve shows the locus of possible combinations of outcomes, as measured by $E(W)$ and $VAR(W)$, that provide the individual with a given level of utility; since these combinations provide the same level of utility the individual is said to be indifferent between them. For instance, combination G, with expected value $E(W_G)$ and variance $VAR(W_G)$, is considered equivalent to combination H with $E(W_H)$ and $VAR(W_H)$; the higher expected value $E(W_G)$ is required to compensate for the higher risk as measured by $VAR(W_G)$.

Any risky prospect whose $E(W)$ and $VAR(W)$ are represented by a point on indifference curve R_1, such as G or H, is preferred to any prospect on R_0, such as F, and any prospect represented by a point on R_2 is preferred to any on R_0 or R_1. For instance, combination H will be preferred to any combination of the same variance but lower expected value, such as F.

The shape of the indifference map is clearly a reflection of how the decision-maker perceives risk. The slope of an indifference curve shows the amount by which E(W) will need to

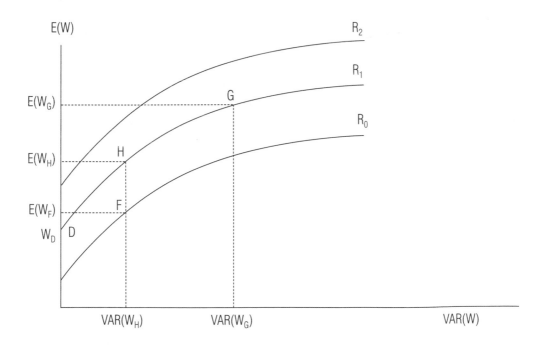

Figure 9.5 A Risk Averse Individual's Indifference Map between Mean and Variance of Wealth

increase to offset any given increase in risk; the larger this amount is, the more risk averse the individual is at the given level of wealth. To illustrate this point, compare points such as D and H; point D represents a situation of zero risk since the variance of wealth is zero, whereas point H represents a higher level of expected wealth, but involves risk as measured by the variance of wealth $VAR(W_H)$. By comparing points D and F we can see that the individual needs to be compensated an amount of wealth $E(W_H)-W_D$ if he is to be indifferent between the zero level of risk associated with D and the level associated with H. In other words, we can think of $E(W_H) - W_D$ as being the total cost of the amount of risk borne by the individual when he moves from D to H along the indifference curve R_1. It can be seen from Figure 9.5 that the steeper the indifference curves the greater the cost of any given level of risk. Furthermore, since the slope of the indifference curve measures the cost of one unit of extra risk, it can be seen from the curvature of the indifference map that as the level of expected wealth rises, the cost per unit of extra risk falls.[4]

While indifference curves are useful for the purpose of the conceptualization of the cost of risk and subjective attitude to risk, constructing such a map would require that the analyst engage in a fairly complex process of choice experimentation with the relevant decision-makers with a view to eliciting from their choices the information necessary to construct the indifference map – a lot easier said than done!

A further problem is that the indifference curves are defined over total wealth, not just a particular project. The risk associated with a particular project is what it adds to the total risk of the portfolio of wealth. Thus adding to the portfolio a project with a high variance, but with an NPV negatively correlated with other projects in the portfolio might actually reduce the variance of wealth (the total NPV of the portfolio). Indeed, in a large, well-diversified investment portfolio it is possible in principle for portfolio risk to be eliminated completely. This is the basis of the argument that governments need not take risk into account in project appraisal because the portfolio of public projects is large and well diversified and any additional project adds nothing to the risk of the overall portfolio. To appreciate this argument, suppose that the fair gamble of h illustrated by Figure 9.4 was to be shared equally among two individuals with identical utility of wealth functions. It can be seen from Figure 9.4 that, because of the curvature of the utility of wealth function, the individual cost of risk associated with the fair gamble $h/2$ is less than half the original cost. This means that sharing the risk between two individuals has reduced its total cost. If the risk were shared among all members of the population, as in the case of a public project, the total cost of risk could, in principle, fall to zero. Needless to say, few individual decision-makers in the public sector subscribe to this view!

---

4   In *Investment, Interest and Capital* J. Hirschliefer points out that at least one of two conditions must be satisfied if the individual's preferences are to be summarized by indifference curves defined on expected value and variance. Either the random variable "wealth" must be normally distributed (in which case its distribution is completely described by the mean and variance) or the utility function must be quadratic (in which case third and higher order moments of the probability distribution of W are not relevant). If both these conditions are satisfied the indifference curves are convex as seen from below, implying that the cost of risk rises as wealth rises. It seems more reasonable that the cost of risk falls as wealth rises (implied by indifference curves which are concave from below as shown in Figure 9.5) and hence that a logarithmic utility function is preferable to the quadratic function.

Portfolio risk can be reduced by spreading risk through judicious selection of projects and the use of financial derivatives. Since risk is traded in this way it is evident that it has a market price. The amount of risk associated with any given asset divided by the market price of risk tells us the premium in expected return that is required to make the asset attractive to investors; just as individuals trade off risk against return along an indifference curve, the market undertakes a similar trade off along a relative price line. The slope of the price line is known as the Beta coefficient, which measures the market price of risk. Clearly it might be possible for the project decision-maker to access this market by investing in the appropriate assets in order to reduce the additional portfolio risk as a result of undertaking the project.

In the following discussion we ignore the above issues, but consider instead how the decision-maker can in practice obtain basic information about the variance of a project's NPV for use in the decision process.

Using @*RISK*© in Spreadsheet Applications

The purpose of this section is to provide the reader with a quick introduction and overview of how the @*RISK*© software add-in can be used to undertake a risk analysis for a net present value calculation.[*]

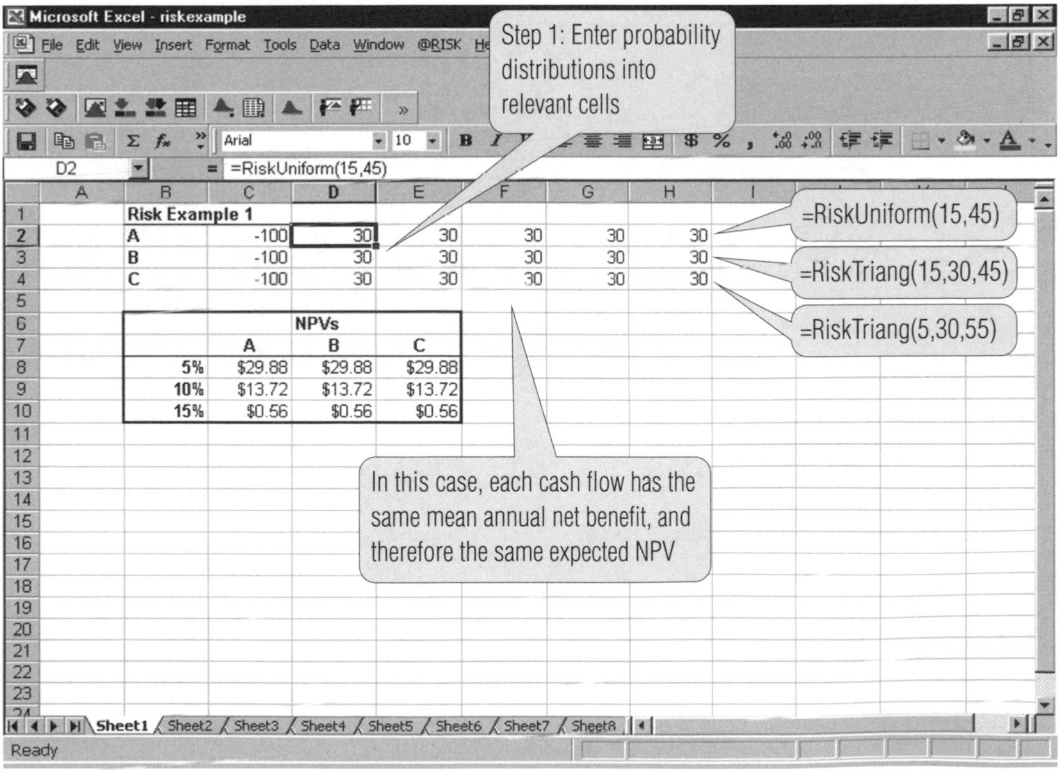

Figure 9.6(a) Entering the Data

* We use @RISK© Version 4.5, Palisade Corporation, NY, USA, 2002.

A simple numerical example is developed, with the reader taken through a number of steps as shown in the screen dumps presented in the following series of figures with text boxes. The example concerns a project with an initial cost of $100, which is known with certainty, and an annual net benefit over a five year period consisting of a random variable with an expected value of $30. Three different probability distributions are used to characterize this random variable and a probability distribution of NPV calculated for each and expressed both as a histogram and a cumulative distribution. A further graph showing how the mean and variance of NPV change as the discount rate is raised is also generated. Some comments on the procedures used follow the presentation of the tables.

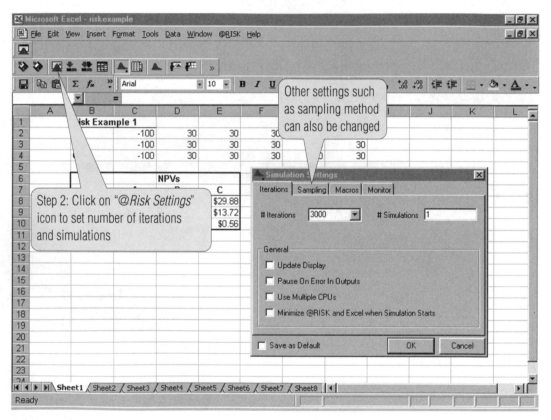

Figure 9.6(b) Entering the Simulation Settings

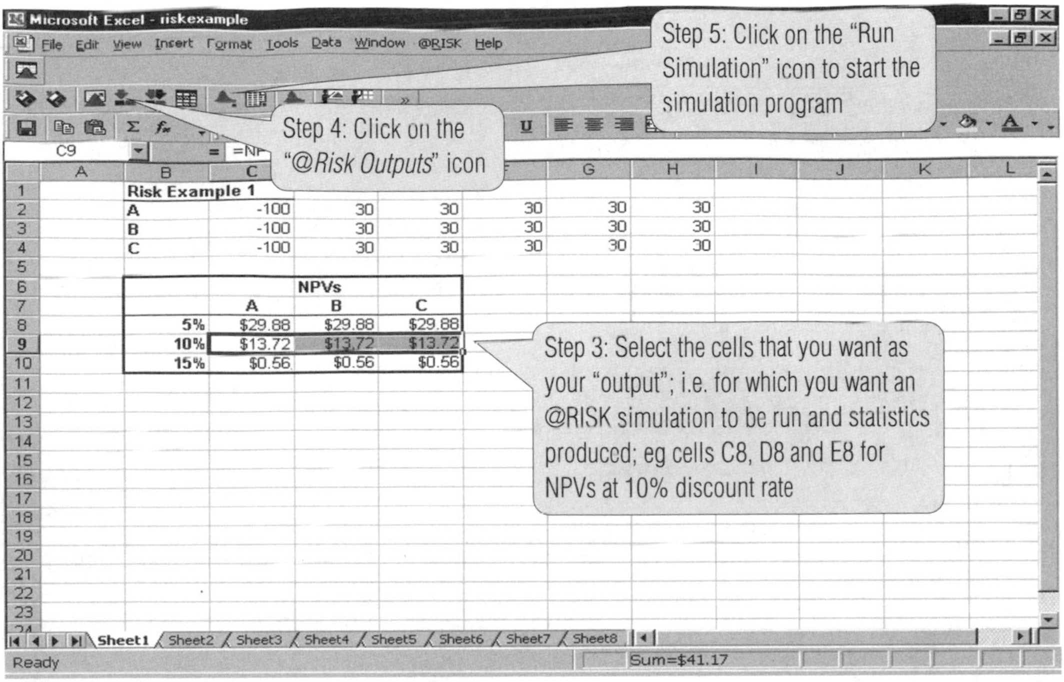

Figure 9.6(c) Running the Simulation

Once the simulation has run, the results will appear as shown below. In this case, we show the results from Example 2.

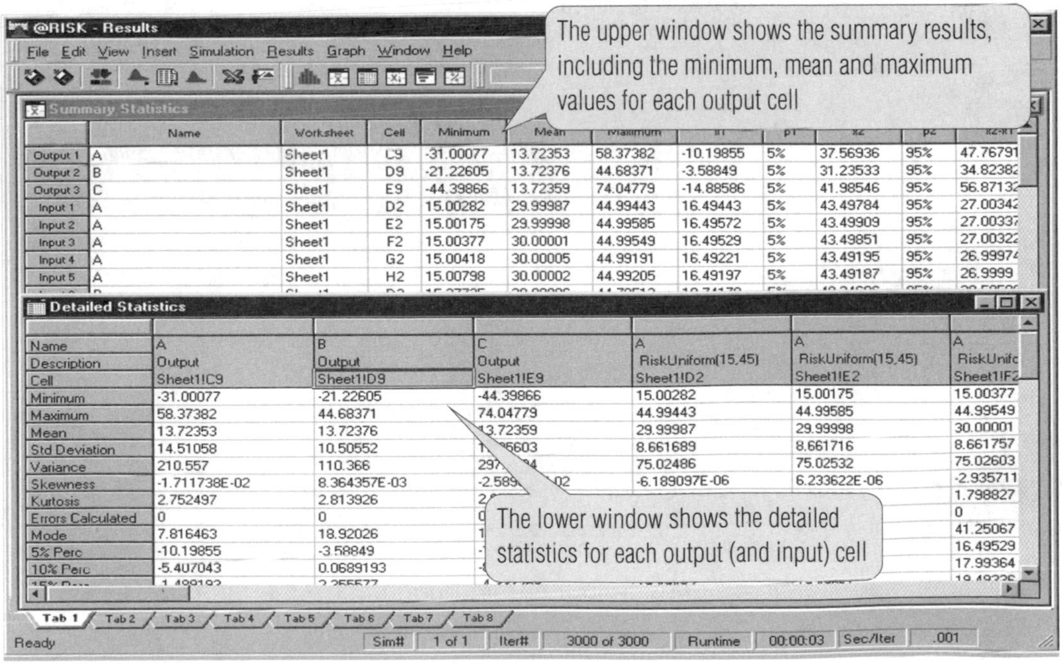

Figure 9.6(d) Reading the Results of the Simulation

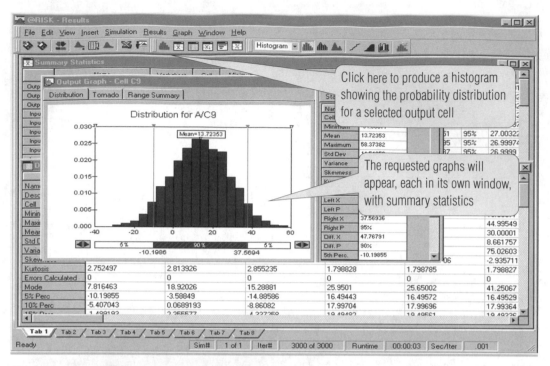

Figure 9.6(e) Graphing the Probability Distribution

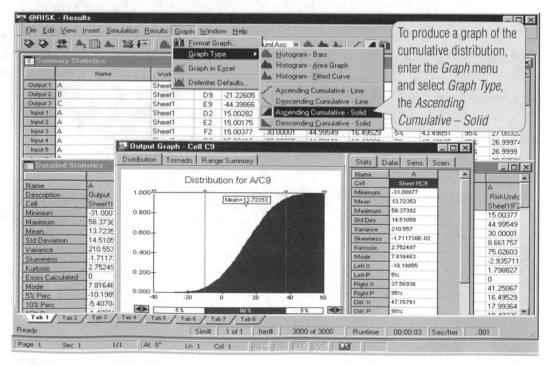

Figure 9.6(f) Generating a Cumulative Probability Distribution

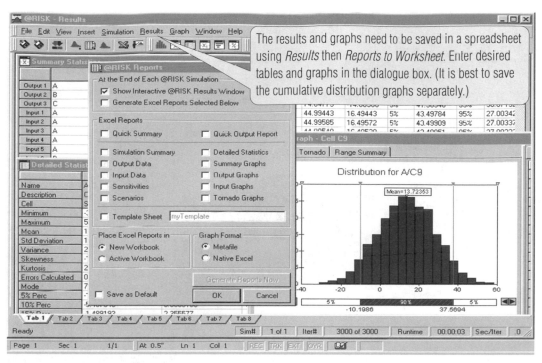

Figure 9.6(g) Saving the Risk Analysis Results to a Spreadsheet

Figure 9.6(h) Selecting a Range of Values as Risk Analysis Outputs

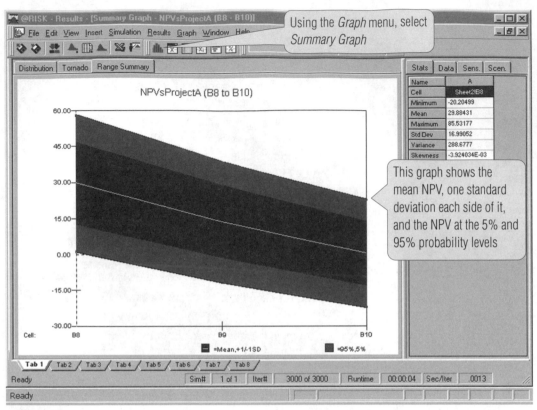

Figure 9.6(i) Producing Summary Graphs for a Range of Outputs

Some Points to Note Using @*RISK*©

In the above example we have assumed in most cases a triangular distribution (*TRIANG*) using estimates of the "minimum", "best guess" and "maximum" values for each input. One problem with this probability distribution is that the two extreme values are assigned a probability of zero and will therefore never be sampled in the simulation. An alternative to this is the *TRIGEN* distribution which allows the analyst to specify the bottom and top percentile values giving the percentage of the total area under the triangle that falls to the left of the entered point. Another alternative to the triangular distribution is the *BETASUBJ* function which requires a minimum, most likely, mean, and maximum value.

In some situations there may be a range of *discrete* values where each value has the same probability of occurrence. Here we would choose the *DUNIFORM* function. On the other hand, if the uniform distribution was *continuous* – one in which any value within the range defined by the minimum and maximum values has equal probability of occurrence – we would use the *UNIFORM* function. (Be careful not to confuse the two.)

With more information about a variable we could use one of the many other distributions available in @*RISK*©, such as "*NORMAL*" for a normal distribution, where we enter the mean and standard deviation for the variable in question. Use of triangular distributions is a rough-and-ready form of risk analysis.

In the preceding example we set our number of iterations at 3000 for the simulation. During the simulation a dialogue box appears indicating whether *convergence* has occurred. If the simulation has converged, an icon showing a smiling face appears; if not, it frowns! Make sure that there is convergence for each output cell. If not, the number of iterations should be increased until convergence is achieved.

We have undertaken one simulation in the preceding examples. It is possible to program @RISK© to run the same set of iterations under a number of scenarios. For instance, the analyst may wish to allow one of the variables to take on three possible values. This is not a variable that varies randomly, as described by a given probability distribution, but rather is a "controllable" or "exogenous" variable, such as a policy variable like a tax rate, a tariff, or a regulated price. It could even be the discount rate. In this instance we use the function "=*RISKSIMTABLE*". This allows us to enter a number of alternative values in a particular cell (let us say three alternative discount rates) and then the simulation is automatically re-run using the same sampled input data for each discount rate scenario. Having entered the three discount rates (or values of other parameters) it is necessary to set the number of simulations required (in this case, three) in the "@Risk Settings" menu, shown earlier when we set the number of iterations. For each simulation a separate and consistent set of probability statistics is produced.

When selecting variables to which an @RISK© probability distribution is to be attached be careful not to introduce an inconsistency by attaching separate distributions to variables that are dependent on each other. As noted earlier in this Chapter, if, in a road transport project, you attached a separate distribution to maintenance cost and use when the former depends (positively) on the latter, you could end up with a nonsensical simulation; another example is where rainfall rises and agricultural yield falls. @RISK© is able to incorporate joint probability distributions by establishing probabilities for each variable conditional on the values selected for others.

Be careful to set up your simulation to allow the program to treat each cell separately in each simulation. If you attach the @RISK© distribution to a variable located in the "Key Variables" or "Inputs" table of your spreadsheet, and then this variable is referred to in each year of the cash flow, what will happen is that during the simulation, the variable will take on the identical value *in each year of the project*. Normally what is required in a simulation is for each year's value to be independent of previous years' values, unless the analyst is programming a scenario where a variable should be related to its value in the previous year. Interest rates or share prices, for instance, are unlikely to take on a random value in each period. It would be better to program such variables so that they are allowed to change *in relation to their level in the previous period*. This is sometimes referred to as a *random walk*, and is easy to program into an @RISK© simulation as demonstrated in the ICP Case Study in the next section.

Incorporating Risk Analysis in the ICP Case Study

Additional Information
In the ICP Case Study you were given an exchange rate of Bt.44 to the US\$, a world price of cotton of US\$0.3 per bale, and a world price of yarn of US\$0.58. Suppose you are concerned

about the uncertainty surrounding future values for each of these variables and have decided to undertake a risk analysis using @RISK© with the following additional information.

- The exchange rate could appreciate or depreciate by 3% in any year, in relation to the previous year's value.
- The US$ world price of cotton and yarn could rise or fall by up to 5% in any year in relation to the previous year's price.
- World cotton and yarn prices can be assumed to be closely correlated with each other, and unrelated to movements in the exchange rate.

This type of risk modeling is best described as a "random walk". Instead of allowing the variable to vary randomly around a best-guess or mean value, we allow it to vary around the value that it took in the previous year. If, in a particular simulation, the exchange rate depreciates to, say, Bt. 47 to the US$ in one year, then the simulation will base the following year's value on a random variation around this new value, and so on.

For the purpose of this analysis it is also assumed that in all cases a triangular distribution would represent a reasonable description of the variable's uncertainty. However, instead of using the *TRIANG* form of this function we decide to use the *TRIGEN* function where it is possible to specify the bottom and top percentile values for the extreme (maximum and minimum) values of the variable, thus allowing the extreme values to have a probability of occurrence greater than zero. For the exchange rate we are informed that these values occur at the 10% and 90% percentile respectively, and for world cotton and yarn prices at the 5% and 95% percentile.

Entering the Risk Analysis Data

Two additional rows need to be entered into the spreadsheet where a "risk factor" formula is entered for each project year. These are shown in rows 21 and 22 of the spreadsheet in Figure 9.7. For the exchange rate (row 21), the formula entered for the first project year, 2000, is "=RiskTrigen(0.97,1,1.03,10,90)", and then, for each subsequent year, "=RiskTrigen(0.97* D21,1*D21,1.03*D21,10,90)". For the world price of cotton and yarn (row 22), the corresponding spreadsheet entries are:

"=RiskTrigen(0.95,1,1.05,5,95)" and "=RiskTrigen(0.95*D22,1*D22,1.05*D22,5,95)".

Whenever there is a cell reference anywhere in the spreadsheet to the value of the exchange rate, or world price of cotton or yarn, this value is multiplied by the corresponding cell containing the formula for the risk factor in that particular year.

The next step is to specify the required output of the analysis. For the purpose of this exercise we shall keep it simple and assume that the only output cell for which a probability distribution is required is the NPV for the Net Cash Flow measuring the Referent Group Benefits. The simulation settings are then set to the required number of iterations; we select 3,000 and the simulation is run.

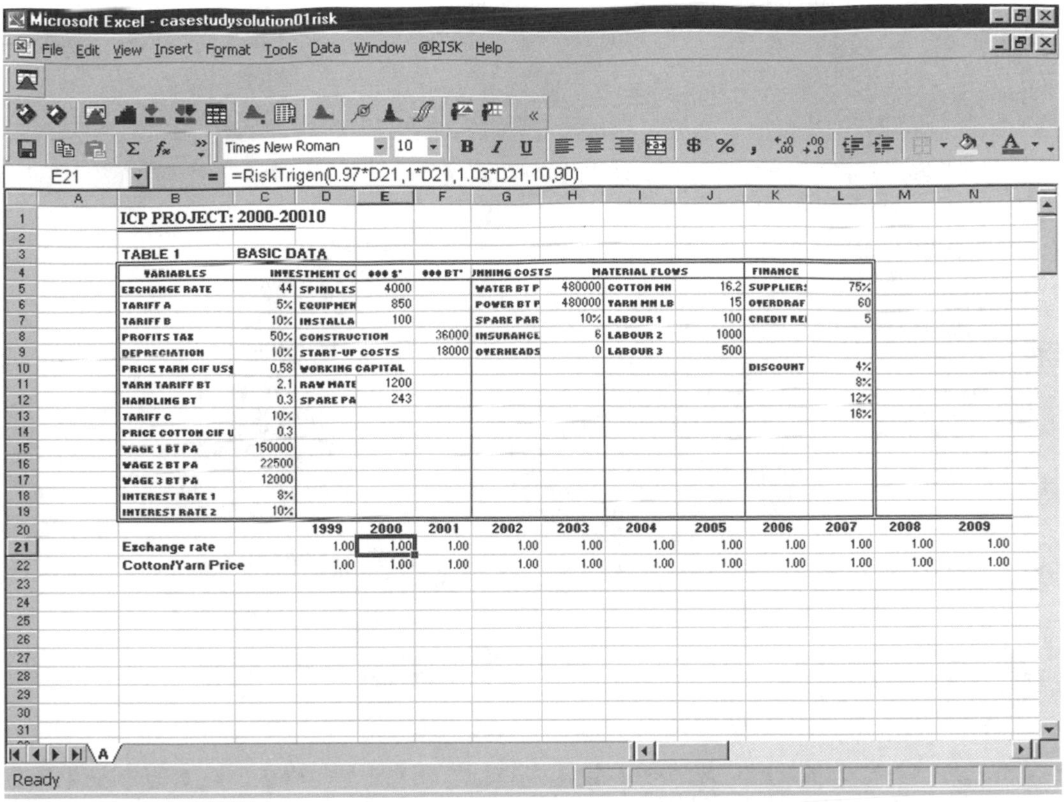

Figure 9.7 ICP Project Risk Analysis: Programming a "Random Walk"

The Results of the Risk Analysis

The results of the simulation are reported in Figure 9.8. The table in the left hand panel shows summary statistics for the project's NPV over the range of discount rates between 4% and 16%. At 4% for instance, it has a maximum of $463.72 million, a minimum of $88.58 million and a mean of $260.38 million. The table also shows the cumulative probability values. These indicate that there is only a 5% probability that the NPV will be less than $181.36 million. In others words, there is a 95% chance that the NPV will be greater than $181.36 million. There is a 95% chance that it will be less than $343.48, or a 5% chance that it will be greater than this amount. The probability distribution for the NPV at a 4% discount rate is represented graphically in the right hand panel of Figure 9.8.

It is possible to present the decision-maker with the full range of possible project outcomes and their associated probabilities, which provides her with a lot more useful information on which to base her final decision than a single point estimate (i.e. mean or mode NPV), or a sensitivity analysis, that would have indicated the possible range of values, but not the probability of the NPV achieving a given level.

As the simulation was undertaken for a range of discount rates, it is also possible to produce a summary graph of NPVs for the project as shown in Figure 9.9.

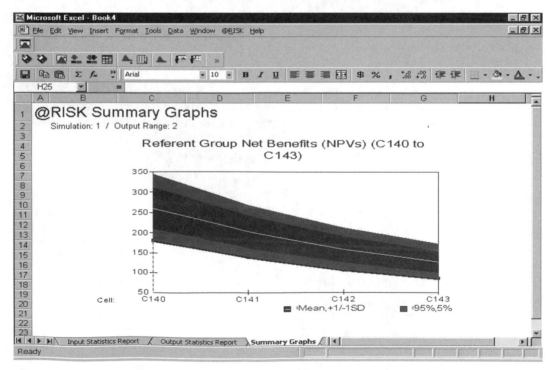

Figure 9.8 ICP Project Risk Analysis: Summary Statistics for Referent Group Net Benefits

The @RISK Output Details Report (Figure 9.8) shows:

@RISK Output Details Report

Output Statistics

Outputs	Referent Group Net Benefits (NPVs)			
Statistics / Cell	4%	8%	12%	16%
Minimum	88.58	65.07	48.46	36.55
Maximum	463.72	362.28	288.08	232.84
Mean	260.38	201.27	158.34	126.61
Standard Deviation	49.91	39.64	32.08	26.41
Variance	2,491.20	1,571.41	1,029.08	697.49
Skewness	0.19	0.19	0.18	0.18
Kurtosis	3.01	3.01	3.00	3.00
Number of Errors	0.00	0.00	0.00	0.00
Mode	242.22	194.48	191.12	121.38
5%	181.36	138.86	107.95	85.52
95%	343.48	267.37	212.47	171.17

Distribution for $ (MN)/C140

Mean=260.3801

181.3585   343.4823

Figure 9.9 ICP Project Risk Analysis: Summary Graph for a Range of Discount Rates

@RISK Summary Graphs

Simulation: 1 / Output Range: 2

Referent Group Net Benefits (NPVs) (C140 to C143)

Cell: C140   C141   C142   C143

=Mean,+1/−1SD   =95%,5%

The discount rates corresponding to the cell references on the horizontal axis (C140–C143) are 4%, 8%, 12% and 16% respectively. The graph shows, at each discount rate:

- the mean NPV values
- the NPVs for one standard deviation each side of the mean
- the NPVs for the 5% and 95% confidence levels.

Further Reading

J. Hirschliefer, *Investment, Interest and Capital* (Prentice Hall, 1970) includes several chapters on investment decision under uncertainty. Two books with a practical focus on risk and project selection are S. Reutlinger, *Techniques for Project Appraisal under Uncertainty* (Johns Hopkins Press, 1970) and J. K. Johnson, *Risk Analysis and Project Selection* (Asian Development Bank, Manila, 1985). A classic paper on dealing with the risk associated with public sector projects is K. J. Arrow and R. C. Lind (1970), "Uncertainty and Evaluation of Public Investment Decisions", *American Economic Review* Vol. 60, pp. 364–378. The *@RISK* manual accompanying the software package *@RISK: Advanced Risk Analysis for Spreadsheets* by Palisade Corporation (1997), Newfield, New York provides a useful discussion of risk modeling. See also Boardman et al., *Cost-Benefit Analysis: Concepts and Practice* (Prentice Hall, 2001), Ch. 7.

Exercises

1. The following table describes the projected net benefits for two projects. (All values in $ millions)

	PROJECT A			PROJECT B		
	Pessimistic	Best Guess	Optimistic	Pessimistic	Best Guess	Optimistic
Year 0	−80	−75	−70	−100	−75	−50
Year 1	−110	−100	−90	−150	−100	−50
Year 2	18	20	22	12	20	28
Year 3	28	30	32	20	30	40
Year 4	28	30	32	25	45	65
Year 5	40	45	50	25	45	65
Year 6	40	45	50	25	45	65
Year 7	40	45	50	25	45	65
Year 8	40	45	50	25	45	65
Year 9	40	45	50	25	45	65
Year 10	55	65	75	35	65	95

(a) Using the NPV decision-rule and assuming a 10% discount rate, which of the two projects would you prefer using the "best guess" estimate of cash flow?

(b) Using the available range of estimates apply an *@RISK©* simulation with a triangular distribution (1000 iterations) to derive the following:

(i)   the mean, minimum, and maximum NPVs for each project;

(ii) a graph of the probability distribution of NPVs for each project;

(iii) a graph of the cumulative (ascending) distribution of NPVs for each project;

(c) Which project would a risk averse decision-maker favour, and why? (Assume a 90% confidence level.)

(d) Which project would a risk-taking decision-maker favour, and why? (Assume a 20% confidence level.)

(e) Would your answers to questions (a), (c) and (d) be any different if the discount rate was set at: (a) 5%; and (b) 15%?

2. Nicole leads an exciting life. Her wealth is a risky prospect which will take the value $100 with probability 0.5, or $36 with probability 0.5. Her utility of wealth function is: $U = W^{0.5}$.

(a) What is the expected value of her wealth?

(b) What is the expected utility of her wealth?

(c) What level of wealth with certainty will give her the same utility as the risky prospect?

(d) What is the cost of the risk associated with the risky prospect?

10

The Social Discount Rate, Cost of Public Funds, and the Value of Information

Introduction

In this Chapter we consider three issues each of which may call for a modification of the following simple net present value rule: in the absence of risk, undertaking any project with a positive net present value (NPV), calculated using the appropriate shadow-prices and discounting at the market rate of interest, will contribute to economic efficiency.

Firstly, the concept of social time preference reflects the view that the market rate of interest does not accurately reflect society's preference for present as opposed to future consumption, and that a discount rate based on a social time preference rate should be used to calculate NPVs from a public interest viewpoint. For reasons which will be discussed below, the social time preference rate is usually judged to be lower than the market rate of interest.

Secondly, the concept of social opportunity cost is based on the notion that, because of tax-induced distortions to the pattern of resource allocation, the opportunity cost to the economy of raising public funds for government expenditures is higher than the nominal amount raised. This suggests that a public project should have a present value of benefits sufficiently large not only to offset project costs (the NPV>0 rule), but also to offset the premium on the cost of public funds if the project is to make a net contribution to efficiency.

Thirdly, the fact that a project has a NPV>0 does not necessarily imply that *now* is the most efficient time to implement it. Because additional information about the project variables – prices, costs etc. – may accrue in the future there could be an advantage to keeping open the option of undertaking the project. Once this option has been exercised it ceases to have any value, and the loss of option value should be taken into account in the decision to proceed.

The Social Rate of Discount

It was argued earlier that the main rationale for social benefit-cost analysis is the existence of market failure. Because of distortions and ill-defined property rights, the actions of private agents operating through the market will not necessarily result in an efficient allocation of resources, thereby creating a possible role for government in the scrutiny and regulation of proposed private projects and the undertaking of public projects. A conspicuous, but unavoidable, market failure is the absence of future generations in the capital markets which determine the quantity of resources to be allocated now to investment to provide consumption goods for the future. If the needs of future generations are not adequately taken into account in the operation of private capital markets, too few investment projects will be undertaken by the private sector. In other words, the private market rate of interest will be too high a hurdle for judging the appropriate rate of return on long-lived private and public projects. This problem could be addressed by using a social time preference rate, lower than the market rate, as the discount rate in social benefit-cost analysis. Such a procedure is in the tradition of constructing shadow-prices to replace private market prices in project appraisal when a significant market failure exists. The effect of using a discount rate that is lower than the market rate of interest will be to both increase the number of potential public sector projects having a positive NPV and, to favour those that are more capital intensive and generate higher rates of saving and reinvestible funds.

At a more fundamental level, we might ask why private markets discount future benefits and costs at all. The simple answer is that interest rates are determined by the interplay of demand for, and supply of, investible funds. The demand for investible funds is determined by the opportunities for investment which exist in the economy, and this issue was considered in detail in Chapter 2. The supply of investible funds is determined by individual preferences for present as opposed to future consumption. The market rate of interest is used by individuals to discount values of future consumption goods for comparison with current consumption values in making choices. From the viewpoint of individual consumers the market or consumption rate of interest needs to be positive for two reasons: consumer time preference and economic growth.

Time preference refers to the fact that individuals discount future utility in making choices, thereby placing less weight on it than on utility enjoyed in the present. Discounting of utility may simply be an expression of tastes, but it may also reflect the fact that the future is uncertain. It will be recalled that one approach to dealing with risk in investment appraisal discussed in Chapter 2 involved adding a risk premium to the discount rate. By adding a risk premium reflecting the probability of the net benefit stream ceasing in any given year, the analyst is able to calculate the expected net present value of the project. Individuals face some probability each year that their utility stream will terminate due to death. In developed economies this probability is quite low: the probability of a middle-aged person dying in the forthcoming year is around one percent. An individual who used this rate to discount future utility in making decisions about present vs. future consumption would, in effect, simply be using her expected total undiscounted utility as a basis for evaluating alternatives.

The second reason for discounting future consumption is the expectation of being wealthier in the future because of economic growth. As noted in the discussion of risk in Chapter 9, it is generally assumed that an individual's utility rises at a decreasing rate as their wealth increases. Diminishing marginal utility reflects the fact that each extra dollar of wealth contributes less to increasing utility as the amount of wealth increases. An individual considering saving, as opposed to spending, an extra dollar has to compare the extra utility which saving that dollar (and using the interest and principal to increase spending in the future) will yield as compared to the extra utility from spending it now. If wealth is expected to be higher in the future, the marginal utility obtained in the future from spending a dollar will be less than the marginal utility obtained from spending it now. This means that for saving a dollar to yield as much extra undiscounted utility as spending it, there must be a positive return to saving, ensuring that a dollar saved converts to more than a dollar's worth of extra consumption in the future. The required rate of return is measured by the product of the growth rate of wealth and the elasticity of the marginal utility of wealth which measures the degree of curvature of the utility of wealth function. This required rate of return can be termed the utility growth factor. Elasticities of the marginal utility of wealth have been calculated for developed economies in the 1–2 range. Combining a value of, say, 1.5 for this parameter with, say, a 2% economic growth rate gives a utility growth factor of around 3%.

In summary, individuals have two reasons for discounting future consumption in making saving and investment decisions. One reason is that the extra future consumption goods will not yield as much extra utility as they would if they were available now. This consideration is accommodated in the present value calculation by the utility growth factor. The other reason is that future utility is worth less to an individual than present utility, either intrinsically because of tastes, or because of the uncertainty which attaches to it through human mortality. This consideration is accommodated by the utility discount factor. The sum of the utility discount factor and the utility growth factor is the *consumption rate of interest*. From the examples cited above the consumption rate of interest in a developed economy could be expected to be around 4% which is similar to observed real rates of interest on government bonds.

When an individual employs a utility discount factor they may be taking account of the possibility that they will not be alive to enjoy the fruits of their investment. Even in that event, however, the investment is still expected to yield a benefit to some member of society. In other words, even if there is no private benefit from the investment, because of the death of the person who undertook it, there is still a social benefit. This suggests that project net benefits should not be subject to a utility discount factor when projects are being assessed from a social viewpoint. Leaving aside the utility discount factor the *social discount rate* would then simply be the utility growth factor – around 3% in the above example.

The above discussion has assumed that individuals care only for their own present and future consumption, and that for this reason it is necessary to use a shadow-rate of interest in the form of the social discount rate to calculate net present values from a social viewpoint. However there is plenty of evidence that individuals do take the needs of future generations into account. People regularly leave substantial bequests to their children, sums in excess of those which could be explained by the difficulty of planning to exhaust one's wealth on the day of one's death. To the extent that the interests of future generations are already factored into market behaviour, the need for an adjustment to the market rate of interest in social benefit-cost analysis becomes less compelling.

The Social Opportunity Cost of Public Funds

Any proposed public or private project is likely to have implications for public funds. In the ICP Case Study considered in the Chapter Appendices, for example, the proposed private project results in increases in government receipts from import duties and company taxes, and these tax revenues were counted as part of the referent group benefits. In practice a large private project could affect the levels of most categories of indirect and direct tax flows. Furthermore, the cost of a proposed public project would be met, wholly or partially, out of public funds. For reasons discussed below the opportunity cost of public funds is higher than the nominal amount involved; in other words, a dollar of public funds raised costs the economy more than a dollar, with the size of the cost premium generally thought to be around 20%. This means that public funds *contributed to* a project, or public funds *generated by* a project, need to be shadow-priced in social benefit-cost analysis to properly reflect their opportunity cost.

Changes in flows of public funds resulting from a project need to be shadow-priced irrespective of whether they are on the revenue or expenditure side of the public accounts. However, for the purposes of this discussion we will consider the opportunity cost of public funds to be expended on undertaking a public project. The shadow-price developed for this purpose can also be used to shadow-price revenues obtained from charges for public goods or services, or accruing as taxes resulting from a private project.

If a public project is to be undertaken it has to be financed, paid for out of public revenues which are obtained from taxes, borrowing or printing money. Each of the latter methods of financing public expenditure imposes costs on the economy which are not included in the measure of the opportunity cost of project inputs at market or shadow-prices. As we saw in Chapter 5, most taxes distort markets and this results in prices not reflecting opportunity costs; higher tax rates, imposed to fund additional public expenditure, increase the degree of distortion and move the allocation of resources further from the efficient pattern. Selling bonds diverts funds from private investment which, because of the tax system, has a higher return to the referent group (the before-tax return) than to the private investor (the after-tax return). Printing money leads to inflation which affects the efficiency of markets and results in an inefficient pattern of resource allocation in the economy.

If the government is rational and informed it will use each of these three sources of funds up to the point at which its marginal cost is equal to the marginal cost of each of the other two. In this way the total cost of collecting any given quantity of public funds is minimized. This implies that if we work out the marginal cost of funds obtained through, say, taxation we can assume that this is the marginal cost of public funds from any source. There is some evidence that governments *are* rational and informed in the way that we are assuming: there has recently been much less reliance on inflation to fund public expenditures than previously. The reason is not so much that the cost of this source has risen but rather that governments are better informed about its costs in terms of economic instability and resource misallocation. Since bond finance eventually leads to higher taxes to pay for interest and principal repayments we may be on reasonably solid ground if we use the marginal cost of tax revenues to approximate the marginal cost of public funds. However in this discussion we will consider both bond and tax finance.

There are three main costs of raising tax revenues: collection costs, compliance costs and deadweight loss: collection costs are costs incurred by the private and public sectors in the battle over the amount of tax due; compliance costs are costs of tax-form-filling incurred by the private sector; and deadweight loss is the cost of changes in economic behaviour induced by the structure of the tax system, with the consequent inefficient allocation of resources. It can be argued that, while collection and compliance costs may be substantial, they do not increase significantly with an increase in tax rates. In other words, in calculating the shadow-price to apply to changes to tax flows, only the deadweight loss needs to be taken into account.

As noted above, the discussion will focus on the opportunity cost of raising an additional amount of tax revenue to fund an additional public project. The benefits of the public project (B) would need to be at least as large as the project opportunity cost (C), plus the deadweight loss, (D), plus any additional collection and compliance costs, to make the project worthwhile. Ignoring additional collection and compliance costs, the NPV rule for deciding to undertake the project is:

$$NPV = B - (C + D) > 0, \text{ or } B - C\left[\frac{(C + D)}{C}\right] > 0,$$

where B, C and D are present values of the benefit, opportunity cost and deadweight loss streams respectively. When the opportunity cost of the project inputs is the same as its nominal cost (i.e. when there is no need to shadow-price project inputs other than public funds), the term $(C+D)/C$ measures the marginal cost of public funds – the extra cost to the economy per extra dollar of tax revenue raised. The marginal cost of public funds can be used to shadow-price the nominal project cost, C, in the NPV calculation. Expressing the NPV rule in the form of a benefit/cost decision-rule gives:

$$\frac{B}{(C + D)} > 1, \text{ or } \frac{B}{C} > \frac{(C + D)}{C},$$

where the shadow-price of public funds replaces unity as the cut-off benefit/cost ratio.

The calculation of the deadweight loss depends on the assumptions made about the incidence of taxation: does it mainly fall on labour, on commodities, or on capital? Many studies have assumed that since eventually all taxes are borne by labour the main deadweight loss stems from distortions to the incentive to work. Some studies have argued that indirect taxes distort consumers' choices among commodities, and some have emphasized the distorting effect of direct taxes on the level and pattern of investment. Notwithstanding the various assumptions made, most studies of the marginal cost of public funds in developed economies such as Australia, Canada, New Zealand, the United Kingdom and the United States find that the cost premium is around 20–25%. The cost of public funds in developing economies is likely to be higher than this because of the additional difficulties associated with designing and running an efficient tax system in these countries.

The Deadweight Loss Resulting from Bond Finance

As an illustration of the cost to the economy of an additional distortion to the allocation of capital, consider a situation in which a public project is to be financed through sale of government bonds to the public. Ignoring risk, private investors will allocate funds between government bonds and private projects until the yields are equalized at the margin. Since the private rate of return on a private project is net of business income tax, the after-business income tax return on private projects will equal the government bond rate. If investment in government bonds displaces investment in private projects, the opportunity cost to the economy of financing the public project is the before-tax return on the displaced private projects. Suppose that investors require a private project to yield an after-tax rate of return equal to the government bond rate of r, and that the business income tax is levied at rate t, then the before-tax rate of return on private projects is given by $r^* = r/(1-t)$. For example, if r is 0.06 and t is 0.4 then the opportunity cost rate of return on private investment is 0.1.

Now suppose that $100 worth of government bonds is sold to the public and that private investors fund the purchase by increasing their saving (reducing their consumption) by $50, and by reducing their investment in private projects by $50. The opportunity cost of the $50 reduction in private consumption is $50, while the opportunity cost of the $50 reduction in private investment is the present value of the forgone before-tax return. Assuming that the private projects are perpetuities, the annual before-tax return is $50r^*$, with a present value of $50(r^*/r)$ at the market rate of interest. Using the interest and tax rates from our example, the present value to the economy of the forgone private investment is $83.33. Thus the cost to the economy of $100 worth of public funds raised through sales of bonds is $133.33, or $1.33 per dollar raised. In other words, raising the $100 in public funds imposes a deadweight loss of $33.33 on the economy. The size of the deadweight loss and the cost premium on public funds is obviously higher the higher is the business income tax rate, and the higher the proportion of funds diverted from private investment as opposed to private consumption.

The example suggests that if the public project is to contribute to economic efficiency the present value of project net benefits will have to exceed the opportunity cost of $133.33 rather than the nominal cost of $100. In other words, the nominal cost of the project, $100, is adjusted by the shadow-price of public funds, 1.33 in the example, in calculating the project NPV in the efficiency benefit-cost analysis. Alternatively, the proposed project could be required to clear a hurdle benefit-cost ratio of 1.33 instead of the customary level of unity. Assuming that the net benefit of the public project is a perpetuity, B, and that the nominal cost, C, is incurred now, the net present value decision-rule becomes:

$$NPV = \frac{B}{r} - 1.33\,C > 0, \text{ and hence } \frac{B}{r} > 1.33\,C.$$

Some analysts have suggested that the opportunity cost of public funds could be accounted for by an upward adjustment to the discount rate used to calculate present values in social benefit-cost analysis. For example, in the case just considered, since 50% of the resources required to undertake the public project are obtained by displacing consumption activity and 50% by displacing investment activity, the appropriate discount rate for the public project is an average of the consumption rate of interest, r, and the before-tax rate of return on private investment, r^*. Assuming that the public project has an initial cost of C and yields an annual net benefit, B, in perpetuity the net present value rule becomes:

$$NPV = \frac{B}{\frac{r^* + r}{2}} - C > 0, \text{ which implies that:}$$

$$\frac{B}{r} > C \left[\frac{(r^* + r)}{2r} \right].$$

Using the values from the above example, the investment decision-rule becomes:

$$\frac{B}{r} > 1.33 \, C$$

which is identical to the shadow-pricing rule developed above.

It appears from the above examples that it makes no difference whether the opportunity cost of public funds is accounted for in social benefit-cost analysis by shadow-pricing the project cost, or by using a shadow-discount rate to calculate project net present value. However the examples deal with the special case of a perpetuity, and when public and private projects with finite lives (longer than two periods) are considered the two methods do not give exactly the same results. Which method is to be preferred? It can be argued that it is better to shadow-price the public project rather than use a shadow-rate of interest. Use of a (higher) shadow-rate of interest as opposed to the consumption rate of interest as the discount rate for public projects will bias the net present value rule against long-lived projects (Example 3.4 in Chapter 3 illustrated the effect of a change in the discount rate on the choice between projects). No such bias exists when the shadow-price of public funds is calculated so as to measure the present value, at the market rate of interest, of the private consumption forgone, both directly and indirectly through reduced private investment, as a result of financing the public project.

The Deadweight Loss Resulting from a Tax Increase on Labour Income

A significant form of deadweight loss associated with a tax increase is generally thought to result from the effect of the tax increase on work incentives. An increase in the tax rate lowers the after-tax wage (the cost of leisure) and makes additional leisure relatively more attractive. However the lower after-tax wage also lowers disposable income and makes additional leisure less affordable. While these two effects work in opposite directions it is likely that a reduction in the after-tax wage will reduce the aggregate amount of labour supplied.

The effect of an increase in a proportional tax rate on labour income can be illustrated by a labour supply curve. Figure 10.1 illustrates the supply of labour in response to the after-tax wage. In Figure 10.1, W is the before-tax wage, which is assumed to be unaffected by the tax increase, W_0 is the initial after-tax wage, and W_1 is the after-tax wage following a tax increase. The effect of the tax increase is to reduce the quantity of labour supplied by an amount measured by the distance $L_1 L_0$ in Figure 10.1.

The cost of each extra dollar of public funds obtained through a tax increase is the cost of the tax increase divided by the additional amount of tax revenues obtained. The cost of the tax increase to the worker is the change in after-tax labour income less the change in the cost of supplying the labour. The cost of supplying an additional unit of labour is the value of that unit of the worker's time in an alternative use, which is measured by the supply curve. In terms of Figure 10.1, the loss of labour income as a result of the tax increase is given by ACDE + $DCL_0 L_1$ but this is partially offset by the reduction in cost, $DCL_0 L_1$, of supplying the labour. The net cost to the worker of the tax increase is given by area ACDE, which represents a loss of producer surplus as discussed in Chapter 7.

The additional tax revenue obtained from the tax increase is measured by area ABDE –

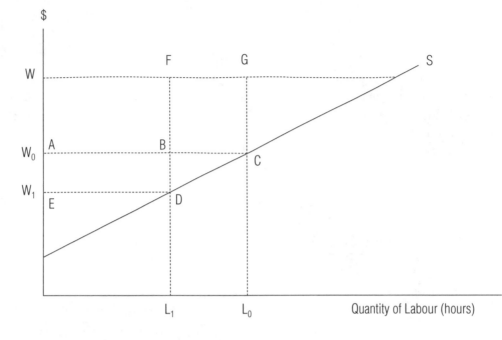

Figure 10.1 Taxation and Labour Supply

FGCB in Figure 10.1. This is the additional tax levied on the new level of labour supply, less the loss of tax levied at the original rate as a result of the reduction in labour supply. The cost of public funds is given by ACDE/(ABDE – FGCB). This can also be expressed as 1+FGCD/(ABDE – FGCB), where FGCD is the deadweight loss caused by the tax increase. In other words, the cost of public funds is greater than $1 per $1 of tax revenue if the deadweight loss is positive.

Why is area FGCD called a deadweight loss? Looking at the question from the point of view of the economy as a whole, there has been a reduction in labour supply and hence a reduction in the value of output (GDP) of FGL_0L_1. This is partially offset by the value, DCL_0L_1, of the additional quantity of leisure, L_0L_1. The net loss to the economy is FGCD.

The cost of public funds can be estimated from information about labour supply and tax rates. However the relevant tax rates are effective marginal tax rates (EMTRs) which incorporate both direct and indirect taxes and include the effects of benefit programs as well as taxation: the effective marginal rate of tax is the increase in tax paid less social security benefit received when household income rises by a dollar. In effect the household is penalized twice when income rises as a result of additional work – it pays more tax and it experiences a reduction in those government benefits which are related to income level. When the marginal tax rate on labour income is calculated on this basis EMTRs can be significant in most income brackets; for example, an Australian study calculated an average EMTR of 47% across income deciles.

As noted above, a rise in the tax rate in order to fund an additional public project causes a decline in the quantity of labour supplied, thereby reducing before-tax incomes and making some households eligible to receive increased benefit levels. How should these increased benefits be financed? It can be argued that the additional tax revenues should be sufficient to fund the additional public project *and* pay any additional benefits required under current programs because of the tax increase. When this requirement is imposed on the funding of an additional public project a larger tax increase is required, with a consequent increase in the deadweight loss and the cost premium.

The size of the reduction in labour supply depends upon how responsive labour supply is to a change in the after-tax wage. An Australian study assumed that, while households in different income deciles would respond differently to a tax increase, the average household would reduce labour supply by 6% in response to a 10% fall in its after-tax wage. Using a simple model of labour supply incorporating this assumption, values corresponding to areas FGCD and (ABDE − FGCB) in the labour supply diagram of Figure 10.1 could be calculated for the average household in each income decile. Aggregate deadweight loss and aggregate additional tax revenues can be calculated by summing across households and their ratio used to calculate the deadweight loss per dollar of additional revenue available to fund public expenditure. A value of $0.19 was obtained in the Australian study, implying that the cost of public funds in Australia is $1.19 per dollar of tax revenue.

The effect of the tax increase on labour supply was considered above. However undertaking the public project may independently affect labour supply. For example, a new road could decrease labour supply by making it easier to get to the beach, or could increase labour supply by making it easier to get to work: in the first case the public project complements leisure activities and in the second it is a substitute for leisure. Furthermore, having access to an additional quantity of a public good as a result of a public project increases households' economic well-being, thereby making leisure seem more affordable; this sort of reaction is termed an "income effect". The net effect of the output of the public project will vary from case to case, but may generally tend to be in the direction of reduced labour supply. In terms of Figure 10.1, this means that the supply curve of labour shifts to the left when the project is undertaken, thereby causing an additional reduction in tax revenues.

If undertaking the project causes a reduction in labour supply, the loss in tax revenues will need to be made up by a further increase in taxation with its associated deadweight loss. Allowing for the income effect of increased public good provision added a further 5% to the Australian estimate of deadweight loss, bringing the estimate of the marginal cost of public funds up to $1.24 per dollar of additional tax revenue to be used to fund an additional public project.

The conclusion of this analysis of the taxation of labour income is that changes in levels of public revenues or expenditures should be shadow-priced in efficiency benefit-cost analysis. In a developed economy the size of the appropriate shadow-price will probably be in the 1.2–1.25 range. In principle the shadow-price should be project-specific, depending on the nature of the project's output as a substitute for (complement to) leisure, but in practice this kind of information is seldom available. Where project-specific labour supply effects are localized they may be insignificant in comparison with the overall cost of the project.

Option Value and the Value of Information

A cost-benefit analysis is a costly exercise which provides information about the efficiency and referent group net benefits of a project normally before the implementation decision is made. In deciding whether to perform a cost-benefit analysis the decision-maker must weigh the benefits of the analysis against its costs – in other words, implicitly do a cost-benefit analysis of the cost-benefit analysis. The question is whether the value of the information obtained through the cost-benefit analysis is high enough to justify incurring the cost of performing the analysis. The value of information can be defined as the excess of the value of the decision which is made with the information over the value of the decision made without the information. Since these values cannot be known with certainty, the value of information is expressed as an expected value. We now consider a simple example of the question of whether or not to delay implementing a project in order to obtain better information before making a decision; delay has a cost, but it also has an expected benefit and the difference between these two values is the expected value of the information obtained through delay.

Suppose that a project involving an irreversible investment of \$K will yield an operating profit of R_0 in the present period, and an expected operating profit of $E(R)$ in perpetuity starting in period 1. The expected annual value in perpetuity of operating profit is given by:

$$E(R) = qR_H + (1-q)R_L,$$

where q is the probability of a high price environment, and R_H and R_L are the annual operating profits in the high and low price environments respectively. The net present value rule developed in Chapter 2 would be to undertake the project if:

$$\frac{E(R)}{r} > (K - R_0)$$

Now suppose that in period 1 information will become available about the project's future profitability; for example, it will become known whether prices will be high or low and hence whether operating profit will be R_H or R_L. Assume that the firm has the option of delaying the project for one period. If it does so and finds that prices turn out to be low it need not suffer a loss by undertaking the project in period 1; alternatively if prices turn out to be high it can undertake the project in period 1 and it will have suffered a loss of profit (R_0) in the present period, but will have benefited from postponing the investment cost by one period. The benefit of waiting derives from the possibility of avoiding a mistake; the cost of waiting is the forgone profit in the present period, net of the lower present value of the capital cost, together with the cost of delaying the start of the future benefit stream by one period. If the benefit of waiting exceeds the cost it is better to wait.

Figure 10.2 illustrates the decision-maker's choice of investing now or waiting for one period. If he invests now he incurs a capital cost, K, receives R_0 revenue in the current period, and, starting in the following period, revenue in perpetuity with an expected value of $E(R) = qR_H + (1-q)R_L$. The expected net present value of investing now is:

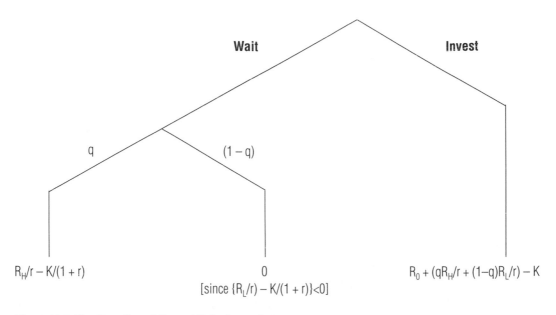

Figure 10.2 The Benefit and Cost of Delaying an Investment

$$NPV(0) = R_0 + \left[\frac{qR_H}{r} + \frac{(1-q)\,R_L}{r} \right] - K$$

where NPV(0) is the NPV at time 0 of undertaking the project at time 0.

If the decision-maker defers the decision for one period he will have the option of not investing if the low price environment eventuates. Assuming that $R_L/r < K - R_L$, he will opt not to undertake the project in the low price environment. This means that there is a $(1-q)$ probability of a zero payoff if he waits. If the high price environment eventuates the project is undertaken in period 1 with a net present value in period 1 of $R_H/r + R_H - K$, or $R_H/r - K/(1+r)$ at time 0. The expected net present value at time 0 of the deferred investment decision is given by:

$$NPV(1) = q \left[\frac{R_H}{r} - \frac{K}{1+r} \right]$$

where NPV(1) is the NPV at time 0 of undertaking the project in period 1. The value to the decision-maker of waiting – "keeping his options open" – is given by the difference between NPV(1) and NPV(0):

$$V_W = K \left[1 - \frac{q}{1+r} \right] - R_0 - \left[\frac{R_L}{r} \right] (1-q).$$

By means of partial differentiation it can be ascertained that the value of waiting increases as K rises, and falls as q, R_L, or R_0 increase. In other words, the larger the capital investment the more an option to delay is worth; however the value of the option falls as the probability of high operating profit increases, as the level of operating profit in the low price environment increases, and as the profit forgone in the initial period increases. The "bad news principle" is illustrated by the fact that a change in R_H, the value of operating profit in the high price environment, does not affect the value of the option of waiting.

For the decision-maker to decide to undertake the project now, the option of waiting must be worthless: $V_W < 0$. From the expression for V_W, and using the expression for E(R) derived earlier, it can be shown that this means that:

$$\frac{E(R)}{r} > (K - R_0) + b$$

$$\text{where } b = q\left[\frac{R_H}{r} - \frac{K}{1+r}\right]$$

On the assumption that the investment project, undertaken in period 1, has a positive NPV at time 0 in the high price environment, b is positive. Since b is positive, the investment decision-rule is to undertake the project if the present value of its expected future returns exceeds the net cost of the investment by some positive amount: ie. undertake the project if NPV > b. This is a more stringent condition that the net present value criterion when the option of delay is not available. Undertaking the project now has to be sufficiently attractive to outweigh the forgone value of the option of delay.

Incorporating the Cost of Public Funds in the ICP Case Study

Provision has already been made in the ICP Case Study for a social rate of discount different from the market rate of interest. The NPV of the project in both the efficiency and referent group analysis was calculated at a range of discount rates, which is expected to include the social rate of discount. If information is available about the appropriate discount rate the corresponding NPV can readily be obtained.

It will now be assumed that the marginal cost of public funds in Thailand is 1.2: this means that a real cost of 0.2 Baht is imposed on the economy for every Baht transferred from the private to the public sector in the form of taxes. To take account of this in the ICP Case Study we start by entering the public funds premium in the variables section of Figure 10.3 (p. 235).

If public funds are to be shadow-priced to reflect a cost premium, this will affect the efficiency and referent group analyses, but not the project and private analyses. In the efficiency analysis no account was taken of direct taxes, such as business income taxes, and outputs and inputs were priced at their marginal values or opportunity costs which, as discussed in Chapter 6, could be either net or gross of tax. In either case, no specific account is taken of indirect tax flows in the efficiency analysis. The referent group analysis, on the other hand, takes explicit account of direct and indirect tax flows because the government is usually a member of the referent group.

To see how the cost premium on public funds can be integrated into the benefit-cost analysis framework, consider first the referent group analysis. In Figure A6.2 Table 5 of the consolidated tables for the ICP project identified a set of indirect and direct tax flows accruing to government as a member of the referent group. It is a simple matter to multiply these flows by a shadow-price of 1.2 to reflect the cost premium on public funds. In Table 5 of Figure 10.3 the 20% premium is added to the net value of import duties received by government in a new row labeled *Indirect Taxes + Premium* and to the profits taxes received by government, in a new row labeled *Direct Taxes + Premium*.

It is now clear that some adjustments are required to the efficiency analysis to reflect the project's net contribution to public revenues. In the absence of a cost premium on public funds, direct taxes net out in the efficiency analysis because they are a cost to one group (the firm) and a benefit to another (the government). However if public funds are to be shadow-priced, the benefit of a given tax flow to government will exceed the cost of the same tax flow to the firm. The difference between the two values is measured by the amount of the tax flow valued at the cost premium.

For example, if the cost premium is 20% then 20% of the direct tax flow needs to be credited as a benefit in the efficiency benefit-cost analysis. The intuition behind this procedure is that the extra tax flow will allow the government to cut taxes elsewhere, or to not raise taxes elsewhere, thereby generating a benefit, or avoiding a cost, to the economy. When the tax flow is entered in the referent group analysis it must be shadow-priced, at 1.2 in the example, to reflect the cost premium on public funds. Thus the NPV of the project will rise by the same amount in both the efficiency and referent group analyses, as a result of shadow-pricing the direct tax flow.

We saw in Chapter 5 that project inputs that are in additional supply, and project output that replaces existing demand should be valued at their net of tax prices in the efficiency benefit-cost analysis. When project inputs are valued at net of tax prices this tends to over-state their costs once a cost premium is to be applied to tax revenues. For example, consider an input with a market price of $P_t = P(1+t)$, where P_t is the gross of tax price, P is the net of tax price, and t is the *ad valorem* tax rate. A quantity, Q, of this input would be costed at PQ in the efficiency analysis. However once a 20% cost premium is applied to public funds an efficiency benefit valued at 0.2PQt is generated by the use of the input. Crediting this efficiency benefit reduces the net cost of the input to the economy to PQ(1–0.2t). In other words, the shadow-price of the input should be reduced from P to P(1–0.2t). In the referent group analysis the tax flow should be shadow-priced at 1.2, with the result that the referent group net benefit increases by 0.2PQt. The effect of these two adjustments is to increase the efficiency and referent group net benefit by 0.2PQt, thereby preserving the requirement that the referent and non-referent group net benefits sum to the efficiency net benefit.

Now consider a project which produces output that replaces existing demand, such as an import-replacing project. Project output is to be priced at its net of tariff price to reflect the fact that as consumers purchase the domestically produced commodity instead of the imported variety, tariff revenues fall. If tariff revenues are to attract a premium in the analysis because of the cost of public funds an additional cost must be attributed to the project. For example, consider an output with a market price of $P_t = P(1+t)$, where P_t is the gross of tariff price, P is the world price, and t is the *ad valorem* tariff. If there were no cost premium on public funds, a quantity, Q, of this input would be costed at PQ in the efficiency analysis. However once a 20% cost premium is applied to public funds an additional efficiency cost of 0.2PQt is generated by the import replacement. Allowing for this additional efficiency cost reduces the net value of the output to the economy to PQ(1–0.2t). In other words, the shadow-price of the output should be reduced from P to P(1–0.2t). In the referent group analysis the reduction in the tariff revenue flow should be shadow-priced at 1.2, with the result that the referent group net benefit also declines by 0.2PQt.

We also saw in Chapter 5 that project output which satisfies additional demand, or project inputs which are diverted from other uses, should be priced at their gross of tax prices in the efficiency benefit-cost analysis. In these circumstances the effects on net tax flows are uncertain. For example, if labour moves from one form of employment to another there may be no change in income tax receipts; and if consumers purchase more of one good they may reduce purchases of other goods with the net result that sales tax revenues do not change. Any net change in tax revenues which does occur from these sources should be adjusted by the cost premium on public funds, which, in our example, would involve increasing any gain or loss by 20% in both the efficiency and referent group benefit-cost analyses. If there is no reason to believe that the net change in tax revenues is large it may be reasonable to ignore the 20% adjustment which, in principle, is required.

It can be concluded from the above discussion that the cost premium on public funds could be incorporated in the efficiency analysis by applying a recomputed set of shadow-prices (as compared with the analysis of Chapter 5) to value the project inputs and outputs. While this procedure would take care of the premium on indirect tax revenues, the direct tax revenue premium would have to be entered directly. Entering the public funds premium directly is much simpler than creating a new set of shadow-prices, and this is the procedure adopted below for both indirect and direct tax revenues. Using this procedure to account for the premium on indirect tax revenues allows the analyst to avoid the complicated set of adjustments to shadow-prices described above.

Turning now to the details of the efficiency analysis in the ICP Case Study, in Table 4 of Figure 10.3 the 20% premium on tariff revenues gained or lost is entered in the row labeled *Indirect Tax Premium*, and the 20% premium on profits taxes lost or gained is entered in the row labeled *Direct Tax Premium*. To simplify the calculation of these values, the former can be derived from the data on import duties in Table 5 and the latter, from ICP's profit taxes as calculated in Table 3 of the spreadsheet in Figure 10.3, together with the public funds premium reported in Table 1.

The effect of these adjustments is a net increase in the project's efficiency benefits, resulting in an increase in the IRR from 23.4% to 24.2%. This increase reflects the fact that the project is a net contributor to public funds. The referent group net benefits increase from $260.4 million to $283.6 million at a 4% discount rate. As a consistency check to verify that the analyst has not made an error in making these adjustments the aggregate referent group benefits at the top of Table 5 in Figure 10.3 (derived by subtracting ICP's cash flow and the overseas lender's cash flow from the efficiency cash flow) should be the same as those on the bottom line (derived by aggregating the sub-referent group members' net cash flows).

ICP PROJECT: 1999-2009

TABLE 1 — KEY INPUT VARIABLES

VARIABLES		INVESTMENT COSTS	000 $'	000 BT	RUNNING COSTS		MATERIAL FLOWS		FINANCE	
EXCHANGE RATE	44	SPINDLES	4000		WATER BT P	480000	COTTON MN LB	16.2	SUPPLIERS CREDIT	75%
TARIFF A	5%	EQUIPMENT	830		POWER BT P	480000	YARN MN LBS	15	OVERDRAFT	60
TARIFF B	10%	INSTALLATION	100		SPARE PART	10%	LABOUR 1	100	CREDIT REPAY YEAI	5
PROFITS TAX	50%	CONSTRUCTION		36000	INSURANCE	6	LABOUR 2	1000		
DEPRECIATION	10%	START-UP COSTS		18000	OVERHEADS	0	LABOUR 3	500		
PRICE YARN CIF US$	0.58	WORKING CAPITAL							DISCOUNT RATES	4%
YARN TARIFF BT	2.1	RAW MATERIALS	1200							8%
HANDLING BT	0.3	SPARE PARTS	243							12%
TARIFF C	10%									16%
PRICE COTTON CIF US$	0.3									
WAGE 1 BT PA	150000	PUB. FUNDS PREMIUM		0.2						
WAGE 2 B1 PA	22500									
WAGE 3 BT PA	12000									
INTEREST RATE 1	8%									
INTEREST RATE 2	10%									

TABLE 2 — PROJECT CALCULATION

YEAR	1999	1999	2000	2001	2002	2003	2004	2005	2006	2007	2008	2009
	'000 US$	MN BT	MN BT	MN BT	MN BT	MN BT	MN BT	MN BT	MN BT	MN BT	MN BT	MN BT
INVESTMENT COSTS												
SPINDLES	-4200.000	-184.800										
EQUIPMENT	-872.500	-39.270										
INSTALLATION	-100.000	-4.400										
CONSTRUCTION		-36.000										
START-UP COSTS		-18.000										
RAW MATERIALS		-58.080										58.080
SPARE PARTS		-11.227										11.227
TOTAL	-282.470	-69.307	0.000	0.000	0.000	0.000	0.000	0.000	0.000	0.000	0.000	69.307
RUNNING COSTS												
WATER		-3.600	-7.200	-7.200	-7.200	-7.200	-7.200	-7.200	-7.200	-7.200	-7.200	-7.200
POWER		-3.600	-7.200	-7.200	-7.200	-7.200	-7.200	-7.200	-7.200	-7.200	-7.200	-7.200
SPARE PARTS		-22.407	-22.407	-22.407	-22.407	-22.407	-22.407	-22.407	-22.407	-22.407	-22.407	-22.407
RAW MATERIALS		-117.612	-235.224	-235.224	-235.224	-235.224	-235.224	-235.224	-235.224	-235.224	-235.224	-235.224
INSURANCE		-6.000	-6.000	-6.000	-6.000	-6.000	-6.000	-6.000	-6.000	-6.000	-6.000	-6.000
LABOUR		-43.500	-43.500	-43.500	-43.500	-43.500	-43.500	-43.500	-43.500	-43.500	-43.500	-43.500
TOTAL		196.719	-321.531	-321.531	-321.531	-321.531	-321.531	-321.531	-321.531	-321.531	-321.531	-321.531
REVENUES												
SALE OF YARN		209.400	418.800	418.800	418.800	418.800	418.800	418.800	418.800	418.800	418.800	418.800
NCF (Project)	282.470	-56.626	97.269	97.269	97.269	97.269	97.269	97.269	97.269	97.269	97.269	166.576

TABLE 3 — PRIVATE CALCULATION

YEAR	1999	1999	2000	2001	2002	2003	2004	2005	2006	2007	2008	2009
	'000 US$	MN BT	MN BT	MN BT	MN BT	MN BT	MN BT	MN BT	MN BT	MN BT	MN BT	MN BT
FINANCIAL FLOWS												
DEPRECIATION			-26.447	-26.447	-26.447	-26.447	-26.447	-26.447	-26.447	-26.447	-26.447	-26.447
INTEREST												
SUPPLIERS CREDIT	3637.500	160.050	-12.804	-10.621	-8.264	-5.719	-2.969					
REPAYMENT			-27.282	-29.464	-31.821	-34.367	-37.116					
BANK OVERDRAFT		60.000	-6.000	-6.000	-6.000	-6.000	-6.000	-6.000	-6.000	-6.000	-6.000	-6.000
REPAYMENT												-60.000
NET OPERATING REVENUE		12.681	97.269	97.269	97.269	97.269	97.269	97.269	97.269	97.269	97.269	97.269
TAXABLE PROFIT		-26.570	54.201	56.558	59.103	61.853	64.822	64.822	64.822	64.822	64.822
PROFIT TAX		13.285	-27.100	-28.279	-29.552	-30.926	-32.411	-32.411	-32.411	-32.411	-32.411
FLOW OF OWN FUNDS	-122.420	-23.426	24.083	22.905	21.632	20.257	58.858	58.858	58.858	58.858	68.165

TABLE 4 — EFFICIENCY CALCULATION

YEAR	1999	1999	2000	2001	2002	2003	2004	2005	2006	2007	2008	2009
	'000 US$	MN BT	MN BT	MN BT	MN BT	MN BT	MN BT	MN BT	MN BT	MN BT	MN BT	MN BT
INVESTMENT COSTS												
SPINDLES	-4000.000	-176.000										
EQUIPMENT	-850.000	-37.400										
INSTALLATION	-100.000	-4.400										
CONSTRUCTION		-18.000										
START-UP COSTS		-18.000										
RAW MATERIALS		-52.800										52.800
SPARE PARTS		-10.692										10.692
TOTAL	-253.800	-63.492	0.000	0.000	0.000	0.000	0.000	0.000	0.000	0.000	0.000	63.492
RUNNING COSTS												
WATER		-3.600	-7.200	-7.200	-7.200	-7.200	-7.200	-7.200	-7.200	-7.200	-7.200	-7.200
POWER		-1.800	-3.600	-3.600	-3.600	-3.600	-3.600	-3.600	-3.600	-3.600	-3.600	-3.600
SPARE PARTS		-21.340	-21.340	-21.340	-21.340	-21.340	-21.340	-21.340	-21.340	-21.340	-21.340	-21.340
RAW MATERIALS		-106.920	-213.840	-213.840	-213.840	-213.840	-213.840	-213.840	-213.840	-213.840	-213.840	-213.840
INSURANCE & RENT		0.000	0.000	0.000	0.000	0.000	0.000	0.000	0.000	0.000	0.000	0.000
LABOUR		-40.500	-40.500	-40.500	-40.500	-40.500	-40.500	-40.500	-40.500	-40.500	-40.500	-40.500
TOTAL		-174.160	-286.480	-286.480	-286.480	-286.480	-286.480	-286.480	-286.480	-286.480	-286.480	-286.480
REVENUES												
SALE OF YARN		191.400	382.800	382.800	382.800	382.800	382.800	382.800	382.800	382.800	382.800	382.800
INDIRECT TAX PREMIUM	2.134	-0.085	-2.710	-2.710	-2.710	-2.710	-2.710	-2.710	-2.710	-2.710	-2.710	-3.873
DIRECT TAX PREMIUM		-2.657	5.420	5.656	5.910	6.185	6.482	6.482	6.482	6.482	6.482
NET EFFICIENCY BENEFIT	-251.666	-48.994	99.030	99.266	99.521	99.795	100.092	100.092	100.092	100.092	162.421

TABLE 5 — REFERENT GROUP ANALYSIS

YEAR	1999	1999	2000	2001	2002	2003	2004	2005	2006	2007	2008	2009
	'000 US$	MN BT	MN BT	MN BT	MN BT	MN BT	MN BT	MN BT	MN BT	MN BT	MN BT	MN BT
TOTAL REFERENT GROUP	30.804	-65.654	34.862	36.276	37.803	39.453	41.234	41.234	41.234	41.234	94.257
IMPORT DUTIES												
YARN		-18.000	-36.000	-36.000	-36.000	-36.000	-36.000	-36.000	-36.000	-36.000	-36.000
COTTON		10.692	21.384	21.384	21.384	21.384	21.384	21.384	21.384	21.384	21.384
EQUIPMENT	1.870											
SPINDLES	8.800											
MATERIALS INVENTORY		5.280										-5.280
SPARES INVENTORY		0.535										-0.535
SPARES		1.067	1.067	1.067	1.067	1.067	1.067	1.067	1.067	1.067	1.067
INDIRECT TAXES+PREMIUM	12.804	-0.512	-16.259	-16.259	-16.259	-16.259	-16.259	-16.259	-16.259	-16.259	-23.236
DIRECT TAXES+PREMIUM		-15.942	32.520	33.935	35.462	37.112	38.893	38.893	38.893	38.893	38.893
(i) TOTAL GOVERNMENT	12.804	-16.454	16.262	17.676	19.203	20.853	22.634	22.634	22.634	22.634	15.657
(ii) POWER SUPPLIER		1.800	3.600	3.600	3.600	3.600	3.600	3.600	3.600	3.600	3.600
(iii) LABOUR	18.000	3.000	3.000	3.000	3.000	3.000	3.000	3.000	3.000	3.000	3.000
(iv) DOMESTIC BANK	0.000	-60.000	6.000	6.000	6.000	6.000	6.000	6.000	6.000	6.000	6.000
												60.000
(v) INSURANCE		6.000	6.000	6.000	6.000	6.000	6.000	6.000	6.000	6.000	6.000
TOTAL REFERENT GROUP	30.804	-65.654	34.862	36.276	37.803	39.453	41.234	41.234	41.234	41.234	94.257

NPV / IRR Summary

	PROJECT		PRIVATE		EFFICIENCY		REFERENT GROUP	
NPV	$(Mn)	IRR (%)	$(Mn)	IRR (%)	NPV $ (MN)	IRR (%)	NPV $ (MN)	IRR (%)
4%	405.3	20.6%	134.5	16.7%	456.5	24.2%	283.6	n/a
8%	259.8		88.7		308.6		219.9	
12%	152.0		40.8		198.9		173.6	
16%	70.7		5.4		115.9		139.3	
0%	605.6		246.6		659.7		372.7	

Figure 10.3 ICP Project Solution with a Premium on Public Funds

Finally, it should be obvious that the way the spreadsheet is structured makes it relatively simple to undertake an analysis of the value of the option of delaying the project. Suppose that there was considerable uncertainty about the future price of yarn, the project output. The NPV of the project under each of a range of possible yarn prices could readily be calculated simply by editing the Key Input Variables Table in Figure 10.3. Values corresponding to R_o, R_H/r and R_L/r in the discussion of the value of information could be obtained and combined with the capital cost and the relevant probabilities to work out the value of the option of delaying the project.

Further Reading

Classic articles on the social discount rate and the opportunity cost of public funds are W. J. Baumol (1968), "On the Social Rate of Discount", *American Economic Review*, Vol. 58, pp. 788–802, and two papers by S. A. Marglin (1963), "The Social Rate of Discount and the Optimal Rate of Investment" and "The Opportunity Costs of Public Investment", *Quarterly Journal of Economics*, Vol. 77, pp. 95–111, and 274–287. For various approaches to estimating the opportunity cost of public funds in a range of OECD countries, see, for example, E. K. Browning (1976), "The Marginal Cost of Public Funds", *Journal of Political Economy*, Vol. 84, pp. 283–298; H. F. Campbell (1975), "Deadweight Loss and Commodity Taxation in Canada", *Canadian Journal of Economics*, Vol. 8, No. 3, pp. 441–447; H. F. Campbell and K. A. Bond (1997), "The Cost of Public Funds in Australia", *The Economic Record*, Vol. 73, No. 220, pp. 22–34; W. E. Diewert and D. A. Lawrence (1995), "The Excess Burden of Taxation in New Zealand", *Agenda*, Vol. 2, No. 1, pp. 27–34, and K. J. Arrow and A. C. Fisher, "Environmental Preservation, Uncertainty, and Irreversibility", *Quarterly Journal of Economics*, 88, (2), pp. 312–31, 1974. Useful articles on the value of delaying an investment decision in order to gather more information are R. S. Pindyck (1991), "Irreversibility, Uncertainty and Investment", *Journal of Economic Literature*, Vol. 29, pp. 1100–1148, especially pages 1100–1118 and J. M. Conrad "Quasi-Option Value and the Expected Value of Information", *Quarterly Journal of Economics*, 44 (4), pp. 813–820, 1980.

Exercises

1. Suppose that a $100 public project is to be financed by the sale of bonds to the public. Purchasers of the bonds increase savings by $80 and reduce private investment by $20. The only tax in the economy is a 50% business income tax.
   (i)   Work out the opportunity cost to the economy of raising the $100 in public funds;
   (ii) The cost premium on public funds represents a deadweight loss to the economy. Which group bears this cost? Explain.

2. Show that if public and private investment projects have two-period lives (a cost this year and a net benefit next year) the two shadow-pricing rules considered in the discussion of bond finance give the same results.

3. Suppose that a competitive economy's labour supply consists of 100 units at the after-tax wage of $3 per unit. The elasticity of labour supply is 0.025, and there is a flat-rate 40%

tax on labour earnings. It is proposed to raise the tax on labour earnings to 50%, and the before-tax wage (which measures the value of the marginal product of labour) is not expected to change.

(i)   How much extra revenue would the tax change yield?

(ii) Work out the cost of the additional deadweight loss imposed on the economy by the tax increase;

(iii) Work out the marginal cost of public funds.

4. A risk-neutral decision-maker is considering making an irreversible investment costing $1200. The proposed project has no operating costs, and will produce 100 units of output per annum in perpetuity, starting one year after the investment cost is incurred. The price at which the output can be sold will either be $1 per unit, with probability 0.5, or $3 per unit, with probability 0.5. The rate of interest is 10% per annum.

(a)   What is the expected NPV of the project if it is undertaken now?

One year from now the price at which the output can be sold will be known with certainty. The project can be delayed for one year, in which case the investment cost is incurred a year from now, and the flow of output starts two years from now.

(b)   What is the expected NPV of the project **now** if it is to be delayed for one year pending the receipt of the price information?

(c)   Should the project be delayed for a year? Explain why or why not.

(d)   What is the value **now** of the option of delaying the project? Explain.

11
Weighting Net Benefits to Account for Income Distribution

Introduction

We have seen in previous chapters how market prices can be adjusted in order to measure accurately project benefits and opportunity costs to the economy as a whole, and how benefit and cost measures can be further adjusted to account for non-market values and externalities. In this chapter we discuss how the valuation of project costs and benefits, and hence the appraisal, evaluation and choice of projects, can also be made to reflect social objectives with respect to the *distribution* of a project's net benefits. We have already discussed in Chapter 10 how concern for the inter-generational distribution of wealth may be reflected in benefit-cost analysis through the choice of discount rate. In this Chapter we are mainly concerned with the distribution of income among members of current generations – *atemporal distribution* – but we will return to the question of inter-generational equity – *inter-temporal distribution* – in the concluding section.

It is probably true to say that there is no country in which the government does not claim to be committed to improving the distribution of income between rich and poor. If there is a choice where two projects have the same net present value but one results in a more equitable distribution of net benefits, then the latter will generally be preferred. The first part of this Chapter concerns the atemporal distribution of income. It examines data on the distribution of income for a hypothetical country, shows how the degree of inequality of income distribution is measured, and then shows how income distributional weights can, in principle, be calculated. In the second part of the Chapter the inter-temporal distribution of income is also considered.

Interpersonal Distribution

We can look at income distribution from a number of different points of view. For example, there is *interpersonal distribution* which refers to distribution between different individuals or households. Table 11.1 shows how income might be distributed among households in a given country. Here we see, for example, that 30.7% of the population earned less than $100 per annum, while 4.5% earned more than $500 per annum. We can refer to these categories as *income groups*.

Table 11.1 Distribution of Households by Annual Income

Annual Income ($\overline{Y}$ = $189)	% Households
Less than $100	30.7
$100 to 200	42.9
$200 to 300	13.4
$300 to 400	5.8
$400 to 500	2.7
More than $500	4.5

Another way of presenting this same information is given in Table 11.2 which shows how much of the country's total income was earned by the different income groups. For example, we see that the richest 10% of the population earned more than 33% of total income, while the poorest 10% earned only 2.45% of total income.

Table 11.2 Income Distribution by Deciles

Households	% of Income
Top 1 per cent	8.31
Top 2 per cent	22.81
Top 10 per cent	33.73
2nd decile	15.49
3rd decile	11.61
4th decile	9.22
5th decile	8.12
6th decile	7.32
7th decile	6.47
8th decile	2.94
9th decile	2.67
Bottom decile	2.45

Inter-sectoral Distribution

Another way of looking at income distribution is by sector, or *inter-sectoral income distribution*. Here we see how income is distributed among households in different sectors of the economy. For example, we might be interested in comparing household income distribution between the rural and urban sectors. Such a comparison is shown in Table 11.3, from which we can see, for example, that a much higher percentage of rural households fall into the poorest income group; 34.2% of rural households had incomes less than $100 compared with 3.8% of urban households. On the other hand, only 1.3% of rural households earned more than $500, compared with 22.2% of urban households.

Table 11.3 Distribution of Income by Sector

Annual Income	Urban Areas	Percentage of Households in Semi-Urban Areas	Rural Areas	All Areas
Less than $100	3.8	15.5	34.2	30.7
$100 to 200	24.4	34.0	47.7	42.9
$200 to 300	25.1	22.3	11.1	13.4
$300 to 400	14.8	11.8	4.3	5.8
$400 to 500	9.7	5.8	1.4	2.7
More than $500	22.2	10.6	1.3	4.5
Mean annual income $\overline{Y}$ ($)	411	270	148	189

Measuring the degree of inequality

To measure the degree of equality or inequality, we use a Lorenz Curve as shown in Figure 11.1. This curve shows the relationship between the cumulative percentage of the population (individuals or households) and the cumulative percentage of income. If there is perfect income equality among all households the Lorenz Curve would be a straight line or diagonal, indicating that x% of the population earns x% of income for all values of x between 0 and 100.

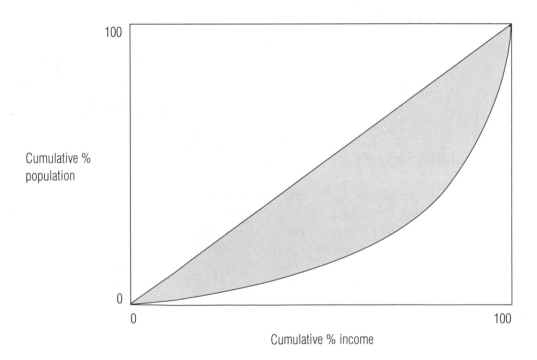

Figure 11.1 The Lorenz Curve

The deviation of the Lorenz Curve from the diagonal indicates the degree of inequality; the greater the extent of the deviation, as shown by the shaded area, the greater the degree of inequality. To compare the degree of inequality among countries a Gini Coefficient is used. This is a measure of the area between the Lorenz Curve and the diagonal (the shaded area in Figure 11.1) expressed as a percentage of the area of the whole triangle below the diagonal. Its value ranges between zero and one. Where there is perfect equality the Gini Coefficient will have a value of zero; the higher its value the more unequal the distribution of income.

Table 11.4 presents the data used to construct a Lorenz Curve. It shows how much of total income (in each sector) is earned by each income group. It shows, for example, that the richest 10% of the rural population earned 27.3% of total rural income, while almost 32% of total urban income was earned by the richest 10% of the urban population. On the other hand, we can also see that in both the rural and the urban sectors, the poorest 10% of the population earned around 3% of total income.

What can we conclude from such information about the distribution of income between the rural and urban sectors? First, we can see that the rural sector contains a higher proportion of poor people, while the urban sector contains a relatively higher proportion of rich people. Second, we can see that within the rural sector income seems to be more evenly distributed than it is within the urban sector. We also see that the Gini Coefficient for income distribution among urban households has a value of 0.4 while for rural households it is 0.3. This confirms that the degree of income inequality is higher for urban than rural households.

Table 11.4 Income Distribution by Percentile

Households	% of total income		
	Urban	**Rural**	**Whole Country**
Top 1%	8.1	6.3	8.3
Top 2%	20.9	17.2	22.8
Top 10%	31.8	27.3	33.7
2nd decile	15.2	15.6	15.5
3rd decile	11.6	12.0	11.6
4th decile	9.7	19.5	9.2
5th decile	8.1	9.8	8.1
6th decile	6.6	8.8	7.3
7th decile	6.1	6.5	6.5
8th decile	4.4	3.6	2.9
9th decile	3.8	2.3	2.7
Bottom decile	2.7	3.0	2.5
Gini Coefficient	0.4	0.3	0.4

Other Measures of Income Distribution

Other ways of comparing the distribution of income include "functional" income distribution and "international" income distribution. "Functional" distribution concerns the way in which income is distributed among the different factors of production in the economy. For example, we might need to compare the relative share of total income accruing to wage-earners, profit-earners, rent-earners, etc. In a poor country it is likely that wage-earners will save a lower proportion of their income than wealthier profit-earners and businesses. Therefore, the higher the share of total income earned by wage-earners, the lower the overall savings level is likely to be. In these circumstances, changing the distribution of income between wage- and profit-earners will change the overall savings rate in the economy.

Within each of these categories there are further sub-categories. For example, within the wage-earning category we have "professionals", "skilled labourers", "semi-skilled labourers", "unskilled labourers", etc. We might be interested in knowing how total wage-income is distributed among these sub-categories. Similarly, we might need to distinguish between different categories of profit-earners. In particular, it is important to know how profits and dividends are shared among nationals and non-nationals, especially if their propensities to remit their earnings overseas differ.

Changing Income Distribution

If government is committed to improving the distribution of income between rich and poor households, regions or sectors, it has a number of policy instruments that could, in principle, be used. Use could be made of fiscal policies to promote a more equitable income distribution. Tax policies could be designed so that the overall incidence of taxation is progressive, in the sense that the higher the individual's income level the higher the proportion of income they contribute in tax. For example, a progressive income tax could be introduced, regressive indirect taxes could be avoided to the extent possible, and subsidies could be paid on essential items of consumption. Moreover, policies of expenditure on health, education, co-operatives and social welfare could be designed so as to deliver a range of social services to low income groups.

In the economics literature there has been much debate on the relationship between economic growth and income distribution and how a more egalitarian distribution of income can best be achieved. It is often the case that political opposition or resistance to income redistribution on the part of the wealthy makes measures such as tax reforms impractical or infeasible. Some commentators argue that only a more egalitarian distribution of productive resources such as land and capital can bring about a more egalitarian distribution of income.

Another way in which changes in income distribution can be effected is through the choice of investment projects. Clearly, the government can affect the distribution of income between sectors and regions of the economy through the sectoral and regional spread of public investment projects. Similarly, the type of investment undertaken can influence the distribution of income among various categories of income-earners. An investment that uses relatively more labour than capital will imply more employment, and perhaps, a larger share of income for the wage-earner versus the profit-earner, and *vice versa*. Similarly, different types of investment will have different implications for the employment (and income) of different types of labour.

It follows that, if the government is aware of the implications of different projects for the distribution of income (whether it be among individuals, regions or sectors), it can indirectly affect the pattern of income distribution through its influence over the choice of investments in the public and private sectors. For instance, the government could choose between, say, one large, capital-intensive scheme or a number of smaller, more labour-intensive projects, to produce a given level of output. Such a choice will have implications for the distribution of income among individuals, categories of income-earners and perhaps regions.

While one investment option could be superior to another from an economic efficiency viewpoint, it might be inferior to the other from a distributional perspective. The final choice among projects will depend on the relative importance that the policy-makers attach to the economic efficiency objective *versus* the income distribution objective. It is to the explicit incorporation of distributional objectives in benefit-cost analysis that we now turn.

The Use of Distributional Weights in Project Analysis: Some Illustrative Examples

Suppose that we are required to advise on the best choice of projects taking into consideration the government's commitment to the twin objectives of economic efficiency and improving income distribution. In Table 11.5 we have before us three possible projects, A, B and C, of which only one can be undertaken.

Table 11.5 Comparing Projects with Different Atemporal Distributions

Project	Referent Group Net Benefits ($NPV)		
	Rich	Poor	Total
A	60	40	100
B	50	30	80
C	20	80	100

Project B can be rejected purely on economic efficiency grounds – its aggregate net referent group benefits (measured at efficiency prices) is less than that of both A and B, *and* the distribution of benefits among the rich and poor is less egalitarian than that of either A or C. So, the question is whether to choose A or C. As long as there is a commitment to select projects in conformity with the objective of improving income distribution, Project C will be preferred. Aggregate net referent group benefits are the same, but the distribution of benefits is more favourable towards the poor in the case of Project C.

Which project would we choose from the two options D and E in Table 11.6?

Table 11.6 Comparing Projects with Different Aggregate Benefits and Distributions

Project	Referent Group Net Benefits ($NPV)		
	Rich	Poor	Total
D	60	40	100
E	40	50	90

Here the choice is much less straightforward. Project D would be preferred on purely economic efficiency grounds, whereas Project E might be preferred on purely distribution grounds. As long as there is a commitment to the objectives of economic efficiency and income distribution, a conflict arises. Choose D and we sacrifice distribution; choose E and we sacrifice efficiency. This choice is a classic example of what economists call a *trade-off*.

At this stage the analyst needs further information to make the relative importance of these objectives explicit in the project selection process. This information takes the form of a particular "weight" or "factor" which can be applied to the additional income that accrues to the poor beneficiary. Let us assume for the moment that we weight each additional dollar of net benefit received by the poor by three times as much as each additional dollar of benefit received by the rich. For example, let us assign a weight of 1.0 to the net benefits accruing to the rich, and a weight of 3.0 to the net benefits accruing to the poor. We can now make an explicit decision on the choice between the two projects as shown in Table 11.7.

Table 11.7 Applying Distributional Weights to Project Net Benefits

Project	Referent Group Net Benefits ($NPV)			Weighted (Social) Benefits ($)		
	Rich	Poor	Total	Rich	Poor	Total
D	60	40	100	(60x1.0)+(40x3.0) = 180		
E	40	50	90	(40x1.0)+(50x3.0) = 190		

Clearly, Project E is favoured, as the total value of its net benefits, adjusted according to the weights described above, exceeds that of Project D. (Distribution weighted net benefits are sometimes referred to as "social net benefits" in the benefit-cost analysis literature.) This need not have been the case, however; it is possible that the weight given to the net benefits accruing to the poor could have been much less than 3.0.

What these simple examples reveal is that:

- in order to make a choice between projects taking into account both the economic efficiency objective and the income distribution objective, we could attach explicit weights to the net benefits accruing to the different categories of project beneficiaries;
- the difference between the weights attached to the net benefits to the rich and the poor would vary according to how much importance the policy-makers gave to the equality of income distribution objective. The greater their commitment to this objective, the greater the difference between the weights.

If the government decided not to attach different distributional weights to the net benefits accruing to different groups, projects would be selected purely on the basis of their aggregate referent group net benefits. What would this imply about the government's objective concerning income redistribution? From what we have seen, it could mean one of two things: either

- it does not regard project selection as an important means of redistributing income, but prefers other more direct measures such as a progressive taxation system; or,
- it does not care about income distribution; i.e. it attaches equal weight (1.0) to net benefits accruing to all referent group members.

The Derivation of Distributional Weights

Theoretical Basis

In the previous section we saw how a system of distributional weights could be used to compare projects that have different income distributional effects. We now need to discuss how, in practice, we might go about the task of deriving such weights.

The approach to this problem most commonly proposed is based on the concept of diminishing marginal utility of consumption. This assumption simply means that the more one has of a particular good, or of consumption in general, the less utility or satisfaction one gets from consuming an additional unit. As one's consumption increases, so the total satisfaction one derives also increases, *but* the amount by which satisfaction increases, as a result of each extra unit of consumption, gradually declines. This can be represented graphically as in Figure 11.2.

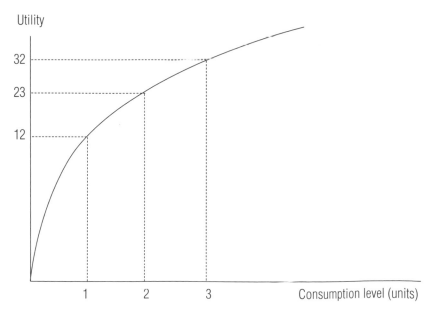

Figure 11.2 Total Utility Curve

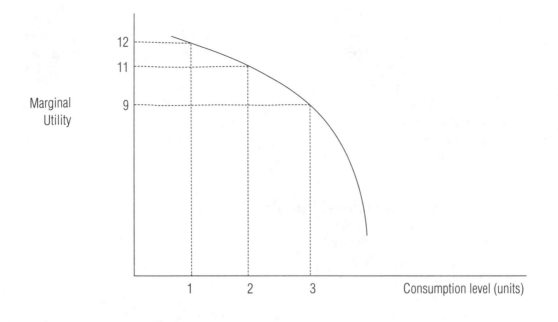

Figure 11.3 Marginal Utility Curve

For consumption of any individual good or service, at a level of, say, 1 unit, total utility might be, say, 12. When consumption increases to 2 units, total utility increases to, say, 23. If consumption were now further increased to 3 units, utility rises to 32. In other words, the extra utility per additional unit gradually decreases – from 12 to 11 to 9 and so on. We call this type of relationship *diminishing marginal utility*, and the concept is represented graphically as in Figure 11.3.

Figure 11.3 shows that the higher the level of consumption of the good, the lower the marginal utility of extra consumption. This concept of diminishing marginal utility is then extended to consumption *in general*. In other words, instead of just considering one good, we now apply this concept to all consumption by stating that, as our *total* consumption level increases, so the extra utility we get from each additional unit of consumption declines. Total consumption can be measured in terms of money ($) spent on consumption commodities. In effect, we are then saying that the higher the level of consumption expenditure of an individual, the less additional utility she will get from each extra dollar's worth of consumption.

We can extend the notion of diminishing marginal utility of consumption to that of diminishing marginal utility of income. The difference between consumption and income is savings. We can assume that the individual chooses her savings level such that the marginal utility of a dollar saved is equal to the marginal utility of a dollar consumed. In other words, the marginal utility of an extra dollar of income equals the marginal utility of an extra dollar saved or consumed. An increase in income would lead to an increase in consumption and savings, and an equal decline in the marginal utility of each.

There is plenty of empirical evidence to support the concept of diminishing marginal utility; for example observed risk averse behaviour follows from the concept of diminishing marginal utility of wealth, as discussed in Chapter 9. It is tempting to draw on the concept to support the following conclusion: if the income of a rich landowner increases by $100 per annum the extra utility he will get will be much less than in the case of a $100 per annum increase in the income of a poor unskilled worker. However that conclusion would be unwarranted as utility itself is not measurable and not comparable across individuals. On the other hand, if all individuals were assumed to be identical in their tastes and capacity for enjoyment we would not need to be able to measure utility to conclude that an extra dollar to the rich generates less additional utility than an extra dollar to the poor; in other words, as income level increases, marginal utility of income declines.

It is from the concept of diminishing marginal utility that distribution weights are rationalised and derived, the idea being that the weight attached to additional consumption by an individual should be based on the marginal utility that she receives at her particular level of income, relative to some base level, and given that marginal utility declines as income and consumption increase, the *higher* the level of income and consumption, the *lower* is the distributional weight. To illustrate this point, consider an individual with the utility function:

$$U = Y^a,$$

where U is the level of utility, Y is the income level, and *a* is a parameter. To simplify the discussion, we shall also assume, for the time being, that all of income is consumed. The extra utility, dU, obtained from a small increase in income, dY, is given by:

$$dU = aY^{(a-1)}dY$$

Since marginal utility is positive, but diminishes as income rises, it is evident that $0<a<1$. It can readily be seen from the expression for marginal utility that *a* is the percentage change in utility resulting from a one percent rise in income.

Now consider the ratio of the change in utility resulting from a small increase in income at income level Y_i to the change at some base level of income Y_b:

$$\frac{dU_i}{dU_b} = \frac{Y_i^{a-1}}{Y_b^{a-1}}$$

The value $(Y_i/Y_b)^{(a-1)}$ is the ratio of the changes in utility resulting from the small change in income at the two income levels. If all individuals had this utility function the value $(Y_i/Y_b)^{(a-1)}$ would express the extra utility gained by an individual at income level *i* from a small increase in income as a multiple of the extra utility which would be gained by an individual at the base level of income from the same small increase. If $Y_i > Y_b$ ($Y_i < Y_b$) the multiple is less (greater) than unity.

Following the above line of reasoning, the appropriate income distribution weight can be expressed in algebraic form as follows (note that we have inverted the ratio discussed in the previous paragraph):

$$d_i = \left(\frac{\bar{Y}}{Y_i}\right)^n$$

where:

d_i	=	the distribution weight for income group i
$\bar{Y}$	=	the average level of income for the economy
Y_i	=	the average income level of group i
n	=	the elasticity (responsiveness) of marginal utility with respect to an increase in income, expressed as the ratio of the percentage fall in marginal utility to the percentage rise in income (note that n is expressed as a positive number and that $n = (1-a)$).

As an example of the use of such weights, suppose that a net beneficiary of a project is in an income group which has a level of income equal to, say, $750 per annum ($Y_i$), and that the national average income is $1500 ($\bar{Y}$); the distribution weight for that individual would then be:

$$d_i = \left(\frac{1500}{750}\right)^n$$

$$= 2^n$$

While the value of d_i finally depends on the value of n, it can be seen that if n takes a value greater than zero, which it must since $0<a<1$, then when the project beneficiary in question enjoys a level of income *below* the national average, the distributional weight applied to her net benefits will be *greater than* one; and if the level of income is *above* the national average the weight will be *less than* one. If $n = 0.8$, then an individual at income level $750 per annum will have her benefits weighted by a factor of 1.74 (i.e. $\left(\frac{1500}{750}\right)^{0.8}$). Someone at an income level of $2500 per annum will have his benefits weighted by a factor of: 0.66 (i.e. $\left(\frac{1500}{2500}\right)^{0.8}$). An additional $1.00 going, for example, to someone earning an income of $4250 per annum would be valued at only 43% of the value of an additional $1.00 going to someone at the average ($1500 per annum) income level. These income distribution weights can be illustrated graphically as in Figure 11.4.

To this point, based on our simple utility function, we have assumed that n in the formula $d_i = \left(\frac{\bar{Y}}{Y_i}\right)^n$ has a value between zero and one. As noted above, n indicates the respon-siveness (or "elasticity") of marginal utility of income with respect to a one unit increase in income. In other words, it indicates how rapidly utility declines as the income level increases. The higher the value of n, the faster the rate at which marginal utility falls. While n must be positive, to be consistent with diminishing marginal utility, the utility function need not take

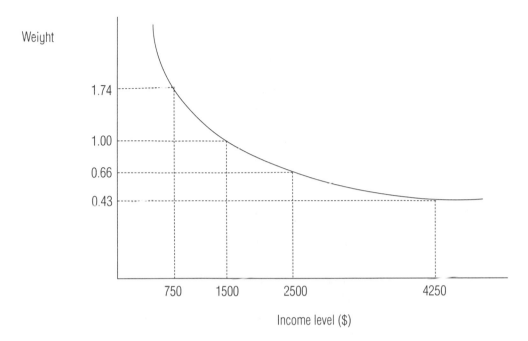

Figure 11.4 Weighting Factors for Extra Income

the particular form we have assumed and there is no theoretical reason why n must be less than unity. Let us now recalculate the values of d_i for various values of n as shown in Table 11.8.

Table 11.8 Responsiveness of Distributional Weights to Changes in n

| | Distributional Weight d_i | | | |
$/Annum	$n = 0$	$n = 1$	$n = 2$	$n = 3$
250	1.00	6.00	36.00	216.00
750	1.00	2.00	4.00	8.00
1250	1.00	1.20	1.44	1.73
1500	1.00	1.00	1.00	1.00
1750	1.00	0.71	0.73	0.63
2250	1.00	0.67	0.44	0.30
2750	1.00	0.55	0.30	0.16
3250	1.00	0.46	0.21	0.10
3750	1.00	0.40	0.16	0.06
4250	1.00	0.35	0.12	0.04

As the value of n increases, the spread of values for the distributional weight increases quite dramatically. For someone in the lowest income group ($250 per annum) the weight increases to 36 when $n = 2$ and to 216 when $n = 3$. For someone in the highest income group ($4250 per annum) the distributional weight falls to 0.12 when $n = 2$, and to 0.04 when $n = 3$.

These calculations are not intended to be prescriptive but rather to illustrate how sensitive the distributional weight is to a change in the assumed value of n. How, then, do we determine the appropriate value of n for a particular economy?

While values of n have been calculated for a range of countries,[1] the estimated values for similar countries (typically in the 1.5 to 2.5 range for developed economies) vary too much to be more than a guide to policy-makers. In practice the choice of value of n represents a value judgement that someone at the policy-making level will have to make if distributional weighting is to be used explicitly. In other words, to express an opinion as to the appropriate value of n is to express an opinion as to the value of an additional dollar in the hands of a rich person, as opposed to a poor person.

The formula $d_i = \left(\dfrac{\bar{Y}}{Y_i} \right)^n$ simply expresses, in algebraic form, the point that the distributional weights we use are determined by *two* factors:

(a)   the relative income/consumption level of the project beneficiaries $\left(\dfrac{\bar{Y}}{Y_i} \right)$; and,

(b)   the value judgement that is made about the extra utility or satisfaction that is gained by project beneficiaries at different income levels; the value of n.

Can the policy-maker or project analyst escape the awkward task of making such a value judgement by simply refraining from using distributional weights at all? Unfortunately, no; as long as we do not apply distributional weights *explicitly*, we are *implicitly* assigning a value $d_i = 1.00$ to each and every project beneficiary, irrespective of how much he earns. And, assigning a value $d_i = 1$ to all income groups implies, as we have seen in Table 11.8, that we are using a value $n = 0$. In other words, we are implicitly assuming that the distribution of the project's benefits do not matter at all. This is as much of a value judgement as the situation in which we assume that distribution *does* matter and we therefore give n a value that is greater than 0.

Some analysts have tried to avoid making a value judgement by turning the question of distributional weights on its head. For example, we saw from Table 11.7 that a distributional weight of approximately 3 justified the selection of project E over project D. If we observe that project E is actually chosen in preference to project D, the weight implicitly used by the decision-maker to value net benefits to low-income groups must be at least 3. In other words, in some circumstances we can infer from the choices the decision-maker makes what she regards as the appropriate or "threshold" distributional weights. This type of threshold analysis can be useful in eliminating patently absurd trade-offs, but it does not provide any independent information about the appropriate weights.

---

1   An estimate of n is a by-product of demand analysis by means of a linear expenditure system. See for example Alan Powell, 'A complete system of consumer demand equations for the Australian economy fitted by a model of additive preferences', *Econometrica*, vol. 34, 1966, pp. 661–675.

Distributional Weighting in Practice

In the ideal situation, distributional weighting of project benefits would be undertaken across all public sector projects being appraised and evaluated as well as, perhaps, being extended to private sector projects being considered by governments for incentives such as subsidies, company tax holidays, relief from import duties, etc. In such a comprehensive system information would be required on two levels.

First, at the national or central level, information on the government's objectives with respect to income distribution (among individuals, regions, or sectors) would have to be translated into a set of explicit distributional weights as discussed above. These weights would then be made available as *national parameters* for project analysts at all levels. This could be described as a *Top-Down* approach, as opposed to the *Bottom-Up* approach mentioned briefly at the end of the previous section and discussed in more detail in the next section.

Second, at the level of the project itself, information on the distributional implications of the potential investment would have to be compiled. For instance, in order to apply the distributional weights that are given to us as national parameters we would need to know the following about the project in question:

(a)   identification of the project's gainers and losers;
(b)   classification of the project's gainers and losers; i.e. to which particular income category they belong; and,
(c)   quantification of gains and losses, i.e. by how much do the net incomes of the gainers and losers increase or decrease?

If information were available to us at all of these levels, we could proceed with the task of distributional weighting. If the analyst has followed the approach recommended in this book it should be evident that the relevant project level information about (a) and (c) already exists, for this is, in effect, what is contained in the *Referent Group analysis* discussed in Chapter 6. We need *only* identify the income group to which each referent group stakeholder belongs and then apply the relevant distributional weight, assuming this is available from the decision-makers.

Regarding the provision of national parameters, however, most governments appear neither able nor willing to translate their stated commitment to income redistribution into a system of explicit weights, and, in most instances, the departments within the various government bodies and other agencies vested with responsibility for appraising and evaluating projects do not possess the authority or power to decide for themselves on the relative importance that should be given to the distribution objective, as opposed to other important objectives such as economic efficiency, especially where these might be in conflict. In the real world, therefore, the project analyst is most likely to be operating in a vacuum as far as such national parameters are concerned.

A Bottom-Up Approach

We prefer to consider benefit-cost analysis and distributional weighting from the perspective of it serving as a potentially powerful means of *identifying* the possible distributional implications of government project selection, and thereby sharpening our understanding of the value judgements implicit in government decisions. In other words, through benefit-cost analysis we can make ourselves, as projects analysts, and the relevant policy-makers more aware of the consequences of decisions concerning project selection. This is essentially the procedure advocated by UNIDO[2] in its *Guidelines for Project Evaluation*, in which the immediate objective is to get the policy-makers to confront the distributional objectives implicit in project choice and to make explicit the value judgements underlying what are essentially political decisions with respect to project choice. In this context, distributional weights can be interpreted as the focus of a dialogue between the analyst and the policy-maker, the main purpose of which is to compel policy-makers to make their assumptions and judgements explicit and consistent.

Example 11.1: Taking Income Distribution into Account in the Analysis of an Irrigation Project

Two alternative designs of an irrigation project have been prepared. They are mutually exclusive and differ chiefly with respect to location. Alternative A would be located in the Central Region where a well-developed infrastructure would keep investment and certain operating costs relatively low. Alternative B would be located in the Southern Region which is both poor and underdeveloped, though equally well-endowed with suitable natural resources for such a project.

The chief differences between the alternatives are:
(1) The capital costs of Project B are significantly higher because of the investment in roads and other infrastructure, and
(2) Project B would bring income and employment to one of the poorer regions of the country, whereas Project A would cost less initially, but would contribute to further inequality of income distribution in the country.

The opportunity cost of unskilled labour in the Southern Region is estimated to be much lower than in the Central Region, but transport costs will be much higher, even after the infrastructure has been established, as distances to markets and sources of input supply are much greater. In addition, supervisory personnel would have to come from the Central Region for some time to come, and they require a wage supplement to offset the harsher living conditions in the Southern Region. The net result is that operating costs, calculated in terms of efficiency prices, would be very similar. As the two projects produce essentially identical outputs and the gross operating benefits are equal, the question is which alternative will the decision-maker prefer?

The decision-maker's initial response may be to choose the project with the higher aggregate referent group net benefit; Project A in Table 11.9. However once the relative income distribution effects of the two projects have been drawn to her attention she may ask the analyst to apply income distributional weights in the comparison of the projects. However, if no national guidelines exist on the appropriate weights the analyst is not in a position to

---

2   United Nations International Development Organization, *Guidelines for Project Evaluation* (United Nations, New York, 1972), Chapter 17, pp. 248–258.

supply this information since it is the preserve of the political sphere (which the decision-maker occupies) rather than a technical matter for the analyst to deal with.

Suppose that the analyst calculated the aggregate referent group benefits of the two projects at three different discount rates, 10%, 15% and 20%, and then worked out what the distributional weight on additional income accruing to the Southern Region would have to be for the weighted NPV of Project B to be at least as much as the unweighted NPV of Project A. The threshold distributional weights for this example are shown in right hand column of Table 11.9.

Table 11.9 Threshold Distributional Weights

Discount Rate	NPV A	NPV B	Threshold Distributional Weight (NPV[A] = NPV[B])
10%	$360	$200	1.8
15%	$315	$150	2.1
20%	$270	$100	2.7

If the appropriate discount rate is 10%, then a distributional weight of at least 1.8 on net benefits will be required for Project B to be preferred to Project A; at 15% the weight would have to be at least 2.1, and at 20% it would have to be at least 2.7. (The reason that the required weight rises as the discount rate increases is that the more capital intensive project (B) becomes relatively less attractive as the cost of capital rises. This issue is discussed further in the following section of this Chapter.) The decision-maker might respond that it seems reasonable to value net benefits generated in the Southern Region at roughly two to three times as much as those generated in the Central Region, and would, therefore, favour alternative B even if the discount rate were as high as 20%.

In the way illustrated by this example, the project analyst has clearly delineated the political component of project formulation and selection, and has facilitated the final choice by spelling out the consequences of the alternatives. Ideally, this approach or dialogue could be repeated for all potential projects. Where inconsistencies appear the project analyst can draw them to the attention of the minister or policy-maker in question and they can be resolved to a point at which the range of implied income distribution parameters has been sufficiently narrowed for some concrete conclusions to be reached as to their appropriate values.

An early attempt to work out implicit distributional weights was undertaken in the United States in the 1960s by Weisbrod (1968) who compared three similar water resource projects (Projects 2 to 4) that had been selected in preference to a project with a higher benefit/cost ratio (Project 1). In each case he was able to disaggregate the project's benefits among four income/racial groups. On the initial assumption that the sum of the net weighted benefits of each of the three chosen projects per dollar of project cost was equal to the sum of the net weighted benefits of the rejected project, he was able to find the values of the implicit distributional weights from the coefficients derived by solving the set of simultaneous equations:

Project 1: 0.36a + 0.63b + 0.007c + 0.003d = 1
Project 2: 0.172a + 0.479b + 0.025c + 0.039d =1
Project 3: 0.161a + 0.294b + 0.066c + 0.33d = 1
Project 4: 0.023a + 0.470b + 0.007c + 0.041d = 1

where the coefficients indicate the proportion of each dollar of a project's benefits accruing to each group and the variables a, b, c and d are the distributional weights for the four groups of project beneficiaries. The equations were solved simultaneously, yielding implicit distributional weights: a = −1.3; b = 2.2; c = 9.3; and, d = −2.0. As a form of sensitivity analysis the exercise was then repeated allowing the net weighted benefits of the three preferred projects (Projects 2 to 4) to vary from 5% to 20% more than the net weighted benefits of Project 1.

In the absence of this kind of analysis, however, the project analyst can perhaps do no more than try to establish, among alternative projects, who the gainers and losers are, how much they gain or lose, and what the efficiency and distributional implications would be of choosing one rather than another project; in other words, prepare a disaggregated referent group benefit-cost analysis along the lines developed in this book.

Worked Example: Incorporating Distributional Effects in the NFG Project

In Chapter 6 it was found that the NFG project generated negative aggregate referent group net benefits (−$201.9 thousand at a 5% discount rate). The results of the disaggregated referent group BCA are reproduced in the first column of Table 11.10. (For the purposes of this example, it will be assumed that the relevant discount rate is 5%.) The second column provides a set of distributional weights (d_i) which are used to calculate the adjusted or weighted net benefits as shown in the last column. The values for d_i were chosen deliberately so that a decision reversal results, as compared with the result based on unweighted net benefits. With net benefits to wage-earners (gainers) being given a relatively high weight of 4, and those to downstream users (losers) a relatively low weight of 0.5, the weighted aggregate net benefit becomes marginally positive ($1.97 thousand).

Table 11.10 Distributional Weighting in the NFG Project

	Net Benefit ($000s)	d_i	Weighted Net Benefit ($000s)
Government	−173.2	1.0	−173.2
Landowners	33.2	0.6	19.92
Wage Earners	53.2	4.0	212.8
Downstream Users	−115.1	0.5	−57.55
Aggregate	−201.9		1.97

In the absence of information about distributional weights we could have considered the threshold values of d_i; i.e. by asking what combination of values for d_i would result in a positive aggregate net benefit. Let us assume, for example, that the policy-makers are satisfied that the d_i value for government revenue/expenditure should be 1, and for landowners it should be 0.6, but that there is less clarity as to the values of d_i for wage-earners and downstream users. We could then construct a trade-off matrix showing what possible combinations of these two d_i values would produce a positive value for aggregate referent group net benefits. An example of such a matrix is shown in Table 11.11.

Table 11.11 Threshold Combinations of Distributional Weights

Combination of d_is	1	2	3
Wage Earners	3.5	3.0	2.5
Downstream Users	0.3	0.05	<0

What this shows is that for any d_i value of less than 4 for wage-earners, the d_i value for downstream users would need to be extremely low for the aggregate (weighted) net benefit to be positive; this would imply that the costs the project imposes on these users are regarded as being relatively unimportant. When wage-earners' d_i is set at 3, the d_i for downstream users would need to be 0.05, and if it is set at 2.5 the d_i for downstream users would need to be negative, which is an unlikely value since it implies that imposing costs on this category of users is actually regarded as an advantage of the project. It is through this type of sensitivity testing and threshold analysis that the analyst can engage in a useful elicitation process with decision-makers.

Incorporating Inter-temporal Distribution Considerations

Until now in this Chapter it has been assumed that the marginal value of a dollar is the same regardless of whether that dollar is consumed or saved; this assumption is based on the supposition that, from an individual viewpoint, income is allocated optimally between consumption and savings. Furthermore, it may be the case that the aggregate effect of individual savings decisions, based on the market rate of interest, is to generate the optimal level of savings in the economy as a whole. However it is legitimate to ask whether, from the viewpoint of society as a whole, an extra dollar that is saved is considered to have the same value as an extra dollar that is consumed, and whether the level of aggregate savings determined by market processes is sufficient.

The answer to the question is related to the question of whether the social time preference rate is different from the market rate of interest, as discussed in Chapter 10. As noted above, individuals use the market rate of interest to make decisions about consumption and saving, and they maximize their individual welfare by saving up to the point at which the present value of extra future consumption resulting from extra saving equals the value of the extra consumption forgone in the present. In other words, at the market rate of interest the present value of an extra dollar consumed is the same as the present value of an extra dollar saved. If, however, the social time preference rate is lower than the market rate, then the present value of a dollar saved is higher than the present value of a dollar consumed. In that event, in determining the relative value of a dollar of benefit to the poor, as opposed to the rich, we need to take into account the fact that the rich save a higher proportion of an additional dollar than do the poor; in other words, while an extra dollar of benefit to the rich may worsen the atemporal distribution of income, it may improve the inter-temporal distribution. Before developing this argument, however, we can review the reasons outlined in Chapter 10 as to why the relative marginal value of savings and consumption might differ.

The argument runs as follows: income that is not consumed by us today, is saved. Savings finance investment, and investment today generates consumable output in the future. Therefore, the decision we make today, regarding how much of our income is spent now on immediate consumption and how much is saved now for future consumption, is essentially a decision about how consumption should be distributed among those living today and those living in the future – *inter-temporal distribution*. Other things being equal, the more that is consumed by us today, the less that is left for future generations to consume, and *vice versa*. If the social time preference rate is lower than the market rate of interest, the present value of the additional benefit that could be generated by one extra dollar of savings is greater than that of the additional benefit generated by one extra dollar of consumption.

Using a social discount rate lower than the market rate of interest will result in raising the NPV of all investment projects, and raising the NPV of projects which are more capital-intensive relative to that of projects which are less capital-intensive (this effect of changing the discount rate was discussed in detail in Chapter 3). However the lower social discount rate makes no allowance for the different effects of projects on saving and reinvestment of project net benefits. This being the case, it becomes important for the project analyst to establish what part of the referent group's net benefits are saved and what parts are consumed, with a view to attaching a weight or premium to that part which is saved.

It cannot be assumed that all members of the referent group save the same proportion of any income gained or lost. It is commonly observed that individuals at higher income levels save a higher percentage of income than individuals at lower income levels. One reason for this is obvious: at some low level of income the individual needs to spend all her income on consumption commodities in order to survive; at higher income levels she can consider the luxury of saving to provide for the future. It follows that a project which largely benefits high-income groups will result in more saving than one which benefits low-income groups (assuming the net benefits are positive). If an extra dollar of saving is worth more to the economy than an extra dollar of consumption, it is possible that the net benefits to a relatively better-off group could be weighted *more* than those to a relatively poorer group, taking into account both the atemporal and inter-temporal distribution effects.

Recalling our discussion of distributional weighting in the previous section, we learned that one extra unit of consumption may not convey the same benefit to all income groups; the higher the income group, the lower the relative value of an additional dollar of consumption, and *vice versa*. This was the rationale for the use of income distributional weights to assign greater value to net benefits accruing to the poor than to the rich. Once we introduce a premium (or shadow-price) on savings we need to make an additional adjustment to the raw estimates of referent group net benefits. As noted above, this adjustment will tend to favour projects that generate relatively more net benefit for the rich, since the rich generally save a higher proportion of any additional dollar of income than do the poor. It is possible that the decision-maker will be faced with a trade-off between a better atemporal and a better inter-temporal distribution of income. Such a case is illustrated by Example 11.2.

Example 11.2: Incorporating Atemporal and Inter-temporal Distributional Effects

Suppose that the effect of two projects can be summarized as follows:

> Project A generates a net referent group benefit of $100. $80 is saved and $20 is consumed by a group with above average income. Assuming that $1.00 saved is worth the same to the economy as $1.20 consumed (i.e. the shadow-price of savings is 1.2), and that the distributional weight for this group is 0.75 then:
>
> Net Benefit (in terms of Dollars of consumption) $= \$80(1.2) + \$20(0.75)$
> $= \$96 + \$15$
> $= \$111$
>
> Project B also has a net benefit of $100. Of this $50 is saved and $50 is consumed by members of the referent group who enjoy an average level of income. As the same shadow-price of saving (1.2) applies, and the sub-group's distributional weight will have a value of 1.0, then:
>
> Net Benefit (in terms of Dollars of consumption) $= \$50(1.2) + \$50(1.0)$
> $= \$60 + \$50$
> $= \$110$

In this instance the combined effect of introducing both distributional weights is to favour the project that benefits the relatively richer group, Project A, whereas in the absence of a shadow-price of savings Project B would have been favoured.

The problem in applying this approach is how to estimate the value of savings relative to consumption – the premium on savings. One method is to consider the implications of the social time preference rate which was discussed in Chapter 10. Suppose that a dollar of saving results in a dollar of investment yielding the market rate of interest, r, in perpetuiy. At the social rate of time preference, r_s , the present value of the investment project's net benefit stream is (r/ r_s); for example if r = 6% and r_s = 5%, the present value generated by a dollar of saving, matched by investment, is $1.2. In other words, the premium on saving is 20% and the shadow-price of savings is 1.2.

Another method is to try to elicit from the decision-makers their implicit premium on savings through the choices they make. For example, we could confront the decision-maker with a number of project options, where a choice would have to be made between an extra dollar saved by any member of society versus an extra dollar consumed by individuals in various income categories. As a result of this process it might be inferred that the decision-maker would be indifferent between whether the extra dollar was saved, or consumed by an individual in a particular income group, Y_i. Since there is a premium on saving there must also be a premium on consumption by individuals in income category Y_i; in other words, the atemporal distributional weight attached to net benefits to this group must exceed unity, reflecting the group's low-income status. Ignoring the small amount of saving that might be undertaken by individuals in this low-income group, we can infer that the atemporal distributional weight (d_i) for that group must be equal to the premium on saving. Let us consider a simple numerical example.

Example 11.3: Deriving the Premium on Savings Indirectly

Consider the hypothetical example in Table 11.12 in which the consumption levels of the different income groups are shown in the first column and the atemporal distributional weights are given in the second column. In this example, the mean level of consumption is $1500.

Table 11.12 Composite Distributional Weights

Consumption $/annum ($C_i$)	Distributional Weight (d_i)
250	6.00
750	2.00
$\underline{C}_c = 1250$	1.20
$\bar{C} = 1500$	1.00
1750	0.71
2250	0.67
2750	0.55

The decision-makers are asked to specify the critical consumption level (C_c). Since a dollar saved is assumed to be more valuable than a dollar consumed by the average income-earner, the critical consumption level nominated by the decision-maker will turn out to be less than the average level. Assume that through a process of iteration that the decision-makers identify consumption level, C_c = $1250, as the critical level at which they place the same value on an additional dollar of an individual's consumption as on a dollar of additional saving. From Table 11.12 it can be seen that the distributional weight for this critical consumption level is 1.2. In other words, a dollar of extra consumption enjoyed by individuals at the critical consumption level is 1.2 times as valuable as each extra dollar consumed by an individual at the average level, and, we now know, is worth the same as an extra dollar of saving. We can therefore conclude that the implicit premium on saving is 1.2. Each extra dollar of saving has to be weighted by a factor of 1.2 in the analysis.

   If the decision-maker's distribution objectives are to be accommodated by a system of atemporal and inter-temporal weights it will be necessary for the analyst to disaggregate net benefit for each referent group gainer or loser into its consumption and savings components, and then weight the consumption component by the atemporal distributional weight and the savings component by the inter-temporal distributional weight (or savings premium). If we were to follow this procedure in the context of the NFG project discussed previously (see Table 11.10), it would be necessary to disaggregate each stakeholder group's net benefits into their consumption and savings components, and then apply the respective d_i to the consumption benefit and the savings premium to the savings benefit of each referent group beneficiary or loser.

It needs to be emphasized that the weighting of savings described above accounts for the different reinvestment rates of project net benefits; it converts savings to the corresponding value of consumption using the savings premium or the social discount rate. The original net benefit stream is still discounted by the social time preference rate as the social discount rate as discussed in Chapter 10. An alternative way of dealing with reinvestment of project net benefits is discussed by Marglin (1963).

Finally it should be noted that once referent group net benefits have been adjusted by a set of distributional weights the adding-up property of the spreadsheet framework will no longer hold: weighted referent group net benefits need not be equal to efficiency less non-referent group net benefits. For this reason we prefer that, where distributional weighting is employed, the weighted net benefits are presented in an additional part of the spreadsheet, and that the decision-maker's attention is drawn to the value judgements implicit in both weighted and unweighted net benefit summaries.

Further Reading

The issues of atemporal and inter-temporal distribution of income are dealt with at length in I. M. D. Little and J. A. Mirrlees, *Manual of Industrial Project Analysis in Developing Countries* (OECD, 1968) and P. Dasgupta, A. Sen and S. Marglin, *Guidelines for Project Evaluation* (United Nations, 1972). For an early study showing how distributional weights can be derived from government's project choices see B. A. Weisbrod, "Income Redistribution Effects and Benefit-Cost Analysis", in S. B. Chase (ed.), *Problems in Public Expenditure Analysis* (The Brookings Institution, 1968). Also see A. C. Harberger, "On the Use of Distributional Weights in Social Cost-Benefit Analysis", *Journal of Political Economy*, 86(2), pp. S87–S120, 1978, and M. Feldstein, "Distributional Equity and the Optimal Structure of Public Prices", *The American Economic Review*, 62(1), pp. 32–36, 1972. On the reinvestment of project net benefits, see S. A. Marglin, "The Opportunity Costs of Public Investment", *Quarterly Journal of Economics*, 77(2): pp. 274–289, 1963.

Exercises

1. From the data in the table on the distribution of income (by quintile) between two States, A and B, you are required to compare the degree of income inequality between the two states using Lorenz Curves and Gini Coefficients.

| | Percentage of Total Disposable Income | |
Quintile	State A	State B
1st	50%	35%
2nd	20%	30%
3rd	15%	25%
4th	10%	6%
5th	5%	4%
Total	100%	100%

2. The data in the table below shows the breakdown of the referent group (RG) benefits for two projects (A and B), and information about each sub-group's income level and marginal propensity to save (mps). In addition you have ascertained that the mean income level is $30,000 per annum, that an appropriate value for n (the elasticity of marginal utility with respect to an increase in income) is 2, and that the premium on savings relative to consumption is 10%.

	RG1	RG2	RG3
Income p.a.	$20,000	$40,000	$90,000
Mps	0.05	0.20	0.60
Net Benefits – A	$10	$20	$90
Net Benefits – B	$20	$30	$40

With this information you are required to calculate and compare the projects' net benefits in terms of:
(i)   unweighted aggregate referent group net benefits;
(ii) aggregate net benefits weighted for atemporal distributional objectives (assuming consumption and savings have the same value at the margin); and,
(iii) aggregate net benefits weighted for both atemporal and inter-temporal distributional objectives.

3. You have been provided with the following information about three public sector projects with a breakdown of the referent group net benefits (unweighted) among the three referent group (RG) categories:

	RG1	RG2	RG3
Project A	$30	$30	$60
Project B	$40	$20	$40
Project C	$40	$30	$10

With the knowledge that all three projects are considered to have equivalent weighted net benefits, and that the three distribution weights are to have an (unweighted) average of 1, you are required to find the implicit values of the three distribution weights for RG1, RG2 and RG3 respectively. (Hint: follow Weisbrod's method and note that the solution value for the weighted net benefit of each project is $100.)

12

Valuation of Non-marketed Goods

Introduction

This Chapter deals with the methods and techniques used by economists to place monetary values on non-marketed goods and services, or, more specifically, those project inputs or outputs which affect the level of economic (material) welfare but which do not have market prices. While the discussion will focus mainly on environmental goods in order to illustrate the issues involved, the Chapter concludes with a brief discussion of various methods of valuing human life.

In previous Chapters we discussed how benefit-cost analysis involves the identification and valuation of a project's costs and benefits. Our analysis has so far been confined to those inputs and outputs that are exchanged through markets and where, in consequence, market prices exist. We recognized in Chapter 5 that the market does not always provide the appropriate measure of value and that shadow-prices sometimes have to be generated in order to better reflect project benefits or opportunity costs. This discussion was essentially about adjusting existing market prices where these were believed to be distorted, due perhaps to government intervention or to imperfections in the structure and functioning of markets. The present Chapter deals with another type of market failure – where there is no market for the input or output in question, and, therefore, no market price at which to value the cost or benefit.

As a starting point it is reasonable to ask why there is no private market for the commodity in question. Markets exist in order to trade ownership of goods and services – hamburgers and machine tools, haircuts and labour services. For economic agents to exchange ownership of a good or service there must exist a reasonably well-defined set of property rights that specify what is being traded. In particular, the good or service must be *excludable*, meaning that it is feasible for the owner to prevent others from enjoying the good or service unless they pay for it. If a commodity is not excludable a private agent would be unlikely to be able to recover the cost of supplying it by charging a price for it – even if some customers purchased the good others could act as *free riders*, enjoying the good without paying for it. Of course excludability is partly a matter of cost – while free-to-air TV is non-excludable, excludability can be achieved by installing a cable system. However if access to a good or service is not excludable at a reasonable cost it will not be traded in private markets. Examples of non-excludable goods are national parks, national defence, and some forms of fire and police protection.

Air and water pollution are further examples of non-excludable goods, which could more accurately be described as "bads", since they detract from rather than contribute to economic welfare. While there is no incentive for economic agents to produce bads – no one would pay for them – they are sometimes generated as a by-product of economic activity and are termed *externalities* to reflect the fact that they are external to the market system. For example, firms and consumers which generate air pollution as a by-product of their production and consumption activities impose a *negative externality* on other consumers and firms. Since access to clean (or polluted) air is non-excludable there is no market mechanism that enables members of the general public to purchase cleaner air, or requires a firm or individual to pay for the air pollution they cause. The former mechanism would provide the "carrot" and the latter the "stick" that would persuade the profit maximizing firm or utility maximizing individual to reduce their level of emissions. In the absence of a market there is no price that can be used to measure the cost of the air pollution generated by a project.

While air pollution is an example of a negative externality, there also exist *positive externalities* – beneficial side-effects of production or consumption activity that are not captured by the market. Examples are pollination of fruit trees as a by-product of honey production, or enjoyment of the output of the neighbour's stereo system. While economic agents would, in principle, be willing to purchase these commodities, in practice there is no need to pay for them because of their non-excludable nature, and hence there is no market for them.

While the above examples deal with non-excludable negative and positive externalities, it can be noted that externalities can also be excludable in nature. The time-honoured example of an excludable (or private) externality concerns a smoker and a non-smoker sharing a railway compartment. In principle this problem can be resolved by negotiation: if it is a "no-smoking" ("smoking") compartment the smoker (non-smoker) pays the non-smoker (smoker) to be allowed to smoke (to limit their smoking). While there is no market in smoking the efficient level can be achieved though negotiation between the two parties. To appreciate the importance of excludability in this example, suppose that a second non-smoker were present: a three-way negotiation would be more difficult (costly), and if we add more non-smokers to the example the bargaining costs would eventually outweigh any benefit that could be achieved by negotiation. In the case of private externalities, such as those involving disputes between neighbours, an efficient solution can be found through bargaining, provided that transactions costs are not too high.

Non-excludability is one of the two main characteristics of a *public good*, with the other main characteristic being non-rivalness. A good or service is *non-rival* in nature if each individual or firm's consumption of a unit of the commodity does not affect the level of benefit derived by others from consumption of the same unit. Examples of non-rival commodities are weather forecasts, views, and film shows. The latter commodity provides an instructive illustration of the market's failure to provide the efficient quantities of non-rival goods and services. Since the costs of showing the film are fixed, regardless of the number of viewers, the theatre owner's incentive is to charge an admission price that maximizes revenue. If that price does not result in filling the theatre, additional customers could benefit from viewing the film without imposing any additional cost. In other words, the service has not been provided up to the efficient level at which marginal benefit equals marginal cost. In principle this problem could be solved by price discrimination – charging different prices to different customers – but in practice theatre owners may be unable to obtain detailed information about customers' willingness-to-pay.

In summary, the private market does not supply efficient levels of goods or bads which are non-excludable and/or non-rival. Provision of public goods is one of the important activities of governments, and is one of the reasons for social benefit-cost analysis: proposed government programs or projects which supply public goods need to be appraised. Furthermore, because many private projects produce non-excludable external effects it cannot be assumed that because they are in the private interest of their proponents they are also in the public interest. Social benefit-cost analysis is used to appraise such projects from a public interest viewpoint before they are allowed to proceed. To be of use the social BCA needs to be able to assess the project's external effects in terms commensurate with its private net benefits. Thus the market failure which provides the major rationale for social BCA at the same time poses one of its major challenges – that of valuation in the absence of market prices.

Valuing Environmental Costs and Benefits

Environmental economics has made substantial progress in recent years in devising and refining non-market valuation methods. The subject area has become extremely wide and increasingly technical in nature. It would not be possible, in a single chapter, to equip the reader with a working knowledge and technical capacity to apply the full range of non-market valuation techniques. This has become a highly specialized aspect of economics, an in-depth study of which could constitute a separate course in itself. In this Chapter the reader will be familiarized with:

- the issues and arguments giving rise to the need for the incorporation of non-market environmental values in BCA
- the range of approaches and techniques available, together with illustrations of how non-market values can be incorporated into the BCA framework developed in the first part of this book
- some of the more important theoretical concepts underlying the valuation methods, and,
- some of the strengths and weaknesses of the various methods.

Environmental Resources as Public Goods

The distinguishing feature of environmental goods is that they possess *public good* characteristics. One of the most commonly cited examples of an environmental good is the air we breathe. This is classified as a *pure public good* as it possesses all three characteristics of a public good. These are:

1. non-rivalry in consumption, implying zero opportunity cost of consumption in the sense that one person's consumption does not affect the availability of the good for others;
2. non-excludability by producers, implying that the suppliers cannot exclude any consumers or other producers who want access to the good; and,
3. non-excludability by consumers, implying that the consumer cannot choose whether or not to access or consume the good.

Many environmental commodities such as air quality, flood protection, noise, and views are pure public goods. At the other end of the spectrum are *private goods*, which meet none of the above three criteria. The goods we buy at the local supermarket are examples of private goods. Each item that any one of us purchases and consumes, leaves one item less for others to consume. A producer owns the right to decide whether or not to sell the good, and we as consumers have the right to decide whether or not we wish to purchase it. In such cases, there is rivalry in consumption and excludability on the part of both producers and consumers.

In between the two extremes lie various forms of "impure" public goods where only one or two of the three criteria are satisfied. A *semi-public good* is defined as one where criteria (1) and (2) are satisfied. There is zero opportunity cost of consumption and producers cannot exclude anyone from using the good, but consumers have the right and ability not to use the good. An example is free-to-air broadcasting: the reception of a station's broadcast by one viewer does not weaken the signal for others; the producer cannot exclude some would-be viewers and include others, but consumers can decide whether or not they want to tune in to the broadcast. As noted earlier, technological change involving the invention and marketing of the decoder by pay-TV broadcasters has allowed some producers to effectively remove the non-excludability characteristic of their TV channels.

An example of a semi-public environmental good is the *common*. In this instance, exploitation of the resource is rival but non-excludable by producers. The resulting form of market failure, described in the economics literature as "the tragedy of the common", accounts for the tendency for unregulated competitive market forces to result in the over-exploitation of natural resource stocks, such as fish stocks. As each producer catches fish he reduces the fish stock, and the catch rates of all fishers fall as a result; in other words, each fisher imposes a negative public externality in production on his fellow fishers. Each fisher could benefit his colleagues by reducing his impact on the fish stock, but has no way of benefiting himself by so doing. Put another way, each fisher could invest in the fish stock (by reducing his catch), but, while the net benefit to the economy of such investment is positive, there is no net benefit to an individual investor. While all fishers may recognize the possibility of increasing the aggregate net benefit derived from the fishery by reducing total fishing effort, the non-excludability of the fishery makes it impossible for any individual to benefit in this way. The result is that the fish stock is over-exploited from an economic viewpoint: the marginal benefit of effort is lower than its marginal cost.

A further case is that of the *non-congestion* public good, where there is no opportunity cost of consumption, but where both producer and consumer excludability apply; uncongested roads are an example of a non-congestion public good. The owners of the road can exclude potential users by introducing a charge, and consumers can elect to use the road or not. As in the earlier example of the movie theatre, charging for access to an uncongested road leads to a lower level of use than the efficient level.

Even where a competitive market economy is free of distortions in the form of regulations or taxes in its markets for *private goods*, there will still be market failure associated with the existence of the various types of *public goods* described above. In these instances there is either no market price at all, or, where there is one it will not reflect the true value or opportunity cost of the good in question. It is this situation that typically characterizes the markets pertaining to environmental goods. To take proper account of environmental costs and benefits in project appraisal it is therefore necessary for the analyst to use some alternative means to the market for eliciting the values society attaches to such costs and benefits. In recent years a wide range of non-market valuation methods has emerged from economics research and the literature, particularly in the field of environmental economics. These methods are examined in later sections of this chapter.

Externalities and the Environment

As noted above, externalities arise where there is no market connection between those taking an action, which has consequences for material welfare, and those affected by that action. The action could be, say, the run-off of nutrients and chemicals from irrigated farmlands into a river resulting in downstream pollution damage. The costs are borne by others, such as the fishers or tourists whose benefits are determined by the quality of the water downstream and perhaps at the adjacent coast where there might be a coral reef. In other words the costs are *external* to the person who causes them and she has no direct financial incentive to avoid making them.

Externalities can also be *positive*. In this case the person taking the action results in another (or others) external to her benefiting from the action. For example if the nutrients in agricultural run-off stimulate the growth of fish stocks, the fishers may benefit from larger catches but the farmers who provided the extra nutrients do not. As the unregulated market either altogether ignores or inaccurately reflects the external costs and benefits associated with a resource's use, there is a need for some form of non-market valuation method to allow the decision-maker to measure the dollar value of the external effect and to allow for the external cost or benefit (to *internalize* it) in appraising alternative project or policy options. Failure to take account of referent group external costs results in the over-utilization of an environmental resource, while failure to account for external benefits leads to under-utilization.

Internalizing externalities, or accounting for them in benefit-cost analysis, is therefore necessary for economic evaluation in the same way as shadow-pricing was required to account for market distortions as discussed in Chapter 5. In this regard, environmental valuation and the inclusion of environmental costs and benefits in BCA should, in principle, be treated as a necessary part of the "bottom line" in economic efficiency analysis. Until recently economics lacked the methods and techniques for non-market valuation which meant that externalities were largely ignored in formal BCA, or, at best, treated qualitatively in the form of an *Environmental Impact Assessment* (EIA), and therefore remained below the "bottom line". With recent advances in non-market valuation techniques there can be no justification today for failing to attempt to quantify and value externalities as part of the shadow-pricing process of BCA.

The development of the benefit-cost analysis of the National Fruit Growers project in Chapter 5 showed how environmental costs could be integrated into the efficiency analysis section of the spreadsheet framework. In Figure 5.14 (p. 116) the annual cost of water pollution is entered in Table 4 of the spreadsheet in the form of a cash flow, along with other project costs estimated at efficiency prices. These costs appear subsequently in the referent group analysis described in Chapter 6 as an annual cost to downstream users of the river. In

Figure 6.2 (p. 136) this cost is entered in the form of a cash flow in Table 5 of the project spreadsheet. It can be seen from this example that environmental costs can be incorporated as an integral part of a social benefit-cost analysis.

Total Economic Value

It is now generally acknowledged that environmental resources contribute value not only to those who use the resource, but also to non-users, who may value the conservation of the resource. The value to non-users could arise for reasons of altruism – the value to one individual from knowing that the asset can be used and enjoyed by others – or for reasons of self-interest – the value to an individual from knowing that the asset will continue to be accessible in the future. For instance, you may be unsure whether you will ever be able to visit Australia's Great Barrier Reef, yet you might feel a significant loss of value if it and the ecosystem it supports were destroyed.

Total Economic Value (TEV) is the term used by economists for describing the range of use and non-use values of a resource, where:

TEV = Direct use value + Indirect use value + Quasi-option value + Existence value +
      Bequest value

It should be noted that the TEV concept is limited to *anthropogenic* values only. In other words, in benefit-cost analysis the resource is valued exclusively in terms of the values it yields to humans; no intrinsic value is attributed to it.

As an illustrative example let us consider the valuation of a coral reef. The sorts of values it provides can be categorized under the components of TEV as shown in Figure 12.1. As we move from the left to the right of the diagram, the values become more difficult to quantify.

Direct Uses usually include the most obvious and important market-based uses such as fisheries (a consumptive use that can include subsistence, artisinal inshore fishing, recreational fishing, and large-scale commercial fishing) and tourism (mainly a non-consumptive use, although it usually includes commercially organised recreational fishing trips). Other consumptive uses can include coral mining for building materials, as well as shell and coral collecting.

Indirect uses include regulatory functions such as storm surge protection, fish nursery and food chain regulation, and, where mangroves form part of the reef's ecosystem, wastewater treatment. Only a few studies have made attempts to value these uses, most notably storm protection values.

Option value is becoming recognized as a significant form of benefit from environmental resources such as coral reefs and forests, as an increasing number of pharmaceutical and medicinal values are discovered. Option value is the value we attach to keeping alive the possibility of one day being able to benefit from the resource. Since it is the value attached to potential use, its current "non-use" value is attributable to its potential use value in the future, which is why we draw it as straddling the "use" and non-use categories in Figure 12.1. Closely related to option value are the important concepts of *uncertainty* and *irreversibility*. There are uncertainties about the possible future discoveries and bio-technological advances to be gained from

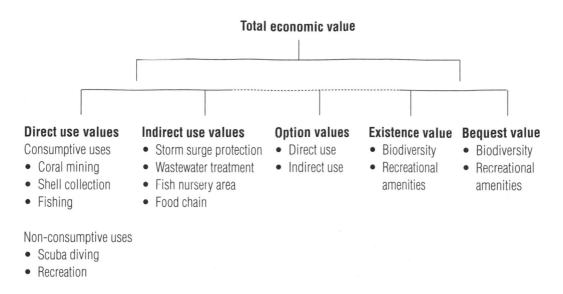

Figure 12.1 Total Economic Value of Coral Reef Ecosystems

ecosystems, which will be lost if we allow irreversible damage to occur. Therefore there may be value to be gained by delaying any action or decision that could cause irreversible degradation. Economists recognize and quantify this "*quasi-option value*" in other areas of economics, such as finance. This same principle was raised in Chapter 10 in the context of the discussion of the value of delaying a decision in the absence of perfect information. If there are unknown potential future benefits from the protection of biodiversity these need to be acknowledged and formally included as part of a BCA.

Existence and bequest values: Economists have come to recognize that individuals may derive value from something even though it is accepted that these individuals will probably never get to "use" or "consume" it. Take the whale, the panda, or South American rainforests for instance. Individuals are prepared to commit funds to the conservation of such natural assets for no other reason than their belief that they ought to remain in existence. Where the individual's satisfaction arises purely from the knowledge that the environmental resource will continue to exist it is labeled *existence value*. Where the individual's satisfaction is attributable to the continued existence of the resource for the future possible benefit of others, either known or unknown to her, we label it *bequest value*.

Using Non-market Values in Benefit-Cost Analysis

It is important to remember that in a BCA framework we are analysing the effects of changes to an existing regime, and that it is the "trade-off" or marginal value of the resource that is relevant, not the total economic value. Again, let us consider the example of a coral reef. If the purpose of the valuation is to provide a dollar value for use in a BCA of alternative management options, what is required is the trade-off of values under competing management scenarios. Resource management is usually about introducing changes at the margin. Most decisions mean that some users (or non-users) gain at the expense of others. Declaring a section of a coral reef that was previously used for, say, commercial fishing and tourism, as a "no-go" marine park implies that the fishing and tourism industries may forgo net benefit, while others may gain from the increase in, say, scientific, biodiversity, existence and/or option values.

What is needed, therefore, is not the total value of each component of TEV but rather their *marginal* values. In the context of our coral reef example this could mean the amount of TEV gained or lost per unit of reef usage or non-usage. If a re-zoning management plan proposes to introduce a no-go marine park of 200 km^2 which means that the area that may be accessed for purposes of tourism is reduced from 2000 km^2 to 1800 km^2 we need to know by how much this marginal reduction in access for tourism affects the value to tourists who are prevented from using it. Knowing only the total value of tourist expenditure or income from tourism is of little help in addressing this issue.

In a BCA of alternative management options, both the incremental benefits (in terms of changes in TEV) and the incremental costs need to be quantified and compared. The net benefits of a given management option (relative to some base case scenario) can be written:

$$NB(M) = (B_m + B_{nm}) - (C_m + C_{nm})$$

where, $NB(M)$ = net benefits *with* management option *vs. without* the option
B_m = incremental benefits for which there is a market
B_{nm} = incremental benefits for which there is no market
C_m = incremental costs for which there is a market
C_{nm} = incremental costs for which there is no market.

In the absence of a budget constraint the decision-rule would be to adopt the option provided that $NB(M) > 0$.

Having established the appropriate decision-support framework within which the estimate of non-market value is to be used, the question of which approach and method of non-market valuation is appropriate can then be addressed. In the context of this book, the decision-support framework is BCA. If another type of framework such as multi-criteria analysis is being used, it may not be appropriate to rely on the same trade-off values or non-market valuation methods.

Methods of Non-market Valuation

Various types of non-market values suggest the need for a variety of valuation methods, which we discuss here in rather broad terms without going into too much detail on the techniques and methodologies involved. It is useful to think in terms of two broad approaches to economic valuation. The *production approach* and the *utility approach*. The production approach can be thought of as a "supply side" approach, while the utility approach is a "demand side" approach. We now consider briefly each of these approaches.

The Production Approach

In a benefit-cost analysis the net benefits of a development project, D, involving an environmental cost can be written:

$$NB(D) = (B - C) - EB$$

where   B = the benefits of the development project
C = the cost of the development project (excluding the environmental cost)
EB = the environmental cost of the project, measured as the forgone benefits resulting from the decline in quantity or quality of the environmental resource.

Following the production approach there are three types of methods for taking account of the environmental cost, EB: the *dose/response method* assesses the forgone environmental benefits by the resulting decline in value of output in the economy; the *opportunity cost method* involves working out the cost of preventing the environmental damage by modifying or forbidding the proposed development project; and the *preventative cost method* involves working out the cost of preventing or mitigating the environmental damage if the project does go ahead. We briefly consider each of these approaches.

The **dose/response method** estimates value by measuring the contribution of the environmental resource to the output of those who rely on it for the production of goods or services. For instance, a firm combines environmental resources of a given quality with manufactured capital goods and labour to produce an output such as tourism services or a harvest of fish. The production function combines natural capital in the form of, say, water quality (Q_1) and reef quality (Q_2), with manufactured capital (K), labour (L) and other purchased inputs (I) to produce the output (X):

$$X = f (K, L, I, Q_1, Q_2)$$

The effect of a change in Q_1 or Q_2 is then gauged by the size of the impact it has on X, and the benefit or cost of that impact measured in the market for commodity X.

For example, to value the impact of agricultural development on land adjacent to a coral reef and a fishery, the analyst would need to model the physical relationship between a pollutant dose, such as run-off of nitrates, and the deterioration in water quality and its subsequent impact on fish stocks and reef quality. She would then need to estimate the production response of users of the fishery and calculate the reduction in net value of the catch. Similarly the value lost or gained from reef-based tourism as a result of changes in reef quality, as opposed to changes in other input levels such as produced capital, material inputs, and labour, would need to be estimated This approach is most readily applicable to environmental resources which have direct market-based uses, such as tourism and fishing. It cannot be used to estimate non-use values.

Another example of the dose/response method is the human capital approach, which measures the value of a change in environmental quality in terms of its impact on human health and the earnings capacity of the individuals affected. This could be used to calculate the costs of air or water pollution (or benefits of reduced pollution) to the extent that these can be accounted for in terms of their impact on human health and productivity.

The **opportunity cost method** is often used when it is not feasible to value the environmental benefits or costs of a project or policy. One method of implementing this approach is to work out the opportunity cost of preventing or limiting the environmental damage by not undertaking or by modifying the proposed project. The following example illustrates this approach.

Example 12.1: The Opportunity Cost Method

Irrigators in a catchment are currently growing 10,000 tons of sugar cane per annum. They receive $150 per ton and their variable costs are $50 per ton. Water quality in the catchment has fallen to a level of 40 points measured on a 0 to 100-point indicator. Three proposals are being considered to improve the catchment's water quality as summarized in Table 12.1. Option 1 involves annual direct costs of $50,000 which raises the index of water quality to 50; option 2 costs $30,000 per annum which raises the water quality index to 65; and option 3 costs $20,000 per annum and raises the water quality index to 85. In addition, irrigators are required to reduce their output of sugar by: 10% under option 1, 20% under option 2, and 40% under option 3. Three questions are posed:

(i) Which option has the lowest total opportunity cost?
(ii) Which option has lowest cost per unit of water quality improvement?
(iii) Why might neither of these represent the most efficient option?

Table 12.1 Hypothetical Water Quality Improvement Project Options

	Input Values		Direct Cost p.a	Output reduction	Quality Index	Total Cost p.a.	Cost/unit Quality Change p.a.
Output (tons)	10,000	Option 1	$50,000	10%	50	$150,000	$15,000
Price ($/ton)	$150	Option 2	$30,000	20%	65	$230,000	$9,200
Costs ($/ton)	$50	Option 3	$20,000	40%	85	$420,000	$9,333

From the table the answers to the three questions can be calculated as follows:
(i) Option 1 has lowest total opportunity cost equal to $150,000. The value of forgone output is $100,000, being 10% of 10,000 at $100 net revenue per annum ($150–50), to which direct costs of $50,000 are added.
(ii) Option 2 has the lowest cost per unit of water quality improvement equal to $9,200 per annum. Total cost is $230,000 per annum, which is divided by the increase in quality index of 25 (65 minus 40).

(iii) We do not know how the value of ecosystem services and other benefits respond to changes in water quality. Without that information we cannot say whether a 10-point improvement in the water quality indicator is worth $150,000, and whether further quality improvements by 15 and 20 points are worth the additional $80,000 and $190,000 respectively.

The opportunity cost method leaves it to the judgement of the decision-maker whether the value to society of a particular level of improvement in water quality is worth its associated opportunity cost. In a threshold analysis the analyst turns that question around by calculating what *minimum* value the associated (unknown) environmental benefits would need to have to justify the choice of a particular option. If decision-makers consider the environmental benefits due to the water quality improvement to be worth at least this amount the option can be selected.

Example 12.2: Threshold Analysis

Suppose the government is considering an application for a development project that will involve degradation of a wetland. The wetland plays an important role in the provision of ecosystem services, such as breeding habitat for some rare species of birds. To replace the wetland elsewhere is estimated to cost $K million. The development project is expected to generate a net income to the referent group (in economic efficiency prices) with an NPV of $40 million (not taking account of the cost of the loss of the wetland). If the same capital was invested elsewhere it would generate net benefits with an NPV of $15 million, implying that the contribution of the wetland's *natural capital* to the project has an NPV of $25 million. What would the present value to society of the wetland's ecosystem services, denoted by $B million, need to be to justify a decision:
(i) to preserve the wetland intact, not allowing the project to proceed;
(ii) to allow the project to proceed without replacing the wetland elsewhere;
(iii) to allow the project to proceed provided the wetland is replaced elsewhere?

The answer to these questions involves choosing among three mutually exclusive projects. As discussed in Chapter 3, the appropriate decision-rule is to choose the project with the highest NPV. If the project does not proceed (Option (i)) the manufactured capital invested elsewhere will yield an NPV of $15 million and the wetland will yield an NPV of $B million. If the project proceeds without replacement (Option (ii)) it yields an NPV of $40 million. If it proceeds with replacement (Option (iii)) the NPV is $(40 + B − K) million. Hence we would choose Option:

(i)   if $15 + B > 40 (i.e. B > 25) *and* $15 + B > 40 + B − K (i.e. K > 25);
(ii) if $40 > 15 + B (i.e. B < 25) *and* $40 > + B − K (i.e. B < K);
(iii) if $40 + B − K > 15 + B (i.e. K < 25) *and* $40 + B − K > 40 (i.e. B>K).

Suppose we have an estimate that K < $25 million: that immediately rules out Option (i); the choice between Options (ii) and (iii) then turns on whether B > K, and it may be possible for the decision-maker to make that judgement without further research.

Both of the above applications of the opportunity cost method provide dollar measures of the cost of environmental preservation, and invite the decision-maker to choose the appropriate level of environmental quality by trading these costs off against benefits measured in physical units. An alternative way of applying the opportunity cost method is to select an objective or target, such as a given level of water quality, and then choose the management option which achieves the target at the least cost. This approach is usually referred to as *Cost-Effectiveness Analysis* (CEA). For example, if the target level of water quality is set at, say, 50 points and its current level is 40 points, a CEA would compare the cost of alternative means of raising water quality by 10 points. The target level of 50 points is treated as a given (by policy-makers), implying no need to measure the value of the benefits associated with the improvement in water quality.

The **preventative cost method** of measuring the cost of environmental damage assumes that the value of the environmental resource is equal to the cost of preventing or mitigating the environmental damage, or replacing or restoring the environmental asset, or relocating the environmental activity. When the quality of an environmental service deteriorates, households react to prevent or mitigate the effects. For instance, if the quality of drinking water deteriorates households might spend money on a water filtration system or on the purchase of bottled water. If noise from air or road traffic increased, households might decide to install double-glazing, or alternatively may decide to relocate. The cost of the preventative measures which households voluntarily undertake provides a minimum estimate of the cost to

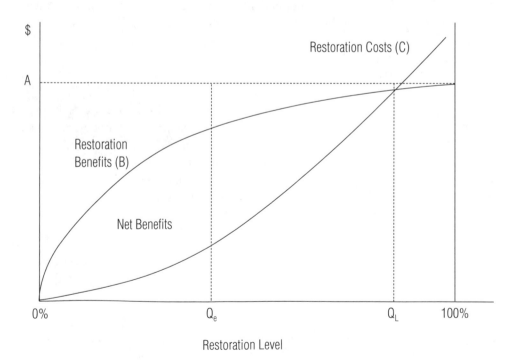

Figure 12.2 Measures of Value using the Replacement Cost Method

the community of the deterioration of the environment. However, it is only if it can be assumed that the averting or preventative expenditure and environmental quality are perfect substitutes, that the change in averting or preventative expenditure can be considered a good measure of the cost of the welfare effects of a change in environmental quality.

The **replacement cost method** infers the value of environmental quality from the cost of restoring or replacing the degraded environment to its level before the damage occurred; for example, the cost of restoring lost vegetation, forests, wetlands, or coral reefs is sometimes used for estimating damages in the legal process. It should be noted that the replacement cost method could well overstate the cost of environmental losses. This is illustrated in Figure 12.2, which records dollar values of restoration benefits and costs against the degree of restoration undertaken.

In this example, restoring beyond level Q_L would imply incurring total costs greater than the benefits. At Q_L total costs and benefits are equal. At Q_e, net benefits are maximized. From an economic efficiency perspective the appropriate level of restoration costs would be Q_e, where marginal benefit equals marginal cost. This analysis assumes that the level of total economic value at each restoration level is known.

It is important to note that all cost of production methods assume that incurring a cost to prevent, avoid or replace produces a benefit at least as great as the value of the environmental cost, or loss of benefit, to society. This could be considered a reasonable assumption when the cost is incurred by private individuals or conservation groups, and when the objective is to assess the value to those individuals or groups. These methods become a lot less acceptable when used to estimate the value of benefits to society as a whole, and to calculate how much governments should spend on the environment.

While the production approaches usually use actual market prices as the basis for valuation, there is no reason why the analyst could not use shadow-prices to gauge the true value of opportunity cost following the methodology developed in previous Chapters of this book. For instance, if the cost of avoiding pollution damage from agricultural run-off is a loss of agricultural output, the loss of net income to the farmers will not reflect the opportunity cost to the economy if agricultural production is subsidized. In this case appropriate shadow-prices should be used.

The Utility Approach

Neoclassical economic theory is grounded on the working assumption that consumers are rational and always make consumption decisions in accordance with the objective of maximizing their individual utility, subject to their income or budget constraint, and given the market prices of all goods and services. As discussed in Chapter 7, the net benefit consumers obtain from consumption activity is measured by *consumer surplus* which is the difference between the amount actually paid for the quantity of the good consumed and the amount that the consumer would be *willing to pay*. The concepts of *consumer surplus* and *willingness to pay* (WTP) can be illustrated by means of a market demand curve for a product, as shown in Figure 12.3.

As discussed in Chapter 7, we can measure the total WTP for a given consumption level, Q_1, by the area $OABQ_1$. If the actual charge to users for access to, say, a park, is P_1 the area OP_1BQ_1 measures the amount actually paid, or total cost. The total benefit, measured by the

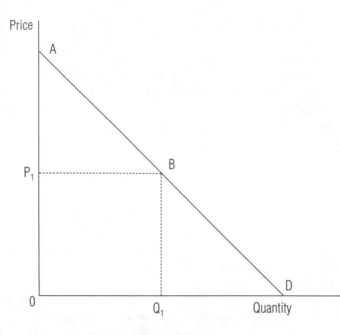

Figure 12.3 Willingness-to-pay and Consumer Surplus

amount of WTP, exceeds the cost by the area of the triangle P_1AB. This area represents the *consumer surplus* (CS), and is the measure of net benefit to the consumers who pay price P_1 for use of the park.

What happens when the good in question is a public good for which there is no market price? As there is no market we cannot actually observe a relationship between price and quantity demanded from market information. Nonetheless it can be assumed that a demand curve for the use of the public good exists, even although the amount actually paid to use it is zero. In that case CS (net benefit) is given by the entire amount of the WTP – the area of the whole triangle ODA under the demand curve in Figure 12.3. It is for this reason that the net benefit of an environmental asset is often equated with WTP, because, in the absence of a price, CS = WTP.

As noted previously, when valuing environmental assets we are more likely to be interested in comparing *changes* in net benefits resulting from changes in the management of these assets at the margin, than in the total asset value. The change in consumer surplus to users of an environmental resource, associated with a proposed project to improve the quality of the resource, is given by the maximum amount of money that society is willing to pay to obtain the improvement rather than do without it. A management option that improves the quality of a resource, is likely to increase consumers' demand for that resource, resulting in a change in consumer surplus. This is illustrated in Figure 12.4, where tourists have access to a coral reef at a price of P_0, and an improvement in reef quality (measured, say, in terms of percentage of reef cover) causes the demand for the reef's services to shift from D_0 to D_1. The resulting change in WTP is given by the entire area between the two demand curves, and the change in CS by the area ABCE.

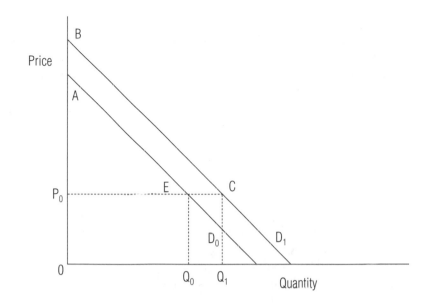

Figure 12.4 Change in Consumer Surplus from Demand Curve Shift

Note that this interpretation of the significance of a demand shift is different from that discussed in Chapter 7 where the demand shift was the result of a change in the price of a substitute or complementary good and where there was no CS change to measure. In the present case the demand shift is a result of a real improvement in the quality of the resource, and reflects an increase in the value of the service offered.

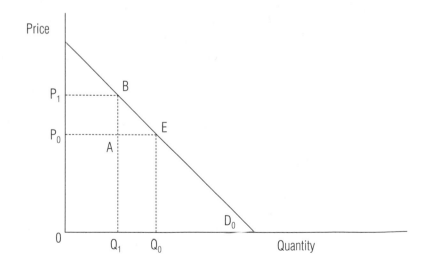

Figure 12.5 Change in Consumer Surplus Resulting from a Price Change

If the management option is a change in price, such as the entrance fee to a park, without any change in the quality of the service offered, the demand curve and WTP do not change. However the change in net benefit to users is measured by the change in CS as illustrated in Figure 12.5. If the access fee rises from P_0 to P_1 and quantity demanded falls from Q_0 to Q_1, CS falls by the amount given by area P_0P_1BE.

It should not be forgotten that, while the change in CS measures the change in net benefit to the consumer as a result of the change in price, in a BCA framework we are interested in the net benefit from the perspective of all members of the referent group, including government. In the above example, access fee revenues change by $P_0P_1BA - Q_0Q_1AE$ and this amount must be included along with the change in consumers' net benefit to arrive at the net benefit or, in this instance, cost to the economy as a whole.

Up to this point the discussion has been limited to instances in which changes in WTP and consumer surplus are attributable only to changes in the value to the users of an environmental resource. It was noted previously that TEV can include both use and non-use values. However, as will be noted in the following discussion about different utility-based valuation methods, not all are capable of capturing and measuring both use and non-use values.

Revealed and Stated Preference Methods

There are essentially two categories of utility valuation methods: the *Revealed Preference Method* and the *Stated Preference Method*. The former uses observations from consumer behaviour as revealed in actual or surrogate markets while the latter uses a survey instrument to construct hypothetical markets in which the respondents are asked to express their preferences.

Revealed Preference Methods

An example of a surrogate market is expenditure on travel. If we observe the amount individuals spend on travel and other associated costs in getting to and from the non-market activity they participate in, such as a day's recreational fishing around the lagoons of the reef, we can infer the value to those individuals of the activity; hence the term **Travel Cost Method** **(TCM)**. By collecting survey-based information from different groups of recreational fishers about the distances traveled, time spent, other associated costs, as well as the frequency of their visits, it is possible to construct a demand curve for recreational fishing. The TCM uses information on total visitation and travel cost to sites to estimate the relationship between cost and numbers of trips. This method assumes that an individual's demand for entrance to a site is related to travel costs in the same way as demand would be related to the level of an entrance fee. As individuals must be using the site to reveal a preference for it, it follows that this method is not capable of measuring non-use values.

Example 12.3: Travel Cost Method

Suppose that individuals A and B have the same money income, have the same tastes, and face the same set of prices of all goods and services except that of access to a National Park. Individual A lives further away from the Park than Individual B and hence incurs a higher travel cost per visit. There is no admission charge to enter the Park. The data in Table 12.2 summarize their annual use of the Park:

Table 12.2 Hypothetical Travel Cost Example

Individual Travel	Cost per Visit	Visits per Year
A	$15	10
B	$5	20

You are asked to calculate:

(i)   approximately how much consumer surplus does Individual A receive per annum from her use of the Park?

(ii) approximately how much consumer surplus does Individual B receive per annum from his use of the Park?

(iii) what is the approximate measure of the annual benefits to A *and* B from their use of the Park?

(iv) why are the measures in (i), (ii) and (iii) "approximate"?

To answer these questions, note that in this simple example there are only two visitors, and they are assumed to have identical characteristics, implying identical demand curves. This means that the pair of (price, quantity) observations lies on the same individual demand curve as shown in Figure 12.6.

Assuming that no park entrance fee is charged:

(i)   consumer surplus for A = 0.5(10×10)=$50

(ii) consumer surplus for B = 0.5(20×20)=$200

(iii) total consumer surplus =$50+200=$250

(iv) the estimate of total consumer surplus is approximate as the demand curve may not be a straight line as assumed here.

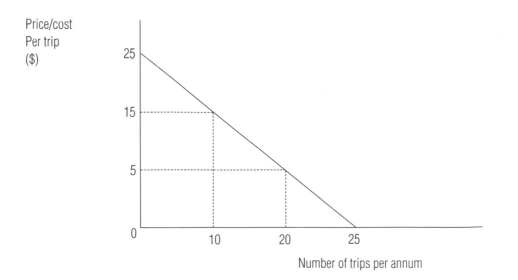

Figure 12.6 Approximate Individual Demand Curve for Park Visits

Since the individuals using the Park will not have identical demand curves, because of different tastes, income levels and prices of other goods they consume, statistical methods must be used to accommodate these differences. For example, the number of visits can be regressed against travel cost, education level, household income, and prices of other goods (such as alternative sites) to get a conditional relationship between the number of visits and price.

The main strengths of the TCM are:

- it is relatively easy to use
- it is well suited to cases where current use values are required
- it is based on actual revealed preference observations.

The main weaknesses of the TCM are:

- it has limited ability to measure the values of individual site attributes
- there are complications when valuing a trip with multiple destinations or purposes (although the multiple site TCM has also been developed)
- biases arise if possible substitute sites are not properly incorporated in the analysis.

Like the TCM, the *Random Utility Method* (RUM) uses trip data and travel costs to estimate a demand function for a recreational site. While the TCM assumes that the demand for a site is continuous – as trip prices fall so the number of trips increases – the RUM method assumes each time an individual undertakes a recreational activity she makes a discrete choice about which site to visit. This approach is often used to value fishing or hunting trips, where the probability of visiting one site, given information about all other sites and the individuals' characteristics, is modeled. From this model it is then possible to estimate the user's per trip benefit which is then multiplied by the number of trips per time period to obtain an estimate of total net benefits.

The main advantage of this method is that, unlike the TCM, it takes explicit account of the existence of substitute sites in situations where individuals swap site choice depending on opportunities available. It also allows for valuation of each attribute of a recreational site visit. The main problem with the RUM is that it does not explain the number of trips made, which means that when the quality of the site changes only the estimate of per trip benefit changes; the number of trips made is assumed to remain constant.

As an alternative to the TCM we can use the behaviour of consumers as revealed in other related markets to infer their preferences for the good in question. The underlying proposition is that an individual's utility for a good or service is derived from the attributes of the good or service in question, and that it is possible to distinguish the value of each attribute. For example, if the quality of an environmental resource, such as air or water, is considered an important attribute entering our choice of house, variations in air or water quality should directly affect relative house prices. For instance, the value to the resident of property frontage on a waterway could be affected by the quality of the water. If we compare house prices in polluted *vs.* non-polluted situations, with controls for price differences attributable to other factors, we should be able to measure the dollar value of differences (and changes) in water quality. When all other effects have been accounted for, any difference in property price is attributed to the differential water quality. This is called the **Hedonic Pricing Method (HPM)**.

To apply the HPM in this instance, data on house prices are gathered to estimate a model that explains variations in house price in terms of a whole set of attributes, one of which is the environmental attribute in question. For example, observed house price can be modeled as a function of house and site characteristics, neighbourhood characteristics, and water quality characteristics. This is the *hedonic price function* which can be expressed as:

$$P_h = P\,(S_i,\, N_j,\, Q_k\,)$$

where, P_h = house price
$\qquad S_i$ = site characteristics
$\qquad N_j$ = neighbourhood characteristics
$\qquad Q_k$ = environmental quality characteristics
and, i = 1…m; j =1…n; and k = 1…1

This first stage of the analysis permits the calculation of an implicit "price" or value for the environmental attribute in terms of its marginal influence on house prices. This relationship is not a demand curve. A second stage in the analysis involves estimating a demand curve for the environmental attribute, using the environmental price and quantity information obtained from the first stage and allowing for socio-economic differences among the sampled house buyers so as to isolate the effect of water quality from other factors, such as income, which affect house prices. This second stage generates an individual demand curve for water quality which can be summed across individuals and used to estimate the benefit (cost) of improved (deteriorating) quality.

Example 12.4: Hedonic Pricing

It is proposed to build a new city ring road which will increase noise levels in two suburbs, A and B, by 6 and 8 units respectively, and reduce noise levels in two others, C and D, by 3 and 10 units respectively. You are required to calculate the environmental cost (or benefit) of the change in traffic noise due to the project. A hedonic pricing model based on sales prices and house characteristics has estimated the percentage fall in the price of the average house in each area which can be attributed to a one unit increase in noise level: these percentage changes are Area A = –0.45; Area B = –0.18; Area C = +0.92; Area D = +0.08. Table 12.3 shows the number of houses in each area and the mean house price prior to the construction of the new road, together with the estimates of the changes in noise levels and the changes in house prices attributable to a one unit change in noise level.

Table 12.3 Impact of Road Noise Changes on Property Values

Area	Mean House Price ($ thousand)	Number of Houses	Change in Noise Level	% Change in house price per unit change in noise level	Total Change in Cost of Noise ($ thousand)
A	$250	76	6	−0.45	513.0
B	$125	124	8	−0.18	223.2
C	$400	64	−3	+0.92	−706.6
D	$100	60	−10	+0.08	−48.0
			Net cost of change in noise levels		−$18.4

The changes in noise levels will result in a net increase in the value of properties of $18.4 thousand as calculated in Table 12.3. This sum is an estimate of the present value of the environmental benefit of the proposed road.

The main advantages of the HPM are:
- it is conceptually intuitive
- it is based on actual revealed preferences.

The main disadvantages of the HPM are:
- it requires a relatively high degree of statistical knowledge and skill to use
- it generally relies on the assumption that the price of the house is given by the sum of the values of its individual attributes, implying a linear relationship among attributes
- it assumes that there is a continuous range of product choices containing all possible combinations of attributes available to each house buyer.

Stated Preference Methods

Other methods attempt to use surveys or other instruments such as focus groups to get consumers to express their view of use and non-use values on the same basis as they would reveal their preferences in actual markets through the price mechanism. A hypothetical situation for the use of an environmental resource is described and the interviewees are asked, contingent on the existence of the situation described to them, how much they would be willing to pay for the use and/or non-use services of the resource, such as recreation or existence.

The most commonly used stated preference method is the *Contingent Valuation Method* (CVM). CVM uses surveys to ask people directly how much they would be willing to pay for a change in the quality or quantity of an environmental resource. The resulting sample mean (or median) WTP is then multiplied by the relevant population to estimate total WTP. CVM is, in principle, a relatively simple method, although state-of-the-art applications have become quite complex.

CVM is susceptible to a number of response biases. These include:
- *hypothetical market bias*: where responses are affected by the fact that it is a hypothetical and not a real market choice, and where individuals may enjoy, for example, "warm glow" effects from overstating their true preferences for an environmental good, or, where they simply want to please the interviewer – "yeah-saying";

- *strategic bias*: where respondents believe that their survey response bids could be used to determine actual charges or expenditures they may understate or overstate their true WTP;
- *design bias*: the way in which the information is presented to the respondents can influence the individuals' responses, especially concerning the specification of the payment vehicle, raising the question of how far preferences can be considered exogenous to the elicitation process; and,
- *part-whole bias*: individuals have been found to offer the same WTP for one component of an environmental asset, say, recreational fishing in one river, as they would for fishing in the entire river system.

With refinements in the design of surveys most of these biases can be avoided or at least minimized, although the debate still continues as to whether individuals are indeed capable of expressing preferences for environmental and other public goods and services on the same basis as they would for private goods in, say, the context of a supermarket or shopping mall.

One of the main advantages of CVM, like other stated preference methods, is that it is capable of estimating both use and non-use values and it can be applied to almost any situation.

Example 12.5: Contingent Valuation Method

A local authority is considering alternative proposals to improve the quality of the water in the main river on which the city is located. The three options are: Option 1, improve river quality to a level suitable for recreational boating; Option 2, improve river quality to a level suitable for recreational fishing; and, Option 3, improve river quality to a level suitable for swimming. The annual costs of the options are estimated at $2 million, $3.25 million, and $4.25 million respectively. A contingent valuation study based on a representative sample of households, including both users and non-users of the river, estimates average annual Willingness to Pay for the three options at $12.5, $17.50, and $25 per household respectively. The city has a total of 200,000 households. Suppose you are required to rank the options in terms of:

(a) maximum aggregate net benefit
(b) maximum net benefit per $ invested

Which of the three options would you recommend and why? The calculation of project net benefit (in $ thousands) and net benefit per dollar cost is shown in Table 12.4.

Table 12.4 Estimating Net Benefits of Improved Water Quality using CVM

	No. of households in population (000's)	Sample WTP/HH ($)	Estimate of total WTP ($000's)	Project Cost ($000's)	Net Benefit ($000's)	NB/$cost
Option 1	200	12.5	2500	2000	500	0.25
Option 2	200	17.5	3500	3250	250	0.08
Option 3	200	25	5000	4250	750	0.18

It can be seen that Option 3 generates the largest annual net benefit of $750,000; the ranking of options on this measure is Option 3 then 1 then 2. However Option 1 yields the highest net benefit per dollar of cost, of $0.25, followed by Option 3 then Option 2. If funds are not rationed then Option 3 would be preferred. If funds are rationed it would be necessary to compare the net benefit per dollar of cost with other projects to determine the cut-off level. For instance, if the cut-off level is more than $0.18, Option 1 would be chosen. If it was less than $0.18 then Option 3 would be chosen. Option 2 would never be preferred as Option 1 costs less and yields a higher value of net benefit.

One of the main limitations of CVM is that it is usually restricted to comparison of only one option with the *status quo*. The *Discrete Choice Modeling* method (DCM), which is another stated preference approach, provides for the comparison of a range of options. DCM is a form of conjoint analysis using choice experiments. The environmental good is described in terms of a set of attributes, where each attribute is allowed to take on a number of possible values over a defined range. All possible combinations of attributes are assembled to derive a large matrix of hypothetical scenarios for the environmental resource. Surveyed individuals are presented with approximately 8–10 choice sets, each containing (usually) two hypothetical options and the *status quo* and asked to select their most preferred. The survey data are used to estimate trade-off values for each attribute, using a multinomial logit model. From the regression results the net benefit of each management option can be calculated.

Example 12.6 Discrete Choice Modeling*

The DCM method was used to value a wetland that provides a number of important ecosystem services including habitats for waterbirds and water filtration for downstream users. With the opening of a dam on the adjacent river, the area of wetland fell from $5000km^2$ to $1200km^2$ and the number of endangered and protected bird species using the wetland fell from 34 to 12. A DCM questionnaire was developed where respondents were informed about the problem and management options were specified. Through a series of focus group meetings with stakeholders, the key attributes characterizing the wetland were identified and, according to an experimental design, possible combinations of levels for each attribute were combined into a number of choice sets, an example of which is shown in Table 12.5.

Table 12.5 Example of a Hypothetical Choice Set

Attribute	Status Quo	Option 1	Option 2
Water rates (one-off increase)	No change	$20 increase	$50 increase
Irrigation related employment	4400 jobs	4350 jobs	4350 jobs
Wetlands area	$1000km^2$	$1250km^2$	$1650km^2$
Waterbirds breeding	Every 4 years	Every 3 years	Every year
Endangered and protected species present	12 species	25 species	15 species

Respondents were required to select their most preferred of the three options in each choice set. This enabled estimation of the relative importance of each attribute. The study

---

* Based on M. Morrison, J. Bennett and R. Blamey, *Valuing Improved Wetland Quality Using Choice Modelling*. Choice Modelling Reports, No. 6. School of Economics and Management, University of New South Wales, Sydney, 1998.

found, for instance, that respondents were willing to pay 13 cents for an extra irrigation related job preserved and about $4 for an additional endangered species to be present. Once the marginal values for each attribute were estimated the actual levels of each attribute corresponding to each policy option under consideration could be used to compute the relative value of each policy option.

Variants of the DCM method include *Contingent Ranking* and *Contingent Rating* where, instead of making a single choice from each set of options, the respondent is required to rank or rate (on a given scale) each hypothetical option in the set.

DCM may be less prone than CVM to bias because of its emphasis on choice among specific alternatives. One advantage of the DCM is that it enables the analyst to derive the trade-off values for, and compare the net incremental benefits of a number of, alternative management interventions in one survey questionnaire. The main disadvantage is that there is no rule as to how attributes should be chosen and over what range their possible values should be allowed to vary. Increasing these complicates the choice experiment enormously.

Alternative Approaches

Criticism of BCA and orthodox methods of environmental valuation has led some economists to propose totally different approaches to valuation and evaluation of environmental resource management options.

Deliberative Value Assessment (DVA) methods treat the *process* of value elicitation as an important factor in determining the validity of the information acquired from surveys. Unlike the traditional methods described above, individuals' valuations are treated as endogenously determined and adaptive, being determined as part of an ongoing activity within the decision-making process itself. In a DVA framework the elicitation of values does not occur independently of the decision-making process itself; it forms part of it. For instance, Citizens' Juries (CJ) can be formed to deliberate on matters of public policy such as the use and management of environmental resources. These juries will include expert witnesses with scientific knowledge, as well as economists, along with, perhaps, the results of their non-market valuations and BCA studies. The jury is required to deliberate and to come to an informed, considered decision on the most acceptable course of action or management intervention to be adopted by the respective authority responsible for the management of the resource. A CJ can be used to pronounce upon a value or to make a specific decision.

A similar approach to a CJ is a multi-criteria analysis (MCA) where each of the relevant stakeholder groups is required to rate or rank alternative performance criteria, with the ranking depending on their preferences and constraints, and then to rate the extent to which they believe alternative management interventions are likely to succeed in achieving the criteria identified.

It could be argued that there is not necessarily any inconsistency between a DVA approach to valuation and evaluation, and what has been prescribed in this Chapter and elsewhere in this book. It is recognized that BCA is essentially an approach to inform the decision-making process. There is no reason why BCA could not also be used in a deliberative, democratic decision-making process, and, where that process gives rise to changes in stake-holders' preferences and choices, there is no reason why the BCA could not be conducted on an iterative and interactive basis, as stakeholders' preferences and valuations evolve. In other words, rejection of utility theory's assumption of fixed preferences, which underlies most non-market valuation methods, does not in itself imply rejection of BCA as a decision-support tool. BCA could and perhaps should play an important part in a Citizens' Jury or other form of DVA. Similarly, valuation methods such as CVM and DCM could equally be adapted to decision-making contexts in which it is recognized that values can be endogenously determined and adaptive.

Another Example of Non-market Valuation – the Value of Life

We chose environmental assets to illustrate the use of the revealed and stated preference approaches to determining values of non-marketed goods and services because environmental valuation is currently a rapidly expanding area of research and application. However in traditional benefit-cost analysis the aspect of non-market valuation which received much of the attention was the valuation of life. A significant benefit of investment in health services or transport infrastructure is the saving of lives, and benefit-cost analyses of these kinds of investments require that a value be placed on a life saved.

Before considering how such a value might be estimated, it should be noted that saving a life really means prolonging a life, and that the number of extra years (the quantity) is an expected value which differs according to the personal characteristics of the individual, including age, sex, standard of living and other factors. Furthermore, the value of each additional year of life (the price or unit value) may also depend on personal characteristics, such as age, which influence the quality of life. Consequently, if we want a summary measure of the "value of a life" we need to average the product of price times quantity over the population distribution.

In some circumstances it is possible to appraise alternative investment proposals while avoiding the question of what a life is worth. For example, if the saving of lives is the only objective and there is a fixed budget to be allocated among alternative project proposals, cost-effectiveness analysis (CEA) can be used for project selection; the set of projects selected, subject to the budget constraint, is the set which maximizes the number of lives saved. However many spending agencies have more than one objective; for example, the transport department wishes to save both lives and travel time and would be unlikely to accept a proposal to virtually eliminate traffic fatalities by imposing a 5 kph speed limit. Furthermore, budgets are not fixed, and distributing investment funds among departments with varied objectives, such as saving lives, saving time, environmental protection, and provision of consumption goods and services, involves being able to make trade-offs.

As in the case of environmental goods and services there are two general approaches to determining the value of life relative to other goods and services. Under the stated preference approach a questionnaire could be used to determine individuals' willingness to trade income for reduced risk of death or improved state of health. Under the revealed preference approach the choices that people actually make could be analysed to determine what value is implicitly being placed on life. We now consider some applications of the latter approach.

The spending decisions of health and transport departments implicitly place values on lives saved, and estimates of these values can be ascertained by comparing expenditures and outcomes at the margin. However there are at least two problems with this approach. First, the outcome is rarely the single product "a life saved". We have already seen that transport departments are also interested in time savings and, in considering the trade-off between these two objectives, information about the value of time saved (another non-marketed good which was discussed in Chapter 5) would be required to estimate the value placed on life. In the case of health expenditures, there is a research component to medical procedures that may justify the discrepancy between the costs of lives saved by transplanting various kinds of organs, such as, for example, hearts and kidneys. The second problem is similar to the one we encountered in Chapter 11 when we were attempting to infer income distributional weights: the decision-maker is seeking independent advice about the value that "should" be attached to life as opposed to information about the values that are implicitly used. These implicit values are a product of expenditure allocation decisions which ideally should be informed by prior information about the value of life.

The expenditure decisions of government departments, such as health and transport, are essentially driven by non-market behaviour. If we turn to spending decisions in the market place we might hope to get better estimates of the value of life. Two promising places to look are in the life insurance market and in the labour market. For example, if a person is willing to accept hazard pay of X per year for working in a risky industry, such as mining, where the chance of accidental death in the course of the year is higher by the probability p than in similar work in a less risky industry, then it could be argued that the value placed on life is X/p. This estimate is based on the assumption that the relationship between the hazard pay premium and the risk is linear, whereas it might reasonably be argued that the fact that I am willing to accept $100 to take a .001 chance of death does not necessarily mean that I am willing to accept only $1000 to take a .01 chance, and $10,000 to take a 0.1 chance. This criticism may not be important if the estimate is to be used to value small changes in probability of death around current levels of risk.

The problem with treating the life insurance industry as a related market is that the sum insured measures the consumer's estimate of the value of her livelihood to the beneficiaries of the policy. However the group of beneficiaries excludes both the individual herself and the general community, and the value of livelihood is not the same as the value of life. Adjustments to the value of the insurance policy, such as adding estimates of the present value of the insured person's forgone consumption expenditures and the difference between the present value of the taxes she would have paid net of the cost of the public services she would have received, might address the former problem but not the latter.

Empirical studies have found a wide range of estimates of the value of life; for example, Usher[1] reports values ranging from $34,000 to $4,500,000 in 1960s US dollars, the former

1   D. Usher, *The Measurement of Economic Growth* (Oxford: B. Blackwell, 1980). See Also B. C. Field and N. D. Olewiler, *Environmental Economics* (McGraw-Hill Ryerson, 1995), Table 7.1 for more estimates.

estimate being based on miners' hazard pay and the latter on the number of military pilots whose lives are expected to be saved by investment in ejector seats. In part the wide range of estimates may reflect the different values placed on different lives, but it is hard to escape the conclusion that there is little coherence among the various decision-making processes involving the saving of lives. In these circumstances, as in some environmental decision-making situations, benefit-cost analysts may have to resort to threshold analysis to inform decision-makers what a life needs to be worth to justify a particular investment.

Further Reading

Most public finance texts include a detailed discussion of public goods and externalities, for example R. Boadway and D. Wildason, *Public Sector Economics* (Little, Brown and Co., 1984). A classic paper on externalities is R. Coase, "The Problem of Social Cost", in R. D. and N. S. Dorfman (eds), *Economics of the Environment* (Norton, 1972) and a classic paper on the common is G. Hardin, "The Tragedy of the Common", *Science*, Vol. 162, 1968, pp. 1243–1248. See also D. L. Weimer and A. R. Vining, *Policy Analysis: Concepts and Practice*, 3rd ed., Chapter 8 (Prentice Hall, 1998). A useful introduction to non-market valuation techniques is J. L. Knetsch and R. K. Davis, "Comparisons of Methods for Recreation Evaluation", in R. D. and N. S. Dorfman (eds), *Economics of the Environment* (Norton, 1972). More recent studies are: R. Cummings, D. Brookshire and W. D. Schulze (eds), *Valuing Environmental Goods* (Rowman and Allanheld, 1986); R. C. Mitchell and R. T. Carson, *Using Surveys to Value Public Goods: the Contingent Valuation Method* (Resources for the Future, 1989); N. Hanley and C. L. Spash, *Cost-Benefit Analysis and the Environment* (Edward Elgar, 1993); G. Garrod and G. Willis, *Economic Valuation and the Environment* (Edward Elgar, 1999). The classic paper in which existence value was first introduced to BCA is J. V. Krutilla, "Conservation Reconsidered", *American Economic Review*, 57 (4), pp. 777–786, 1967. For the subsequent debate on this, see papers by Rosenthal and Nelson, and Kopp in *Journal of Policy Analysis and Management*, 11 (1), 1992.

Exercises

1. Manufacturers in an urban environment are currently producing 25,000 widgets per annum. Their gross revenue is $300 per widget and their variable costs are $125 per widget. Air quality in the city has fallen to a level of 20 points measured on a 0 to 100 point indicator. Three proposals are being considered to improve the city's air quality. Option 1 involves annual direct costs of $100,000 which raises the index of air quality to 32; option 2 costs $130,000 per annum which raises the air quality index to 42; and option 3 costs $150,000 per annum and raises the air quality index to 50. In addition, producers are required to reduce their output of widgets by: 5% under option 1, 10% under option 2, and 15% under option 3. Three questions are posed:
   (i)   Which option has the lowest total opportunity cost?
   (ii) Which option has lowest cost per unit of air quality improvement?
   (iii) Why might neither of these represent the most efficient option?

2. Individuals A and B have the same money income, have the same tastes, and face the same set of prices of all goods and services except that of access to a National Park. Individual A lives further away from the Park than Individual B and hence incurs a higher travel cost per visit. There is no admission charge to enter the Park. The following data summarize their annual use of the Park:

Individual	Travel Cost per Visit	Number of Visits p.a.
A	$20	5
B	$10	10

(i) approximately how much consumer surplus does Individual A receive per annum from her use of the Park?

(ii) approximately how much consumer surplus does Individual B receive per annum from his use of the Park?

(iii) what is the approximate measure of the annual benefits to A *and* B from their use of the Park?

(iv) why are the measures in (i), (ii) and (iii) "approximate"?

3. A contingent valuation study was used to value improvements to a coral reef, where, at present, the reef quality, measured in terms of percentage of reef cover, is so poor that the local residents can no longer rely on the reef for their supply of fish. The study sample, which included users (one-third) and non-users, found the following estimates of average WTP.

Scenario	Mean WTP ($ per annum) Whole sample	Local users	Others	
1 Increase reef cover to	50%	$25	$45	$15
2 increase reef cover to	75%	$40	$70	$25
3 increase reef cover to	100%	$53.5	$95	$33

(i) construct a demand curve for reef quality for: users; others; and the whole sample and discuss the forms of these curves;

(ii) explain how this information could be used in a BCA to compare management options to improve the quality of the reef.

4. Using the data provided in Example 12.4, calculate the net benefits of an alternative road proposal that results in increased noise levels in Areas A and B of 5 and 10 decibels respectively, and decreased noise levels in Areas C and D of 2 and 8 decibels respectively.

13
Economic Impact Analysis

Introduction

A large project, such as construction of a major highway or development of a large mine, will have a significant impact on the economy. The spending in the construction and operating phases will generate income and employment, and public sector decision-makers often take these effects into account in deciding whether or not to undertake the project. An economic impact analysis is a different procedure from a cost-benefit analysis in that it attempts to predict, but not evaluate, the effects of a project. Since the data assembled in the course of a cost-benefit analysis are often used as inputs to an economic impact analysis the two types of analyses tend to become related in the minds of decision-makers and may be undertaken by the same group of analysts.

In this Chapter we survey briefly three approaches to economic impact analysis: the income multiplier approach; the inter-industry model; and the computable general equilibrium model. Use of the latter two approaches involves a degree of technical expertise and would generally not be undertaken by the non-specialist. In discussing economic impacts we emphasize that these are not the same as the costs or benefits measured by a cost-benefit analysis. However there may be costs and benefits associated with the project's economic impact and the decision-maker may wish to take these into account.

The decision whether or not to take the multiplier or flow-on effects into account in the evaluation should be based on an assessment of the extent to which similar such effects would or would not occur in the absence of the project in question. When choosing between alternative projects this would depend on the extent to which the multiplier effects can be expected to vary significantly between the alternatives; when faced with an accept vs. reject decision for a discrete project the analyst would need to assess whether the same investment in the alternative, next best use could be expected to generate multiplier effects of the same or similar magnitude. These points are taken up again in the discussion of the multiplier effects.

Multiplier Analysis

The Closed Economy
For simplicity, the concept of the national income multiplier can be developed in the context of a closed economy – one that does not engage in foreign trade. This simplifying assumption will be dropped later in the discussion.

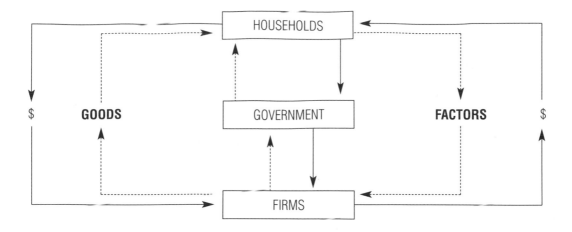

Figure 13.1 The Circular Flow of Income

The value of the gross product of an economy can be measured in two equivalent ways: as the value of all the goods and services produced by the economy in a given time period, usually a year; or as the value of the incomes to factors of production – labour, capital and land – generated in the course of producing those goods and services. The two measures are equivalent because of the concept of the circular flow of income, already referred to in Chapter 7. Figure 13.1 shows the flow of income from firms (the sector which demands the services of factors of production, and supplies goods and services) to the household sector (the sector which demands goods and services, and supplies the services of factors of production), and the flow of expenditures from households to firms. It also shows the activities of government which collects tax revenues and allocates them to the funding of purchases of goods and services from firms for the use of the household sector.

While the concept of the circular flow of income implies that it is always identically true that the flow of income equals the flow of expenditure, there is only one level of income which can be sustained by any given level of demand for goods and services. This equilibrium level of income can be calculated by means of the equilibrium condition:

$$Y = C + I + G$$

In this expression, Y is the equilibrium level of income and C, I and G are expenditures on the three types of goods and services produced by the economy – consumption goods and services, investment goods, and government goods and services.

In applying the equilibrium condition we need to distinguish between those variables that are explained by this simple model of national income determination, and those that are not. The former variables, Y and C in this model, are termed **endogenous**, i.e. determined by the model, and the latter, I and G, are **exogenous**, or autonomous i.e. determined in a manner not explained by the model.

Consumption expenditure can be related to income by means of a consumption function:

$$C = A + bY$$

In this expression A is the level of autonomous consumption expenditure, and b is the marginal propensity to consume – the proportion of an additional dollar of income that is consumed, as opposed to saved. Since income must be either saved or consumed, the savings function can be written as:

$$S = (1 - b)Y - A,$$

where $(1 - b)$ is the marginal propensity to save – the proportion of an extra dollar of income that households will save. When the income level $Y > A/(1 - b)$, savings are positive, but when $Y < A/(1 - b)$ savings are negative (ie. being run down) because households are financing a portion of their consumption expenditure out of past savings. In either event, according to the consumption function a proportion $1 - b$ of any additional dollar of income earned will be saved.

When the above information is substituted into the equilibrium condition, it becomes:

$$Y = A^* + bY + I^* + G^*,$$

where the starred values indicate exogenous variables. This expression can be simplified by collecting the Y terms on the LHS of the equation and solving for the equilibrium level of income:

$$Y = (1/(1 - b))(A^* + I^* + G^*).$$

If we know the level of expenditure chosen by government, the level of investment expenditure chosen by firms, and the level of autonomous consumption, we can work out the equilibrium level of national income.

The term $1/(1 - b)$ is termed the national income multiplier because it determines the equilibrium level of income as a multiple of the sum of the autonomous expenditures. It also relates changes in national income to changes in the level of autonomous expenditure. For example, suppose that a firm decided to undertake an additional investment project, the change in the level of national income could be calculated as:

$$dY = (1/(1 - b)) \, dI^*.$$

To consider the implications of this result, suppose that $b = 0.9$ and that $dI^* = \$100$, then $dY = \$1000$. In other words, an additional expenditure of $100 on autonomous investment results in a $1000 increase in the equilibrium level of national income.

The intuition behind this striking result of the model can be seen by following the moncy trail left by the increase in the level of autonomous investment. When an extra $100 is spent it represents $100 of extra income to households, of which $100b is spent, and this amount in turn represents extra income to households, of which $100b^2$ is spent, and so on. The total increase in expenditure (or income) is given by:

$$dY = 100 + 100b + 100b^2 + 100b^3 + 100b^4 + 100b^5 + \ldots\ldots\ldots\ldots$$

The sum of this geometric progression can be calculated in the usual way to give:

$$dY = 100/(1 - b).$$

It will be evident from this example that, in theory, the only thing that prevents income rising without limit in response to an increase in autonomous expenditure is the fact that a proportion $(1 - b)$ leaks out of the expenditure cycle at each round. The lower the value of b the less the proportion of any income increase that is passed on in the form of expenditure to generate further increases in income.

Now consider an economy in which there are two types of leakages – into household savings and into tax revenues. In this model consumption expenditure can be related to disposable income:

$$C = A^* + b(Y - T^*)$$

where T^* represents taxes paid by households to government. Now the equilibrium level of income is given by:

$$Y = (1/(1 - b))(A^* + I^* + G^* - bT^*).$$

Suppose that the government decided to increase expenditure by some amount dG^*, and to finance it by printing money rather than by raising taxes. The resulting increase in national income would be:

$$dY = (1/(1 - b))dG^*$$

If, on the other hand, the government decided to raise taxes in order to finance the additional expenditure, the increase in national income would be:

$$dY = (1/(1 - b))(dG^* - bdT^*).$$

If the additional expenditure was fully funded by the tax increase, $dG^* = dT^*$, and the increase in national income would be:

$$dY = (1/(1 - b))(1 - b)dG^* = dG^*.$$

This latter expression demonstrates that the "balanced budget multiplier" – the national income multiplier to be applied to an increase in government expenditure fully funded by an increase in taxes – is unity when the level of taxation is autonomous. The reason for this is that, in the round after the initial expenditure, the increase in household consumption which would have occurred in the absence of a tax increase, bdG^*, is offset by the reduction in household expenditure caused by the tax increase, bdT^*, and these effects cancel out in the case of a balanced budget. It should be noted that when the level of tax collected varies with income, the balanced budget multiplier will still be positive, but less than unity because of the leakage of income into treasury coffers.

To this point we have established that an additional public or private project, which represents an increase in the level of autonomous expenditure, will have a multiplier effect on the equilibrium level of national income. In the simple example presented above, a \$100 project raises national income by \$1000, which seems to imply that in addition to the \$100 worth of project output there is an additional \$900 worth of benefit from the project. However we have to be skeptical of this interpretation of the result of the model because it fails to distinguish between real and nominal increases in national income.

If the economy is at full employment no increase in real national income is possible; in other words, no net increase in the volume of goods and services produced is possible because there are no additional factor inputs which can be allocated to production. In that event the increase in the equilibrium level of national income (product) would be purely nominal, consisting simply of the same volume of goods valued at higher prices resulting from inflation. If the national product in real terms is denoted by the flow of goods, Q, and the price level by P, we can express national income or product by PQ, and the increase in national income by:

$$dY = PdQ + QdP,$$

where the term PdQ represents a real benefit to the economy in the form of higher output, and the term QdP represents the increase in the valuation of the original level of production as a result of inflation. Clearly in a social benefit-cost analysis we would be interested only in the former outcome since individuals benefit from increased availability of goods and services, but not from higher prices. At full employment, $dQ = 0$ and there is no benefit to be measured.

Now suppose that the economy is at less than full employment. Then some fraction of the increase in national income resulting from the multiplier effect represents an increase in the value of output of goods and services. However before we could count this as a benefit of the project we would need to determine what that fraction is, and how much of it represents a net benefit. In an economy beset by structural unemployment, where the skills of the unemployed do not match the skills required by business, it may not be possible to increase real output and the multiplier effect may be simply to raise the price level. Determining the fraction of the multiplier effect which represents an increase in output is clearly not a simple matter. Furthermore, as argued in Chapter 5, unemployed resources may have an opportunity cost. Unemployed individuals may value their leisure time, or value goods and services, such as food or home and car repairs, that they produce outside the market economy. The net gain to the unemployed is the wage less the value of such items. This was recognized in Chapter 5 by shadow-pricing the labour used in a project at less than the wage rate, but at more than zero. A similar shadow-price should also be used in assessing the net benefit of any induced changes in real output level as a result of the project.

It must be emphasized that the income and employment multiplier effects will normally last only for the duration of the activity in question. For instance, if the investment and construction phase of a project is limited to one or two years, the associated flow-on impact on output and employment will be limited to that two-year period. It is often the case that policy makers/politicians overlook their relatively short duration when referring to the income and employment impacts of a project.

Finally, it must be recognized that any increase in autonomous expenditure will generate a multiplier effect, so that in comparisons among projects the multiplier effects can generally be ignored, unless, of course, it is evident that the magnitude of the multiplier effects varies significantly among the alternatives being considered.

The Open Economy

For an economy which imports and exports goods and services, the national income equilibrium condition is given by:

$$Y = C + I + G + X - M.$$

This expanded form of the condition recognizes that only domestic production of goods and services generates income in the economy. The imported components of C, I, G and X, totaling M in aggregate, are therefore subtracted from the total value of goods and services produced. Exports can be regarded as exogenous – determined by foreign demand – while expenditure on imported goods and services will be positively related to income.

The multiplier for this open economy can be determined as before by substituting the behavioural relations into the equilibrium condition and solving for equilibrium national income. The behavioural relations are the consumption function:

$$C = A^* + b(Y - T),$$

the import function:

$$M = mY,$$

and a tax function that allows tax collections to rise as income rises:

$$T = tY.$$

Incorporating this relationship between T and Y recognizes that the tax system imposes a brake on the expansion of the economy by increasing the tax leakage as income rises.

The equilibrium level of income in this model is given by:

$$Y = (1/[1 - b(1 - t) + m])(A^* + I^* + G^* + X^*).$$

Some plausible values for b, t and m can be selected as follows. For a mixed economy in which the government sector produces 30% of total production of goods and services, the value of t will be around 0.3; for an open economy for which 25% of the value of goods and services consumed is imported, the value of m will be around 0.25; and household saving out of disposable income can be assumed to be 10% as before, giving a value of 0.9 for b. Using these values a multiplier of 1.45 is obtained. This is considerably lower than the value obtained for the closed economy model because of the addition of the tax and import leakages. The implication of this result is that an additional $100 of government expenditure, not matched by any change in the tax regime, would increase national income by $145, consisting of the $100 expenditure plus second and additional round effects totaling $45.

This more realistic model suggests that multiplier effects are in reality much smaller than in our closed economy model. Again, as noted above, we need to recognize that some of the increase in equilibrium income may simply reflect price changes, and that any increase in real income – the volume of goods and services produced in the economy – may come at some opportunity cost so that the net benefit is lower than the real increase in income.

As noted above, the size of the multiplier falls as the size of the leakages from the economy increases. Since the smaller the region, the larger the import leakage it can be concluded that regional multipliers will be smaller than state multipliers, and state multipliers smaller than national multipliers. A relatively small region might easily import half of the value of the goods and services it consumes. Substituting the value $m = 0.5$ into the above multiplier model reduces the value of the multiplier to 1.06. Furthermore, a relatively small region may not get the full benefit of the initial round of expenditure. For example, suppose an additional tourist spends $100, represented as $dX^* = \$100$ in the national income multiplier model. However a portion of this expenditure may immediately leak out of the region without generating any first-round income increase at all. Suppose that half of the expenditure simply goes to the national head office of a hotel chain so that the amount of additional income generated in the region – income to service providers such as hotel, restaurant and transport staff – is only $50. Now if we apply the multiplier we find that the rise in regional income is only $53.

If multiplier effects are relatively small, and have to be qualified by distinguishing real from nominal effects, and netting out opportunity costs, it might be asked why various client groups are often keen to have them estimated. One industry which often emphasizes these effects is the tourism industry, since it usually operates at below capacity. For a hotel, or a bus tour which has vacant places the marginal cost of serving an additional customer is very low. This means that almost the whole of the induced rise in regional income constitutes a net benefit to business. This case is similar to the case of an economy with significant unemployment where multiplier-induced increases in income are real, as opposed to nominal, and the net benefit is similar to the gross benefit because of the low opportunity cost of additional factor services.

Governments often emphasize job creation as a consequence of increased public expenditure. Additional jobs are created to the extent that the increase in national income is real as opposed to nominal. A real increase in income is obtained by drawing otherwise unemployed resources into market activity, whereas a nominal increase involves simply shifting the existing labour force around from one job to another. A "jobs multiplier" can be constructed by using the ratio of the number of jobs to the national income in conjunction with the national income multiplier. For example, suppose that the ratio of employment to income, L/Y, is denoted by k. Using the relations $L = kY$, and $dL = k\,dY$, the multiplier relationship can be expanded to predict the number of jobs created, providing that the increase in income is real as opposed to nominal:

$$dL = k\,dY = k\,(1/[1 - b(1 - t) + m])\,d\,G^*,$$

where $(k/[1 - b(1 - t) + m])$ is the employment multiplier. For example, if the average wage, Y/L, is \$25,000 the value of k is 0.00004 and the value of the employment multiplier in the national income model is 0.000058. This means that, according to the model, an extra \$1 million of government expenditure would create 58 new jobs.

Inter-Industry Analysis

More detailed estimates of the economic impact of a proposed project can be obtained on an industry basis by using an input-output model which takes into account inter-industry sales and purchases of intermediate inputs. The input-output model measures the impact of any increase in final demand expenditure (an increase in the value of an exogenous variable) on the level of output of each industry. As in the case of the multiplier model, these impacts are not predictions or forecasts, because other events may occur to counter or magnify the industry impacts, but they indicate the likely size and direction of the effects of the increase in final demand. Governments are interested in this information because of concern for the welfare of particular industries which may exhibit high unemployment or be located in economically depressed regions.

Inter-industry analysis recognizes that each industry uses two types of inputs to produce its output: factors of production such as land, labour and capital; and intermediate inputs consisting of goods and services produced by itself or by other industries. The value of the gross output of each industry equals the value of output used as intermediate inputs plus the value of output used in final demand. Inter-industry transactions net out of national income transactions since a revenue for one industry represents a cost to another, or, in terms of the national income model, because all inter-industry transactions occur within the *Firms* sector of Figure 13.1 and do not form part of the circular flow of income. Each industry's contribution to national income is measured by the value of the final demand goods it supplies, or, equivalently by the value of the factor incomes it generates. This contribution is referred to as "value added" since it measures the difference between the value of the goods and services the industry sells and the value of the goods and services it buys.

In modeling inter-industry transactions we distinguish between the value of goods produced by industry i, x_i, and the value of its production that enters final demand, y_i. If the coefficient a_{ij} is used to represent the sales of industry i to industry j per dollar's worth of output of industry j, then total sales of industry i to industry j can be represented by:

$$x_{ij} = a_{ij}x_j,$$

And total value of output of industry i can be written as:

$$x_i = \sum_j a_{ij}x_j + y_i.$$

A disadvantage of the input-output model as described here is the assumption of a set of fixed relationships between inputs and output. A more general approach would allow the input-output coefficients to vary with the level of output, or over time with technological change.

In order to illustrate how the input-output model is constructed, consider an economy consisting of three industries. Using the above relation we can write a set of equations determining the gross output of each industry:

$$a_{11}x_1 + a_{12}x_2 + a_{13}x_3 + y_1 = x_1$$
$$a_{21}x_1 + a_{22}x_2 + a_{23}x_3 + y_2 = x_2$$
$$a_{31}x_1 + a_{32}x_2 + a_{33}x_3 + y_3 = x_3$$

This set of equations can be simplified to:

$$(1 - a_{11})x_1 - a_{12}x_2 - a_{13}x_3 = y_1$$
$$-a_{21}x_1 + (1 - a_{22})x_2 - a_{23}x_3 = y_2$$
$$-a_{31}x_1 - a_{32}x_2 + (1 - a_{33})x_3 = y_3$$

which can be written in matrix form as:

$$(I - A)X = Y$$

where I is the identity matrix (a matrix with '1' on the diagonal and '0' elsewhere), A is the matrix of inter-industry coefficients, a_{ij}, X is the vector of industry gross output values, and Y is the vector of values of final demands for industry outputs. Solving this equation in the usual way (by pre-multiplying both sides by $(I - A)^{-1}$) an equation relating gross industry outputs to final demands can be obtained:

$$X = (I - A)^{-1} Y.$$

This equation can be used to predict the effect on industry output of any change in final demand. For example, if a private investment project were to involve specified increases in final demands for the outputs of the three industries, the effects on gross industry outputs could be calculated.

Table 13.1 illustrates the inter-industry structure of a three-industry closed economy.

Table 13.1: Inter-Industry Structure of a Small Closed Economy

		Sales			Final Demand	Gross Output
		1	2	3		
Purchases	1	100	400	300	200	1000
	2	0	400	900	700	2000
	3	0	0	600	2400	3000
Value Added		900	1200	1200	3300	
Gross Output		1000	2000	3000		

Note that the sum of inter-industry sales plus value added equals the value of the gross output of each industry. Similarly the sum of inter-industry purchases plus final demand sales also equals the value of gross output. The inter-industry coefficients a_{ij} are obtained as the ratios of inter-industry purchases to the value of the gross output of each industry. Expressed in the form of the matrix A, these are:

$$A = \begin{bmatrix} 0.1 & 0.2 & 0.1 \\ 0 & 0.2 & 0.3 \\ 0 & 0 & 0.2 \end{bmatrix}$$

We now construct the matrix $(I - A)$:

$$(I - A) = \begin{bmatrix} 0.9 & -0.2 & -0.1 \\ 0 & 0.8 & -0.3 \\ 0 & 0 & 0.8 \end{bmatrix}$$

and, using the *MINVERSE* function in *EXCEL*©, we obtain the inverse matrix:

$$(I - A)^{-1} \doteq \begin{bmatrix} 1.11 & 0.28 & 0.24 \\ 0 & 1.25 & 0.47 \\ 0 & 0 & 1.25 \end{bmatrix}$$

We can now write down the set of relations $X = (I - A)^{-1}Y$:

$$x_1 = 1.11y_1 + 0.28y_2 + 0.24y_3$$
$$x_2 = 1.25y_2 + 0.47y_3$$
$$x_3 = 1.25y_3$$

which relates the value of gross output of each industry to the value of final demand for its product. This set of equations can also be written in the form of changes in values of gross output in response to changes in values of final demand:

$$dx_1 = 1.11dy_1 + 0.28dy_2 + 0.24dy_3$$
$$dx_2 = 1.25dy_2 + 0.47dy_3$$
$$dx_3 = 1.25dy_3.$$

Suppose that a public or private project costs $100, consisting of expenditures of $20, $30 and $50 on the goods and services produced by industries 1, 2 and 3 respectively. Using the above set of equations we can calculate the effects on the values of gross output of industries 1, 2 and 3:

$$dx_1 = 42.6, \; dx_2 = 61.0 \text{ and } dx_3 = 62.5.$$

Note that the total increase in the value of gross output exceeds the $100 increase in the value of final demand because each industry needs to produce enough output to satisfy inter-industry flows as well as final demand.

Inter-industry Analysis and the National Income Multiplier

The estimates of increases in values of industry output obtained above are first-round effects only. In increasing their output levels industries will hire additional services of factors of production and so the incomes paid to the owners of these factors – land, labour and capital – will rise. As predicted by the multiplier model some of this additional income will be spent, thereby generating a second and subsequent rounds of increases in final demands, leading to an eventual increase in national income in excess of the original $100 increase in the exogenously determined level of final demand.

The input-output model can be modified to incorporate multiplier effects by adding a set of equations which play the same role as the consumption function in the multiplier model. Suppose that the final demand for the outputs of the three industries is given by:

$$y_1 = 0.2y + g_1$$
$$y_2 = 0.3y + g_2$$
$$y_3 = 0.4y + g_3$$

Where y is the level of national income and g_i is the autonomous levels of demand for the output of each industry. Recall that it was changes in these levels of autonomous demand, resulting from the expenditures associated with the public or private project, that set off the first round effects on the values of gross output of the three industries. Each of the above equations can be thought of as an industry-specific consumption function, where the coefficient on y plays the role of the coefficient b in the aggregate consumption function and g_i plays the role of A* (p. 293). By summing the equations we can see that:

$$\sum_i y_i = 0.9y + \sum_i g_i$$

where 0.9 is the marginal propensity to consume, as in our earlier illustrative model of national income determination.

Now consider the system of inter-industry equations $Y = (I - A)X$, and replace Y by the set of industry-specific expenditure functions and rearrange to get:

$$0.9x_1 - 0.2x_2 - 0.1x_3 - 0.2y = g_1$$
$$0x_1 + 0.8x_2 - 0.3x_3 - 0.3y = g_2$$
$$0x_1 - 0x_2 + 0.8x_3 - 0.4y = g_3$$

We now have a set of three equations in four unknowns, the x_i and y. In order to close the system we need to add the condition, derived from the concept of circular flow of national income, which determines equilibrium: the value of final demand output should equal the value added in producing this output – the value of factor incomes paid by the industries. The values added can be expressed as proportions of the values of the outputs of the three industries:

$$y = 0.9x_1 + 0.6x_2 + 0.4x_3.$$

When this equation is added to the other three and the system solved (using Cramer's Rule and the *MDETERM* function in *EXCEL$^©$*) for national income, y, the following result is obtained:

$$y = 10(g_1 + g_2 + g_3).$$

In other words, the equilibrium level of national income is ten times the sum of the levels of autonomous demands, i.e. the multiplier is 10, as we saw earlier in our illustrative closed-economy national income determination model (p. 290). A change in the level of autonomous demand for any one of the goods would produce a ten-fold change in the level of equilibrium national income.

Inter-industry Analysis and Employment

In the above discussion the input-output model was used to calculate the effect on national income of an increase in autonomous demand for the three goods produced in the economy. The model can be extended to calculate the effect of the demand increase on employment of factors of production.

Suppose that the level of input of factor of production i to industry j is given by:

$$v_{ij} = b_{ij} x_j$$

Where b_{ij} is a coefficient and x_j is gross output of industry j as before. Supposing that there are two inputs, labour and capital for example, total input levels are given by:

$$v_1 = b_{11}x_1 + b_{12}x_2 + b_{13}x_3$$
$$v_2 = b_{21}x_1 + b_{22}x_2 + b_{23}x_3$$

Or, in matrix notation, $V = BX$, where V is the vector of factor inputs, B the matrix of employment coefficients, and X the vector of industry outputs. However, we already know that $X = (1 - A)^{-1}Y$ and so we can write $F = B (1 - A)^{-1}Y$, a set of equations which relates the levels of inputs of the two factors to the levels of final demand for the three goods. Any change in the level of autonomous demand for any of the three goods can be traced back through this system of equations to calculate the effects on the levels of the factor inputs.

For example, let the matrix of factor input coefficients be:

$$B = \begin{bmatrix} 0.6 & 2 & 1.2 \\ 0.5 & 0.4 & 0.3 \end{bmatrix}$$

We can now solve for V, using the $MMULT$ operation in $EXCEL^{©}$:

$$V = \begin{bmatrix} v_1 \\ v_2 \end{bmatrix} = \begin{bmatrix} 0.6 & 2 & 1.2 \\ 0.5 & 0.4 & 0.3 \end{bmatrix} \begin{bmatrix} 1.11 & 0.28 & 0.24 \\ 0 & 1.25 & 0.47 \\ 0 & 0 & 1.25 \end{bmatrix} \begin{bmatrix} y_1 \\ y_2 \\ y_3 \end{bmatrix}$$

to get the following result:

$$v_1 = 0.67y_1 + 2.67y_2 + 2.58y_3$$
$$v_2 = 0.56y_1 + 0.64y_2 + 0.68y_3.$$

Now suppose that input v_1 represents labour, and that the increases in the levels of y_i are $20, $30 and $50 respectively, then the increase in employment – the number of jobs created in the first round – is given by:

$$dv_1 = 0.67*20 + 2.67*30 + 2.58*50 = 222.5.$$

The above calculation takes account of first-round effects only. If second and subsequent round effects were also to be considered, this can be done by solving the input-output multiplier model for the levels of final demand, y_i, for both the original and the new levels of autonomous expenditures, g_i. The two sets of y_i estimates could then be used to calculate two sets of estimates of employment levels of the two factors, v_i, and the difference between these values would indicate the extra employment resulting from the original change in the levels of autonomous expenditures and the subsequent multiplier effects in the economy.

General Equilibrium Analysis

A general equilibrium in an economy is a situation in which all markets clear in the sense that, at the prevailing prices, quantity supplied of each good or factor of production equals quantity demanded. This implies that, at the equilibrium prices, no economic agent has any incentive to change the quantity they supply or demand of any good or factor. In principle a situation of equilibrium will continue until there is a change in the value of some exogenous variable, such as a tax rate or level of autonomous government expenditure. A computable general equilibrium (CGE) model can be constructed to determine the equilibrium values of prices and quantities traded in the economy, and to calculate the changes in these values which would result from some change in an exogenous variable. For example, a large project could involve a significant change in the exogenously determined level of investment, which, in turn, could cause changes in the values of variables of interest to the policy-maker –

employment, the wage level, the exchange rate and so on. A CGE model could be used in this way to assess the economic impact of a large project.

It is beyond the scope of this discussion to consider in detail the structure of CGE models. However simple CGE models can be constructed from information contained in the input-output model and it is useful to consider in principle how the model described in the previous section of this Chapter could be developed into a CGE model. Our simple input-output model was of a closed economy producing three commodities and using two factors of production. The model could be solved for the equilibrium values of the two inputs and the three outputs. In a general equilibrium model values are calculated as the product of two variables – price and quantity. Equilibrium in such a model with three commodities and two factors consists of five equilibrium prices and five equilibrium quantities. In order to solve for the values of these 10 variables, a system of 10 equations is required.

Three of the required equations can be obtained from the input-output coefficients by assuming that competition in the economy ensures that total revenue equals total cost; this means that for each industry the value of its sales equals the value of the intermediate inputs and factors of production used to produce the quantity of the commodity sold. Two more equations are obtained from the factor markets where factor prices have to be set at levels at which the quantities of factors supplied by households equal the quantities demanded by industries; this means, for example, that the market wage has to be sufficiently high to ensure that the total quantity of labour supplied is sufficient to meet the demands of the three industries. Three equations are obtained from the markets for commodities in final demand; commodity prices must be at a level at which the quantities demanded by households are equal to the final demand quantities supplied by industries. An income equation is required to ensure that the income households receive from the supply of factors of production to industries is equal to their expenditure on final demand goods. Lastly, since the CGE model determines relative prices only, the price of either one commodity or one factor must be set at an arbitrary level – for example, the wage could be set equal to 1 – or the price level, as measured by some price index, must be set equal to an arbitrary value. In either event, this normalization adds one more equation to the model and completes the system of 10 equations required to solve for the 10 variables.

It will be evident that the model described above is very limited in that it contains no government or foreign sector. However our purpose here is simply to convey the flavour of such models rather than to provide a recipe for constructing one. The solution to a CGE model is often expressed in terms of a set of proportionate changes in the values of variables of interest (solving for rates of change is a way of linearizing a non-linear model). For example, in the analysis of the impact of a significant exogenously driven expansion of an export sector of an economy the model might predict that the exchange rate would appreciate (the value of the domestic currency would rise in terms of US\$), the domestic price level would fall, and the wage rate would fall. The first step in interpreting these results is to ask whether they are consistent with international trade theory: the exchange rate rises because of an increase in exports; prices of imported consumer goods fall in domestic currency terms, leading to consumers substituting imports for domestically produced goods; the wage falls because of a net decline in employment owing to the fact that the capital-intensive exporting sector is unable to absorb all the labour released by the shrinking domestic consumer goods sector. Since the direction of changes predicted by the CGE model is consistent with economic theory, we can have some confidence in the results and turn our attention to the magnitudes of the changes predicted.

Case Study: The Impact of the ICP Project on the Economy

An economic impact analysis would estimate the effect of the proposed ICP project on Thailand's gross national product. As noted earlier, the gross impact of the project may be larger than its net impact to the extent that project outlays reflect expenditures that are simply displaced from other areas of the economy. We will consider the gross impact first, and then the net impact of the project.

It will be recalled from the discussion of the national income multiplier that money which leaks out of the circular flow of income as savings and taxes has no further impact on the level of national income. A large proportion of the ICP project expenditures is in this category since they represent imports of capital inputs, such as machinery, and intermediate inputs, such as cotton. Only expenditures on inputs sourced from within the economy will have multiplier effects on national income through their effects on consumers' incomes and expenditures. For example, receipt of wages will stimulate spending by workers; receipt of rent will stimulate spending by landlords; and receipt of service fees by banking and insurance companies, and water and power utilities, will, eventually, stimulate spending by shareholders of these institutions. Applying the multiplier to the total of these categories of expenditure in each year will provide an estimate of the gross impact of the project in that year.

The net impact of the project on GNP will be lower than the gross impact because some of the above expenditures are simply displaced from other sectors of the economy. For example, the analysis of the opportunity cost of the project inputs established that the wages paid to skilled labour and the rent paid to the landlord would have been paid in the absence of the project. Any gross multiplier effects attributed to these expenditures cancel out in the analysis of net impact. The most significant net impact of the project on the economy probably results from the wages paid to unskilled labour. The unskilled wage bill could be adjusted by the national income multiplier to provide an estimate of this impact.

As discussed earlier, it is important not to confuse "net impact" with "net benefit". The first-round net benefits resulting from employment of each unit of unskilled labour have already been included in the estimate of referent group benefits as the difference between the wage and the shadow-price. There could be additional net benefits to the extent that additional spending by unskilled labour generates additional demand for the services of unskilled labour, additional wages, and hence further spending. However, as far as the case study is concerned, these additional net benefits are likely to be relatively small and it is unlikely that the results of this kind of impact analysis would affect the decision about the project.

Because of the importance of the distinction between net benefit and net impact, the reporting of impact effects derived from multiplier, input-output or CGE models should not be integrated with the cash flow analysis and social benefit-cost analysis results. An appropriate format is a separate statement of impact assessment results, including an assessment of both their expected longevity/duration and their net impact relative to the scenario without the project.

Further Reading

A good discussion of national income determination and the inter-industry model is contained in T. F. Dernburg and J. D. Dernburg, *Macroeconomic Analysis: an Introduction to Comparative Statics and Dynamics* (Addison-Wesley, 1969).

Exercises

1. An advertising campaign is expected to increase expenditures of foreign tourists in Far North Queensland (FNQ) by $100 million per annum. You have been asked to estimate the economic impact of this increase on the FNQ economy. You are told that out of any extra dollar earned by FNQers they pay 30 cents in taxes. Out of any dollar increase in disposable (after-tax) income they save 20 cents and spend 30 cents on goods produced outside of FNQ. It is estimated that 30 cents of every dollar spent by foreign tourists accrues as income to non-residents of FNQ, such as national hotel chain headquarters.
    (a) Develop and explain a simple model of the FNQ economy which can be used to estimate the impact of the advertising campaign on FNQ's Gross Regional Product (GRP);
    (b) Use the data provided above to estimate the FNQ multiplier and calculate the size of the increase in FNQ's GRP;
    (c) If the FNQ GRP per capita is $50,000, what is the likely size of the employment effects in FNQ of the advertising campaign?

2. Suppose that the inter-industry structure of a three-commodity, two-factor closed economy is described by the following Table:

Inter-Industry Structure of a Small Closed Economy

		Sales			Final Demand	Gross Output
		1	2	3		
Purchases	1	300	200	200	300	1000
	2	0	300	700	1000	2000
	3	0	0	600	2400	3000
Value Added		700	1500	1500	3700	
Gross Output		1000	2000	3000		

Work out the first-round effects on industry outputs of an exogenous $100 increase in final demand for the output of industry 2.

14
Writing the Benefit-Cost Analysis Report

Introduction

If benefit-cost analysis is to assist in the decision-making process the analyst must be able to convey and interpret the main findings of the benefit-cost analysis in a style that is user-friendly and meaningful to the decision-makers. The analyst should never lose sight of the fact that the findings of a BCA are intended to inform the decision-making process. BCA is a *decision-support* tool; not a *decision-making* tool. To this end it is imperative that the report provides the decision-maker with information about the project and the analysis which is directly relevant to the decision that has to be made, and to the context in which it is to be used.

There is no blue-print for report writing, as every project or policy decision will be different in various respects, as will the decision-making context and framework within which the analyst will be operating. Good report writing is essentially an art that can be developed and refined through practical experience. The purpose of this final Chapter is to identify what we consider to be some of the key principles the analyst should follow when preparing a report and to illustrate how these might be applied in the drafting of a report on the ICP Project we have used in previous chapters as a case study. As an illustration, we have selected the report prepared by one of our postgraduate students at the University of Queensland, Australia, who has kindly given us permission to use it in this way. In the sections below we explain why we consider this study an example of good BCA reporting. The report itself, along with the appended spreadsheet tables, is reproduced in its original form (with the exception of a few minor editorial corrections) as an Appendix to this chapter. Note that the report consists of an *Executive Summary*, four main sections – *Introduction*, *Methodology*, *Analysis* and *Conclusion* – and an *Appendix* containing the printouts of the spreadsheet tables.

Before commenting on this report, we should note that the starting point for the exercise was the ICP Case Study problem appended to Chapter 4. This starting point is already some way along the path which the analyst must follow. As in any area of investigation, framing the questions to be answered is an important first step. The ICP Case Study asked for an analysis of seven different scenarios involving two different locations and various tax regimes. These scenarios would have been established in discussions between the analyst and the client about the terms of reference for the study. It must not be assumed that the analyst plays a passive role in developing the terms of reference. As noted in Chapter 1, the benefit-cost analyst may play an important role in project design by asking pertinent questions about the options which are available. This significant contribution to the decision-making process is sometimes referred to as *scoping* the project.

The Executive Summary

The Executive Summary should not be written until the analyst has completed a draft of the rest of the report. The Executive Summary is, as its title indicates, written for the decision-makers' benefit. These are usually senior civil servants and/or politicians who are, most likely, not technical experts in the field, and who will, most probably, not be reading the rest of the report. It is reasonable to assume that they will not want to read more than a page or two. The report manages to highlight the main issues, summarize the main findings, and make a recommendation in one page. The executive summary begins with a succinct description of the project, its purpose, the players, and the decision to be made. It then describes the options, discusses the form of analysis undertaken and the main findings, and makes some recommendations for the minister's consideration. In this instance the writer has chosen not to include a summary table, but has instead reported some of the results in the text. Given that this report will constitute a major input into a negotiation process between the government of Thailand and ICP, the Executive Summary could have incorporated a summary table showing the trade-off between ICP's private net benefit and the Referent Group net benefits over the seven project options, perhaps at one discount rate. As the subsequent analysis shows, in this case this is a clear example of a zero-sum-game where each additional dollar gained by ICP represents an equivalent loss in net benefit by the Referent Group.

The Introduction

Bearing in mind that the main body of the report is written independently of the Executive Summary, the Introduction provides a brief summary of the report, the players, the options to be analysed and compared. This section should not contain too much detail about the project and the information used to undertake the analysis, but should rather aim to provide the reader with a fairly general description of what the project is about and what decision the analysis intends to inform.

The Methodology

While it is imperative that any report of this sort should provide an account of the methodology used in the analysis, it is not necessary for the report to contain a detailed account of what BCA is about. It should be assumed that the reader is already familiar with the concept and principles of BCA. However, as conventions, terms and approaches can vary quite considerably, the writer has been careful to point out in sub-section 2.1 exactly what is meant by *Project, Private, Efficiency,* and *Referent Group Analysis,* in anticipation that the reader will need to have this information to follow the rest of the report. Sub-section 2.2 explains what decision criteria are used and over what range the discount rates are allowed to vary in the sensitivity analysis. She is also mindful to refer the reader (sub-section 2.3) to the *Key Variables* table in the spreadsheet (attached as an appendix table) where all the input data and assumptions are contained.

The main assumptions on which the findings of the analysis rest are summarized in sub-section 2.4. It should be noted that this section does not attempt to summarize each and every piece of input information but instead focuses on those assumptions that are perhaps most open to the analyst's interpretation and discretion. This includes assumptions underlying the estimation of shadow-prices for the efficiency analysis, as well as other unknowns such as the projected exchange rate, possible future tax changes, and so on.

Since the analysis was an exercise there was no need to comment on the quality of the data, but in a real world situation it is worth detailing the sources of the data used in the analysis and reporting any verification process that was followed. This information could be included in a data appendix.

The Analysis

This section presents the findings of the analysis. It does not discuss in detail how the cash flows were derived, as this detail is contained in the spreadsheet tables in the Appendix. Tables A14.1 to A14.4 summarize the NPVs and IRR for each project option, in terms of the four types of BCA we undertake: Project, Private, Efficiency, and Referent Group. In terms of the decision to be made in this case, the two analyses that are really important are the Private BCA which shows how much ICP stands to gain or lose under each option, and the Referent Group BCA, which is what matters from the Government of Thailand's perspective. The writer has chosen, for sake of completeness, to summarize the results for the project and the Efficiency BCA as well. These are not really important to the decision and could well have been omitted, or perhaps mentioned briefly in passing. However in general their relevance will depend on the context. If, for instance, we were reporting on a project that is being funded by a multilateral agency such as the World Bank or a multilateral regional bank such as the Asian or African Development Bank, the agency could well be interested in knowing how the project performed in global efficiency terms, in which case reporting also on the Efficiency BCA would be required.

It should also be noted that a sensitivity analysis was undertaken under each option (not reported in this edited version), and it was established that the ranking of options from both ICP and the government's perspective is not unambiguous. At a discount rate around 20% there is a switching of the ranking of options, which could be significant for ICP's decision as 20% is not outside the possible bounds of a private investor's required rate of return.

The Conclusion

Note that the conclusion does not merely summarize what has already been said elsewhere in the report. It synthesizes the main findings, discusses their relevance and explores their possible implications for the government's negotiations and decision-making. Attention is also drawn to areas where further, more detailed work might be undertaken before a final decision is reached. In this instance the writer has also made a fairly concrete recommendation in favour of option 2, although in the context of her other recommendations, it is qualified and should not be interpreted as the final word.

Other Points

Because the ICP Case Study is designed as an exercise to be undertaken on the basis of Chapters 1–6, the report does not deal with any of the issues covered in Chapters 7–13: the possibility of changes in output or input prices as a result of the project; the shadow-price of foreign exchange; risk analysis; the cost of public funds; income distribution effects; non-market valuation; and economic impact analysis. In a real world situation all these issues would need to be explored with the client in the scoping process and sources of information identified if these issues were to be included in the analysis.

APPENDIX TO CHAPTER 14:
Report on International Cloth Products Ltd: Spinning Mill Proposal

Prepared by ANGELA McINTOSH*

EXECUTIVE SUMMARY

International Cloth Products Ltd (ICP), a foreign-owned textile firm, proposes to invest in a spinning mill in Thailand at the end of 1999. The mill will have a capacity of 15 million pounds of yarn, which will satisfy ICP's current demand for 10 million pounds, as well as demand from other Thai textile firms of approximately five million pounds.

ICP is seeking a concession from the Government to induce it to invest in Thailand. ICP has suggested that it is likely to invest in the Bangkok area if it receives either duty-free entry of cotton *or* a ten year exemption from profits tax. The Government would prefer the mill to be located in Southern Thailand, due to the policy to disperse industries to "deprived areas". ICP will consider locating the mill in Southern Thailand if it is given duty-free entry of cotton *and* a ten year exemption from profits tax.

The report considers the following options:
- Option 1: Bangkok – No Concessions;
- Option 2: Bangkok – No Duties;
- Option 3: Bangkok – No Profits Tax;
- Option 4: Southern Thailand – No Concessions;
- Option 5: Southern Thailand – No Duties;
- Option 6: Southern Thailand – No Profits Tax; and
- Option 7: Southern Thailand – No Duties, No Profits Tax.

---

* Written as an assignment while studying as a postgraduate student at the University of Queensland (2001).

Using Social Benefit-Cost Analysis methodology, each Option can be ranked according to efficiency from: the market perspective; ICP's perspective; the economy as a whole; and from Thailand's perspective. Based on the data from the analyses, Options 4 and 7 can clearly be rejected. Option 4 offers the best outcome for Thailand, but offers ICP no incentive and is ranked last from ICP's perspective. Conversely, Option 7 (ICP's highest ranked Option) will be disastrous for Thailand, with negative net present values for all discount rates.

Option 2, however, warrants serious consideration. This Option (Bangkok – No Duties on Imported Cotton) satisfies ICP's request to receive one concession if it invests in the Bangkok area. It is ranked fourth from both ICP's and Thailand's perspectives and, although in terms of the economy as a whole it is not as efficient as any of the Southern Thailand options, the differences between Options 1–3 and Options 4–7 in efficiency terms are relatively small (IRR 22% compared to IRR 23%).

Unless ICP can be convinced to accept Option 5 (ranked fifth from ICP's perspective and third from Thailand's perspective), none of the Southern Thailand options seems likely, unless a different set of alternatives, including subsidization of any investment in Southern Thailand, is considered. However, to determine whether or not other options are viable would require further, detailed analysis and direction from the Minister. Therefore, Option 2 is the recommended Option.

1. INTRODUCTION

This report examines a proposal by International Cloth Products Ltd (ICP) to invest in a spinning mill in Thailand at the end of 1999. ICP is a foreign-owned textile firm that manufactures cloth products (textile prints, finished and unfinished cloth) in the Bangkok area of central Thailand. It currently imports 10 million pounds (lbs) of cotton yarn each year. However, if the proposed spinning mill (with a capacity of 15 million lbs of yarn) goes ahead, ICP will be able to supply its own demand, as well as approximately five million lbs of yarn to other textile firms in Thailand. There appears to be an existing market for the excess supply, as Thailand's textile industry currently imports around 16.5 million lbs of cotton yarn per annum.

ICP is seeking a concession from the Government to induce it to invest in Thailand. ICP has suggested that it is likely to invest in the Bangkok area if it receives either duty-free entry of cotton *or* a ten year exemption from profits tax. Although ICP has indicated its preference to locate the mill adjacent to its existing plant in the Bangkok area, it will consider locating the mill in Southern Thailand (consistent with the Government's policy to disperse industries to "deprived areas") if it is given both concessions – that is, duty-free entry of cotton *and* a ten year exemption from profits tax. To accommodate the variety of alternatives open to the Government and ICP regarding the proposed spinning mill, the following options have been considered:

- **Option 1: Bangkok – No Concessions** (duties and profits tax paid by ICP);
- **Option 2: Bangkok – No Duties** (i.e. duty free entry of cotton);
- **Option 3: Bangkok – No Profits Tax;**

- Option 4: Southern Thailand – No Concessions;
- Option 5: Southern Thailand – No Duties;
- Option 6: Southern Thailand – No Profits Tax; and
- Option 7: Southern Thailand – No Duties, No Profits Tax.

2. METHODOLOGY

2.1 Social Benefit-Cost Analysis

The Social Benefit-Cost Analysis methodology is designed to provide information about the level and distribution of the costs and benefits of each identified alternative. Four different points of view are taken into account

1. **Project Analysis:** The project benefit-cost analysis values all project inputs and outputs at private market prices (does not include tax, interest on loans etc.) and determines whether the project is efficient from a market perspective.

2. **Private Analysis:** The private benefit-cost analysis examines the proposed project from the private firm's perspective by taking the project analysis and netting out tax, interest and debt flows.

3. **Efficiency Analysis:** The efficiency analysis is similar to the project analysis, except that "shadow-prices" are used where applicable. Shadow-prices are used to adjust the observed, imperfect market price to measure the marginal benefit or marginal cost. They are not the prices at which project inputs or outputs are actually traded. For example, minimum wages represent a labour market imperfection. If the labour input is additional to the current supply (for example, taken from the existing, unskilled labour pool), then it is priced at the "shadow-wage". Alternatively, if the labour input is reallocated from another market (for example, skilled labour), then the market rate is used. Another example is taxes, which also distort the market and therefore should not be included in the efficiency analysis.

    The efficiency analysis determines whether the project is an efficient allocation of resources across all groups impacted by the proposal – if the monetary benefits of the proposal exceed the amount required to theoretically compensate those who are adversely affected by the project, then the project is deemed to be an efficient allocation of resources (a potential Pareto improvement).

4. **Referent Group Analysis:** The referent group is comprised of the stakeholder/s that are deemed to be relevant. For this project the referent group can be broadly categorised as Thailand. The referent group analysis also examines the distributional effects of the proposal on the members of the referent group. The referent group for the proposal at hand can be broken down into the following sub-groups: the domestic bank, the Thai Government, domestic labour likely to be engaged on the project; the Electricity Corporation of Thailand and the domestic insurance company. There are two methods of determining referent group impacts. Method A involves identifying the costs and benefits for each

member of the referent group, while method B involves subtracting the non-referent group net benefits from the efficiency analysis. If the results of method A equal those for method B, then the analysis is shown to be internally consistent.

2.2 Discounted Cash Flows, Internal Rate of Return

Each of the four components (project, private, efficiency and referent group) has been assessed using discounted cash flows: see Tables A14.7 to A14.13. Cash flows have been projected over each year of the project (from 1999–2000) and then discounted back to present value (1999) amounts using discount rates of 4%, 8%, 12%, 16% and 20%. These different discount rates allow a sensitivity analysis to be undertaken of the net present values (NPV) for each discount rate. As the discount rates increase, the NPVs decrease. If the net present value is greater than zero, then for the relevant discount rate, the project is worth undertaking.

The internal rate of return (IRR) has also been determined for each component of the analysis. The IRR represents the discount rate that reduces the NPV to zero. If the IRR exceeds the discount rate, then the project should usually be accepted. This issue is discussed further in section 3.2 (Private Analysis).

2.3 Key Variables

Key variables for Option 1 are set out in Table A14.5 and these variables have been used to analyse each option. Every item identified in these attachments may be varied and may, indeed, change over time (see section 2.4 (Assumptions)).

Options 1 and 4 set out the base cases for Bangkok and Southern Thailand, respectively, in that they have all duties and taxes included. Options 2 and 5 have the duty on imported raw cotton reduced to 0% (compared to 10% in Options 1, 3, 4 and 6). Options 3 and 6 have the tax on profits reduced from 50% to 0%. Option 7 examines the costs and benefits for each component of the analysis should ICP locate in Southern Thailand with concessions on both duties and profits tax granted (cotton import duty 0% and profits tax 0%).

2.4 Assumptions

For any benefit-cost analysis, a number of assumptions need to be made. For this proposal, the following key assumptions have been made:

Operating Costs Generally

Operating costs have been assumed to remain constant over the life of the project. This may or may not be the case. For example, the cost of imported cotton may change with changes in world prices and other market forces. Similarly, the cost of labour (skilled and unskilled), electricity, water, spare parts, insurance and rent may all change over time. However, undertaking a sensitivity analysis (using different discount rates) helps to mitigate this potential problem.

Shadow-Prices

The shadow wage for labour has been assumed by the Government to be 50% of the market cost in Bangkok and zero in Southern Thailand. This may change over time, especially if the Government's "deprived area" policy is successful (e.g. shadow wages in deprived areas could increase).

The variable cost to the Electricity Corporation of Thailand of supplying power to ICP for the proposed mill is estimated to be 50% of the standard rate. In the absence of information on the supply of electricity to Southern Thailand, this shadow-rate has also been used to cost electricity in the efficiency analyses for Options 4–7 (the Bangkok standard rate of electricity has also been used for the other components of the analysis). Further information on alternative electricity providers could be found through a company search, or Government contacts. In terms of supply costs, the relevant supplier could be approached to obtain the information or, alternatively, annual reports may be a useful source of information.

Insurance has been shadow-priced at zero, as the insurance risk has been assumed to be widely spread. This may change over time. An examination of workplace health and safety incidents could be undertaken to find data on accidents in spinning mills to determine whether employee insurance premiums are likely to change. Additionally, insurance costs and shadow-prices have been applied equally across all options. However, Southern Thailand may have peculiarities that warrant different rates being applied. Further research of insurance companies could be undertaken to determine whether insurance premiums in Southern Thailand are higher or lower than those in Bangkok. For example, Southern Thailand may have different rates of crime and weather conditions, factors which may affect an insurance premium.

Interest on Loan

ICP intends to finance 75% of imported spindles and equipment under foreign credit. The interest component of this loan (8%) has not been calculated on a reducing balance.

Profits Tax, Import Duties

Like profits tax, import duties on spindles, ancillary equipment, working capital and imported cotton are assumed to be fixed for the length of the project. However, these rates may change over time. It would be prudent to check with the Government's Treasury to determine whether increases or decreases in taxes/duties are planned or likely over the coming decade, including the introduction of new taxes/duties. Of course if the Government changes, any forecasted rates may also change.

Depreciation

The rules for depreciation are assumed to be fixed (at a rate of 10%). However, it may be useful to check with the appropriate accounting body whether any review of accounting standards is planned for the near future and/or if different depreciation methods are planned to be introduced during the life of the project.

Foreign Exchange Rate

The exchange rate is assumed to be fixed at Bt.44=US$1 for the life of the project. This assumption is correct if exchange rates are fixed in Thailand. If, on the other hand, Thailand has a floating exchange rate, then depending on monetary policy and global impacts, the rate may or may not fluctuate. Again, the sensitivity analysis mitigates against this potential problem.

Sunk Costs

ICP currently incurs 7.5 million Baht per annum in overheads. This can be considered a "sunk cost" and has not been included in the analysis.

Production Capacity

It is assumed that ICP will operate at 50% capacity for the first year and 100% for every year after that. An examination of ICP's business plan and project implementation plan would be prudent to verify these assumptions.

3. ANALYSIS

Each of the four components of the Social Benefit-Cost Analysis is examined separately below, for each Option. The information in this section is taken from Appendix Tables A14.7 to A14.3.

3.1 Project Analysis

Table A14.1: Project Analysis

Discount Rates (for NPV):		4%	8%	12%	16%	20%	RANK	IRR	RANK
	Option 1	405.3	259.8	152.0	70.7	8.3	3	21%	3
BANGKOK	Option 2	568.5	393.4	263.3	164.8	89.0	1	26%	1
	Option 3	405.3	259.8	152.0	70.7	8.3	3	21%	3
	Option 4	341.4	200.9	96.9	18.5	–41.7	4	17%	4
SOUTHERN THAILAND	Option 5	504.5	334.5	208.2	112.6	39.1	2	23%	2
	Option 6	341.4	200.9	96.9	18.5	–41.7	4	17%	4
	Option 7	504.5	334.5	208.2	112.6	39.1	2	23%	2

From the market perspective, Option 2 is preferred over the other options, with Options 5 and 7 ranked equal second. This is the case for both the NPV and IRR calculations. NPVs for all Options are positive, except for Options 4 and 6 when a discount rate of 20% is used. This is because the IRR for those Options is 17%.

3.2 Private Analysis

Table A14.2: Private Analysis

Discount Rates (for NPV):		4%	8%	12%	16%	20%	RANK	IRR	RANK
	Option 1	154.5	88.7	40.8	5.4	−21.1	6	17%	6
BANGKOK	Option 2	236.1	155.4	96.4	52.5	19.2	4	23%	3
	Option 3	361.2	252.9	173.3	113.8	68.6	2	29%	2
	Option 4	119.1	53.7	6.2	−28.9	−55.2	7	13%	7
SOUTHERN THAILAND	Option 5	200.7	120.5	61.8	18.2	−14.8	5	18%	5
	Option 6	296.7	194.0	118.6	62.4	19.8	3	22%	4
	Option 7	459.9	327.5	229.9	156.5	100.5	1	31%	1

Not surprisingly, Option 7 is the most favourable option for ICP. This is because the costs of relocating to Southern Thailand are outweighed by the benefits of not having to pay profits tax or import duty on imported cotton. Option 3 is the next best option for ICP. Deciding on the third ranking is different when comparing the NPV and IRR results for Options 2 and 6. This is due to a phenomenon called "switching", which occurs because the NPV curves of these mutually exclusive projects cross one another.

It is not possible to determine precisely whether ICP would prefer Option 2 over Option 6 and *vice versa* because information on the cost of capital has not been supplied. If the cost of capital is greater than 20.27%, then Option 2 would be preferred over Option 6; and if the cost of capital is less than 20.27%, then Option 6 would be preferred to Option 2. The easiest way of obtaining this information would be to approach ICP directly. However, in the absence of that information, the NPV decision-rule is preferred over the IRR rule and so Option 6 is preferred over Option 2. Just as Option 7 was not a surprising first choice, neither is Option 4 for last place, with additional costs, no concessionary benefits and negative NPVs at discount rates of 16% and 20%.

3.3 Efficiency Analysis

Table A14.3: Efficiency Analysis

Discount Rates (for NPV):		4%	8%	12%	16%	20%	RANK	IRR	RANK
	Option 1	408.9	269.8	166.6	88.7	28.9		22%	
BANGKOK	Option 2	408.9	269.8	166.6	88.7	28.9	2	22%	2
	Option 3	408.9	269.8	166.6	88.7	28.9		22%	
	Option 4	408.1	271.4	170.1	93.6	39.4		23%	
SOUTHERN THAILAND	Option 5	408.1	271.4	170.1	93.6	39.4	1	23%	1
	Option 6	408.1	271.4	170.1	93.6	39.4		23%	
	Option 7	408.1	271.4	170.1	93.6	39.4		23%	

All Options involve efficient allocation of resources across all groups impacted by the proposal, with the Southern Thailand Options ranking slightly higher than the Bangkok Options. Of course, this analysis does not take into account any distributional effects.

3.4 Referent Group Analysis

Table A14.4: Referent Group Analysis

Discount Rates (for NPV):		4%	8%	12%	16%	20%	RANK (not 20%)	IRR
	Option 1	236.0	181.1	141.4	112.1	90.2	2	N/A
BANGKOK	Option 2	154.5	114.3	85.7	65.0	49.8	4	N/A
	Option 3	29.3	16.9	8.9	3.7	0.5	6	N/A
	Option 4	270.1	217.7	179.9	152.1	131.4	1	N/A
SOUTHERN THAILAND	Option 5	188.5	150.9	124.3	105.0	91.0	3	N/A
	Option 6	92.5	77.5	67.5	60.9	56.4	5	N/A
	Option 7	−70.7	−56.1	−43.8	−33.3	−24.3	7	N/A

As would be expected, the Option that ranked lowest in the Private Analysis (Option 4) is ranked first in the Referent Group Analysis: not only will the Government enjoy receiving cotton import duties and profits tax under this Option, but many unskilled workers will earn significantly more than they currently do. Conversely, Option 7 (ICP's highest ranked Option) will be disastrous for the Referent Group, with negative NPVs for all discount rates.

It is noted that the NPV rankings are consistent for all discount rates except 20%. Again, by plotting the NPV curves, it would be possible to observe that they cross at different points, explaining this anomaly.

IRRs are not applicable because the net benefit streams for all the referent group analyses have more than one change of sign (i.e. positive, negative, positive), leading to an inaccurate result. The reason for this sign change is due to negative cash flows for the domestic bank and the Government in 2000 (all other cash flows are positive) for the referent group members.

4. CONCLUSION

Based on the data from the analyses, Options 4 and 7 can clearly be rejected. Option 4 offers the best outcome for the referent group, but offers ICP no incentive and is ranked last in terms of the Private analysis. Conversely Option 7 is clearly unacceptable to the referent group. Option 2, however, warrants serious consideration. This Option: Bangkok – No Duties on Imported Cotton satisfies ICP's request to receive one concession if it invests in the Bangkok area. It is ranked fourth in both the Private and Referent Group analyses and, although in terms of the Efficiency analysis it is not as efficient as any of the Southern Thailand options, the differences between Options 1-3 and Options 4–7 in efficiency terms are relatively small (IRR 22% compared to IRR 23%). Option 2 is also preferred over Option 3 (which also satisfies ICP's request for a concession). Option 3 is ranked sixth in the Referent Group ranking.

Unless ICP can be convinced to accept Option 5 (ranked fifth from ICP's perspective and third from Thailand's perspective), none of the Southern Thailand options seem likely. A further alternative that could be considered is subsidizing ICP for some or all of the costs to move the spinning mill to Southern Thailand. This could potentially be coupled with a reduction in import duties on raw materials. Moving to Southern Thailand involves an additional injection of up-front funds in 1999 which are not discounted. It can be seen from the Private Cash Flows in Tables A14.7 and A14.10 that the costs to ICP between 2001 and 2004 are less in Southern Thailand than in Bangkok. However, to determine whether or not other options are viable, further detailed analysis and direction from the Minister would be required.

Therefore, Option 2 is the recommended Option.

Table A14.5 Summary Information

SUMMARY INFORMATION

Net Present Values

	Discount Rates	Project					Private					Efficiency					Referent				
		4%	8%	12%	16%	20%	4%	8%	12%	16%	20%	4%	8%	12%	16%	20%	4%	8%	12%	16%	20%
Bangkok	Option 1	405.3	259.8	152.0	70.7	8.3	154.5	88.7	40.8	5.4	-21.1	408.9	269.8	166.6	88.7	28.9	236.0	181.1	141.4	112.1	90.2
	Option 2	568.5	393.4	263.3	164.8	89.0	236.1	155.4	96.4	52.5	19.2	408.9	269.8	166.6	88.7	28.9	154.5	114.3	85.7	66.0	49.8
	Option 3	405.3	259.8	152.0	70.7	8.3	361.2	252.9	173.3	113.8	68.6	408.9	269.8	166.6	88.7	28.9	29.3	16.9	8.9	3.7	0.5
Southern	Option 4	341.4	200.9	96.9	18.5	-41.7	119.1	53.7	6.2	-28.9	-55.2	408.1	271.4	170.1	93.6	34.9	270.1	217.7	179.9	152.1	131.4
	Option 5	504.5	334.5	208.2	112.6	39.1	200.7	120.5	61.8	18.2	-14.8	408.1	271.4	170.1	93.6	34.9	188.5	150.9	124.3	105.0	91.0
Thailand	Option 6	341.4	200.9	96.9	18.5	-41.7	296.7	194.0	118.6	62.4	19.8	408.1	271.4	170.1	93.6	34.9	92.5	77.5	67.5	60.9	56.4
	Option 7	504.5	334.5	208.2	112.6	39.1	459.9	327.5	229.9	156.5	100.5	408.1	271.4	170.1	93.6	34.9	-70.7	-56.1	-43.8	-33.3	-24.3

Internal Rates of Return

		Project	Private	Efficiency	Referent
Bangkok	Option 1	21%	17%	22%	N/A
	Option 2	26%	23%	22%	N/A
	Option 3	21%	29%	22%	N/A
Southern	Option 4	17%	13%	23%	N/A
	Option 5	23%	18%	23%	N/A
Thailand	Option 6	17%	22%	23%	N/A
	Option 7	23%	31%	23%	N/A

Table A14.6 Option 1: Bangkok – No Concessions – Key Variables

OPTION 1 (BANGKOK - NO CONCESSIONS): KEY VARIABLES						

Exchange Rate Bt/1US$	44					
ICP Capacity (lbs of yarn)	15,000,000					
ICP demand for yarn (lbs)	10,000,000					
ICP yarn for sale (lbs)	5,000,000					

Capacity Output		Discount Rates				
1999	nil	1	4%			
2000	50%	2	8%			
2001-2009	100%	3	12%			
		4	16%			
		5	20%			

REVENUES

	Rates	Cost Savings	Yarn Sales			
CIF price of yarn/lb ($US)	0.58					
CIF price of yarn/lb (Bt)	25.52	255,200,000	127,600,000			
Import Duty/lb yarn (Bt)	2.10	21,000,000	10,500,000			
Cstms Charges/lb yarn (Bt	0.30	3,000,000	1,500,000			
TOTAL		279,200,000	139,600,000			

INVESTMENT COSTS: BANGKOK

		No. (units)	Cost (US$)	Cost (Bt)	Import Duty	Total Cost (Bt)	Shadow Price
Fixed Investment	*[1999]*						
Spindles		40,000	4,000,000	176,000,000	5%	184,800,000	176,000,000
Ancillary equipment			850,000	37,400,000	5%	39,270,000	37,400,000
Installation	(skilled)		100,000	4,400,000		4,400,000	4,400,000
Building Construction	(unskilled)		818,182	36,000,000		36,000,000	18,000,000
Start-up Costs	(skilled)		409,091	18,000,000		18,000,000	18,000,000
TOTAL						282,470,000	253,800,000

Working Capital	*[2000]*						
3 months' raw materials			1,200,000	52,800,000	10%	58,080,000	52,800,000
1 year's spare parts			243,000	10,692,000	5%	11,226,600	10,692,000
TOTAL						69,306,600	63,492,000

OPERATING COSTS: BANGKOK

Note: water, power and raw materials cost 50% in 2000, with all other costs 100%.		No.	Cost (US$)	Cost (Bt)	Import Duty	Total Cost (Bt)	
Raw Materials	*[2000 on]*		0.30				
Imported Cotton (lbs)		16,200,000	4,860,000	213,840,000	10%	235,224,000	

		No.	Cost p.a (Bt)	Total Cost (Bt)	Bangkok Shadow Price		
Labour	*[2000 on]*	(employees)	(/employee)		50%		
Supervisors & Technicians		100	150,000	15,000,000	15,000,000		
Other Skilled Workers		1,000	22,500	22,500,000	22,500,000		
Unskilled Workers		500	12,000	6,000,000	3,000,000		
TOTAL		1,600		43,500,000	40,500,000		

Fuel, Water, Spare Parts	*[2000 on]*	(lbs of yarn)	(/million lbs)		50%		
Water		15,000,000	480,000	7,200,000	7,200,000		
Electricity		15,000,000	480,000	7,200,000	3,600,000		
TOTAL				14,400,000	10,800,000		

Spare Parts			10%	22,407,000	21,340,000		
(% of equipment + 5% duty)	*[2000 on]*						
TOTAL				22,407,000	21,340,000		

Insurance and Rent							
Insurance	*[2000 on]*			3,000,000	0		
Rent	*[2000 on]*			3,000,000	3,000,000		
TOTAL				6,000,000	3,000,000		

FINANCING

		Amount (Bt)	Interest (p/a)	Term (yrs)	Interest on O'Draft		
Loan for Spindles & Equip	*foreign*	160,050,000	8%	5			
Working Capital Overdraft	*local*	60,000,000	10%	9	-6,000,000		

TAXES & DEPRECIATION

		Rate (%)	Initial Fxd Inv Costs	Dep'n Expense			
Profits Tax		50%					
Depreciation	*[2000 on]*	10%	264,470,000	26,447,000			

Table A14.7 Option 1: Bangkok – No Concessions

OPTION 1: BANGKOK - NO CONCESSIONS

Project Cash Flow

	1999	2000	2001	2002	2003	2004	2005	2006	2007	2008	2009
Investment Costs											
Fixed Investment	-282.5										
Working Capital		-69.3									69.3
TOTAL	-282.5	-69.3	0.0	0.0	0.0	0.0	0.0	0.0	0.0	0.0	69.3
Operating Costs											
Raw Materials		-117.6	-235.2	-235.2	-235.2	-235.2	-235.2	-235.2	-235.2	-235.2	-235.2
Labour		-43.5	-43.5	-43.5	-43.5	-43.5	-43.5	-43.5	-43.5	-43.5	-43.5
Fuel, Water		-7.2	-14.4	-14.4	-14.4	-14.4	-14.4	-14.4	-14.4	-14.4	-14.4
Spare Parts		-22.4	-22.4	-22.4	-22.4	-22.4	-22.4	-22.4	-22.4	-22.4	-22.4
Insurance and Rent		-6.0	-6.0	-6.0	-6.0	-6.0	-6.0	-6.0	-6.0	-6.0	-6.0
TOTAL		-196.7	-321.5	-321.5	-321.5	-321.5	-321.5	-321.5	-321.5	-321.5	-321.5
Revenues											
Cost Savings		139.6	279.2	279.2	279.2	279.2	279.2	279.2	279.2	279.2	279.2
Yarn Sales		69.8	139.6	139.6	139.6	139.6	139.6	139.6	139.6	139.6	139.6
TOTAL		209.4	418.8	418.8	418.8	418.8	418.8	418.8	418.8	418.8	418.8
NET CASH FLOW	-282.5	-56.6	97.3	97.3	97.3	97.3	97.3	97.3	97.3	97.3	166.6

Discount Rates	4%	8%	12%	16%	20%
NPV	405.3	259.8	152.0	70.7	8.3
IRR	21%				

Private Cash Flow

		1	2	3	4	5	6	7	8	9	10
FINANCING	1999	2000	2001	2002	2003	2004	2005	2006	2007	2008	2009
Principal											
Loan	160.1	-27.3	-29.5	-31.8	-34.4	-37.1					
Overdraft		60.0									-60.0
Interest											
Loan		-12.8	-10.6	-8.3	-5.7	-3.0					
Overdraft			-6.0	-6.0	-6.0	-6.0	-6.0	-6.0	-6.0	-6.0	-6.0
NET FINANCING FLOW	160.1	19.9	-46.1	-46.1	-46.1	-46.1	-6.0	-6.0	-6.0	-6.0	-66.0
NCF (Equity, Pre-Tax)	-122.4	-36.7	51.2	51.2	51.2	51.2	91.3	91.3	91.3	91.3	100.6
TAXES											
Revenues		209.4	418.8	418.8	418.8	418.8	418.8	418.8	418.8	418.8	418.8
Operating Costs		-196.7	-321.5	-321.5	-321.5	-321.5	-321.5	-321.5	-321.5	-321.5	-321.5
Depreciation		-26.4	-26.4	-26.4	-26.4	-26.4	-26.4	-26.4	-26.4	-26.4	-26.4
Interest on Loans		-12.8	-16.6	-14.3	-11.7	-9.0	-6.0	-6.0	-6.0	-6.0	-6.0
PROFITS BEFORE TAX		-26.6	54.2	56.6	59.1	61.9	64.8	64.8	64.8	64.8	64.8
TAX CASH FLOWS		13.3	-27.1	-28.3	-29.6	-30.9	-32.4	-32.4	-32.4	-32.4	-32.4
EQUITY AFTER TAX											
PRIVATE CASH FLOW	-122.4	-23.4	24.1	22.9	21.6	20.3	58.9	58.9	58.9	58.9	68.2

Discount Rates	4%	8%	12%	16%	20%
NPV	154.5	88.7	40.8	5.4	-21.1
IRR	17%				

Table A14.7 (cont.)

OPTION 1(cont.): BANGKOK - NO CONCESSION

Efficiency Analysis

	1999	2000	2001	2002	2003	2004	2005	2006	2007	2008	2009
INPUTS											
Investment Costs											
Fixed Investment	-253.8										
Working Capital		-63.5									63.5
TOTAL	**-253.8**	**-63.5**	**0.0**	**0.0**	**0.0**	**0.0**	**0.0**	**0.0**	**0.0**	**0.0**	**63.5**
Operating Costs											
Raw Materials		-106.9	-213.8	-213.8	-213.8	-213.8	-213.8	-213.8	-213.8	-213.8	-213.8
Labour		-40.5	-40.5	-40.5	-40.5	-40.5	-40.5	-40.5	-40.5	-40.5	-40.5
Fuel, Water		-5.4	-10.8	-10.8	-10.8	-10.8	-10.8	-10.8	-10.8	-10.8	-10.8
Spare Parts		-21.3	-21.3	-21.3	-21.3	-21.3	-21.3	-21.3	-21.3	-21.3	-21.3
Insurance and Rent		-3.0	-3.0	-3.0	-3.0	-3.0	-3.0	-3.0	-3.0	-3.0	-3.0
TOTAL		**-177.2**	**-289.5**	**-289.5**	**-289.5**	**-289.5**	**-289.5**	**-289.5**	**-289.5**	**-289.5**	**-289.5**
OUTPUTS											
Revenues											
Cost Savings		127.6	255.2	255.2	255.2	255.2	255.2	255.2	255.2	255.2	255.2
Yarn Sales		63.8	127.6	127.6	127.6	127.6	127.6	127.6	127.6	127.6	127.6
TOTAL		**191.4**	**382.8**	**382.8**	**382.8**	**382.8**	**382.8**	**382.8**	**382.8**	**382.8**	**382.8**
EFFICIENCY ANALYSIS	**-253.8**	**-49.3**	**93.3**	**93.3**	**93.3**	**93.3**	**93.3**	**93.3**	**93.3**	**93.3**	**156.8**

Discount Rates	4%	8%	12%	16%	20%
NPV	408.9	269.8	166.6	88.7	28.9
IRR	22%				

Referent Group Analysis

METHOD A:

	1999	2000	2001	2002	2003	2004	2005	2006	2007	2008	2009
Domestic Bank											
Overdraft	-60.0										60.0
Interest from Overdraft		6.0	6.0	6.0	6.0	6.0	6.0	6.0	6.0	6.0	6.0
Thai Government											
Lost Import Duties		-18.0	-36.0	-36.0	-36.0	-36.0	-36.0	-36.0	-36.0	-36.0	-36.0
Spindles I.Duty	8.8										
Equipment I.Duty	1.9										
WCap Raw Materials I.Duty		5.3									-5.3
WCap Spare Parts I.Duty		0.5									-0.5
Imported Cotton I.Duty		10.7	21.4	21.4	21.4	21.4	21.4	21.4	21.4	21.4	21.4
Spare Parts Duty		1.1	1.1	1.1	1.1	1.1	1.1	1.1	1.1	1.1	1.1
Profits Tax		-13.3	27.1	28.3	29.6	30.9	32.4	32.4	32.4	32.4	32.4
Domestic Labour											
Initial Labour	18.0										
Ongoing Labour		3.0	3.0	3.0	3.0	3.0	3.0	3.0	3.0	3.0	3.0
Domestic Electricity Corp											
Electricity		1.8	3.6	3.6	3.6	3.6	3.6	3.6	3.6	3.6	3.6
Domestic Insurance Co											
Insurance		3.0	3.0	3.0	3.0	3.0	3.0	3.0	3.0	3.0	3.0
TOTAL	**28.7**	**-65.9**	**29.2**	**30.3**	**31.6**	**33.0**	**34.5**	**34.5**	**34.5**	**34.5**	**88.6**

METHOD B:

	1999	2000	2001	2002	2003	2004	2005	2006	2007	2008	2009
Efficiency Analysis	-253.8	-49.3	93.3	93.3	93.3	93.3	93.3	93.3	93.3	93.3	156.8
Less Non-Referent Grp											
ICP	-122.4	-23.4	24.1	22.9	21.6	20.3	58.9	58.9	58.9	58.9	68.2
Foreign Credit - Principal	-160.1	27.3	29.5	31.8	34.4	37.1					
Foreign Credit - Interest		12.8	10.6	8.3	5.7	3.0					
TOTAL	**28.7**	**-65.9**	**29.2**	**30.3**	**31.6**	**33.0**	**34.5**	**34.5**	**34.5**	**34.5**	**88.6**

Discount Rates	4%	8%	12%	16%	20%
NPV	236.0	181.1	141.4	112.1	90.2
IRR	N/A				

Table A14.8 Option 2: Bangkok – No Duties

OPTION 2: BANGKOK - NO DUTIES										
Project Cash Flow										
	1999	2000	2001	2002	2003	2004	2005	2006	2007	2008	2009
Investment Costs											
Fixed Investment	-282.5										
Working Capital		-69.3									69.3
TOTAL	-282.5	-69.3	0.0	0.0	0.0	0.0	0.0	0.0	0.0	0.0	69.3
Operating Costs											
Raw Materials		-106.9	-213.8	-213.8	-213.8	-213.8	-213.8	-213.8	-213.8	-213.8	-213.8
Labour		-43.5	-43.5	-43.5	-43.5	-43.5	-43.5	-43.5	-43.5	-43.5	-43.5
Fuel, Water		-7.2	-14.4	-14.4	-14.4	-14.4	-14.4	-14.4	-14.4	-14.4	-14.4
Spare Parts		-22.4	-22.4	-22.4	-22.4	-22.4	-22.4	-22.4	-22.4	-22.4	-22.4
Insurance and Rent		-6.0	-6.0	-6.0	-6.0	-6.0	-6.0	-6.0	-6.0	-6.0	-6.0
TOTAL		-186.0	-300.1	-300.1	-300.1	-300.1	-300.1	-300.1	-300.1	-300.1	-300.1
Revenues											
Cost Savings		139.6	279.2	279.2	279.2	279.2	279.2	279.2	279.2	279.2	279.2
Yarn Sales		69.8	139.6	139.6	139.6	139.6	139.6	139.6	139.6	139.6	139.6
TOTAL		209.4	418.8	418.8	418.8	418.8	418.8	418.8	418.8	418.8	418.8
NET CASH FLOW	-282.5	-45.9	118.7	118.7	118.7	118.7	118.7	118.7	118.7	118.7	188.0

Discount Rates	4%	8%	12%	16%	20%
NPV	568.5	393.4	263.3	164.8	89.0
IRR	26%				

Private Cash Flow										
		1	2	3	4	5	6	7	8	9	10
FINANCING	1999	2000	2001	2002	2003	2004	2005	2006	2007	2008	2009
Principal											
Loan	160.1	-27.3	-29.5	-31.8	-34.4	-37.1					
Overdraft		60.0									-60.0
Interest											
Loan		-12.8	-10.6	-8.3	-5.7	-3.0					
Overdraft			-6.0	-6.0	-6.0	-6.0	-6.0	-6.0	-6.0	-6.0	-6.0
NET FINANCING FLOW	160.1	19.9	-46.1	-46.1	-46.1	-46.1	-6.0	-6.0	-6.0	-6.0	-66.0
NCF (Equity, Pre-Tax)	-122.4	-26.0	72.6	72.6	72.6	72.6	112.7	112.7	112.7	112.7	122.0
TAXES											
Revenues		209.4	418.8	418.8	418.8	418.8	418.8	418.8	418.8	418.8	418.8
Operating Costs		-186.0	-300.1	-300.1	-300.1	-300.1	-300.1	-300.1	-300.1	-300.1	-300.1
Depreciation		-26.4	-26.4	-26.4	-26.4	-26.4	-26.4	-26.4	-26.4	-26.4	-26.4
Interest on Loans		-12.8	-16.6	-14.3	-11.7	-9.0	-6.0	-6.0	-6.0	-6.0	-6.0
PROFITS BEFORE TAX		-15.9	75.6	77.9	80.5	83.2	86.2	86.2	86.2	86.2	86.2
TAX CASH FLOWS		7.9	-37.8	-39.0	-40.2	-41.6	-43.1	-43.1	-43.1	-43.1	-43.1
EQUITY AFTER TAX											
PRIVATE CASH FLOW	-122.4	-18.1	34.8	33.6	32.3	30.9	69.6	69.6	69.6	69.6	78.9

Discount Rates	4%	8%	12%	16%	20%
NPV	236.1	155.4	96.4	52.5	19.2
IRR	23%				

Table A14.8 (cont.)

OPTION 2 (cont.): BANGKOK - NO DUTIES

Efficiency Analysis

	1999	2000	2001	2002	2003	2004	2005	2006	2007	2008	2009
INPUTS											
Investment Costs											
Fixed Investment	-253.8										
Working Capital		-63.5									63.5
TOTAL	**-253.8**	**-63.5**	**0.0**	**0.0**	**0.0**	**0.0**	**0.0**	**0.0**	**0.0**	**0.0**	**63.5**
Operating Costs											
Raw Materials		-106.9	-213.8	-213.8	-213.8	-213.8	-213.8	-213.8	-213.8	-213.8	-213.8
Labour		-40.5	-40.5	-40.5	-40.5	-40.5	-40.5	-40.5	-40.5	-40.5	-40.5
Fuel, Water		-5.4	-10.8	-10.8	-10.8	-10.0	-10.8	-10.8	-10.8	-10.8	-10.8
Spare Parts		-21.3	-21.3	-21.3	-21.3	-21.3	-21.3	-21.3	-21.3	-21.3	-21.3
Insurance and Rent		-3.0	-3.0	-3.0	-3.0	-3.0	-3.0	-3.0	-3.0	-3.0	-3.0
TOTAL		**-177.2**	**-289.5**	**-289.5**	**-289.5**	**-289.5**	**-289.5**	**-289.5**	**-289.5**	**-289.5**	**289.5**
OUTPUTS											
Revenues											
Cost Savings		127.6	255.2	255.2	255.2	255.2	255.2	255.2	255.2	255.2	255.2
Yarn Sales		63.8	127.6	127.6	127.6	127.6	127.6	127.6	127.6	127.6	127.6
TOTAL		**191.4**	**382.8**	**382.8**	**382.8**	**382.8**	**382.8**	**382.8**	**382.8**	**382.8**	**382.8**
EFFICIENCY ANALYSIS	**-253.8**	**-49.3**	**93.3**	**93.3**	**93.3**	**93.3**	**93.3**	**93.3**	**93.3**	**93.3**	**156.8**

Discount Rates	4%	8%	12%	16%	20%
NPV	408.9	269.8	166.6	88.7	28.9
IRR	22%				

Referent Group Analysis

METHOD A:

	1999	2000	2001	2002	2003	2004	2005	2006	2007	2008	2009
Domestic Bank											
Overdraft		-60.0									60.0
Interest from Overdraft			6.0	6.0	6.0	6.0	6.0	6.0	6.0	6.0	6.0
Thai Government											
Lost Import Duties		-18.0	-36.0	-36.0	-36.0	-36.0	-36.0	-36.0	-36.0	-36.0	-36.0
Spindles I.Duty	8.8										
Equipment I.Duty	1.9										
WCap Raw Materials I.Duty		5.3									-5.3
WCap Spare Parts I.Duty		0.5									-0.5
Imported Cotton I.Duty		0.0	0.0	0.0	0.0	0.0	0.0	0.0	0.0	0.0	0.0
Spare Parts Duty		1.1	1.1	1.1	1.1	1.1	1.1	1.1	1.1	1.1	1.1
Profits Tax		-7.9	37.8	39.0	40.2	41.6	43.1	43.1	43.1	43.1	43.1
Domestic Labour											
Initial Labour	18.0										
Ongoing Labour		3.0	3.0	3.0	3.0	3.0	3.0	3.0	3.0	3.0	3.0
Domestic Electricity Corp											
Electricity		1.8	3.6	3.6	3.6	3.6	3.6	3.6	3.6	3.6	3.6
Domestic Insurance Co											
Insurance		3.0	3.0	3.0	3.0	3.0	3.0	3.0	3.0	3.0	3.0
TOTAL	**28.7**	**-71.3**	**18.5**	**19.6**	**20.9**	**22.3**	**23.8**	**23.8**	**23.8**	**23.8**	**78.0**

METHOD B:

	1999	2000	2001	2002	2003	2004	2005	2006	2007	2008	2009
Efficiency Analysis	-253.8	-49.3	93.3	93.3	93.3	93.3	93.3	93.3	93.3	93.3	156.8
Less Non-Referent Grp											
ICP	-122.4	-18.1	34.8	33.6	32.3	30.9	69.6	69.6	69.6	69.6	78.9
Foreign Credit - Principal	-160.1	27.3	29.5	31.8	34.4	37.1					
Foreign Credit - Interest		12.8	10.6	8.3	5.7	3.0					
TOTAL	**28.7**	**-71.3**	**18.5**	**19.6**	**20.9**	**22.3**	**23.8**	**23.8**	**23.8**	**23.8**	**78.0**

Discount Rates	4%	8%	12%	16%	20%
NPV	154.5	114.3	85.7	65.0	49.8
IRR	N/A				

Table A14.9 Option 3: Bangkok – No Profits Tax

OPTION 3: BANGKOK - NO PROFITS TAX

Project Cash Flow

	1999	2000	2001	2002	2003	2004	2005	2006	2007	2008	2009
Investment Costs											
Fixed Investment	-282.5										
Working Capital		-69.3									69.3
TOTAL	-282.5	-69.3	0.0	0.0	0.0	0.0	0.0	0.0	0.0	0.0	69.3
Operating Costs											
Raw Materials		-117.6	-235.2	-235.2	-235.2	-235.2	-235.2	-235.2	-235.2	-235.2	-235.2
Labour		-43.5	-43.5	-43.5	-43.5	-43.5	-43.5	-43.5	-43.5	-43.5	-43.5
Fuel, Water		-7.2	-14.4	-14.4	-14.4	-14.4	-14.4	-14.4	-14.4	-14.4	-14.4
Spare Parts		-22.4	-22.4	-22.4	-22.4	-22.4	-22.4	-22.4	-22.4	-22.4	-22.4
Insurance and Rent		-6.0	-6.0	-6.0	-6.0	-6.0	-6.0	-6.0	-6.0	-6.0	-6.0
TOTAL		-196.7	-321.5	-321.5	-321.5	-321.5	-321.5	-321.5	-321.5	-321.5	-321.5
Revenues											
Cost Savings		139.6	279.2	279.2	279.2	279.2	279.2	279.2	279.2	279.2	279.2
Yarn Sales		69.8	139.6	139.6	139.6	139.6	139.6	139.6	139.6	139.6	139.6
TOTAL		209.4	418.8	418.8	418.8	418.8	418.8	418.8	418.8	418.8	418.8
NET CASH FLOW	-282.5	-56.6	97.3	97.3	97.3	97.3	97.3	97.3	97.3	97.3	166.6

Discount Rates	4%	8%	12%	16%	20%
NPV	405.3	259.8	152.0	70.7	8.3
IRR	21%				

Private Cash Flow

	1	2	3	4	5	6	7	8	9	10
FINANCING	1999	2000	2001	2002	2003	2004	2005	2006	2007	2008	2009
Principal											
Loan	160.1	-27.3	-29.5	-31.8	-34.4	-37.1					
Overdraft		60.0									-60.0
Interest											
Loan		-12.8	-10.6	-8.3	-5.7	-3.0					
Overdraft			-6.0	-6.0	-6.0	-6.0	-6.0	-6.0	-6.0	-6.0	-6.0
NET FINANCING FLOW	160.1	19.9	-46.1	-46.1	-46.1	-46.1	-6.0	-6.0	-6.0	-6.0	-66.0
NCF (Equity, Pre-Tax)	-122.4	-36.7	51.2	51.2	51.2	51.2	91.3	91.3	91.3	91.3	100.6
TAXES											
Revenues		209.4	418.8	418.8	418.8	418.8	418.8	418.8	418.8	418.8	418.8
Operating Costs		-196.7	-321.5	-321.5	-321.5	-321.5	-321.5	-321.5	-321.5	-321.5	-321.5
Depreciation		-26.4	-26.4	-26.4	-26.4	-26.4	-26.4	-26.4	-26.4	-26.4	-26.4
Interest on Loans		-12.8	-16.6	-14.3	-11.7	-9.0	-6.0	-6.0	-6.0	-6.0	-6.0
PROFITS BEFORE TAX		-26.6	54.2	56.6	59.1	61.9	64.8	64.8	64.8	64.8	64.8
TAX CASH FLOWS		0.0	0.0	0.0	0.0	0.0	0.0	0.0	0.0	0.0	0.0
EQUITY AFTER TAX											
PRIVATE CASH FLOW	-122.4	-36.7	51.2	51.2	51.2	51.2	91.3	91.3	91.3	91.3	100.6

Discount Rates	4%	8%	12%	16%	20%
NPV	361.2	252.9	173.3	113.8	68.6
IRR	29%				

Table A14.9 (cont.)

OPTION 3: BANGKOK - NO PROFITS TAX

Efficiency Analysis

	1999	2000	2001	2002	2003	2004	2005	2006	2007	2008	2009
INPUTS											
Investment Costs											
Fixed Investment	-253.8										
Working Capital		-63.5									63.5
TOTAL	**-253.8**	**-63.5**	**0.0**	**0.0**	**0.0**	**0.0**	**0.0**	**0.0**	**0.0**	**0.0**	**63.5**
Operating Costs											
Raw Materials		-106.9	-213.8	-213.8	-213.8	-213.8	-213.8	-213.8	-213.8	-213.8	-213.8
Labour		-40.5	-40.5	-40.5	-40.5	-40.5	-40.5	-40.5	-40.5	-40.5	-40.5
Fuel, Water		-5.4	-10.8	-10.8	-10.8	-10.8	-10.8	-10.8	-10.8	-10.8	-10.8
Spare Parts		-21.3	-21.3	-21.3	-21.3	-21.3	-21.3	-21.3	-21.3	-21.3	-21.3
Insurance and Rent		-3.0	-3.0	-3.0	-3.0	-3.0	-3.0	-3.0	-3.0	-3.0	-3.0
TOTAL		**-177.2**	**-289.5**	**-289.5**	**-289.5**	**-289.5**	**-289.5**	**-289.5**	**-289.5**	**-289.5**	**-289.5**
OUTPUTS											
Revenues											
Cost Savings		127.6	255.2	255.2	255.2	255.2	255.2	255.2	255.2	255.2	255.2
Yarn Sales		63.8	127.6	127.6	127.6	127.6	127.6	127.6	127.6	127.6	127.6
TOTAL		**191.4**	**382.8**	**382.8**	**382.8**	**382.8**	**382.8**	**382.8**	**382.8**	**382.8**	**382.8**
EFFICIENCY ANALYSIS	**-253.8**	**-49.3**	**93.3**	**93.3**	**93.3**	**93.3**	**93.3**	**93.3**	**93.3**	**93.3**	**156.8**

Discount Rates	4%	8%	12%	16%	20%
NPV	408.9	269.8	166.6	88.7	28.9
IRR	22%				

Referent Group Analysis

METHOD A:

	1999	2000	2001	2002	2003	2004	2005	2006	2007	2008	2009
Domestic Bank											
Overdraft		-60.0									60.0
Interest from Overdraft			6.0	6.0	6.0	6.0	6.0	6.0	6.0	6.0	6.0
Thai Government											
Lost Import Duties		-18.0	-36.0	-36.0	-36.0	-36.0	-36.0	-36.0	-36.0	-36.0	-36.0
Spindles I.Duty	8.8										
Equipment I.Duty	1.9										
WCap Raw Materials I.Duty		5.3									-5.3
WCap Spare Parts I.Duty		0.5									-0.5
Imported Cotton I.Duty		10.7	21.4	21.4	21.4	21.4	21.4	21.4	21.4	21.4	21.4
Spare Parts Duty		1.1	1.1	1.1	1.1	1.1	1.1	1.1	1.1	1.1	1.1
Profits Tax		0.0	0.0	0.0	0.0	0.0	0.0	0.0	0.0	0.0	0.0
Domestic Labour											
Initial Labour	18.0										
Ongoing Labour		3.0	3.0	3.0	3.0	3.0	3.0	3.0	3.0	3.0	3.0
Domestic Electricity Corp											
Electricity		1.8	3.6	3.6	3.6	3.6	3.6	3.6	3.6	3.6	3.6
Domestic Insurance Co											
Insurance		3.0	3.0	3.0	3.0	3.0	3.0	3.0	3.0	3.0	3.0
TOTAL	**28.7**	**-52.6**	**2.1**	**2.1**	**2.1**	**2.1**	**2.1**	**2.1**	**2.1**	**2.1**	**56.2**

METHOD B:	1999	2000	2001	2002	2003	2004	2005	2006	2007	2008	2009
Efficiency Analysis	-253.8	-49.3	93.3	93.3	93.3	93.3	93.3	93.3	93.3	93.3	156.8
Less Non-Referent Grp											
ICP	-122.4	-36.7	51.2	51.2	51.2	51.2	91.3	91.3	91.3	91.3	100.6
Foreign Credit - Principal	-160.1	27.3	29.5	31.8	34.4	37.1					
Foreign Credit - Interest		12.8	10.6	8.3	5.7	3.0					
TOTAL	**28.7**	**-52.6**	**2.1**	**2.1**	**2.1**	**2.1**	**2.1**	**2.1**	**2.1**	**2.1**	**56.2**

Discount Rates	4%	8%	12%	16%	20%
NPV	29.3	16.9	8.9	3.7	0.5
IRR	N/A				

Table A14.10 Option 4: Southern Thailand – No Concessions

OPTION 4: SOUTHERN THAILAND - NO CONCESSIONS

Project Cash Flow

	1999	2000	2001	2002	2003	2004	2005	2006	2007	2008	2009
Investment Costs											
Fixed Investment	-318.8										
Working Capital		-69.3									69.3
TOTAL	-318.8	-69.3	0.0	0.0	0.0	0.0	0.0	0.0	0.0	0.0	69.3
Operating Costs											
Raw Materials		-117.6	-235.2	-235.2	-235.2	-235.2	-235.2	-235.2	-235.2	-235.2	-235.2
Transport		-1.9	-3.8	-3.8	-3.8	-3.8	-3.8	-3.8	-3.8	-3.8	-3.8
Labour		-42.8	-42.8	-42.8	-42.8	-42.8	-42.8	-42.8	-42.8	-42.8	-42.8
Fuel, Water		-7.2	-14.4	-14.4	-14.4	-14.4	-14.4	-14.4	-14.4	-14.4	-14.4
Spare Parts		-23.0	-23.0	-23.0	-23.0	-23.0	-23.0	-23.0	-23.0	-23.0	-23.0
Insurance and Rent		-6.0	-6.0	-6.0	-6.0	-6.0	-6.0	-6.0	-6.0	-6.0	-6.0
TOTAL		-198.5	-325.2	-325.2	-325.2	-325.2	-325.2	-325.2	-325.2	-325.2	-325.2
Revenues											
Cost Savings		139.6	279.2	279.2	279.2	279.2	279.2	279.2	279.2	279.2	279.2
Yarn Sales		69.8	139.6	139.6	139.6	139.6	139.6	139.6	139.6	139.6	139.6
TOTAL		209.4	418.8	418.8	418.8	418.8	418.8	418.8	418.8	418.8	418.8
NET CASH FLOW	-318.8	-58.4	93.6	93.6	93.6	93.6	93.6	93.6	93.6	93.6	162.9

Discount Rates	4%	8%	12%	16%	20%
NPV	341.4	200.9	96.9	18.5	-41.7
IRR	17%				

Private Cash Flow

		1	2	3	4	5	6	7	8	9	10
FINANCING	1999	2000	2001	2002	2003	2004	2005	2006	2007	2008	2009
Principal											
Loan	164.6	-28.0	-30.3	-32.7	-35.3	-38.2					
Overdraft		60.0									-60.0
Interest											
Loan		-13.2	-10.9	-8.5	-5.9	-3.1					
Overdraft			-6.0	-6.0	-6.0	-6.0	-6.0	-6.0	-6.0	-6.0	-6.0
NET FINANCING FLOW	164.6	18.8	-47.2	-47.2	-47.2	-47.2	-6.0	-6.0	-6.0	-6.0	-66.0
NCF (Equity, Pre-Tax)	-154.2	-39.6	46.4	46.4	46.4	46.4	87.6	87.6	87.6	87.6	96.9
TAXES											
Revenues		209.4	418.8	418.8	418.8	418.8	418.8	418.8	418.8	418.8	418.8
Operating Costs		-198.5	-325.2	-325.2	-325.2	-325.2	-325.2	-325.2	-325.2	-325.2	-325.2
Depreciation		-30.1	-30.1	-30.1	-30.1	-30.1	-30.1	-30.1	-30.1	-30.1	-30.1
Interest on Loans		-13.2	-16.9	-14.5	-11.9	-9.1	-6.0	-6.0	-6.0	-6.0	-6.0
PROFITS BEFORE TAX		-32.3	46.6	49.1	51.7	54.5	57.6	57.6	57.6	57.6	57.6
TAX CASH FLOWS		16.2	-23.3	-24.5	-25.8	-27.3	-28.8	-28.8	-28.8	-28.8	-28.8
EQUITY AFTER TAX											
PRIVATE CASH FLOW	-154.2	-23.4	23.1	21.9	20.6	19.2	58.9	58.9	58.9	58.9	68.2

Discount Rates	4%	8%	12%	16%	20%
NPV	119.1	53.7	6.2	-28.9	-55.2
IRR	13%				

Table A14.10 (cont.)

OPTION 4 (cont.): SOUTHERN THAILAND - NO CONCESSIONS

Efficiency Analysis

	1999	2000	2001	2002	2003	2004	2005	2006	2007	2008	2009
INPUTS											
Investment Costs											
Fixed Investment	-241.8										
Working Capital		-63.5									63.5
TOTAL	**-241.8**	**-63.5**	**0.0**	**0.0**	**0.0**	**0.0**	**0.0**	**0.0**	**0.0**	**0.0**	**63.5**
Operating Costs											
Raw Materials		-106.9	-213.8	-213.8	-213.8	-213.8	-213.8	-213.8	-213.8	-213.8	-213.8
Transport		-1.9	-3.8	-3.8	-3.8	-3.8	-3.8	-3.8	-3.8	-3.8	-3.8
Labour		-38.0	-38.0	-38.0	-38.0	-38.0	-38.0	-38.0	-38.0	-38.0	-38.0
Fuel, Water		-5.4	-10.8	-10.8	-10.8	-10.8	-10.8	-10.8	-10.8	-10.8	-10.8
Spare Parts		-21.9	-21.9	-21.9	-21.9	-21.9	-21.9	-21.9	-21.9	-21.9	-21.9
Insurance and Rent		-3.0	-3.0	-3.0	-3.0	-3.0	-3.0	-3.0	-3.0	-3.0	-3.0
TOTAL		**-177.1**	**-291.3**	**-291.3**	**-291.3**	**-291.3**	**-291.3**	**-291.3**	**-291.3**	**-291.3**	**-291.3**
OUTPUTS											
Revenues											
Cost Savings		127.6	255.2	255.2	255.2	255.2	255.2	255.2	255.2	255.2	255.2
Yarn Sales		63.8	127.6	127.6	127.6	127.6	127.6	127.6	127.6	127.6	127.6
TOTAL		**191.4**	**382.8**	**382.8**	**382.8**	**382.8**	**382.8**	**382.8**	**382.8**	**382.8**	**382.8**
EFFICIENCY ANALYSIS	**-241.8**	**-49.2**	**91.5**	**91.5**	**91.5**	**91.5**	**91.5**	**91.5**	**91.5**	**91.5**	**155.0**

Discount Rates	4%	8%	12%	16%	20%
NPV	**408.1**	**271.4**	**170.1**	**93.6**	**34.9**
IRR	**23%**				

Referent Group Analysis

METHOD A:

	1999	2000	2001	2002	2003	2004	2005	2006	2007	2008	2009
Domestic Bank											
Overdraft		-60.0									60.0
Interest from Overdraft			6.0	6.0	6.0	6.0	6.0	6.0	6.0	6.0	6.0
Thai Government											
Lost Import Duties		-18.0	-36.0	-36.0	-36.0	-36.0	-36.0	-36.0	-36.0	-36.0	-36.0
Spindles I.Duty	8.8										
Equipment I.Duty	2.2										
WCap Raw Materials I.Duty		5.3									-5.3
WCap Spare Parts I.Duty		0.5									-0.5
Imported Cotton I.Duty		10.7	21.4	21.4	21.4	21.4	21.4	21.4	21.4	21.4	21.4
Spare Parts Duty		1.1	1.1	1.1	1.1	1.1	1.1	1.1	1.1	1.1	1.1
Profits Tax		-16.2	23.3	24.5	25.8	27.3	28.8	28.8	28.8	28.8	28.8
Domestic Labour											
Initial Labour	66.0										
Ongoing Labour		4.8	4.8	4.8	4.8	4.8	4.8	4.8	4.8	4.8	4.8
Domestic Electricity Corp											
Electricity		1.8	3.6	3.6	3.6	3.6	3.6	3.6	3.6	3.6	3.6
Domestic Insurance Co											
Insurance		3.0	3.0	3.0	3.0	3.0	3.0	3.0	3.0	3.0	3.0
TOTAL	**77.0**	**-67.0**	**27.2**	**28.4**	**29.7**	**31.1**	**32.7**	**32.7**	**32.7**	**32.7**	**86.8**

METHOD B:

	1999	2000	2001	2002	2003	2004	2005	2006	2007	2008	2009
Efficiency Analysis	-241.8	-49.2	91.5	91.5	91.5	91.5	91.5	91.5	91.5	91.5	155.0
Less Non-Referent Grp											
ICP	-154.2	-23.4	23.1	21.9	20.6	19.2	58.9	58.9	58.9	58.9	68.2
Foreign Credit - Principal	-164.6	28.0	30.3	32.7	35.3	30.2					
Foreign Credit - Interest		13.2	10.9	8.5	5.9	3.1					
TOTAL	**77.0**	**-67.0**	**27.2**	**28.4**	**29.7**	**31.1**	**32.7**	**32.7**	**32.7**	**32.7**	**86.8**

Discount Rates	4%	8%	12%	16%	20%
NPV	**270.1**	**217.7**	**179.9**	**152.1**	**131.4**
IRR	**N/A**				

Table A14.11 Option 5: Southern Thailand – No Duties

OPTION 5: SOUTHERN THAILAND - NO DUTIES											
Project Cash Flow											
	1999	2000	2001	2002	2003	2004	2005	2006	2007	2008	2009
Investment Costs											
Fixed Investment	-318.8										
Working Capital		-69.3									69.3
TOTAL	**-318.8**	**-69.3**	**0.0**	**0.0**	**0.0**	**0.0**	**0.0**	**0.0**	**0.0**	**0.0**	**69.3**
Operating Costs											
Raw Materials		-106.9	-213.8	-213.8	-213.8	-213.8	-213.8	-213.8	-213.8	-213.8	-213.8
Transport		-1.9	-3.8	-3.8	-3.8	-3.8	-3.8	-3.8	-3.8	-3.8	-3.8
Labour		-42.8	-42.8	-42.8	-42.8	-42.8	-42.8	-42.8	-42.8	-42.8	-42.8
Fuel, Water		-7.2	-14.4	-14.4	-14.4	-14.4	-14.4	-14.4	-14.4	-14.4	-14.4
Spare Parts		-23.0	-23.0	-23.0	-23.0	-23.0	-23.0	-23.0	-23.0	-23.0	-23.0
Insurance and Rent		-6.0	-6.0	-6.0	-6.0	-6.0	-6.0	-6.0	-6.0	-6.0	-6.0
TOTAL		**-187.8**	**-303.8**	**-303.8**	**-303.8**	**-303.8**	**-303.8**	**-303.8**	**-303.8**	**-303.8**	**-303.8**
Revenues											
Cost Savings		139.6	279.2	279.2	279.2	279.2	279.2	279.2	279.2	279.2	279.2
Yarn Sales		69.8	139.6	139.6	139.6	139.6	139.6	139.6	139.6	139.6	139.6
TOTAL		**209.4**	**418.8**	**418.8**	**418.8**	**418.8**	**418.8**	**418.8**	**418.8**	**418.8**	**418.8**
NET CASH FLOW	**-318.8**	**-47.7**	**115.0**	**115.0**	**115.0**	**115.0**	**115.0**	**115.0**	**115.0**	**115.0**	**184.3**

Discount Rates	4%	8%	12%	16%	20%
NPV	504.5	334.5	208.2	112.6	39.1
IRR	23%				

Private Cash Flow											
		1	2	3	4	5	6	7	8	9	10
FINANCING	1999	2000	2001	2002	2003	2004	2005	2006	2007	2008	2009
Principal											
Loan	164.6	-28.0	-30.3	-32.7	-35.3	-38.2					
Overdraft		60.0									-60.0
Interest											
Loan		-13.2	-10.9	-8.5	-5.9	-3.1					
Overdraft			-6.0	-6.0	-6.0	-6.0	-6.0	-6.0	-6.0	-6.0	-6.0
NET FINANCING FLOW	**164.6**	**18.8**	**-47.2**	**-47.2**	**-47.2**	**-47.2**	**-6.0**	**-6.0**	**-6.0**	**-6.0**	**-66.0**
NCF (Equity, Pre-Tax)	**-154.2**	**-28.9**	**67.8**	**67.8**	**67.8**	**67.8**	**109.0**	**109.0**	**109.0**	**109.0**	**118.3**
TAXES											
Revenues		209.4	418.8	418.8	418.8	418.8	418.8	418.8	418.8	418.8	418.8
Operating Costs		-187.8	-303.8	-303.8	-303.8	-303.8	-303.8	-303.8	-303.8	-303.8	-303.8
Depreciation		-30.1	-30.1	-30.1	-30.1	-30.1	-30.1	-30.1	-30.1	-30.1	-30.1
Interest on Loans		-13.2	-16.9	-14.5	-11.9	-9.1	-6.0	-6.0	-6.0	-6.0	-6.0
PROFITS BEFORE TAX		**-21.6**	**68.0**	**70.4**	**73.1**	**75.9**	**78.9**	**78.9**	**78.9**	**78.9**	**78.9**
TAX CASH FLOWS		**10.8**	**-34.0**	**-35.2**	**-36.5**	**-37.9**	**-39.5**	**-39.5**	**-39.5**	**-39.5**	**-39.5**
EQUITY AFTER TAX											
PRIVATE CASH FLOW	**-154.2**	**-18.1**	**33.8**	**32.6**	**31.3**	**29.9**	**69.6**	**69.6**	**69.6**	**69.6**	**78.9**

Discount Rates	4%	8%	12%	16%	20%
NPV	200.7	120.5	61.8	18.2	-14.8
IRR	18%				

Table A14.11 (*cont.*)

OPTION 5 (cont.): SOUTHERN THAILAND - NO DUTIES

Efficiency Analysis

	1999	2000	2001	2002	2003	2004	2005	2006	2007	2008	2009
INPUTS											
Investment Costs											
Fixed Investment	-241.8										
Working Capital		-63.5									63.5
TOTAL	**-241.8**	**-63.5**	**0.0**	**0.0**	**0.0**	**0.0**	**0.0**	**0.0**	**0.0**	**0.0**	**63.5**
Operating Costs											
Raw Materials		-106.9	-213.8	-213.8	-213.8	-213.8	-213.8	-213.8	-213.8	-213.8	-213.8
Transport		-1.9	-3.8	-3.8	-3.8	-3.8	-3.8	3.8	-3.8	-3.8	-3.8
Labour		-38.0	-38.0	-38.0	-38.0	-38.0	-38.0	-38.0	-38.0	-38.0	-38.0
Fuel, Water		-5.4	-10.8	-10.8	-10.8	-10.8	-10.8	-10.8	-10.8	-10.8	-10.8
Spare Parts		-21.9	-21.9	-21.9	-21.9	-21.9	-21.9	-21.9	-21.9	-21.9	-21.9
Insurance and Rent		-3.0	-3.0	-3.0	-3.0	-3.0	-3.0	-3.0	-3.0	-3.0	3.0
TOTAL		**-177.1**	**-291.3**	**-291.3**	**-291.3**	**-291.3**	**291.3**	**-291.3**	**-291.3**	**-291.3**	**-291.3**
OUTPUTS											
Revenues											
Cost Savings		127.6	255.2	255.2	255.2	255.2	255.2	255.2	255.2	255.2	255.2
Yarn Sales		63.8	127.6	127.6	127.6	127.6	127.6	127.6	127.6	127.6	127.6
TOTAL		**191.4**	**382.8**	**382.8**	**382.8**	**382.8**	**382.8**	**382.8**	**382.8**	**382.8**	**382.8**
EFFICIENCY ANALYSIS	**-241.8**	**-49.2**	**91.5**	**91.5**	**91.5**	**91.5**	**91.5**	**91.5**	**91.5**	**91.5**	**155.0**

Discount Rates	4%	8%	12%	16%	20%
NPV	**408.1**	**271.4**	**170.1**	**93.6**	**34.9**
IRR	**23%**				

Referent Group Analysis

METHOD A:

	1999	2000	2001	2002	2003	2004	2005	2006	2007	2008	2009
Domestic Bank											
Overdraft		-60.0									60.0
Interest from Overdraft			6.0	6.0	6.0	6.0	6.0	6.0	6.0	6.0	6.0
Thai Government											
Lost Import Duties		-18.0	-36.0	-36.0	-36.0	-36.0	-36.0	-36.0	-36.0	-36.0	-36.0
Spindles I.Duty	8.8										
Equipment I.Duty	2.2										
WCap Raw Materials I.Duty		5.3									-5.3
WCap Spare Parts I.Duty		0.5									-0.5
Imported Cotton I.Duty		0.0	0.0	0.0	0.0	0.0	0.0	0.0	0.0	0.0	0.0
Spare Parts Duty		1.1	1.1	1.1	1.1	1.1	1.1	1.1	1.1	1.1	1.1
Profits Tax		-10.8	34.0	35.2	36.5	37.9	39.5	39.5	39.5	39.5	39.5
Domestic Labour											
Initial Labour	66.0										
Ongoing Labour		4.8	4.8	4.8	4.8	4.8	4.8	4.8	4.8	4.8	4.8
Domestic Electricity Corp											
Electricity		1.8	3.6	3.6	3.6	3.6	3.6	3.6	3.6	3.6	3.6
Domestic Insurance Co											
Insurance		3.0	3.0	3.0	3.0	3.0	3.0	3.0	3.0	3.0	3.0
TOTAL	**77.0**	**-72.3**	**16.5**	**17.7**	**19.0**	**20.4**	**22.0**	**22.0**	**22.0**	**22.0**	**76.2**

METHOD B:

	1999	2000	2001	2002	2003	2004	2005	2006	2007	2008	2009
Efficiency Analysis	**-241.8**	**-49.2**	**91.5**	**91.5**	**91.5**	**91.5**	**91.5**	**91.5**	**91.5**	**91.5**	**155.0**
Less Non-Referent Grp											
ICP	-154.2	-18.1	33.8	32.6	31.3	29.9	69.6	69.6	69.6	69.6	78.9
Foreign Credit - Principal	-164.6	28.0	30.3	32.7	35.3	38.2					
Foreign Credit - Interest		13.2	10.9	8.5	5.9	3.1					
TOTAL	**77.0**	**-72.3**	**16.5**	**17.7**	**19.0**	**20.4**	**22.0**	**22.0**	**22.0**	**22.0**	**76.2**

Discount Rates	4%	8%	12%	16%	20%
NPV	**188.5**	**150.9**	**124.3**	**105.0**	**91.0**
IRR	**N/A**				

Table A14.12 Option 6: Southern Thailand – No Profits Tax

OPTION 6: SOUTHERN THAILAND - NO PROFITS TAX

Project Cash Flow

	1999	2000	2001	2002	2003	2004	2005	2006	2007	2008	2009
Investment Costs											
Fixed Investment	-318.8										
Working Capital		-69.3									69.3
TOTAL	**-318.8**	**-69.3**	**0.0**	**0.0**	**0.0**	**0.0**	**0.0**	**0.0**	**0.0**	**0.0**	**69.3**
Operating Costs											
Raw Materials		-117.6	-235.2	-235.2	-235.2	-235.2	-235.2	-235.2	-235.2	-235.2	-235.2
Transport		-1.9	-3.8	-3.8	-3.8	-3.8	-3.8	-3.8	-3.8	-3.8	-3.8
Labour		-42.8	-42.8	-42.8	-42.8	-42.8	-42.8	-42.8	-42.8	-42.8	-42.8
Fuel, Water		-7.2	-14.4	-14.4	-14.4	-14.4	-14.4	-14.4	-14.4	-14.4	-14.4
Spare Parts		-23.0	-23.0	-23.0	-23.0	-23.0	-23.0	-23.0	-23.0	-23.0	-23.0
Insurance and Rent		-6.0	-6.0	-6.0	-6.0	-6.0	-6.0	-6.0	-6.0	-6.0	-6.0
TOTAL		**-198.5**	**-325.2**	**-325.2**	**-325.2**	**-325.2**	**-325.2**	**-325.2**	**-325.2**	**-325.2**	**-325.2**
Revenues											
Cost Savings		139.6	279.2	279.2	279.2	279.2	279.2	279.2	279.2	279.2	279.2
Yarn Sales		69.8	139.6	139.6	139.6	139.6	139.6	139.6	139.6	139.6	139.6
TOTAL		**209.4**	**418.8**	**418.8**	**418.8**	**418.8**	**418.8**	**418.8**	**418.8**	**418.8**	**418.8**
NET CASH FLOW	**-318.8**	**-58.4**	**93.6**	**93.6**	**93.6**	**93.6**	**93.6**	**93.6**	**93.6**	**93.6**	**162.9**

Discount Rates	4%	8%	12%	16%	20%
NPV	341.4	200.9	96.9	18.5	-41.7
IRR	17%				

Private Cash Flow

	1	2	3	4	5	6	7	8	9	10
FINANCING	1999	2000	2001	2002	2003	2004	2005	2006	2007	2008	2009
Principal											
Loan	164.6	-28.0	-30.3	-32.7	-35.3	-38.2					
Overdraft		60.0									-60.0
Interest											
Loan		-13.2	-10.9	-8.5	-5.9	-3.1					
Overdraft			-6.0	-6.0	-6.0	-6.0	-6.0	-6.0	-6.0	-6.0	-6.0
NET FINANCING FLOW	**164.6**	**18.8**	**-47.2**	**-47.2**	**-47.2**	**-47.2**	**-6.0**	**-6.0**	**-6.0**	**-6.0**	**-66.0**
NCF (Equity, Pre-Tax)	**-154.2**	**-39.6**	**46.4**	**46.4**	**46.4**	**46.4**	**87.6**	**87.6**	**87.6**	**87.6**	**96.9**
TAXES											
Revenues		209.4	418.8	418.8	418.8	418.8	418.8	418.8	418.8	418.8	418.8
Operating Costs		-198.5	-325.2	-325.2	-325.2	-325.2	-325.2	-325.2	-325.2	-325.2	-325.2
Depreciation		-30.1	-30.1	-30.1	-30.1	-30.1	-30.1	-30.1	-30.1	-30.1	-30.1
Interest on Loans		-13.2	-16.9	-14.5	-11.9	-9.1	-6.0	-6.0	-6.0	-6.0	-6.0
PROFITS BEFORE TAX		**-32.3**	**46.6**	**49.1**	**51.7**	**54.5**	**57.6**	**57.6**	**57.6**	**57.6**	**57.6**
TAX CASH FLOWS		**0.0**	**0.0**	**0.0**	**0.0**	**0.0**	**0.0**	**0.0**	**0.0**	**0.0**	**0.0**
EQUITY AFTER TAX											
PRIVATE CASH FLOW	**-154.2**	**-39.6**	**46.4**	**46.4**	**46.4**	**46.4**	**87.6**	**87.6**	**87.6**	**87.6**	**96.9**

Discount Rates	4%	8%	12%	16%	20%
NPV	296.7	194.0	118.6	62.4	19.8
IRR	22%				

Table A14.12 (cont.)

OPTION 6 (cont.): SOUTHERN THAILAND - NO PROFITS TAX

Efficiency Analysis

	1999	2000	2001	2002	2003	2004	2005	2006	2007	2008	2009
INPUTS											
Investment Costs											
Fixed Investment	-241.8										
Working Capital		-63.5									63.5
TOTAL	-241.8	-63.5	0.0	0.0	0.0	0.0	0.0	0.0	0.0	0.0	63.5
Operating Costs											
Raw Materials		-106.9	-213.8	-213.8	-213.8	-213.8	-213.8	-213.8	-213.8	-213.8	-213.8
Transport		-1.9	-3.8	-3.8	-3.8	-3.8	-3.8	-3.8	-3.8	3.8	-3.8
Labour		-38.0	-38.0	-38.0	-38.0	-38.0	-38.0	-38.0	-38.0	-38.0	-38.0
Fuel, Water		-5.4	-10.8	-10.8	-10.8	-10.8	-10.8	-10.8	-10.8	-10.8	-10.8
Spare Parto		-21.9	-21.9	-21.9	-21.9	-21.9	-21.9	-21.9	-21.9	-21.9	-21.9
Insurance and Rent		-3.0	-3.0	-3.0	-3.0	-3.0	-3.0	-3.0	-3.0	-3.0	-3.0
TOTAL		-177.1	-291.3	-291.3	-291.3	-291.3	-291.3	-291.3	-291.3	-291.3	-291.3
OUTPUTS											
Revenues											
Cost Savings		127.6	255.2	255.2	255.2	255.2	255.2	255.2	255.2	255.2	255.2
Yarn Sales		63.8	127.6	127.6	127.6	127.6	127.6	127.6	127.6	127.6	127.6
TOTAL		191.4	382.8	382.8	382.8	382.8	382.8	382.8	382.8	382.8	382.8
EFFICIENCY ANALYSIS	-241.8	-49.2	91.5	91.5	91.5	91.5	91.5	91.5	91.5	91.5	155.0

Discount Rates	4%	8%	12%	16%	20%
NPV	408.1	271.4	170.1	93.6	34.9
IRR	23%				

Referent Group Analysis

METHOD A:

	1999	2000	2001	2002	2003	2004	2005	2006	2007	2008	2009
Domestic Bank											
Overdraft		-60.0									60.0
Interest from Overdraft			6.0	6.0	6.0	6.0	6.0	6.0	6.0	6.0	6.0
Thai Government											
Lost Import Duties		18.0	-36.0	-36.0	-36.0	-36.0	-36.0	-36.0	-36.0	-36.0	-36.0
Spindles I.Duty	8.8										
Equipment I.Duty	2.2										
WCap Raw Materials I.Duty		5.3									-5.3
WCap Spare Parts I.Duty		0.5									-0.5
Imported Cotton I.Duty		10.7	21.4	21.4	21.4	21.4	21.4	21.4	21.4	21.4	21.4
Spare Parts Duty		1.1	1.1	1.1	1.1	1.1	1.1	1.1	1.1	1.1	1.1
Profits Tax		0.0	0.0	0.0	0.0	0.0	0.0	0.0	0.0	0.0	0.0
Domestic Labour											
Initial Labour	66.0										
Ongoing Labour		4.8	4.8	4.8	4.8	4.8	4.8	4.8	4.8	4.8	4.8
Domestic Electricity Corp											
Electricity		1.8	3.6	3.6	3.6	3.6	3.6	3.6	3.6	3.6	3.6
Domestic Insurance Co											
Insurance		3.0	3.0	3.0	3.0	3.0	3.0	3.0	3.0	3.0	3.0
TOTAL	77.0	-50.8	3.9	3.9	3.9	3.9	3.9	3.9	3.9	3.9	58.1

METHOD B:

	1999	2000	2001	2002	2003	2004	2005	2006	2007	2008	2009
Efficiency Analysis	-241.8	-49.2	91.5	91.5	91.5	91.5	91.5	91.5	91.5	91.5	155.0
Less Non-Referent Grp											
ICP	-154.2	-39.6	46.4	46.4	46.4	46.4	87.6	87.6	87.6	87.6	96.9
Foreign Credit - Principal	-164.6	28.0	30.3	32.7	35.3	38.2					
Foreign Credit - Interest		13.2	10.9	8.5	5.9	3.1					
TOTAL	77.0	-50.8	3.9	3.9	3.9	3.9	3.9	3.9	3.9	3.9	58.1

Discount Rates	4%	8%	12%	16%	20%
NPV	92.5	77.5	67.5	60.9	56.4
IRR	N/A				

Table A14.13   Option 7: Southern Thailand – No Duties, No Profits Tax

OPTION 7: SOUTHERN THAILAND - NO DUTIES, NO PROFITS TAX

Project Cash Flow

	1999	2000	2001	2002	2003	2004	2005	2006	2007	2008	2009
Investment Costs											
Fixed Investment	-318.8										
Working Capital		-69.3									69.3
TOTAL	**-318.8**	**-69.3**	**0.0**	**0.0**	**0.0**	**0.0**	**0.0**	**0.0**	**0.0**	**0.0**	**69.3**
Operating Costs											
Raw Materials		-106.9	-213.8	-213.8	-213.8	-213.8	-213.8	-213.8	-213.8	-213.8	-213.8
Transport		-1.9	-3.8	-3.8	-3.8	-3.8	-3.8	-3.8	-3.8	-3.8	-3.8
Labour		-42.8	-42.8	-42.8	-42.8	-42.8	-42.8	-42.8	-42.8	-42.8	-42.8
Fuel, Water		-7.2	-14.4	-14.4	-14.4	-14.4	-14.4	-14.4	-14.4	-14.4	-14.4
Spare Parts		-23.0	-23.0	-23.0	-23.0	-23.0	-23.0	-23.0	-23.0	-23.0	-23.0
Insurance and Rent		-6.0	-6.0	-6.0	-6.0	-6.0	-6.0	-6.0	-6.0	-6.0	-6.0
TOTAL		**-187.8**	**-303.8**	**-303.8**	**-303.8**	**-303.8**	**-303.8**	**-303.8**	**-303.8**	**-303.8**	**-303.8**
Revenues											
Cost Savings		139.6	279.2	279.2	279.2	279.2	279.2	279.2	279.2	279.2	279.2
Yarn Sales		69.8	139.6	139.6	139.6	139.6	139.6	139.6	139.6	139.6	139.6
TOTAL		**209.4**	**418.8**	**418.8**	**418.8**	**418.8**	**418.8**	**418.8**	**418.8**	**418.8**	**418.8**
NET CASH FLOW	**-318.8**	**-47.7**	**115.0**	**115.0**	**115.0**	**115.0**	**115.0**	**115.0**	**115.0**	**115.0**	**184.3**

Discount Rates	4%	8%	12%	16%	20%
NPV	504.5	334.5	208.2	112.6	39.1
IRR	23%				

Private Cash Flow

	1	2	3	4	5	6	7	8	9	10
	1999	2000	2001	2002	2003	2004	2005	2006	2007	2008	2009
FINANCING											
Principal											
Loan	164.6	-28.0	-30.3	-32.7	-35.3	-38.2					
Overdraft		60.0									-60.0
Interest											
Loan		-13.2	-10.9	-8.5	-5.9	-3.1					
Overdraft			-6.0	-6.0	-6.0	-6.0	-6.0	-6.0	-6.0	-6.0	-6.0
NET FINANCING FLOW	**164.6**	**18.8**	**-47.2**	**-47.2**	**-47.2**	**-47.2**	**-6.0**	**-6.0**	**-6.0**	**-6.0**	**-66.0**
NCF (Equity, Pre-Tax)	**-154.2**	**-28.9**	**67.8**	**67.8**	**67.8**	**67.8**	**109.0**	**109.0**	**109.0**	**109.0**	**118.3**
TAXES											
Revenues		209.4	418.8	418.8	418.8	418.8	418.8	418.8	418.8	418.8	418.8
Operating Costs		-187.8	-303.8	-303.8	-303.8	-303.8	-303.8	-303.8	-303.8	-303.8	-303.8
Depreciation		-30.1	-30.1	-30.1	-30.1	-30.1	-30.1	-30.1	-30.1	-30.1	-30.1
Interest on Loans		-13.2	-16.9	-14.5	-11.9	-9.1	-6.0	-6.0	-6.0	-6.0	-6.0
PROFITS BEFORE TAX		**-21.6**	**68.0**	**70.4**	**73.1**	**75.9**	**78.9**	**78.9**	**78.9**	**78.9**	**78.9**
TAX CASH FLOWS		**0.0**	**0.0**	**0.0**	**0.0**	**0.0**	**0.0**	**0.0**	**0.0**	**0.0**	**0.0**
EQUITY AFTER TAX											
PRIVATE CASH FLOW	**-154.2**	**-28.9**	**67.8**	**67.8**	**67.8**	**67.8**	**109.0**	**109.0**	**109.0**	**109.0**	**118.3**

Discount Rates	4%	8%	12%	16%	20%
NPV	459.9	327.5	229.9	156.5	100.5
IRR	31%				

Table A14.13 *(cont.)*

OPTION 7 (cont.): SOUTHERN THAILAND - NO DUTIES, NO PROFITS TAX

Efficiency Analysis

	1999	2000	2001	2002	2003	2004	2005	2006	2007	2008	2009
INPUTS											
Investment Costs											
Fixed Investment	-241.8										
Working Capital		-63.5									63.5
TOTAL	**-241.8**	**-63.5**	**0.0**	**0.0**	**0.0**	**0.0**	**0.0**	**0.0**	**0.0**	**0.0**	**63.5**
Operating Costs											
Raw Materials		-106.9	-213.8	-213.8	-213.8	-213.8	-213.8	-213.8	-213.8	-213.8	-213.8
Transport		-1.9	-3.8	-3.8	-3.8	-3.8	-3.0	-3.8	-3.8	-3.8	-3.8
Labour		-38.0	-38.0	-38.0	-38.0	-38.0	-38.0	-38.0	-38.0	-38.0	-38.0
Fuel, Water		-5.4	-10.8	-10.8	-10.8	-10.8	-10.8	-10.8	-10.8	-10.8	-10.8
Spare Parts		-21.9	-21.9	-21.9	-21.9	-21.9	-21.9	-21.9	-21.9	-21.9	-21.9
Insurance and Rent		-3.0	-3.0	-3.0	-3.0	-3.0	-3.0	-3.0	-3.0	-3.0	-3.0
TOTAL		**-177.1**	**-291.3**	**-291.3**	**-291.3**	**-291.3**	**-291.3**	**-291.3**	**-291.3**	**-291.3**	**-291.3**
OUTPUTS											
Revenues											
Cost Savings		127.6	255.2	255.2	255.2	255.2	255.2	255.2	255.2	255.2	255.2
Yarn Sales		63.8	127.6	127.6	127.6	127.6	127.6	127.6	127.6	127.6	127.6
TOTAL		**191.4**	**382.8**	**382.8**	**382.8**	**382.8**	**382.8**	**382.8**	**382.8**	**382.8**	**382.8**
EFFICIENCY ANALYSIS	**-241.8**	**-49.2**	**91.5**	**91.5**	**91.5**	**91.5**	**91.5**	**91.5**	**91.5**	**91.5**	**155.0**

Discount Rates	4%	8%	12%	16%	20%
NPV	408.1	271.4	170.1	93.6	34.9
IRR	23%				

Referent Group Analysis

METHOD A:

	1999	2000	2001	2002	2003	2004	2005	2006	2007	2008	2009
Domestic Bank											
Overdraft		-60.0									60.0
Interest from Overdraft			6.0	6.0	6.0	6.0	6.0	6.0	6.0	6.0	6.0
Thai Government											
Lost Import Duties		-18.0	-36.0	-36.0	-36.0	-36.0	-36.0	-36.0	-36.0	-36.0	-36.0
Spindles I.Duty	8.8										
Equipment I.Duty	2.2										
WCap Raw Materials I.Duty		5.3									-5.3
WCap Spare Parts I.Duty		0.5									-0.5
Imported Cotton I.Duty		0.0	0.0	0.0	0.0	0.0	0.0	0.0	0.0	0.0	0.0
Spare Parts Duty		1.1	1.1	1.1	1.1	1.1	1.1	1.1	1.1	1.1	1.1
Profits Tax		0.0	0.0	0.0	0.0	0.0	0.0	0.0	0.0	0.0	0.0
Domestic Labour											
Initial Labour	66.0										
Ongoing Labour		4.8	4.8	4.8	4.8	4.8	4.8	4.8	4.8	4.8	4.8
Domestic Electricity Corp											
Electricity		1.8	3.6	3.6	3.6	3.6	3.6	3.6	3.6	3.6	3.6
Domestic Insurance Co											
Insurance		3.0	3.0	3.0	3.0	3.0	3.0	3.0	3.0	3.0	3.0
TOTAL	**77.0**	**-61.5**	**-17.5**	**-17.5**	**-17.5**	**-17.5**	**-17.5**	**-17.5**	**-17.5**	**-17.5**	**36.7**

METHOD B:

	1999	2000	2001	2002	2003	2004	2005	2006	2007	2008	2009
Efficiency Analysis	-241.8	-49.2	91.5	91.5	91.5	91.5	91.5	91.5	91.5	91.5	155.0
Less Non-Referent Grp											
ICP	-154.2	-28.9	67.8	67.8	67.8	67.8	109.0	109.0	109.0	109.0	118.3
Foreign Credit - Principal	-164.6	28.0	30.3	32.7	35.3	38.2					
Foreign Credit - Interest		13.2	10.9	8.5	5.9	3.1					
TOTAL	**77.0**	**-61.5**	**-17.5**	**-17.5**	**-17.5**	**-17.5**	**-17.5**	**-17.5**	**-17.5**	**-17.5**	**36.7**

Discount Rates	4%	8%	12%	16%	20%
NPV	-70.7	-56.1	-43.8	-33.3	-24.3
IRR	N/A				

Case Study Assignment

International Mining Corporation (IMC) Copper Mining Project[1]

Project Description

The Government of Indonesia is considering a proposed joint venture with a foreign investor, International Mining Corporation (IMC), to develop a new copper mine in the mountainous and remote Eastern Province (EP) where recent geological surveys have revealed significant copper deposits. Under the proposal, Eastern Province Mining Limited (EPML), in which the Government of Indonesia (GOI) will hold 30% of the shares, will mine and mill the copper ore on site. The concentrate will then be transported (in slurry form) by pipeline to a dedicated port facility at the mouth of the Eastern Province River, from where it will be shipped to Japan for refining and sale on the world market. Although the main product is copper, the concentrate will also contain some quantities of gold and silver that will also be extracted from the concentrate at the refining stage and sold on the world market.

Eastern Province is a low-income region with a population of 5 million and a per capita income of around US$300 per annum, considered the least developed part of the country. The local population living in the area rely mainly on subsistence agriculture and fishing for their livelihoods. At present there is very little economic or social infrastructure in the area, which means that apart from on-site investment in the mine, mill and tailings dam, EPML will need to make substantial off-site investments in infrastructure and logistics, such as transport equipment, the construction of roads, bridges, wharfs, an airstrip, storage facilities, housing, power generation and supply, as well as the establishment of a school, hospital, shops, recreational facilities and other amenities for the locally engaged and expatriate employees and families. The GOI is eager for the project to proceed as it is expected to provide a significant injection of investment in the region, as well as opportunities for training and employment of local workers and some inter-state, migrant workers from other underdeveloped areas of the EP and elsewhere in Indonesia.

It is also expected that the project will generate some backward linkages into the local economy. EPML will be required to sub-contract certain services to locally based contractors and to buy some of its supplies locally, such as food. Under the proposal the local landowners are to be compensated for the use of their land for mining-related activities, and priority is to be given to the local population for employment and training by EPML. Part of the compensation payments are to be paid into the Eastern Province Development Trust Fund that will be used to finance development projects in the EP region once the fund is established. EPML will also pay royalties to GOI, based on the value of its mineral sales net of transportation, treatment and refining costs.

---

1 This assignment case study is hypothetical and is not based on the activities of an actual company. Any similarity with regard to the activities or name of an actual company is unintended. As a guide to the instructor it should be noted that it is of a higher degree of difficulty than the ICP Case Study.

Although IMC has a strong interest in the project, it is concerned that the additional off-site costs associated with the establishment and operation of the extensive economic and social infrastructure will reduce the profitability of the project significantly. It is also felt that much of EPML's off-site investment will be of significant benefit to the local population. In its proposal to GOI it has argued that it will only participate in the project if it is granted concessions in the form of:

- exemption from import duties on all imported goods (all inputs are currently subject to a 10% *ad valorem* duty levied on the c.i.f. price);
- a tax holiday in the form of exemption from company taxes over the first 10 years of the mine's operation;
- lower royalties;
- a smaller share of equity for GOI.

The Treasury Department of Indonesia is not in favour of these concessions, especially as IMC has no obligation to reinvest its after-tax profits in Indonesia and there are no restrictions on the remittance of profits to its overseas shareholders.

You have been contracted by GOI to advise on the project. You are required to prepare a report based on a benefit-cost analysis of the project in which you estimate the net benefits of the project from the perspective of the people of Indonesia – the referent group. As this report is also to be used to inform GOI in its negotiations with IMC you are required to consider a number of scenarios in which you show the net benefits to both the referent group and IMC.

You should assume that the initial investment begins during 2003 and that the project will come to an end – the mine will be closed down completely – at the end of 2020. GOI uses a discount rate of 6% (real) for public sector investment appraisal, and requires sensitivity analysis over a range of discount rates from 5–10% (real).

All available details of the project are provided in the following sections. Where information is missing or ambiguous you are required to make what you consider the most reasonable assumption, which should be discussed explicitly in the text of your report. All values should be reported in thousands of New Rupiah; our assumed 'new' currency of Indonesia, which exchanges at Rp2.5 to US$1.0 (to simplify conversions and calculations). All prices are in constant 2003 prices. Assume that relative prices are unaffected by inflation.

The report should contain an Executive Summary of approximately one page in length, and should be no more than 10 pages in total, including tables and charts. Printouts of the detailed spreadsheets should be attached in an appendix, and should also be provided in electronic format on disk. For an example of a completed report, see the Appendix to Chapter 14.

Investment Costs

The project is an open cut mining operation with most material drilled and blasted. EPML will begin the construction stage of the project in 2003. Mining, milling and the overseas refining operations are expected to begin three years later, in 2006.

Total initial investment in the project amounts to approximately US$1.25 billion, consisting of both on-site and off-site expenditure and involving a combination of imported and locally produced goods, local and expatriate labour, and is spread over three years: 25% in 2003; 45% in 2004; and, 30% in 2005. A detailed breakdown is provided in Table 1.

Table 1: Details of Initial Capital Expenditure, 2003–2005
(All amounts in Rp000s unless otherwise stated)

Item	Composition		
	Imports US$000s (cif)[1]	Local Materials[2]	Labour[3]
Roads	11,800	48,750	81,250
Buildings	3,800	17,000	14,875
Wharf	3,275	6,750	6,750
Airstrip	950	2,656	5,313
Power Supplies	73,000	28,750	57,500
Facilities	18,000	75,000	125,000
Mining Equip.	470,000	71,875	71,875
Milling Equip.	83,000	27,000	13,500
Logistics Equip.	92,500	37,500	75,000
Other Equip.	5,500	7,500	7,500
Construction	5,000	30,000	105,000
Excavation		16,500	88,000

[1] Import duties are 10% *ad valorem*.
[2] Consisting exclusively of locally manufactured materials (65%), contractors' margins (15%), local skilled labour (5%) and local unskilled labour (15%).
[3] Consisting of a mixture of expatriate salaries (40%), local managerial and professional wages (10%), local skilled (30%), and local unskilled (20%).

It should be noted that there are both direct labour and indirect labour inputs to be considered in the efficiency analysis.

During the operation of the mine certain items of infrastructure and equipment will need to be replaced as shown in Table 2.

Table 2: Details of Replacement Capital Expenditure, 2009–2017
(All amounts in Rp000s unless otherwise stated)

ITEM	2009	2013	2017
Imported Equipment US$000s (cif)[1]	6,612	8,264	4,959
Local Materials[2]	12,500	25,000	12,500
Installation[3]	12,500	18,750	12,500

[1] Import duties are 10% *ad valorem*.
[2] Composition as for Table 1.
[3] Consisting exclusively of labour – composition as for Table 1.

Working capital consisting of a mixture of imported equipment spares (60%), fuel supplies (35%) and locally produced materials (5%) is to be built up from a level of approximately Rp25 million in 2004 to Rp75 million in 2005, and maintained at that level over the remainder of the project's life until 2020 when it is to be completely run down (or sold off at cost). See Table 3 for details.

Table 3 Composition of Additions to Working Capital
(All amounts in Rp000s unless otherwise stated)

	2004	2005
Imported Equipment US$000s (cif)[1]	6,600	10,909
Fuel US$000s (cif)	3,182	6,364
Local Materials[2]	1,250	2,500

[1] Import duties are 10% *ad valorem*.
[2] Composition as for Table 1.

Salvage Values, Depreciation Rates and Provision for Rehabilitation

For the purpose of this study it should be assumed that the mine and mill equipment has a salvage value at the end of the project life amounting to 10% of the initial cost. Off-site infrastructure (including construction but excluding excavation costs) has an end-value amounting to 30% of its initial cost; logistic and other equipment has an end-value equal to 20% of its initial cost. Under Indonesian tax legislation IMC is permitted to depreciate all initial investment over the 15 year operating life of the project, starting in 2006, using the straight-line method. Replacement investment is depreciated over the 3 years following the year of the investment, also using the straight-line method, and is assumed to have no salvage value.

It is also understood that EPML will need to rehabilitate the mine site and the Eastern Province Catchment Area on closure of the mine. It is expected that this will cost Rp625 million, in year 2020. EPML is permitted to include an annual provision for rehabilitation as an operating expense for tax purposes. You should treat this as a sinking fund with an annual real interest rate of 7%.

The Output

In the first year of operations, 2006, it is expected that 25% of full capacity will be reached; in the second year, 50%; in the third year 75%; and, in the fourth year 100%. Based on the geological information available, EPML expects to operate the mine at full capacity until the end of 2020.

When operating at full capacity the mine is expected to extract 85 million tons of material per annum. It is believed that this will consist of 40% ore and 60% waste. When milled, a concentrate equal to 2% of the ore tonnage is produced for treatment at a refinery. EPML will contract out the treatment to a refinery in Japan, and will sell the refined minerals on the world markets. Refined copper produced can be expected to amount to 30% of the weight of the concentrate, and currently sells on the world market at US$1.25 per pound (lb). Refined silver equivalent to 0.004% and gold equivalent to 0.0025% of the weight of the concentrate are also extracted during the refining process. In world markets the current price of gold averages around US$290 per ounce, while the price of silver averages around US$5 per ounce.

As noted earlier, the company will invest in substantial off-site infrastructure including roads, utilities and community amenities such as a school, clinic and recreational facilities for its staff. It is understood that the extended families of IMC employees and local landowners will also have access to and benefit from most of these. In the opinion of an expert in the area the value of the additional benefits to the local communities from these amenities could reasonably be estimated as the equivalent of 30% of the annual overhead expenditure on "Utilities" and "Community Services" (Rp110 million). The use of these amenities by the wider (non-employee) community should be treated as an additional "output" of the project and its value added to the mineral output in the Efficiency Analysis, and as an equivalent gain in the Referent Group Analysis.

Operating Costs

Overheads, Insurance and Compensation: Total overheads, including all transportation of inputs and outputs, but excluding compensation payments and provision for rehabilitation, are expected to total about Rp410 million per annum, with effect from 2004. The full details of these are provided in Table 4. As IMC has another operation in Indonesia and will be running the project administration from the same head office in Jakarta, a significant part of the overhead costs itemised in Table 4 (50%) are already being incurred.

Table 4 Composition of Annual Overhead Costs
          (All amounts in Rp000s unless otherwise stated)

	Expatriate Wages	Local Skilled	Local Unskilled	Local Materials[1]
Administration	45,500	6,500	3,250	9,750
Management	49,500	5,500		
Transport & Engineering	54,000	27,000	13,500	40,500
Maintenance	18,000	7,500	1,500	3,000
Utilities	15,000	30,000	15,000	15,000
Community Services	3,500	7,000	14,000	10,500
Other		3,000	3,000	9,000

[1] Composition as for Table 1.

The company will have to increase its existing insurance premium from US$100,000 to US$200,000 per annum. This is paid to an overseas company. No taxes or duties apply.

It has been agreed with GOI and representatives of the local clans inhabiting the catchment area that EPML will make annual compensation payments into a development trust fund amounting to Rp30 million per annum (in real terms) once operations begin in 2006. This is to be treated as compensation for use of communally held land by the mine and its associated activities. A university study has estimated that this level of compensation represents approximately twice the opportunity cost of the land resources affected by the mine, based on their present uses.

Mining and Milling: Mining and milling costs consist of a number of on-site activities including operations, maintenance, engineering, training, metallurgy and port operations. They consist of a combination of fixed and variable cost and can be disaggregated by type of input as shown in Table 5.

Table 5 Composition of Mining and Milling Costs
(All amounts in Rp000s unless otherwise stated)

	Imports US$000s (cif)	Local Materials[1]	Expatriate Labour	Skilled Labour	Unskilled Labour
Mining - Fixed	10,455	12,575	5,925	12,000	8,400
Mining – Variable per thousand ton material	0.1230	0.1479	0.0700	0.1424	0.1000
Milling – Fixed	7,710	8,900	3,900	9,250	5,700
Milling – Variable per thousand ton ore	0.6235	0.2618	0.1150	0.2735	0.1675

[1] Composition as for Table 1.

Freight: In addition to the costs of handling and transportation of the concentrate by pipeline in slurry form to the port (included under milling costs), the concentrate needs to be shipped to Japan. EPML will pay US$25 per ton of concentrate for freighting it to the refinery gate.

Treatment: The concentrate is treated before being refined at a charge by the Japanese refinery of US$95 per ton of concentrate.

Refining: Once treated the copper is refined at US$0.10 per lb of refined copper produced. The refining of gold and silver is charged at US$5 and US$3 respectively per fine ounce produced.

Royalties: EPML pays royalties to GOI. These are 2% of the fob value of sales; i.e. the gross value of sales less the cost of freight to Japan, and the cost of treatment and refining in Japan.

Taxation: EPML will pay corporate taxes of 30% on net profits. For purposes of calculating taxes losses incurred in one year may be offset against IMC's other operations in Indonesia. Royalties, interest payments, depreciation and provision for rehabilitation may also be treated as tax deductible expenses.

Finance: The initial investment (2003 to 2005) will be financed partly by debt (US$500 million) and the remainder through IMC's own funds. The US$500 million loan (repayable in US dollars) is to be raised in 2003 on the capital market at a fixed interest rate of 7% per annum (in real terms), repayable as an annuity over 15 years, beginning in 2006. IMC has negotiated an interest-free period of grace until the beginning of 2006.

In the preliminary negotiations GOI has indicated that it expects to be allocated a 30% share of the equity in EPML, without making any contribution to the equity capital. Dividends are to be calculated on the basis of the net cash after debt service, royalties, tax, and provision for depreciation and rehabilitation, and will only be paid in those years in which this balance is positive.

Referent Group Stakeholders

The referent group consists of all parties engaged in the project except the following: IMC, the Japanese shipping and refining company, the foreign bank, the overseas insurance company, and expatriate labour. The referent group analysis should show the net benefits on a disaggregated basis (i.e. by stakeholder group) as the GOI is concerned to know how the benefits of the project will be distributed. You are advised to set up separate working tables to calculate the net benefits for some stakeholder groups (i.e. GOI, unskilled labour, and local contractors) as each has numerous sources of net benefit, making the calculation rather complex.

Efficiency Pricing

Labour
Various categories of labour cost enter the analysis: the direct costs of those employed on the project and the indirect costs of labour inputs in other components of project cost. The details of these are provided in the preceding sections. For the purpose of efficiency pricing it should be noted that for only one category of labour can the opportunity cost be considered significantly different from the market price; viz. unskilled labour. A recent study by a labour economist at the local university estimates the opportunity cost of unskilled labour in the Eastern Province at 20% of the legal minimum wage (which is the wage paid by the company and associated operations). In the efficiency analysis you should price all unskilled labour accordingly.

Local Contractors
As part of its policy of promoting small-scale local enterprises, the GOI has stipulated that local contractors should be engaged by the project wherever possible. It is envisaged that they will be engaged primarily for the supply of locally produced and non-tradeable goods and services. It has been estimated that 25% of the income they earn as "contractors' margin" (i.e. as a mark-up or commission from these activities) is a rent (a payment in excess of opportunity cost) attributable to the market power they have. In the efficiency analysis this needs to be taken into account.

HINT: *As unskilled labour and/or contractors' margins also enter as cost components of "Local Materials" which is, in turn, a major input in a number of expenditure items, it is important that all the items of expenditure of which unskilled labour and local materials are components are entered in Table 1 of the spreadsheet on a disaggregated basis. This should simplify the subsequent re-valuation of these items in terms of efficiency prices. This re-valuation can be undertaken as part of Table 1 to simplify the remainder of the spreadsheet.*

Conversions and Assumptions

For the purpose of this study you should use the following conversions:
    2204.62 pounds (lbs) per ton
    32.1507 ounces (oz.) per kilogram
    1000 kilograms (kg.) per ton

Any other information requirements will need to be based on your own assumptions. It is essential that these are made explicit in your report.

Scenarios and Sensitivity Analysis

Once you have undertaken a complete BCA for the Base Case Scenario (Project, Private, Efficiency, and Referent Group Analysis) you need to calculate the net benefits to IMC and to the Referent Group under a number of alternative policy scenarios, as you are also required to provide GOI with information and advice for its negotiations with IMC. The policy variables IMC wishes to discuss in the negotiations are: company taxes; import duties; royalties; and GOI's share of equity (dividends payable).

You should consider, at least, the following scenarios in addition to the base case:

1. exemption from all duties
2. exemption from company taxes
3. exemption from duties and taxes
4. exemption from royalties
5. reducing GOI's equity to 10%
6. both (4) and (5)
7. all concessions (1) to (5).

Your final report should comment on the relative attractiveness (ranking) of these from GOI and IMC's perspective, and should offer advice to GOI on how you expect the negotiations to proceed, based on these calculations.

You should also identify those variables (other than the above) to which the project's net benefits are most sensitive and discuss the possible implications for the project if their actual values moved within a band of, say, 10–20% around the estimated "best guess" values.

The sample report included as the Appendix to Chapter 14 is a guide to the appropriate presentation of your report.

Appendix 2: Discount and Annuity Tables

DISCOUNT FACTORS

Period/discount rate

	1%	2%	3%	4%	5%	6%	7%	8%	9%	10%	11%	12%	13%	14%	15%	16%	17%	18%	19%	20%	25%	30%
1	0.990	0.980	0.971	0.962	0.952	0.943	0.935	0.926	0.917	0.909	0.901	0.893	0.885	0.877	0.870	0.862	0.855	0.847	0.840	0.833	0.800	0.769
2	0.980	0.961	0.943	0.925	0.907	0.890	0.873	0.857	0.842	0.826	0.812	0.797	0.783	0.769	0.756	0.743	0.731	0.718	0.706	0.694	0.640	0.592
3	0.971	0.942	0.915	0.889	0.864	0.840	0.816	0.794	0.772	0.751	0.731	0.712	0.693	0.675	0.658	0.641	0.624	0.609	0.593	0.579	0.512	0.455
4	0.961	0.924	0.888	0.855	0.823	0.792	0.763	0.735	0.708	0.683	0.659	0.636	0.613	0.592	0.572	0.552	0.534	0.516	0.499	0.482	0.410	0.350
5	0.951	0.906	0.863	0.822	0.784	0.747	0.713	0.681	0.650	0.621	0.593	0.567	0.543	0.519	0.497	0.476	0.456	0.437	0.419	0.402	0.328	0.269
6	0.942	0.888	0.837	0.790	0.746	0.705	0.666	0.630	0.596	0.564	0.535	0.507	0.480	0.456	0.432	0.410	0.390	0.370	0.352	0.335	0.262	0.207
7	0.933	0.871	0.813	0.760	0.711	0.665	0.623	0.583	0.547	0.513	0.482	0.452	0.425	0.400	0.376	0.354	0.333	0.314	0.296	0.279	0.210	0.159
8	0.923	0.853	0.789	0.731	0.677	0.627	0.582	0.540	0.502	0.467	0.434	0.404	0.376	0.351	0.327	0.305	0.285	0.266	0.249	0.233	0.168	0.123
9	0.914	0.837	0.766	0.703	0.645	0.592	0.544	0.500	0.460	0.424	0.391	0.361	0.333	0.308	0.284	0.263	0.243	0.225	0.209	0.194	0.134	0.094
10	0.905	0.820	0.744	0.676	0.614	0.558	0.508	0.463	0.422	0.386	0.352	0.322	0.295	0.270	0.247	0.227	0.208	0.191	0.176	0.162	0.107	0.073
11	0.896	0.804	0.722	0.650	0.585	0.527	0.475	0.429	0.388	0.350	0.317	0.287	0.261	0.237	0.215	0.195	0.178	0.162	0.148	0.135	0.086	0.056
12	0.887	0.788	0.701	0.625	0.557	0.497	0.444	0.397	0.356	0.319	0.286	0.257	0.231	0.208	0.187	0.168	0.152	0.137	0.124	0.112	0.069	0.043
13	0.879	0.773	0.681	0.601	0.530	0.469	0.415	0.368	0.326	0.290	0.258	0.229	0.204	0.182	0.163	0.145	0.130	0.116	0.104	0.093	0.055	0.033
14	0.870	0.758	0.661	0.577	0.505	0.442	0.388	0.340	0.299	0.263	0.232	0.205	0.181	0.160	0.141	0.125	0.111	0.099	0.088	0.078	0.044	0.025
15	0.861	0.743	0.642	0.555	0.481	0.417	0.362	0.315	0.275	0.239	0.209	0.183	0.160	0.140	0.123	0.108	0.095	0.084	0.074	0.065	0.035	0.020
16	0.853	0.728	0.623	0.534	0.458	0.394	0.339	0.292	0.252	0.218	0.188	0.163	0.141	0.123	0.107	0.093	0.081	0.071	0.062	0.054	0.028	0.015
17	0.844	0.714	0.605	0.513	0.436	0.371	0.317	0.270	0.231	0.198	0.170	0.146	0.125	0.108	0.093	0.080	0.069	0.060	0.052	0.045	0.023	0.012
18	0.836	0.700	0.587	0.494	0.416	0.350	0.296	0.250	0.212	0.180	0.153	0.130	0.111	0.095	0.081	0.069	0.059	0.051	0.044	0.038	0.018	0.009
19	0.828	0.686	0.570	0.475	0.396	0.331	0.277	0.232	0.194	0.164	0.138	0.116	0.098	0.083	0.070	0.060	0.051	0.043	0.037	0.031	0.014	0.007
20	0.820	0.673	0.554	0.456	0.377	0.312	0.258	0.215	0.178	0.149	0.124	0.104	0.087	0.073	0.061	0.051	0.043	0.037	0.031	0.026	0.012	0.005
21	0.811	0.660	0.538	0.439	0.359	0.294	0.242	0.199	0.164	0.135	0.112	0.093	0.077	0.064	0.053	0.044	0.037	0.031	0.026	0.022	0.009	0.004
22	0.803	0.647	0.522	0.422	0.342	0.278	0.226	0.184	0.150	0.123	0.101	0.083	0.068	0.056	0.046	0.038	0.032	0.026	0.022	0.018	0.007	0.003
23	0.795	0.634	0.507	0.406	0.326	0.262	0.211	0.170	0.138	0.112	0.091	0.074	0.060	0.049	0.040	0.033	0.027	0.022	0.018	0.015	0.006	0.002
24	0.788	0.622	0.492	0.390	0.310	0.247	0.197	0.158	0.126	0.102	0.082	0.066	0.053	0.043	0.035	0.028	0.023	0.019	0.015	0.013	0.005	0.002
25	0.780	0.610	0.478	0.375	0.295	0.233	0.184	0.146	0.116	0.092	0.074	0.059	0.047	0.038	0.030	0.024	0.020	0.016	0.013	0.010	0.004	0.001
26	0.772	0.598	0.464	0.361	0.281	0.220	0.172	0.135	0.106	0.084	0.066	0.053	0.042	0.033	0.026	0.021	0.017	0.014	0.011	0.009	0.003	0.001
27	0.764	0.586	0.450	0.347	0.268	0.207	0.161	0.125	0.098	0.076	0.060	0.047	0.037	0.029	0.023	0.018	0.014	0.011	0.009	0.007	0.002	0.001
28	0.757	0.574	0.437	0.333	0.255	0.196	0.150	0.116	0.090	0.069	0.054	0.042	0.033	0.026	0.020	0.016	0.012	0.010	0.008	0.006	0.002	0.001
29	0.749	0.563	0.424	0.321	0.243	0.185	0.141	0.107	0.082	0.063	0.048	0.037	0.029	0.022	0.017	0.014	0.011	0.008	0.006	0.005	0.002	0.000
30	0.742	0.552	0.412	0.308	0.231	0.174	0.131	0.099	0.075	0.057	0.044	0.033	0.026	0.020	0.015	0.012	0.009	0.007	0.005	0.004	0.001	0.000
40	0.672	0.453	0.307	0.208	0.142	0.097	0.067	0.046	0.032	0.022	0.015	0.011	0.008	0.005	0.004	0.003	0.002	0.001	0.001	0.001	0.000	0.000
50	0.608	0.372	0.228	0.141	0.087	0.054	0.034	0.021	0.013	0.009	0.005	0.003	0.002	0.001	0.001	0.001	0.000	0.000	0.000	0.000	0.000	0.000

ANNUITY FACTORS

Period/discount rate

Period	1%	2%	3%	4%	5%	6%	7%	8%	9%	10%	11%	12%	13%	14%	15%	16%	17%	18%	19%	20%	25%	30%
1	0.990	0.980	0.971	0.962	0.952	0.943	0.935	0.926	0.917	0.909	0.901	0.893	0.885	0.877	0.870	0.862	0.855	0.847	0.840	0.833	0.800	0.769
2	1.970	1.942	1.913	1.886	1.859	1.833	1.808	1.783	1.759	1.736	1.713	1.690	1.668	1.647	1.626	1.605	1.585	1.566	1.547	1.528	1.440	1.361
3	2.941	2.884	2.829	2.775	2.723	2.673	2.624	2.577	2.531	2.487	2.444	2.402	2.361	2.322	2.283	2.246	2.210	2.174	2.140	2.106	1.952	1.816
4	3.902	3.808	3.717	3.630	3.546	3.465	3.387	3.312	3.240	3.170	3.102	3.037	2.974	2.914	2.855	2.798	2.743	2.690	2.639	2.589	2.362	2.166
5	4.853	4.713	4.580	4.452	4.329	4.212	4.100	3.993	3.890	3.791	3.696	3.605	3.517	3.433	3.352	3.274	3.199	3.127	3.058	2.991	2.689	2.436
6	5.795	5.601	5.417	5.242	5.076	4.917	4.767	4.623	4.486	4.355	4.231	4.111	3.998	3.889	3.784	3.685	3.589	3.498	3.410	3.326	2.951	2.643
7	6.728	6.472	6.230	6.002	5.786	5.582	5.389	5.206	5.033	4.868	4.712	4.564	4.423	4.288	4.160	4.039	3.922	3.812	3.706	3.605	3.161	2.802
8	7.652	7.325	7.020	6.733	6.463	6.210	5.971	5.747	5.535	5.335	5.146	4.968	4.799	4.639	4.487	4.344	4.207	4.078	3.954	3.837	3.329	2.925
9	8.566	8.162	7.786	7.435	7.108	6.802	6.515	6.247	5.995	5.759	5.537	5.328	5.132	4.946	4.772	4.607	4.451	4.303	4.163	4.031	3.463	3.019
10	9.471	8.983	8.530	8.111	7.722	7.360	7.024	6.710	6.418	6.145	5.889	5.650	5.426	5.216	5.019	4.833	4.659	4.494	4.339	4.192	3.571	3.092
11	10.368	9.787	9.253	8.760	8.306	7.887	7.499	7.139	6.805	6.495	6.207	5.938	5.687	5.453	5.234	5.029	4.836	4.656	4.486	4.327	3.656	3.147
12	11.255	10.575	9.954	9.385	8.863	8.384	7.943	7.536	7.161	6.814	6.492	6.194	5.918	5.660	5.421	5.197	4.988	4.793	4.611	4.439	3.725	3.190
13	12.134	11.348	10.635	9.986	9.394	8.853	8.358	7.904	7.487	7.103	6.750	6.424	6.122	5.842	5.583	5.342	5.118	4.910	4.715	4.533	3.780	3.223
14	13.004	12.106	11.296	10.563	9.899	9.295	8.745	8.244	7.786	7.367	6.982	6.628	6.302	6.002	5.724	5.468	5.229	5.008	4.802	4.611	3.824	3.249
15	13.865	12.849	11.938	11.118	10.380	9.712	9.108	8.559	8.061	7.606	7.191	6.811	6.462	6.142	5.847	5.575	5.324	5.092	4.876	4.675	3.859	3.268
16	14.718	13.578	12.561	11.652	10.838	10.106	9.447	8.851	8.313	7.824	7.379	6.974	6.604	6.265	5.954	5.668	5.405	5.162	4.938	4.730	3.887	3.283
17	15.562	14.292	13.166	12.166	11.274	10.477	9.763	9.122	8.544	8.022	7.549	7.120	6.729	6.373	6.047	5.749	5.475	5.222	4.990	4.775	3.910	3.295
18	16.398	14.992	13.754	12.659	11.690	10.828	10.059	9.372	8.756	8.201	7.702	7.250	6.840	6.467	6.128	5.818	5.534	5.273	5.033	4.812	3.928	3.304
19	17.226	15.678	14.324	13.134	12.085	11.158	10.336	9.604	8.950	8.365	7.839	7.366	6.938	6.550	6.198	5.877	5.584	5.316	5.070	4.843	3.942	3.311
20	18.046	16.351	14.877	13.590	12.462	11.470	10.594	9.818	9.129	8.514	7.963	7.469	7.025	6.623	6.259	5.929	5.628	5.353	5.101	4.870	3.954	3.316
21	18.857	17.011	15.415	14.029	12.821	11.764	10.836	10.017	9.292	8.649	8.075	7.562	7.102	6.687	6.312	5.973	5.665	5.384	5.127	4.891	3.963	3.320
22	19.660	17.658	15.937	14.451	13.163	12.042	11.061	10.201	9.442	8.772	8.176	7.645	7.170	6.743	6.359	6.011	5.696	5.410	5.149	4.909	3.970	3.323
23	20.456	18.292	16.444	14.857	13.489	12.303	11.272	10.371	9.580	8.883	8.266	7.718	7.230	6.792	6.399	6.044	5.723	5.432	5.167	4.925	3.976	3.325
24	21.243	18.914	16.936	15.247	13.799	12.550	11.469	10.529	9.707	8.985	8.348	7.784	7.283	6.835	6.434	6.073	5.746	5.451	5.182	4.937	3.981	3.327
25	22.023	19.523	17.413	15.622	14.094	12.783	11.654	10.675	9.823	9.077	8.422	7.843	7.330	6.873	6.464	6.097	5.766	5.467	5.195	4.948	3.985	3.329
26	22.795	20.121	17.877	15.983	14.375	13.003	11.826	10.810	9.929	9.161	8.488	7.896	7.372	6.906	6.491	6.118	5.783	5.480	5.206	4.956	3.988	3.330
27	23.560	20.707	18.327	16.330	14.643	13.211	11.987	10.935	10.027	9.237	8.548	7.943	7.409	6.935	6.514	6.136	5.798	5.492	5.215	4.964	3.990	3.331
28	24.316	21.281	18.764	16.663	14.898	13.406	12.137	11.051	10.116	9.307	8.602	7.984	7.441	6.961	6.534	6.152	5.810	5.502	5.223	4.970	3.992	3.331
29	25.066	21.844	19.188	16.984	15.141	13.591	12.278	11.158	10.198	9.370	8.650	8.022	7.470	6.983	6.551	6.166	5.820	5.510	5.229	4.975	3.994	3.332
30	25.808	22.396	19.600	17.292	15.372	13.765	12.409	11.258	10.274	9.427	8.694	8.055	7.496	7.003	6.566	6.177	5.829	5.517	5.235	4.979	3.995	3.332
40	32.835	27.355	23.115	19.793	17.159	15.046	13.332	11.925	10.757	9.779	8.951	8.244	7.634	7.105	6.642	6.233	5.871	5.548	5.258	4.997	3.999	3.333
50	39.196	31.424	25.730	21.482	18.256	15.762	13.801	12.233	10.962	9.915	9.042	8.304	7.675	7.133	6.661	6.246	5.880	5.554	5.262	4.999	4.000	3.333

Index